The Gallipoli
Experience
Reconsidered

The Gallipoli Experience Reconsidered

Peter Liddle

Pen & Sword
MILITARY

First published in Great Britain in 2015 by
Pen & Sword Military
an imprint of
Pen & Sword Books Ltd
47 Church Street
Barnsley
South Yorkshire
S70 2AS

ISBN 978 1 78340 039 3

A CIP catalogue record for this book is available from the British Library

Typeset in Ehrhardt by
Mac Style, Bridlington, East Yorkshire
Printed and bound in the UK by CPI Group (UK) Ltd, Croydon,
CRO 4YY

Pen & Sword Books Ltd incorporates the imprints of Pen & Sword
Archaeology, Atlas, Aviation, Battleground, Discovery, Family History,
History, Maritime, Military, Naval, Politics, Railways, Select,
Transport, True Crime, and Fiction, Frontline Books, Leo Cooper,
Praetorian Press, Seaforth Publishing and Wharncliffe.

For a complete list of Pen & Sword titles please contact
PEN & SWORD BOOKS LIMITED
47 Church Street, Barnsley, South Yorkshire, S70 2AS, England
E-mail: enquiries@pen-and-sword.co.uk
Website: www.pen-and-sword.co.uk

Contents

List of Plates

Acknowledgements

First, I renew my thanks to all those who made the forerunner of this book possible when it was published in 1976 – Gallipoli veterans and their families in all corners of Britain, in Australia and New Zealand, in France, in Germany, in Newfoundland and in Turkey. I have clear memories of interviews, of documents, of generous hospitality and, more particularly abroad, of help given by people in all stages of life to enable me to plan logistically to meet 'men who were there' and research in documentary collections. In a collective sense the Gallipoli Association in the United Kingdom, recently founded when I began my research, was invaluable in contacting British veterans and still today admirably keeps alive a consciousness of the importance of the campaign.

Second, Sunderland Polytechnic, now Sunderland University, was in so many ways supportive of the work I was undertaking in trying to rescue evidence of personal experience in the Great War, with Gallipoli being the initial focus. The enormous privilege of a sabbatical year and financial assistance, augmented by the Priestman Trust and the British Academy, enabled travel to be undertaken which otherwise could only have been wistfully imagined.

Third, with regard to the original research, I acknowledge appreciatively the help of staff in all the archives listed in the unpublished sources for this book. I cannot recall a single instance of disappointment in this respect and now I would like to add my thanks to Richard Davies and staff in Special Collections, the Liddle Collection, Brotherton Library, the University of Leeds, to Gavin J. Edgerley-Harris, Curator of the Gurkha Museum in Winchester, and to Mrs A.J. Tottle, a museum assistant there, to Larysa Bolton at the Manchester Regiment Museum in Ashton-under-Lyne, to Celia Green at the Regimental Museum of the Royal Welsh Regiment in Brecon, Colin Parr concerning the Dorset Yeomanry Regiment in the Keep Military Museum, Dorchester and the Wingfield Digby photograph collection there, Ian Martin at the Museum of the King's Own Scottish Borderers, Berwick, Colonel Mike Glover and Sarah Stevenson at the Museum of the Lancashire Fusiliers in Bury, and Lynda Powell, at the Museum of the Green Howards in Richmond, Yorkshire. Some of these museums, despite the evident achievements of staff and volunteers in display to the public, in conservation and in the excellence of service to researchers, are run on a shoestring – in one extraordinary case without that shoestring. Our order of priorities in times of financial constraint will never win universal agreement but in important affairs, our defence as a nation most notably, we have an embarrassingly poor record of leaving things until it is almost too late. It may be ineffectual for an historian to challenge national, regional and local authorities by suggesting that the failure to show interest in, and respect for, our past, is no way properly to manage our present nor sensibly prepare for our future, but is this not the case?

I thank John Prust for access to his personal collection of photographs, and most particularly Matthew Richardson, in the Manx Heritage Centre, a former colleague and long-time friend, for shrewd advice and for providing me with material which would otherwise have been beyond my reach.

The idea of reconsidering the original *Men of Gallipoli* came from my more recent publishers, Pen and Sword. Rupert Harding of Pen and Sword has given me every help. I have thoroughly enjoyed the challenge and have appreciated the opportunity. I am happy to express my gratitude to Pen and Sword editor Stephen Chumbley for his eagle-eyed, sound observations throughout his examination of the text.

Finally and more personally, when *Men of Gallipoli* was written thirty-seven years ago, my then wife, Sheila, and our children, Steven and Alison, had 'lived' with Gallipoli. Sincerely I thank them for their support and forbearance – 'beyond the call of duty' comes uncomfortably to mind. Now, in this new book, I have been blessed in the presentation of the text by my wife, Louise, who, over many years, has made so many tasks achievable and so much happiness assured.

To all those who have helped me I remain grateful. It is my hope that this reconsideration of the campaign captures the essence of the Dardanelles/Gallipoli experience and that it makes fair judgements. The book is dedicated in affectionate respect to the memory of so many Gallipoli men who became friends.

Peter Liddle,
Mickley,
North Yorkshire.
December 2013

Introduction

Within my work to rescue personal experience evidence of the First World War, my first concentrated attention was drawn to the Gallipoli Campaign. My books on Gallipoli, three in all now, grew out of that special focus and commitment to the experience of the men who served on the Peninsula or in the surrounding waters. From 1967 I had been endeavouring to track down these men in the United Kingdom, in France, Australia, New Zealand, Eire, Newfoundland, and in Turkey, Germany and Austria. Quite apart from the intense fascination of meeting Gallipoli men, research in each country seemed to offer rich food for thought; the reporter in Australia who as I arrived at a State airport terminal greeted me with the challenge in unmistakable accent: 'Gallipoli, yes, where Churchill sent the expendable colonials!' Then in France, amidst the warmth of a gathering with senior naval officers who had served as young men in the Dardanelles, the chill in the air when, thoughtlessly, I turned to ask about their experience in the Second World War.

The research took me to France four times, to Australasia and to Turkey. With the help of agencies, notably the Gallipoli Association in Britain, and individuals, I managed to contact 650 or so veterans who provided me with original diaries, letters and photographs, as well as recollections of their service. A complete list of these men appears at the end of the book.

From the first, my intention was to build an archive for posterity of the material being collected and then to use it in a book which would faithfully portray the experience of the young officers, soldiers and naval ratings serving on and around the Peninsula. Both intentions were in due course accomplished; the book, *Men of Gallipoli*, was published in 1976, the archive became, in 1988, the Liddle Collection of First World War Archival Materials in the Library of the University of Leeds.

For the book, I additionally consulted personal and official documents in archives in Britain, France and Australasia, and, as would be expected, official histories, biographies, monographs, unit histories, journal articles and published autobiographical accounts.

The research was an exciting, enriching experience and I have, for example, satisfying memories of confirming the authenticity of a Marseilles citizen's dramatic story of escape from the sinking French battleship *Bouvet*, with his 1915 evidence in a dusty file in the French Naval Archives in Paris. On a Tasmanian farmstead, in an elegant Parisian flat, in a South Shields council house and even on an otherwise empty Pacific beach in New Zealand, conversation with men who were at Helles, Anzac or Suvla in 1915 brought me close, I felt, to their experience.

Of course, there were and always will be academic problems in using recollections. But when all account has been taken of the fallibility of memory, there is still the stark newness and intensity of the experience of active military service in a man's impressionable youth, and this deserves, on occasion even demands, consideration. To contest that 1915 in the Dardanelles – and of course on other fronts – left an ineffaceable impression on many, would not just be mean-spirited but, again and again, easily disproved by corroborative evidence from the time.

The examination I was assisted in making of the Peninsula and of Kum Kale in 1972 helped in placing the material I was gathering into a topographical context. Despite afforestation at Anzac and farming at Helles, it was relatively easy to be carried back in eye and mind to 1915. A map shows Achi Baba's height to be insignificant, yet actually seeing its shouldered bulk dominating the view from the cliffs above any of the Helles landing beaches, leaves one in no doubt of its vital importance as a strategic objective. Then the contorted Anzac landscape illuminatingly reveals a forbidding stark face from the sea off Ari Burnu, and the Suvla bowl or amphitheatre, seen from the shore or from the heights of the Anzac beachhead, takes on an evocative aspect from which any account of the events of August 1915 derives added import. To see the still exposed position at the Nek or the slightly raised shingle bank below Seddel Bahr castle and then, in the heat of the summer, the dried Salt Lake and the tinder-like scrub under a burning sun, helps to dissolve the years which have passed since the soldier diarist made his record of the historic events in which he was engaged.

So much for the range of sources from which *Men of Gallipoli* was drawn, but what about its academic justification? Can it be claimed convincingly that Gallipoli provided a sufficiently different soldiering experience with regard to circumstance and performance to justify a detailed concentration on the service of the individual there? Well, I think there are grounds for considering that Gallipoli offered and demanded quite distinctive soldiering, however many similarities there may be with the fighting in France and to an extent in Macedonia, Mesopotamia and Palestine. Patently the naval officer and rating have no parallel 1914–18 service remotely to compare with that of the Dardanelles. Tsingtao, Tanga or Zeebrugge/Ostend, may come to mind, only to be summarily dismissed as quite different again.

Gallipoli was the only major 'alternative' campaign which held any possibility of a quick dramatic victory. In both the documentation and the memories of those who took part there is ample evidence of an anticipation of great events. The sheer might of the naval commitment which the soldiers first glimpsed as they entered Mudros harbour was an inspiring sight engendering a consciousness of involvement in the challenge of a major enterprise. For most men it was to be their first experience under fire, precipitating a maturity which would leave its mark. Following the drama of the landings there were to be further tests, generally fruitless and costly assaults on entrenched positions in the tradition being established on the Western Front, but there were also distinctive operations, such as the seizing of Gurkha Bluff on the left flank at Helles, the night advance up the unreconnoitred Anzac gullies in August, or the aggressive mining activities so unlike the slow gestation of similar activity in France.

There does not, for example, seem to be any parallel on another front to the sheer concentrated ferocity of the hand bombing at Quinn's or Courtney's Post in May or to the prolonged fighting from entrenched positions where at some points only a sandbagged barricade separated the opposing troops. Such conditions actually led to the construction and regular use of catapults. For an August attack at Anzac, troops even dug assault tunnels to reduce further the narrow but fearsome no man's land over which they were to charge, a tactic almost two years ahead of its employment in France.

There was individual enterprise like that of John Simpson Kirkpatrick with his donkey at Anzac, transporting wounded men unable to walk to the dressing station, the night-time reconnaissance of no man's land to the North of the Anzac beachhead to help plan the August outflanking move to strike for the heights, or that of the silent forays by Gurkhas to secure grim evidence of the sudden death of a Turkish sniper.

It is scarcely surprising that the geographical conditions which so dominated the campaign, strategically and tactically, should also determine trench living conditions. With Achi Baba, Sari Bair and the encircling hills at Suvla standing as a constant challenge, at once depressingly unreachable and demonstrably near, the Allied soldiers were confined to beachheads, relatively small at Helles, almost ridiculously so at Anzac. Not even the Mesopotamian seasonal river flooding or the Bulgarian barrier of the Grand Couronne so circumscribed freedom of Allied movement. Each occupied sector of the Peninsula was open to shell-fire; rest areas, or being 'out of the line in reserve', must have been terms defying acceptance by the soldier arriving on the Peninsula following service in France.

The land held by the British and French at Helles was, at its widest point, little more than two miles across, and the distance from the front line at Helles to the extreme point of the Peninsula, Cape Tekke Tepe, was just over three miles. At Anzac the crescent-shaped wedge was still more restricted, particularly from the front line to the rear. At Suvla, sufficient of the plain was won to secure a greater degree of space, but concealment of men, material and tactical movement was even less possible, as the tiny hillocks were too low to hide any movement from the W Hills, still less from observation from Chunuk Bair. Within these three confined areas, attack and defence had to be planned and carried out, supplies accumulated and distributed, communications maintained, troop movements made, bomb factories and tactical schools run, field dressing and casualty clearing stations as well as field hospitals set up. Even a primitive airfield at Helles, of course under observation and shell-fire, was constructed. A narrow-gauge railway, water-purifying plants, bakeries, cookhouses and plans for a funicular railway at Anzac, are further evidence of an altogether remarkable situation.

For men on the Peninsula, mail was irregular, parcel contents often spoiled, and, despite sea-bathing, no one could keep clean. There was no proper leave, and, to re-affirm, there were no real base areas for rest, relaxation and recuperation. Shell-ruined Armentières in France, or even Summerhill camp in Salonika, held possibilities utterly beyond the reach of the Peninsula and while the islands of Imbros or Lemnos afforded safety, they were without recreational facilities. It might be appropriately mentioned here that monastic seclusion from women was the lot of all who set foot on the Peninsula. Neither sight nor sound of an Amiens red light district, still less an authorised brothel, not even a countrywoman at a well to attempt conversation with, nor, for the wounded before evacuation, a nurse. There is significance in the late-August entry of a published Western Front diary: 'Whenever I get depressed … I keep repeating to myself, "Thank God I didn't go to the Dardanelles".'[1]

Permanently living in dugouts or trenches was something to which one simply had to become accustomed, but the summer heat and the impossibility of burying the dead who fell in no man's land produced a plague of flies gorged from their feeding grounds of corpses, open latrines, mugs of tea and runny jam on bread. The resultant dysentery or enteric fever was a curse comparable to that of malaria in Salonika and unparalleled in scale by disease on any other front except East Africa. Certainly on no front did such suffering occur as a result of suddenly severe weather conditions as at Suvla and Anzac in the November storm. In addition to all this, it was Gallipoli, on 25 April, and to some extent in August, which shared with Mesopotamia the melancholy distinction of illustrating most clearly the woefully inadequate medical arrangements to deal with the wounded. There was small compensation for these miseries in the unusual degree of informality in Peninsula service life. Away from the front line, there was freedom to bathe, though frequently under shelling, freedom to scrounge or to visit friends in other units. Individual or collective cooking enterprise, from parcels getting through unspoiled, was not infrequently an alternative to Army rations deficient as the latter were in variety, imagination and dietary need, and, it must be said in extenuation, by the exceptional difficulty of supplying and cooking for large numbers.

Viewed from a wider perspective than that of its being a distinctive personal experience, the Dardanelles/Gallipoli campaign was of enormous and lasting significance. A combined operation involving a British and a French naval squadron and including the most powerful modern battleship afloat, carried out seven separate landings with five divisions of troops from Britain, France, North and West Africa, Australia and New Zealand. The scale of the initial landings was an operation unmatched in the Great War and 25 April 1915 was a day of epic drama fit to rank with any day in the history of twentieth-century British warfare except perhaps 6 June 1944. It might be added that as far as British political and military planning was concerned, Norway in the Second World War in 1940, Sicily in 1943 and of course on a greater scale, Normandy in 1944, illustrate how far lessons from unforgotten Gallipoli had or had not been learned.

One of the most fascinating aspects of the campaign is the richly varied ethnic background of the Allied troops involved. There were English, Scots, Welsh, Irish, Australians, New Zealanders including Maoris, Newfoundlanders, Gurkhas, Sikhs, Punjabis, Jewish Palestinians mostly by origin from Russia, a small number from what was then Ceylon, and Frenchmen, men of the varied races of the French Foreign Legion, and Algerians, Moroccans and Senegalese. Their different languages and cultures, their prejudices and their ideals, their varied military training and experience, had to be fused to serve a common military purpose.

For Australians and New Zealanders above all, Gallipoli earned a singular distinction; and 25 April, the day when Australian and New Zealand troops first saw action as separately identified units, despatched by the instruction of their own Governments, was later chosen as the day on which these two nations commemorate the service and sacrifice of their armed forces in two world wars.[2] Bill Gammage, in *The Broken Years*, wrote: 'Anzac provided a glorious focus for specifically nationalist sentiment; it was a peculiarly Australian achievement which until then had been lacking and in the eyes of contemporaries it made Australia a nation at last with international recognition, national heroes, a national day and a worthy tradition. It established an ethos which seemed to express the best of both nation and Empire, and this inevitably reduced the imperial attachment of Australians.'[3] For Australia and New Zealand, it is universally recognized that their emergent nationhood had been forged in the crucible of Gallipoli.

If this were not enough to make special claim for soldier service on the Peninsula, then there is Gallipoli's legendary reputation for being a ruinously ill-judged venture, for scandalously incompetent military leadership and for the hapless heroism of some troops and slothful inadequacy of others. Of this reputation and the degree to which it can be substantiated, much more later.

The Gallipoli Experience Reconsidered follows *Men of Gallipoli* in emphasising the individual rather than his unit or his nationality, but leans toward an awareness that the evidence, unless specifically stated otherwise, is likely to have representational validity in both respects. Endeavouring to let those who participated in a campaign speak for themselves is sometimes described as 'history from the bottom up'. I am not entirely comfortable with such a description because nothing happens in military matters without an order from above. The chain of military command stretching from a commander-in-chief descends to the very bottom reaches of its length activating a lance-corporal of a platoon to supervise his men doing whatever they have been ordered to do. The soldier's consciousness of his officers may indeed be limited to the officer in command of his platoon, or perhaps as high as his battalion's commanding officer, but soldier and officer are both following orders from above and this to all intents and purposes will determine their experience. Top and bottom are not to be separated so easily and I have tried to bear this in mind as well as the fact that Generals – and Admirals – were themselves following instructions, those of their political masters.

It is a soldier's lot to do what he is told. He will grumble but he will do it, and even when he is ordered to do something which seems against all sense, for a host of reasons he will still obediently try to do it. I might add here that while those reasons will include army discipline and training, may well include unspoken ideals of regimental pride, regional or national patriotism – God, King and Country – the collective requirement of not letting one's comrades down will be pre-eminent. If predictable costly failure were then to ensue, bitter resentment on occasion found virulent expression in letters, surprisingly escaping censorship, proof of the censor's fallibility, over-work or, just possibly, of his own angry agreement.

Briefly to return to the question of High Command, I have tried to keep all matters of senior authority in mind, dealing with them as seemed fitting for this book without letting it draw me towards an attempt to write 'a history of the campaign with some idea of what it was like to go through it'. This has been done often, sometimes notably well, by Robert Rhodes James, long ago, and recently by Peter Hart in his superbly informative, richly descriptive and challengingly judgemental *Gallipoli*. What was required of the men who were there, what did they record at the time of their experience, and what outstanding recollections did they retain; this is at the heart of *The Gallipoli Experience Reconsidered* but it requires throughout an informed awareness of the context in which the men's service is being measured.

My thinking about Gallipoli did not stop with the publication of *Men of Gallipoli* in 1976. I prepared an illustrated book on the campaign in 1982, *Gallipoli; Pens, Pencils and Cameras at War* – I have to say this book was rather poorly presented – and then still more evidence and reflection in chapters of several books in which I had tried to distil the essence of First World War active service experience. I made another research visit to the Peninsula, thought about the conclusions of other historians, and put forward further considerations in various forms.

It had been exciting in 1976 handing the manuscript over for publication when so much of the evidence I put forward I had unearthed myself, but now, not far short of forty years later, it is also exciting and satisfying to know that the structure, information, assessments and writing of this new book are, in my judgement, much improved on that of its progenitor.

The law-courts of history never pronounce a final verdict and what is attempted here in the context of this book with regard to matters of enduring contention – the Dardanelles/Gallipoli concept and execution – has no such unachievable goal. It is simply to be as fair to political and military High Command as I have striven to be to the men on shore, on deck, there at the time.

1. The Aegean and the Western and Central Ottoman Empire.

Prologue: Gestation and Political Responsibility

No one reading the deliberations of the British War Council late in 1914, or from the memoirs or biographies of the men there conferring, can have any doubt that the deepest anxiety and perplexity were afflicting those charged with delivering a successful outcome to the war. The Secretary of State for War, Lord Kitchener, uniquely, in this position, a soldier, and as such both deferred to and resented by the politicians filling all the other ministries and posts in the War Council, is quoted in a colleague's memoirs, starkly stating of the deadlock in France and Belgium: 'I don't know what is to be done, this isn't war.'[1] With Britain's key minister for the strategic direction of the war at a loss, arguments were put forward for a complete change of focus away from Belgium and France. One such project was for a British landing on the German island of Borkum, drawing the Allied-sympathetic Danes into the war and an attack on Schleswig-Holstein, this new threat to Germany being vastly augmented by a projected Russian landing on the German coast. Landings on the Belgian and even the neutral Dutch coast were considered, and a plan to tempt the Greeks into a military landing on the Gallipoli Peninsula allowing the Royal Navy to make its way through the Dardanelles to the Sea of Marmara and so to Constantinople. Another idea, associated with Kitchener himself, was for a landing at Alexandretta on the Eastern Mediterranean coast, designed to sever the Ottoman Empire's rail link south to Baghdad. Success here would at once cut the Turks from Syria, remove any threat to the Suez Canal and render vulnerable Ottoman control of the oil-rich Arabian Gulf.

An attack approaching Austria-Hungary's southern flank through a landing at Salonika in still-neutral Greece, or from a port on the Dalmatian coast, was a consideration too, the pet project of Lloyd George, in the early nurturing of both his inveterate opposition to British Generals on the Western Front and his budding ambition to take control of the direction of the war effort by capturing the British Premiership.

Such ventures, even in the strategic dilemma being faced, had flaws outweighing their attractions. What gave a different, indirect strategy, more chance of acceptance was a combination of circumstance and persuasive theoretical argument. The idea of an attack at the Dardanelles potentially leading to a naval threat to Constantinople itself, possibly removing by revolution the Ottoman Empire from the war, was first put to the War Council by Winston Churchill, First Lord of the Admiralty, on 25 November. He advocated the move as the best way of frustrating immediately any Turkish designs on Egypt and the Suez Canal. He had stated, and it was generally understood, that a considerable body of troops would be needed to take full advantage of the Navy's destruction of the defences of the Narrows and threat to the Ottoman capital. There were simply not the troops available for so ambitious a plan but the ensuing weeks of continued frustration in France and Belgium were to generate such a measure of strategic desperation that the idea was revived just immediately before a serious war emergency arose for Russia on her Armenian front with Turkey, an appeal being made for Allied aid in distracting the Turks from concentration on this front. In such a way was Churchill offered a liberating opportunity to race in with a modified Dardanelles project – and then off to take advantage of it like a latter-day Italian moped bag-snatcher.

The persuasive theoretical argument had been advanced by the Secretary to the War Council, Lieutenant-Colonel Maurice Hankey, just before the Russian plea arrived. On Boxing Day, Hankey, addressing the predicament facing the War Council, prepared a memorandum on the strategic options available. He expanded widely and convincingly on that directed towards the Dardanelles. In essence he put forward that the defeat of the Ottoman Empire would answer the immediate problem of aiding Russia on her Armenian front, and open the Black Sea for Russian wheat to reach Britain and France and for Entente arms and munitions to reach Russia, sustaining her war effort. There was much more: Serbia might be assisted against an impending onslaught by the Central Powers; by success against the Turks, Italy, Bulgaria and Romania, might be drawn into alliance with the Triple Entente; Greece, whose army would be needed, might be drawn in as well; Egypt and the Suez Canal would be made secure, and the oil fields of the Gulf too. Further afield, the German/Turkish diplomatic, propaganda and military threat to India would be expunged. As a final, and it has to be said, even more optimistic bonus, British naval power could be brought up the Danube to threaten the very heart of the Habsburg domains.

It is easy to see this as a house of cards subject to the slightest tremor, but we do no justice to Hankey if we were to ignore the War Council's all-consuming preoccupation with a strategy alternative to that of the costly commitment, without prospect of end, to the Western Front. It was at this stage that the new circumstance intervened and brought opportunity available for seizure. Under dangerous pressure from the Turks on the Caucasus front, Grand Duke Nicholas, on 2 January 1915, appealed urgently for help from Russia's Western allies for some military demonstration against the Turks which might help to forestall imminent disaster.

Kitchener was all too aware that his New Armies were far from fully trained and certainly unready for deployment to an active service front. He had but a single Regular Army division 'spare', held in readiness for Western Front emergency, and, not incidentally, he had infuriated Sir John French, in command of the British force there, with his stated conviction that victory was not be won in France until the New Armies were ready. Kitchener knew he could send no soldiers to the aid of Russia, but called upon Churchill at the Admiralty to see whether naval assistance might be offered. The two men agreed that a naval demonstration might be made at the Dardanelles with the implication that this might lead to a direct warship threat before Constantinople.

From idea to initiation, matters now moved with a speed rendering inappropriate any comparison to the germination of seeds. How ironic it is that the Turkish threat to Russia which created the opportunity snatched so imaginatively by Churchill – though some would say so foolishly – vanished swiftly in Russian counter-attack!

Churchill organised from the Admiralty an immediate enquiry of the Officer in Command of the Eastern Mediterranean Squadron, Sir Sackville Carden, whether he were to judge that bombardment of the forts at the Dardanelles would allow ships to proceed through the Narrows, emphasising that 'the importance of the results would justify severe loss'. Churchill used Carden's cautious response that success could not be expected from a sudden strike, but that the Narrows 'might be forced by extended operations with a large number of ships' to plan an attractive proposal for the War Council. Carden's battleships were old pre-dreadnoughts, no longer considered suitable for combat with the German High Seas Fleet in the North Sea. The word 'expendable' had not been used in Churchill's signal but the implication was clear.

It must be stated that the issue of whether the First Lord's proposal were to have been deliberately deceptive in its attraction has earned the scornful derision of some historians but a rejoinder might be that they themselves underestimate the Allied crisis and enjoy the benefit of hindsight in the laceration of their culprit.

George Cassar, in his fine book *Kitchener's War*, has identified a meeting arranged by Churchill, almost certainly on 12 January, with Kitchener, Fisher, the First Sea Lord, and with Admiral of the Fleet, Sir Arthur Wilson, as the occasion when Churchill's case for a purely naval assault on the forts at the entrance to the Dardanelles and then those of the Narrows, was endorsed. Churchill's persuasive advocacy the following day at the War Council was but a formality, considered Cassar.[2]

The military economy of the proposition put forward by Churchill, based on Carden's plan progressively to demolish the forts using old battleships, won acceptance of the idea from Fisher, and then that no troops were called for, removed the likelihood of Kitchener's opposition. Kitchener himself, at the War Council on 13 January, was to add a third argument in favour of the scheme, in that if success were not visibly within reach, the operation could be considered as a demonstration and at that stage called off without loss of face. However, a naval success, continued Churchill at the meeting on 13 January, and the appearance of British warships off the Golden Horn at Constantinople, were likely to stimulate internal revolution, taking the Ottoman Empire out of the war and leading to the realization of potentially massive benefits – all danger to Egypt removed, direct assistance to Russia now possible, and Balkan countries in all likelihood won from neutrality to the Allied cause. Fisher, predictably unpredictable, stifling his doubts and his resentment that his Baltic assault predilection was not shared, seemed strikingly to endorse Churchill's proposal by offering the Navy's newest superdreadnought, HMS *Queen Elizabeth*, whose 15in guns could be calibrated on the Turkish forts.

The War Council left its own legacy to what is now almost a century-old debate on the Dardanelles/Gallipoli concept with its conclusion on 13 January that 'the

Admiralty should prepare a naval expedition to invade and take the Gallipoli Peninsula'. The 'invading' and the 'taking' of even so small an area of land as the Gallipoli Peninsula, by the Navy, unsupported by troops, have been terminological hostages to fortune ever since.

In such a manner the gamble at the Dardanelles was authorised by the Prime Minister, H.H. Asquith, by Lord Kitchener, by Sir John Fisher and their colleagues on the War Council. Significantly, if further evidence were needed of the Allied bewilderment facing a war without prospect of victory, and then enthusiasm at seeing a way forward after all, the French Cabinet too, was within a short time to back the idea with French naval support, and later military, despite the colossal demands being incurred in holding the German advance into France and attempting to hurl it back.

With regard to Anglo-French unity in the direction of the war during Kitchener's time at the War Office, it might appropriately be added that Kitchener was never free, neither by obligation nor instinct, from his acceptance that Britain must do all she could to take a greater share of the Western Front burden as yet borne so inequitably by France. However, an early biographer stated that: 'Left to himself (he) would have selected, as all his friends knew, some point in the Near East, and would have launched an attack with every man and gun and shell which could have been begged, borrowed or stolen from the Western Front.'[3] If his biographer, Reginald, Viscount Esher, were right here, it is surely still more inexplicable that Kitchener ordered no such study of the means to achieve military success in the alternative area chosen.

Returning to the gamble now agreed, a not unreasonable contemporary analogy to the War Council's desperate dilemma encouraging a venture into the unknown, might be drawn from a range of circumstances; a hard-up family's project for emigration, agreed under persuasion by all the senior members; a potentially advantageous but risky business enterprise for those with drained capital, similarly endorsed; less happily comparable, a criminal conspiracy, handshake-sealed; such enterprises leaving all those involved awaiting success, the sharing of benefits and credit for the concept, but then, later, faced instead by failure and the perceived self-protective necessity to distance oneself from the idea in the first place. From puzzlement to temptation, attraction, commitment, and then, with disaster the unanticipated result, the undignified rush for disentanglement, best achieved, it would seem, by the shovelling of manure onto those left without spade or overalls. Churchill, of course symbolically without spade or overalls, was in due time to be subjected to the judgemental manure liberally directed at him but was of the conviction that some was thrown by those who had let him down and who deserved the derision in full measure too.

The concept as outlined above was to evolve, not remain fixed like a chilled cadaver for autopsy, but first we can deal almost summarily with the issue of responsibility for the gamble being risked on 13 January. With Churchill and, in a sense, Hankey, was Kitchener responsible? Of course he was. Asquith, the Prime Minister? By definition. And all the members of the War Council who endorsed the Dardanelles conclusions of their meetings at different stages before and during the campaign, were they all responsible? Indeed they were and the French Government too. If collective responsibility might have brought collective credit, it certainly confers collective blame, no matter the subsequently attempted shameless evasions.

What about responsibility as the nature of the venture changed, the Navy failing to deliver the goods, as will be related below, and Churchill declaring he would not be held responsible if at a decisive juncture troops were needed and were not made available? On 9 February at the War Council, Kitchener promised that if the Navy were to require assistance at a later stage, troops would be made available, but when Churchill pressed for them, the War Minister's response, on 24 February, offered rebuke to Churchill and delight to generations of historians. He enquired of Churchill his purpose in the gathering together of troops for an operation to be carried through by the Navy.

The issue of British and French troops being deployed to the Balkan region had already been raised inter-governmentally in relation to attempts to persuade Greece to enter the war and concern about how to aid Serbia, and it might be said too that Kitchener was recognizing what had on 25 November been acknowledged that an attack on Turkey at the Dardanelles would at some stage need troops. However, the conclusion to the deliberations of 13 January quite specifically referred to the Navy and Admiralty alone. Churchill would shove relentlessly at the door of troop commitment but it was unlatched by Kitchener.

Some days before the commencement on 19 February of the naval bombardment at the entrance to the Straits, Churchill, urged by consensus at the Admiralty, began the lobbying of Kitchener for the troops he had indicated he would make available. Kitchener responded positively and at the War Council of 16 February he ordered the dispatch of the 29th Division east to the island of Lemnos, leased by the Greek Government as a base for operations in the area. Kitchener also announced that the Australian and New Zealand troops in Egypt would, if necessary, be deployed there too. The French, who had warships under British overall command preparing for the bombardment, then followed Kitchener's example with the commitment of a division for the Dardanelles. Regrettably, Churchill, who was to quarrel fiercely with Fisher – not entirely Churchill's fault here however – now interfered in matters wholly within Kitchener's responsibility, and their working relationship was soured. There was going to be more than enough for Churchill 'legitimately' to quarrel with Kitchener over very soon as the latter changed his mind over the 29th Division's availability for the Dardanelles, though fortunately for Churchill this reversal was itself reversed. Again it is the American historian, George Cassar, who, in his excellent biographies of both Asquith and Kitchener, lays out graphically the occasions when the Prime Minister had to summon Churchill and Kitchener to his office in an attempt to broker agreement and even, on one occasion to Churchill's acute discomfort, to administer rebuke. The accounts read as if the meetings took place in the Headmaster's study in an endeavour to get the Head's two Senior Prefects to work together for the good of the School.

While it may be reasonable to charge Asquith with a lack of dynamic leadership at the War Council, we might remember the drain on his energies in keeping some of his most important ministers from behaving like fighting cats, or, in Fisher's case on a celebrated occasion, like a sulking, uncontactable prima donna on the eve of a performance. All this, and Lloyd George's duplicitous scheming has scarcely been mentioned! If anyone were due a sugar-lump of sympathy before his dose of criticism, it is Asquith.

Asquith was no natural leader in time of war. By inclination and by reason of his circumstance as a wartime Premier, he was reliant upon Kitchener, his appointed Secretary of State for War, and in accord with the latter's assessment that the fulfilling of Britain's Western Front responsibility must not be risked. But, with his keen analytical mind, was he not too easily persuaded to look for answers in the Near East, as, temporarily, did Kitchener? Asquith may be criticised too for presiding over rambling War Council discussions, most notably that of 13 January, the critically important formal meeting even accepting Cassar's account that the unminuted meeting of principals, probably the previous day, had made the Dardanelles a 'done deal'.

Churchill held to his conviction that great gains would accrue from a success in the area but had he not won acceptance of his plan by deluding his colleagues from their previous generally agreed understanding that troops would be needed at some stage? By a balancing irony, had not Kitchener always known that though prospects for victory in France might look depressingly distant, it was in France where Germany would have to be beaten and there really were insufficient troops available for effective deployment elsewhere? It seems that he was swayed into accord by Admiralty confidence that the Navy could do the job, especially with the presence of the 15in guns of *Queen Elizabeth*, and that the naval attack merited his support, the troops merely there for securing the gains achieved.

Kitchener had, however, associated himself with a military expansion of the idea and ordered no staff study of what might be required and whether it were available or needed for France. Were there the men, howitzers, guns, ammunition, medical and other support services for a campaign in the Near East? With a British attack planned for early March on the Western Front at Neuve Chapelle, a major French offensive too, and reason to anticipate a German attack somewhere along the British line, could France and Belgium really be put on the back burner for speculative gains at the Dardanelles?

In fact it was Churchill's impetuosity in proclaiming by Press communiqué, without sanction from the Prime Minister or the War Council, that the first day of the bombardment on 19 February had gone well, thus announcing the deed to the world, which rendered cessation of the action in the event of naval failure out of the question. The communiqué was not just without higher authority, it was decidedly optimistic. The embarrassed members of the War Council were committed to seeing the venture through and it was also now generally realized that this meant, with all surprise jettisoned, military expansion of the project. Whether Churchill were endeavouring to influence Balkan countries to throw off their neutrality (or at least leanings towards the Central Powers), or whether Churchill were positioning himself to seize the laurels of success, is a matter for debate but he shares with no-one else responsibility for this decisive action with its momentous consequences.

At the War Council on 24 February Kitchener reacted to the changed circumstance with impetuosity to match Churchill's in stating that if the Navy could not force the Straits unaided, the Army should see the business through. His following phrase was ironically prescient: 'The effect of a defeat in the Orient would be very serious.' Churchill, a prime mover indeed, but he had no authority over the Army and here is Kitchener's unequivocal sanction.

To move back six weeks or so and from the War Office to the Admiralty and the First Sea Lord, Sir John Fisher, Fisher's mind, even in its mood swings, super-heated personal attachments, enmities, and resentful turning away from the Baltic, was surely, when in its sub-eruptive moments, concentrated to the exclusion of almost everything else, on the priority of the North Sea, husbanding the resources of the Grand Fleet and bringing the High Seas Fleet to battle. Churchill may have made a grand gesture to a distinguished sailor in drawing him out of retirement at the age of seventy-four – and, in Fisher's case, a popular response in accepting the appointment – but the Navy had so far disappointed the nation. Even with some achievements there had been embarrassments, defeat at Coronel and the shelling of Hartlepool, Whitby and Scarborough not least. Fisher, senior in age, had his reputation to recover and protect, Churchill, senior in office and with identifiable personal embarrassments too, like the Antwerp enterprise, had his reputation to re-make. The political marriage of these two great figures was scarcely made in Heaven.

Fisher initially stifled his doubts, and boomed his approval for the Dardanelles. Later he sat in official meetings in sulky silence while informally growling his disenchantment. He claimed that, from Jellicoe to the Admiralty charwomen, everyone knew of his opposition. This opposition grew into simmering fury as the Dardanelles scheme developed. As early as 19 January he wrote to Sir John Jellicoe, the Commander-in-Chief of the Grand Fleet: 'and now the Cabinet have decided on taking the Dardanelles solely with the Navy using fifteen battleships and thirty-other vessels and keeping out their three battlecruisers and a flotilla of destroyers – all urgently required at the decisive theatre at home! There is only one way out and that is to resign! But you say "No" which simply means I am a consenting party to that which I absolutely disapprove. I don't agree with one single step taken.'[4] This letter, one of several on the same theme, illustrates his equivocal position. Resignation, withdrawal of it under persuasion, threats to resign – how on earth was that to be managed by the First Lord and the Prime Minister? With difficulty, is an inadequate assessment. The tragic influence of the split between Churchill and Fisher over Dardanelles policy stands as a factor limiting what chances there were of success in the critical months until Fisher's resignation on 15 May.

Though written a long time ago, by a man himself with a mixed reputation in his trade as an historian, A.J.P. Taylor makes a chastening but broadly fair judgement in stating:

It was a rush job from first to last. Once Churchill took up the idea, he exaggerated both the ease with which it could be carried through and the rewards which it would bring. There was no enquiry into the means available. Churchill merely assumed that battleships could force the Straits unaided. When this failed, he assumed that there was a powerful army available for Gallipoli and assumed also that this inhospitable Peninsula presented no formidable military obstacles. Beyond this, he assumed also that the fall of Constantinople would inflict a mortal blow on Germany. All these assumptions were wrong.[5]

There are phrases of blame here which cannot exclusively be addressed to Churchill, like the responsibility for ensuring that there were the military means available, but the driving force behind the widening of the original idea of the naval strike was indubitably Churchill.

Each member of the War Council can be indicted from the record of the meetings, and perhaps one of the most embarrassing pieces of evidence is the statement of the Foreign Secretary, Sir Edward Grey, on 8 January that the Turks would be paralysed with fear when they heard that the forts were being destroyed one by one.[6] However, as an illustration of matchless irony and the shameless perfidy of politicians, a private comment from Lloyd George to his secretary/mistress, Frances Stevenson, on 15 May, would be hard to beat: 'It is the Nemesis of the man who has fought for the war for years. When the war came he saw in it the chance of success for himself and has accordingly entered on a risky campaign without caring a straw for the misery and hardship it would bring to thousands, in the hope that he would prove to be the outstanding man in this war.'[7] Hankey's notes, it scarcely needs adding, record no opposition by Lloyd George in the meetings during which the vital decisions were taken.

Russian responsibility too should be noted: the decisive impulse towards Gallipoli had been a Russian request for help. There is in addition some irony in the thought that British success in the Dardanelles would have given Russia Constantinople, which British diplomatic, military and naval effort for a hundred years had striven to withhold.[8] Furthermore, Russia vetoed any idea of a Greek contingent being involved with the scheme as it might seem an inducement for their competing claim on the control of the waterway from the Bosporus to the Dardanelles. George Cassar observes that not only did the British and French fail to agree on the political objectives to be secured but they never seriously considered whether Russia could help and if so by what means.[9] The assistance in due course of the Russian cruiser *Askold* can scarcely be considered a major contribution to the Allied naval and military commitment.

French support for what was essentially a British concept seems at first remarkable, even attractively loyal, until the realization dawns that French interests in the Eastern Mediterranean, most particularly with regard to Syria, coveted by France but under Ottoman overlordship, were of prime concern, so joint action in the area was the only way to ensure that Britain, traditional competitor as she was, secured no advantage in the region. Nonetheless the French fell for Churchill's blandishments without consulting their Admiral in the Eastern Mediterranean, Boué de Lapeyrère, and without regard for their previously agreed primacy in this sea. A French source quite fairly outlines the Churchill logic: 'Churchill in his passion to succeed ignored advice which did not support his argument',[10] but no contrary advice came from the French before the military landings in April.

It was recognized that the pedigree of a British assault on the Straits was lengthy. Admiral Duckworth in 1807 had actually breached the Dardanelles but had been severely mauled on his return journey from an unyielding Constantinople. At the time of the Russo-Turkish War in the late 1870s there had been an examination of the problems associated with British involvement in the Dardanelles, and in 1907 a Joint Staff appreciation had seen too many obstacles in the way of a combined operation to offer much chance of a worthwhile success. The Admiralty had however qualified the joint assessment by accepting that such an operation might be forced upon them and that, if this were the case, they were not as gloomy as the War Office appeared to be about the prospects.

The project was raised again in September 1914 as a result of the equivocal Turkish diplomatic position and the escape of the German warships, *Goeben* and *Breslau* to the Dardanelles and then, by secret collusion between Germany and the Ottoman Empire, through to the Sea of Marmara and so to Constantinople. The British military attaché in Constantinople, Lieutenant-Colonel Cunliffe Owen, prepared a paper on the subject and was quite clear that the 'more directions in which Great Britain's energies are scattered, so much the better for German policy'.[11] He drew attention to the need for British-Russian co-operation and suggested that the Persian Gulf might be a better place to strike than the Dardanelles.

As a result of this memorandum the question of the feasibility of an attack was studied by the Director of Military Operations at the War Office, General Callwell. His opinion was that 'considering the strength of the Turkish garrison and the large force already mobilized in European Turkey, he did not regard it as a feasible military operation and that he believed this to be the War Office view'.[12]

The background to Churchill's own ideas on the Dardanelles is interesting. He had sent a memorandum to the Cabinet in 1911 which stated that: 'It is no longer possible to force the Dardanelles ... nobody would expose a modern fleet to such perils.'[13] He had conceded at the War Council on 25 November 1914 that an attack on the Gallipoli Peninsula would be 'a very difficult operation requiring a large force',[14] and he had written to Fisher on 10 December 1914 concerning the latter's projected Zeebrugge landing, a project attractive to Sir John French too: 'I am shy of landings under fire ... unless there is no other way.'[15] In the light of such evidence, Churchill's logic, judgement and memory seem exposed by his confident assertion at the War Council of 6 April 1915 that 'he anticipated no difficulty in effecting a landing'.[16]

Ashmead Bartlett seems to provide an acceptable analysis of the development of Churchill's thinking:

It not infrequently happens that men of dominating imagination are apt to jump to the conclusion that successful accomplishment must follow as a natural corollary to a brilliant scheme which has suddenly germinated in their minds ... Mr Churchill realized how far-reaching would be the result if Constantinople were captured, but there is little evidence that he ever carefully considered what forces were necessary to ensure victory or weighed the consequences of failure.[17]

In considering whether the Gallipoli idea were a 'strategic conception surpassing others in promise',[18] one must surely recognize that a proper evaluation of the practical problems involved in its execution should have been an essential part of such an assessment. Granville Fortescue wrote caustically that 'it is the lack of foresight shown by the mind that conceived the plan of smashing a channel through to the Black Sea which is appalling'.[19] J.F.C. Fuller separates and then links the factors involved with dismissive logic. 'As a problem of pure strategy it was brilliant. But without a powerful Greek army to back it, it was amateurish because England was not capable of fighting on two fronts and the British army was neither equipped nor trained to fight in a theatre such as Gallipoli.'[20] Of course both had the benefit of hindsight, Fortescue fuelled by the immediacy of the cost and shame of failure.

It may be claimed that the true Gallipoli concept involved naval action alone and that only over-cautious leadership and unfortunate weather conditions robbed Churchill's idea of the success it deserved. A.J. Marder has argued persuasively that the stakes were sufficiently high to justify a renewal of the naval attack in April once the new *Beagle* class destroyers were available for fast minesweeping.[21] But had the Allied squadron got through, it would then, almost certainly in a damaged condition, have had to deal with the German-Turkish fleet in the Sea of Marmara. If successful there, but with ammunition surely severely depleted and re-supply problematical, would internal revolution in Constantinople automatically have followed threat of bombardment? The likelihood of Constantinople being shelled into submission is questionable, and the fleet was not equipped for a military occupation.

There is no generally-accepted agreement on the likelihood of internal revolution bringing an end to the Turkish administration, despite American Ambassador Morgenthau's clear support of this view in his memoirs.[22] One is left therefore with uneasy speculation over the Allied ships, short of coal, oil, ammunition, food and water, having to withdraw. The return to the Aegean, with the Narrows unguarded by an Allied military force, would almost certainly have been fraught with hazard.

There are further practical matters which would appear to weaken the case for success being within reach of an assault by the Navy alone. The questionable effectiveness of naval gunfire against coastal forts is one major point which does not seem to have been sufficiently considered at the time. It was maintained that the new development in long-range naval gunnery rendered obsolete the long-accepted dictum that ships were matched unequally against forts. It was anticipated that aeroplanes and balloons would compensate for the lack of adequate observation of fire effectiveness in long-range bombardment. Improved fire control and range-finding would assist in ensuring accuracy in firing at a stationary target from a ship as a pitching, rolling gun-platform. In the event the need for demolition by a shore party soon proved how limited were the results which could be expected from naval gunfire. The low-trajectory high-explosive shells, unless scoring – against the odds – a direct hit on a gun emplacement, either over-shot or merely plunged into the low, broad banks of earth which protected the guns of the forts.

The validity of striking at Turkey through the Dardanelles is probably a more finely balanced issue than its chief protagonists and antagonists declare, but, in 1915, planning and practical considerations had been insufficiently considered. As far as the involvement of the Army is concerned, the Gallipoli commitment was undertaken by the War Council at the very time when the Neuve Chapelle offensive on the Western Front was being planned. Success or failure there would require more of everything which was to be committed, men, guns, howitzers and munitions. The official historian of the Gallipoli campaign accepted that planning for offensives on two fronts was unrealistic. In his memoirs, Sir William Robertson, not of course an unbiased source in the debate over the Western or an alternative front, bemoaned the failure of politicians and soldiers to agree on the decisive front.

The French, even in their support of Gallipoli, had of course no doubt about which was the decisive front as far as they were concerned. Their Gallipoli Commander-in-Chief, General d'Amade, was informed within five days of landing on the Peninsula that despite his desperate need for ammunition 'the needs of the armies of the N.E. [Western Front] – always considerable and urgent – must take priority'.[23]

Examining the crucial question of troop deployment, Fuller cryptically comments that: 'No sooner had the Government made up their mind not to use troops than they decided to use them, and after they had arrived at this decision they decided to carry out the naval attack without them.'[24] The significance of this vacillating folly as Fuller saw it, was re-dissected by Paul Guinn. 'In retrospect it is easy to see that the contrasting views and consequent semi-deliberate misunderstandings on the function of troops at the Dardanelles were largely responsible for the manifest inadequacy of the Mediterranean Expeditionary Force (MEF) for the task it had actually to perform ... were indeed responsible for the ultimate failure of the entire campaign.'[25]

Attempting to measure the degree of desperation in the War Council and trying as best one can to remove the benefit of hindsight – the first difficult and the second, nigh impossible – is challenging to the historian recognizing that he has some responsibility to offer objective judgement as to whether the Dardanelles venture were a viable proposition. Peter Hart has no doubt: 'One thing was certain: Germany would never be beaten by an ill-conceived adventure launched against Turkey. There was no back door to Germany; no easy route to victory; no Allies propping her up, the removal of which would trigger a sudden collapse. Germany operated on interior lines of communications and, even in the event of a Turkish defeat, would have rushed reinforcements to the Austrians to make the Balkan mountain ranges all but impregnable.'[26]

It does indeed seem to the author of this book, that, as sanctioned on 13 January, there were too many unknowns to justify the endeavour, unknowns with regard to what the Navy could achieve against the obstacles in its way, and unknowns with regard to the likelihood of the benefits predicted from success. Altogether the in-built difficulties of the venture, the competence and obduracy of the Turks had been critically underestimated.

Plunging into the Sargasso Sea of speculation, success might have been achieved with some definite material benefit to the Allied conduct of the war, if, from the first, a combined operation had been decided upon, the necessary resources calculated, found to be 'spare' and made available, joint planning thoroughly undertaken, and some measure of surprise achieved. (I am turning a blind eye to the November 1914 shelling at the entrance to the Dardanelles ordered by Churchill!) However, I simply have to add a response to this flight of fancy: 'Would that the circumstance of war allowed the untroubled building of such castles in the air.'

Russian collapse might have been delayed in the event of a decisive Allied victory over the Turks. Austrian defeat might just have been accelerated, but scarcely by a united Balkan coalition comprised of such disparate, mutually-hostile elements. British food supplies would have been made a little more secure, but the idea of British naval power being exercised to any extent up the Danube is far-fetched. There were no suitable vessels to implement the idea, unless it were considered that Fisher's prized North Sea landing craft could have been used. There would have been a considerable economy of men and munitions through the closing of the Turkish fronts, but it is unsound to conclude that the newly available reinforcements for the Western Front would have led to a breakthrough there. Relatedly, the idea that Germany would denude to danger level her Western Front resources to support her threatened Allies thus opening the opportunity for the Entente to break through there, is simply unconvincing.[27]

Briefly to look at the other side of the Dardanelles/Western Front case, it is optimistic to pretend that the full Gallipoli landing force of 75,000 would have made a significant difference had these troops been used in the 1915 attacks at Neuve Chapelle, Aubers Ridge or Loos. The enormous troop commitment to the Somme offensive in the following year was to win no breakthrough.

As it was planned and carried out, the attack on the Dardanelles with its subsequent land campaign had limited prospect of success and was launched with unrealistic hopes. A heavy price was to be paid for the pursuit of an elusive prospect. This is not to deny that there may have been at least some compensatory benefit emerging at a later date from the 1915 endeavour. The Turkish army was severely drained of its strength. Turkish successes in Mesopotamia and in Egypt and Palestine in 1916 could not be exploited. Exhaustion with consequent defeat was to attend their efforts to combat 1917 British reinforcements on those fronts. Nevertheless no sophistry can disguise the Allied naval and military defeat in the Dardanelles and on the Gallipoli Peninsula. By politicians and then commanders in the field, the difficulty of neutralising defence of the Narrows and driving the Turk from the even so slight a finger of the Turkish homeland as the Gallipoli Peninsula, had been seriously miscalculated. The ships would attack and be withdrawn, the soldiers would be landed and, in due course, withdrawn too. Defeat could not be clearer.

2. The Gallipoli Peninsula and the Dardanelles.

Chapter 1

Preliminaries

The Dardanelles is the narrow stretch of water which links the Sea of Marmara to the Aegean, separating the continents of Europe and Asia. This waterway, which provides the vital Mediterranean outlet for the Black Sea via the Bosporus, has Turkish territory on both shores. The tongue of land which forms the northern shore is the Gallipoli Peninsula, named after the village of Gallipoli (Gelibolu) on its southern shore.

At the outbreak of the First World War on 4 August 1914 the area immediately became involved in the action owing to the presence in the Mediterranean of the German battlecruiser *Goeben* and the light cruiser *Breslau*, which escaped from the British and French Mediterranean squadrons, slipped through the Dardanelles and arrived off Constantinople on 9 August.

William Cave, serving as a Chief Petty Officer in HMS *Dublin*, the cruiser which, though far outmatched, had come nearest to forcing the *Goeben* to action in the chase for the Dardanelles, wrote of the disappointment aboard the *Dublin* at that time. He had been range-taker on the upper navigating bridge, where he worked and slept during the search.

Our gun crews were itching to justify our winning the Mediterranean Fleet Battle Practice Cup just prior to the outbreak of the war. The order of 'All guns with lyddite – load' was greeted with cheers from all hands. Within I suppose ten seconds the breach workers had removed the fuse caps and 'guns ready' was reported from all our 8- and 6-inch guns. Next came the torpedo orders 'Flood out bar'. Both port and starboard 21-inch torpedo tubes, previously loaded, were ready to fire. It was very early in the morning and I could only get approximate ranges in that light. Strangely *Goeben* and *Breslau* hadn't put out smoke screens and we could only presume they hadn't seen us. When we were within 6,000 yards and were positioning for torpedo attack, the two destroyers *Beagle* and *Bulldog* were ordered into position as at a boat race by Captain Kelly shouting through a megaphone from the starboard boat-deck 'Back *Bulldog*', 'Up *Beagle*'. Then we were spotted and the German ships sheered off to port exposing only an end on view. As they could now turn if they so wished and have us at their mercy, all we could do was to turn away and present our stern view to them. When we heard the order 'Cooks of messes to the galley for cocoa' we knew that we had failed in our chance secretly to approach and damage or sink *Goeben*. The guns remained loaded but not all the company showed frustration in cursing, some were actually in tears.

Stopping colliers from entering the Straits to coal *Goeben* and *Breslau*, range-keeping exercises and practice firings were to be poor compensation, though Cave asserted that *Dublin* had drawn fire from the Peninsula even before the end of August. When preparing for 'hands to bathe', the ship had been shelled and thus could lay claim to being the war's first British target for Turkish shells.

The story of the escape of the *Goeben* is told in a book by Redmond McLaughlin,[1] in which the author makes use of Admiral Souchon's memoirs concerning the herculean efforts to coal his ship at Messina, when music in the form of martial airs, extra rations, stirring speeches, etc., had been used to increase the work rate. The exhaustion and danger from scalding the overworked stokers are also mentioned in the book, which uses the evidence of a crew member's published memoirs to show that four stokers were killed during their labours in the chase.[2] Hans von Mohl, a gunnery officer in *Breslau*, recalled the state of tension on the ship, exemplified by his reply on being asked what their destination was – 'Heaven or Hell!'

During the days of the chase, numerous pertinent and impertinent articles appeared in *The Tenedos Times*, the monthly journal of the Mediterranean Destroyer Flotilla. An advertisement read, 'What offers? Two cross-bred Racers, *Goeben* and *Breslau*, both by Germany out of Kiel. Have been regularly hunted this season. Owing to the War, owner unable to use same. Apply B. F. Turk Esq., "The Dumping Ground", Chanak.' Then, with apologies to Lewis Carroll, there appeared a parody which included these verses:

> The *Goeben* and the *Breslau*
>   In the Sea of Marmara lay.
> They wept like anything to see
>   Those silent watchers grey.
> 'We're sold to Turkey now,' they cried.
>   'Why won't they go away?'
>
> 'If Turkey keeps the Straits shut up
>   To ships for half a year
> Do you suppose,' the *Breslau* said,
>   'Those ships outside would clear?'
> 'I doubt it,' said the *Goeben*,
>   'They'd still be there, I fear.'[3]

Some might see it permissible to regard the Anglo-German-Ottoman diplomacy before the Turks declared their hand, as a card game with players making persuasive gifts and costly gaffes. This is not appropriate. The German 'gift' – *Goeben* and *Breslau* – had nowhere else to go than the Dardanelles for Ottoman employment, and the British 'gaffe' of withholding from the Turks two dreadnoughts being built and completed in Britain and already paid-for by them, was made on the reasonable judgement of the uncomfortably narrow advantage held by the British Grand Fleet over the German High Seas Fleet. Yes, the 'gift' and the 'gaffe' contributed to the developing denouement but to attribute generosity or shrewdness to one and folly to the other will not do. The charge of bad faith against Britain has to stand and it is explained if not excused by *Realpolitik*, something well-understood by her adversary.

A signal from the Admiralty on 21 September to Vice-Admiral Carden, commander of the British Eastern Mediterranean Naval Squadron, affirmed that his 'sole duty is to sink *Goeben* and *Breslau*, no matter what flag they fly, if they come out of the Dardanelles',[4] but he was unable to put the order into effect. Government and Admiralty indicated their awareness of the approaching certainty of Turkey joining the Central Powers with a message to Carden on the 26th: 'You are authorized to attack any Turkish ships of war emerging from the Dardanelles',[5] and on the following day war was declared between Turkey and the Triple Entente of Britain, France and Russia, thus putting Egypt and the vital Suez Canal in real danger.

On 2 November, a wireless message from the Admiralty informed Carden that 'without risking the ships, demonstration is to be made by bombardment on the earliest suitable day by your armoured ships against the forts at the entrance of the Dardanelles at a range of 14,000 to 12,000 yards. Ships should keep under way, approaching as soon after daylight as possible, retirement should be made before fire from the forts becomes effective.'[6] On the same day Carden prepared his orders, and they included the provision that ships were not to fire more than eight rounds per turret unless otherwise ordered by signal that rapid fire was necessary to keep the ships undamaged.

Cave has described his experience in the bombardment led by the flagship *Indefatigable* and *Indomitable*, together with the French ships led by Admiral Guépratte's flagship, *Suffren*.

> It seemed to me to be a deliberate bombardment of practically every building in sight [the Seddel Bahr area of Cape Helles], care being taken not to hit the minaret. This would be because of its use for range-finding and also perhaps because of a wish not to offend religious sensibilities. The main target was certainly the fort, which we made a mess of, culminating in a huge explosion. There had been sporadic return fire from several positions but we certainly weren't hit and it was all a most one-sided affair.

In April 1919 the Dardanelles Committee of investigators interviewed the Turkish officer in command of the defences of the Dardanelles in 1914, Djevad Pasha. He confirmed that the attack had 'caused more damage than any succeeding attack including that of 18 March',[7] and he accepted that *Suffren*'s shelling of the Kum Kale battery had caused hits on the gun emplacements, though no casualties were caused.

The bombardment was not followed up, and so the period of frustrating inaction was prolonged. The entrance to the Dardanelles was patrolled, as was the Gulf of Smyrna, and the French squadron was reinforced by the old battleships *Gaulois*, *Charlemagne*, *St Louis* and *Bouvet*. British destroyers attacked and drove back two Turkish gunboats and two torpedo boats on 5 November but otherwise it was the same interminable wait for *Goeben* and *Breslau* or for new Admiralty orders.

Former officers from *Gaulois* suggested to the author that the lack of any relations between the British and French crews at this time increased the tendency of the young French officers to blame the British in general and the Admiralty in particular for the inaction. These sentiments were aggravated by technical disagreements over gunnery, in which the French preferred the effectiveness of salvoes to the more deliberate and economical British fire of turret by turret. The British method allowed for observation and correction. Unlike the French and British soldiers who were to serve on the Peninsula, the sailors had little opportunity for fraternization, but some necessary exchange did take place and it is pleasant to read the letters of appreciation from British signal officers and ratings to Admiral Guépratte following upon attachment to French ships. In an undated letter from Mess 26 of the British flagship HMS *Indefatigable*, Signalman Madden wrote:

> Please excuse the liberty I am taking in writing to you but as you told us we would be always your friends perhaps you will not mind. When we left *Suffren* I was too moved and touched to say much and so I write now and express my gratitude for all the kindness of the Admiral, officers and men bestowed on me while serving aboard your flagship. Never as long as I live will I forget it. My wish is that you will get the opportunity to distinguish yourself and so be able to rise to one of the highest in the French Navy.[8]

An English officer, H.D. Farquharson, who served aboard the French cruiser *Jaureguiberry* in April 1915, wrote the first half of his letter in French and then continued, 'I can express myself better in English so I will tell you that I feel deeply indebted to you not only for your extreme kindness you showed to me and to my countrymen but for having given me the chance in assisting at a great event in history.' Farquharson concluded: 'Hoping we shall soon meet in Constantinople and that I may have the chance of entertaining you in London.'[9]

There is no doubt that this consciousness of participating in great events and the consequent sense of exhilaration were shared by many of the Army officers and men at the 25 April landings, and indeed there is abundant evidence that the Kitchener volunteers when they left England for the Suvla landing were imbued with the same spirit.

In December and January two undersea exploits were successively to lift and then lower morale in the Allied squadron, which was now officially under the command of Admiral Carden. The sinking by the British submarine *B 11* of the Turkish battleship *Messudieh* and the subsequent loss of the French submarine *Saphir* were the two events responsible for this fluctuating morale.

The submarine service was still in its infancy and the problems of mines, nets and currents facing the 143-foot-long *B 11*, built in 1906 with a complement of twelve or thirteen,[10] were serious. There was danger from petrol leaks and exhaust leak of carbon monoxide from the engine, which could cause, quite suddenly, the complete collapse of the crew members. The batteries had to be recharged on the surface, and submerged speed was not much more than 6½ knots. There was no escape from the submarine except by surfacing and getting out through the conning-tower, and all these factors combined to make the task of using effectively one of her four precious torpedoes a difficult one. Nevertheless, the competitive eagerness of officers and crew at this early date, and later the wonderful exploits of Nasmith and Boyle, are well documented.

Norman Holbrook provided the author with a vivid account of the *B 11*'s successful mission, the substance of which is fully confirmed in the official naval history.[11] With recently renewed batteries, *B 11* was sent up the Straits on 13 December.

As a fisherman I knew that despite the strength of the current in midstream if I crept in close to the [north] shore there would be slack water. We dived to 60 feet at the Narrows, waited a while and then moved up and through. I came up to periscope depth and saw on the starboard quarter a large old Turkish battleship. We went down again but the tide got us and swept us into Sari Siglar Bay and now the ship [*Messudieh*] was on our port bow. I altered course and it needed full speed to combat the current and get into position for a shot. I fired one torpedo and then had to reduce speed because the lights were getting low and obviously our batteries were failing. We then found ourselves aground stern first and I could see the ship down by the stern and smoke from the shore suggesting that fire was being directed at us. By using full revs, we got off but I couldn't see the way out of the bay. I looked for the farthest bit of land through the periscope but the coxswain said the spirit compass lenses had packed up and all he could see was black spots. I told him to follow them and at full [submerged] speed in twenty minutes a sea horizon appeared on our port hand. We made for it and were more or less swept out of the Straits having dived of course through the Narrows. We had been under water for over nine hours. What a wonderful crew – each a first class man – but we had been very very lucky.

B 11 had successfully navigated and negotiated about forty-five miles within the Straits on the entire trip, and avoided five lines of mines, nets and Turkish patrolling torpedo boats, to say nothing of the shore batteries which sighted her as she ran aground in Sari Siglar Bay. This in itself was a major achievement, which the sinking of the *Messudieh* crowned.[12] Lieutenant Holbrook was awarded the VC and all his men were decorated. Admiral Guépratte informed Vice-Admiral Carden that he had recommended that Holbrook should become a Member of the Order of the Legion of Honour, and in his appreciation of this distinction the submarine commander wrote to the French Admiral, 'it is impossible for me to tell you how much I appreciate receiving such a letter, especially from the Admiral of our most noble Allies. It is most gracious of you to have written to the Commander-in-chief about me and should the Government of the French Republic confer upon me that high distinction, the Legion of Honour, I shall be one of the proudest officers in His Majesty's Navy. I am afraid the small service I have done is not worthy of such high distinction.'[13]

Sadly, *B 11*'s success was balanced by the tragedy of the French submarine *Saphir*. The *Saphir* ran aground in the Straits, near Chanak, and was lost on 15

January. English sources indicate that she was lost owing to the failure to combat the bewildering change of water density as the fresh waters of the Marmara met the salt water at the Mediterranean end of the Straits. Paul Chack and Jean-Jacques Antier[14] give a far fuller explanation. At first the *Saphir* had sprung a small leak and, with the level of water rising, the pumps worked to keep the accumulation of water to manageable proportions. In the middle of a minefield the cables of the mines scraped the hull, then two mines bumped against the thin sheet of the submarine without exploding. An hour later the same noises were heard, and Lieutenant Henri Fournier, in command, brought the submarine to periscope depth. His compass lenses were obscured but he could see he was in the middle of a minefield. He dived again and, steering by auxiliary compass, found himself aground on a beach at an angle of 35°, with his hydroplanes on the beach in full view of the enemy. The submarine began to slide down till it was at an angle of 50°, the accumulators spilled their acid and the boat was filled with noxious fumes. In this situation it settled on the bottom in sixty metres of water. The leakage of water had become a cascade under a pressure which threatened to split the hull. Emptying the ballast tanks failed to raise the boat. Water was now entering from many leaks. All efforts to move *Saphir* failed, but then the bows rose and, totally out of control and balance, broke the surface off Chanak. Two Turkish batteries started firing. One of *Saphir*'s electric motors was still capable of work and Fournier refilled the ballast tanks and went down to sixteen metres, but could not keep on an even keel. The crew destroyed the secret code books and slowly *Saphir* resurfaced. Standing on the bridge while under fire, Fournier directed his submarine into midstream to sink her in deep water. As he was moving into midstream he attempted to fire torpedoes at two gunboats firing on him but the boat's position in the water prevented this. With flag flying and the crew swimming to shore Fournier remained standing under a hail of fire as *Saphir*, with her ballast tanks opened, sank beneath him. One of the sailors stayed till the end to help him as Fournier couldn't swim, but it was cold and the man was obviously exhausted. Fournier himself let go of his helper and drowned. Thirteen of the crew of twenty-seven were saved. The differing fortunes of *B II* and *Saphir* show the perils and strain which the crews of these submarines suffered before the improved equipment of newer boats appeared at the Dardanelles.

The loss of *Saphir*[15] cast a particular shadow of concern which is indicated by the earliest official intimation that something was wrong. In a signal made at 11.09 a.m. on 16 January 1915, the destroyer *Blenheim* reported to Vice-Admiral Carden, 'Saphir has not been seen since 5.30 a.m. 15 January when she was seen to trim and dive near "Z" [a patrol position]. I am searching Rabbit Island and coast of Imbros Island but I consider she has gone up Dardanelles although she was informed not to go without orders.'[16] On the same day Carden wrote to Guépratte, 'I am sending you copy of a signal just received from *Blenheim* about *Saphir*. I hope she is all right … I do not propose to make any signal as yet to the Comm.-in-Chief but please do not let that affect your action if you wish to do so.'[17] Within two days further information became available and there is clearly no recrimination as Carden wrote to Guépratte on the 18th, 'I am very unhappy about your gallant *Saphir*, it was most courageous and dashing. I trust they are all saved', and on 1 February, 'She had done splendidly you see, having ascended so far'. However, before Carden went with *Indefatigable* to Malta for the ship's refit, in temporarily handing over command of the Eastern Mediterranean Squadron to Admiral Guépratte, one of the requests he made in writing was that 'the submarines have orders that they are not to enter the Dardanelles without permission from Captain Coode'.[18]

Chapter 2

The February Bombardments

On 25 November 1914, at a meeting of the War Council, the First Lord of the Admiralty, Winston Churchill, raised the question of safeguarding Egypt by striking at Turkey through the Dardanelles.[1] Though no such action was endorsed at this meeting, Churchill's thoughts were later, as has been related, given significant support in a memorandum by the Secretary to the War Council, Maurice Hankey. Some consider Hankey's celebrated Boxing Day Memorandum the real inception of the Gallipoli campaign because Hankey argued for a blow at Germany's ally, Turkey: 'There ought to be no insuperable obstacle to the occupation of Constantinople, the Dardanelles and Bosporus.'[2]

Whether Churchill and Hankey would have had sufficient support for their ideas to be put into effect at that stage is by no means sure. For such a venture Hankey had laid down certain necessary conditions, such as the co-operation of Greece, Bulgaria and Russia, together with the involvement of three British army corps. However the question is hypothetical, because on 2 January 1915 an appeal for action which would divert the Turks from concentrating on their offensive against the Russians in the Caucasus was made by Grand Duke Nicholas.

By letter to Churchill, Lord Kitchener, the Secretary of State for War, accepted that 'the only place that a demonstration might have some effect in stopping reinforcements going east would be the Dardanelles',[3] and the First Sea Lord, Fisher, who really favoured schemes much nearer to hand, now saw an attack on the Dardanelles as an element in a new design for a major diplomatic, naval and military offensive on Turkey. It was however Churchill who provided the essential 'evidence' to support his own view. Churchill sent carefully-worded telegrams to Admiral Carden raising the question of the feasibility of forcing the Dardanelles and leaving Carden with little option but to admit that the Dardanelles 'might be forced by extended operations with large numbers of ships'. Acquainted with Carden's reply, the War Council of 8 January resolved that an attempt should be made 'to bombard and take the Gallipoli Peninsula with Constantinople as its objective'.[4]

Apart from the immediate pressure of a Russian request for assistance, the case for an attempt on the Dardanelles was that the successful passage of the British Navy through the Straits into the Marmara and the navigation of these waters to Constantinople would stimulate the latent revolutionary atmosphere within the capital and lead to developments of outstanding advantage to the Allies. The Turkish Government would surrender, or be overthrown, or flee to Asia. As Constantinople possessed the only munitions factories in the Ottoman Empire, even if formal surrender were not obtained, Turkish military resistance would be broken. The threat to the Suez Canal would disappear and the way towards the exploitation of Palestine and Syria would be open. The Mesopotamian advance from the Persian Gulf would be so much more secure, and Russia could withdraw her troops from the Caucasus in order to stiffen her resistance to the Austrians and Germans. The German eastward expansion, financial, political and military, would be halted and the Berlin–Baghdad railway axed, thus reducing the threat to India.

Even greater possibilities were considered. It was not merely that Russian wheat would be freed to assist her Allies and that Russia herself would be aided by war materiel. It was hoped that British sea power, by means of the Danubian waterway, would be brought to bear in central and south-eastern Europe, and Germany forced into bolstering her Austrian ally, who was now threatened by the British Navy and a rejuvenated Russian 'steamroller'. In consequence, Germany would have to withdraw troops from the Western Front, and this would probably facilitate an Allied breakthrough.

In the Balkans, it was anticipated that Serbia would be rescued from the danger of Austro-German defeat, and Greece actively influenced to join the Allies, Romania likewise, and perhaps Italy too. Certainly Bulgaria would be tempted away from Teutonic inveiglement so that a united Balkan coalition would face Austria. Not surprisingly it was considered that the advent of these conditions would speedily bring a victorious end to the war.

Lord Kitchener had made it clear that there were no troops available for the opening of a new front, but Churchill had stressed that no troops would be needed and old ships would be used. The economy of the whole scheme went far to securing War Council unanimity.[5] It should be noted that at the crucial War Council of 8 January 1915 it was also resolved that 'if the position in the Western theatre becomes, in the Spring, one of stalemate, British troops should be dispatched to another theatre and objective, and that adequate investigation and preparation would be taken with that purpose in view'.[6] Kitchener had declared that such an expedition might need 150,000 men, and at the War Council of 9 February he assured members that 'if the Navy required the assistance of the land forces at a later stage, that assistance would be forthcoming'.[7]

Meanwhile a plan was drawn up for the progressive bombardment of the outer forts of the Dardanelles. The French were invited to take part and on 2 February the French Minister of Marine, Augagneur, replied to Churchill that there was nothing in the project to which he had the least objection. The plans seemed to Augagneur to be 'conceived with prudence and foresight, allowing the halting of the operations without any loss of prestige if difficulties were encountered'.[8]

The necessary strengthening of the Allied squadrons in the eastern Mediterranean took place in late January and early February 1915. On 25 January, *Inflexible*, fresh from the Falkland Islands victory of 8 December, had relieved *Indefatigable* as Carden's flagship. The old battleship *Triumph* arrived on 15 February from the successful Tsingtao action[9] and further battleships of a similar vintage, *Vengeance*, *Cornwallis* and *Albion*, arrived in time for the beginning of the new operations on 19 February. The French ships had been augmented by the arrival of the battleships, *Bouvet*, *Charlemagne* and *Gaulois*.

There are interesting comparisons in the active-service experience of the complements of some of the British ships. Stewart and Peshall, both of whom served in *Cornwallis*, state in *The Immortal Gamble*[10] that their captain was the only man on board who had been in action, whereas the crew of *Inflexible* had had naval battle experience and *Triumph* had bombarded forts and assisted in the landing of troops.[11] With regard to the question of morale, the recollections of Pierre Vallet, in 1915 an ensign on board *Gaulois*, suggest that the fine *esprit de corps* of his ship was attributable to the fact that so many of the crew were Bretons and that there was a healthy mixture of the experience of older reservists and the devil-may-care approach of those who were much younger.

The plan for 19 February was detailed and involved an initial bombardment at long range of the forts on both sides of the entrance to the Straits, followed by a closer-range bombardment to overwhelm the forts and allow the beginning of minesweeping operations. Ships were intended to keep under way when firing and some of the fire was to be indirect, with other ships doing the necessary spotting. In the event it was found that the fire was too inaccurate from the moving ships and all were ordered to anchor for firing.

The activity on board a ship in action is vividly illustrated in *With the Fleet in the Dardanelles*. The author, W.H. Price, who had been a chaplain in HMS *Triumph* in 1914–15, reminded the reader of the battle preparation orders before action: 'Wash clothes as convenient this afternoon. All men are to wear clean clothes and flannels tomorrow.' These instructions were considered essential by the naval surgeons because dirty clothes led to septic wounds.

> Any vulnerable part of the ship had to be protected by sandbags. Hammocks had to be packed here and there to prevent shell splinters striking men who must be exposed … decks are speedily cleared at the sounding of 'General Quarters'. Hoses are rigged to keep a running stream of water over the woodwork and thus minimize the possibility of fire. Watertight doors are shut, but not before the surgeons and their attendants have moved the sick from the 'Sick Bay' into a place of safety below armour, and taken their instruments and stretchers to their station. The gun crews are in their turrets and casemates, the control officers have climbed into the foretop, the ammunition supply parties find their way to the magazine, half a dozen men take their places in the Transmission Station. Somewhere hidden in the heart of the ship, the 'black squad' are stoking their furnaces. Engineers, electricians, carpenters, and armourers each has his post.[12]

Price was in the 'fore-cross passage' with the medical party during the action of 19 February. He described the heated, crowded depths of this area and the dimly lit ammunition passages along which the shells were transported to the hoists by overhead rails. Some of the shells, in the lulls between firing, were chalked with drawings or messages conveying vulgar greetings to the Sultan.

The private diary for 19 February of Midshipman William-Powlett, on board *Vengeance*, replacing *Cornwallis*, which was ordered out of action at 11.30 a.m. because her damaged capstan prevented her from firing at anchor, recorded his experience as *Vengeance* closed in for shorter-range observation.

> Suddenly No. 1 Fort opened fire on us. We turned round to port and made off westwards, slowly firing on No. 1 with our starboard 6-inch. I did not realize that the shells were falling so close to us. At first they fell short and then over till they picked up our range. A 1 [turret] had a misfire as we were going away. I was rather nervous as I wasn't quite sure what would be the right thing to do. We tried every circuit but none succeeded. So I had it taken out and thrown overboard. I had never had to deal with such a thing before and was terrified it was going to explode. I could hear the shells whistling over us. Just as we were getting out of range one pitched about ten yards off starboard bow. Another splintered the foreyard. All this time Admiral de Robeck had been dodging round the conning tower.

Needless to say the midshipman's official log is a more sober statement of fact, and is less obviously from the pen of a fifteen-year-old lad.

The 19 February bombardment, though augmented by the newly-arrived *Queen Elizabeth*, achieved disappointing results, and bad weather caused the postponement of further operations till the 25th. The contemporary notes of a young French officer on board *Suffren*, Rene Sagnier, show that he had no illusions about the results of the action. The outer forts appeared to have been silenced, but they had not been seriously damaged. The English were misled as to the effectiveness of their fire, which by its slow deliberation and equally slow plan of progressive destruction of the forts were to lose interminable time. 'Nothing has been gained from the day's action – it will have to be done all over again.' Sagnier went on to remark that *Triumph*'s task of indirect firing, first when making way and then at anchor in the current, could not usefully be carried out, and that to attempt such an action showed the ignorance of the British command.

Midshipman Seyeux in *Gaulois* recorded in his diary on 19 February that he had received his baptism of fire. With evident interest he had noticed a 'ship to shelter aeroplanes' – it must have been the Royal Navy's first seaplane carrier, the *Ark Royal* – and saw one of the aeroplanes rise into the air and circle over the Turkish hills. It was fired on, but the 'large bird' was well away from the exploding shells. The midshipman wrote that the fire of the English *Inflexible* was not well-aimed, though some of her shells fell on target. He makes similar criticism of the French *Suffren*, but remarked that the fire of the *Vengeance* was good. A gunnery officer in *Gaulois*, Jean Deffez, noted in his diary that the day was the 199th of the war but the first day of action for his ship. It was his baptism of fire also. He noted the large number of English ships and the eagerness of the men around him for real action and their disappointment that their ship was used only for support and observation. The solemn silence affected them all before the firing broke out. There was frustration as the noise of the firing increased, but they were not to take part until the end of the day's action when they returned the fire of one of the Turkish forts. Pierre Vallet recalled that, with his gun team entombed in a small ammunition magazine on the same ship, they were not at the time unduly conscious that, in the event of an order to abandon ship, escape would have been a very tricky business as they attempted to scale the ladder leading from their depths.

The diaries of Englishmen and Frenchmen in the Allied squadron on 20 February have a clear common concern – impatience and disappointment that the weather had changed and that there were strong winds and quite a high sea. When the bombardment could be resumed on 25 February, Midshipman William-Powlett noted in his private diary the German press report that the British Admiral's ship had been sunk in the attack. In fact both the British battleships with admirals aboard – *Inflexible* with Vice-Admiral Carden and *Vengeance* with Vice-Admiral de Robeck – were in action again on the 25th. William-Powlett described watching the effect of *Queen Elizabeth's* fire from *Vengeance:* 'It was beautiful to see the 15-inch [shells] bursting and the damage done … At 1 p.m. *Cornwallis* and us prepared for the first run. I felt extremely nervous but I was all right once we got on the move.' In the event the experience was not to be unduly unnerving as there was only desultory fire in reply and by dusk 'it was a fine sight to see all the forts ablaze.'

The general scheme of the bombardment on 25 February was the same as that of the 19th, with long-range shelling followed by an attempt at short-range to destroy the forts. *Queen Elizabeth*, *Agamemnon*, *Irresistible* and *Gaulois* were the principal ships carrying out the first phase of the work, with *Vengeance*, *Cornwallis*, *Suffren*, *Charlemagne*, *Albion* and *Triumph* tackling the shorter-range work, though there were other ships involved, like *Dublin*, which was engaged in spotting for *Queen Elizabeth*. The heavy fire under which *Gaulois* came, and the effect this had on her relatively raw crew, were illustrated by the entry for 25 February in the diary of Jean Deffez: 'From where I was sheltering I could see two severely shocked men. Was this to be my last hour and this was the end of *Gaulois?* We certainly didn't fear death but we didn't look on the thought of horrible wounds with any pleasure. When we saw how near the shells were, as fountains of water were thrown up around us, we were without any doubt feeling the strain.'

The *Mitchell Report* stated that this bombardment put out of action at least 30 per cent of the guns at Kum Kale and 50 per cent of those in Seddel Bahr. Turkish military authorities interviewed in 1919 by the Dardanelles Committee gave evidence for the *Mitchell Report* which accepted that 'the batteries and ammunition dumps were all destroyed, but none of the magazines touched. The forts were evacuated because the short-range fire had destroyed them entirely. The morale of the defenders was perfect, it was said, and there was no shortage of ammunition. The crews of the guns felt natural grief at the loss of their comrades and the destruction of guns and ammunition, but were not in any way shaken in their morale or in their opinion of the strength of the defences.'[13] However exaggerated this Turkish evidence may be, in view of the fact that demolition parties found a lot of work to do, particularly at Kum Kale, it was realized by those on the spot at all levels that short-range bombardment could not be relied on to render a fort completely useless and beyond repair. Demolition by shore party was the next essential preparation for minesweeping and in fact the first shore party landed on 26 February.

Chapter 3

Landing Parties and Minesweepers

During the afternoon of 26 February, a destroyer towed in cutters from HMS *Irresistible* to Seddel Bahr beach. Thirty sailors and forty-five Marines were in this party and their task was to destroy the big guns and torpedo tubes in the fort. The *Mitchell Report* gave details about the means of destruction and how they were landed:

> It was decided to use 90 lb. of gun-cotton per gun. The wet gun-cotton for these charges was broken up and made into 30-lb. charges in canvas hoses about 9½ inches in diameter (just less than the bore of the guns). These hoses were fitted with canvas straps, so that they could be carried on the shoulders, leaving the hands free for a rifle or other small gear. A tin tube, obtained from the 16¼-lb. tins of wet gun-cotton, was fitted in each hose for the ultimate insertion of the dry gun-cotton primer. These latter were carried separately, and to provide for eventualities, fitted with two detonators, one for electrical and one for time-fuse firing.[1]

In the event all six guns were rendered useless, but no torpedo tubes could be found. From *Irresistible*, Midshipman L.A.K. Boswell, was late on deck when the demolition party was leaving and being called back for reprimand by the Captain, who had spotted him sliding down a life-line into the cutter. Boswell avoided disappointment on the second and third occasions by being well on time to depart for Kum Kale and Seddel Bahr respectively. At Kum Kale, the enemy gunners had fled and, under a covering guard of *Irresistible*'s Royal Marines, the sailors had gone from gun to gun and taken cover as each one was destroyed by individual charges. Slight opposition at Seddel Bahr led the Marines to respond with small-arms fire.

On the afternoon of the 26th there was an enormous explosion when charges to destroy the first four guns were detonated simultaneously. From HMS *Cornwallis* it was an impressive sight and sound. 'We had never heard anything like it. There was a sudden crack, as loud and dull as thunder, and an enormous rolling cloud of white smoke that swelled and swelled. Stones and masonry in chunks flew out into the sea for hundreds of yards. When we could distinguish anything, we realized that practically the whole fort had gone – a ruin marked it. The battery had disappeared.'[2]

Midshipman William-Powlett recorded in his diary the progress of the demolition party sent from *Vengeance* to Kum Kale at the same time as the *Irresistible* party left for Seddel Bahr. He began as if about to give a detached account of some exciting manoeuvre, but the end is rather different.

They landed by the pier at No. 6 [Fort] and got into scattered formation immediately. 'A' Company was left in Kum Kale while the remainder proceeded up to No. 4. They were fired on by Turks in the windmills at Yeni Shehr which were soon brought down by us and *Dublin*. It was a fine sight to see the windmills crumple up and fall down. When the party got to No. 4 Fort they smashed up a searchlight and several wires connecting mines but did not blow up the guns. On the way back they were cut off by some Turks in a cemetery. We had some difficulty in finding the point of aim owing to the wrong bearing being passed up. The captain got furious and came and trained the gun himself. He cursed me and told me I ought to have turned Mr C – out. It was rather a difficult position. The Turks were driven off and our Marines got back to their boats. I did not expect half of them to come back. Only one was killed and three wounded. The one killed I am afraid was mutilated – the Turks venting their whole wrath on him. His head was smashed in, four bullet holes in his face, one in his wrist, one in shoulder and one in the knee – this was an explosive bullet and had blown his knee cap off. Both his legs were broken and a bayonet wound in his abdomen. One [Marine] was wounded in the eye and subsequently had it taken out, one in the shoulder and one in the chin.

The midshipman recorded the formal burial on the 27th of the mutilated Marine, Sergeant Turnbull. That very day two tubes of the *Vengeance*'s boilers burst and five men were burned so seriously that two died. A worse accident had been prevented by one of the men wrapping a sack round his scalded head and dashing in this condition up a ladder to turn off a stop-valve. William-Powlett, fifteen years old, in this precipitated process of maturing into an experienced officer, shows an understandable readiness to seek a lighter-hearted recollection of the day when he describes with an amusing sketch having seen one of the officers looking 'so funny walking in the latest overall oilskin blown out like a balloon'.

A further landing for demolition purposes was carried out by a party from *Irresistible* on 27 February and despite stronger opposition six howitzers were destroyed. On 1 March a successful operation was carried out from *Irresistible* on Kum Kale Fort 4 to complete work begun by the *Vengeance* party on the 26th, and this assisted the bombardment already begun of the Turkish defences in the Straits. The progressive destruction of these defences was essential to allow the British North Sea trawlers and the French vessels to sweep a safe passage further and further up the Straits. None of the Turkish guns was put out of action in these bombardments and their deceptive silence was because of economy of use of ammunition and the temporary evacuation of forts when deemed necessary. The *Mitchell Report* again makes significant observations on the effectiveness of the Allied bombardment. Only a direct hit would knock out a gun, and 12in guns at a range of between 10,000 and 12,000 yards had a 2 per cent chance of a direct hit if the firing were done under anchor, in a calm sea, with new guns and perfect observation. What success could be expected with the ships manoeuvring, old guns, a choppy sea and salvo firing impossible because of the need for economy? Even the indirect bombardment of Forts 13 and 17 by *Queen Elizabeth*'s 15in shells fired over the Peninsula from near Gaba Tepe on 5 and 6 March, though causing great alarm to the defenders, did little serious damage because the seaplane-spotting was a failure[3] and spotting by other ships proved an inadequate substitute. It is noteworthy that one seaplane pilot, Geoffrey Bromet, acknowledging the difficulty of estimating from the air the damage done to the forts, thought that: 'Shrapnel ought to be used to clear away the personnel before common shell, (i.e. high explosive) is resorted to.'

In the meantime the attempted shore demolition continued, but on 4 March had met with a considerable check. On the previous day a reconnaissance had been undertaken at the Camber, Seddel Bahr. On the 4th, Marines were landed from *Scorpion* and *Wolverine* at Kum Kale, from *Lord Nelson* to destroy Fort 4, from *Irresistible* to destroy the bridge over the River Mendere, and from *Inflexible* and *Ocean* on the northern shore. The Turks were now in greater strength and anticipated this landing. All the disadvantages of landing a small force against a stronger one expecting an attack were illustrated in the failure to make any progress on the Peninsula side. There was a tactical failure at Kum Kale too and it was followed by a high percentage of casualties. A seaman on board *Lord Nelson*, George Keeler, recorded in his diary:

> Demolishing party from our ship landed at Kum Kale and met halfway by a hail of bullets from enemy concealed in trenches and houses. We continued to bombard heavily doing considerable damage whilst party tried to reach forts and blow up guns etc. – but they found road to fort commanded by enemy well entrenched so eventually had to retire as they were only twenty-seven to hundreds of Turks. Much difficulty was found in the retirement as there was very little cover available and a movement from anyone was a signal for a hail of bullets. The two killed from our ship were P.O. Newlands and Cummings, signalman. It was rotten to see the way that they struggled back fighting all the way along the beach. I could see them through the range-finder, crawling through the water. The Marine Brigade suffered more severely, several killed and wounded, one of which died as they brought him off to the ship. We finished embarking troops at dark but we could not find out where our party had got to until later when they were reported on board the *Irresistible*.

Midshipman Boswell, was with the *Irresistible* party and recalled that the Turks were certainly prepared on this occasion. The Royal Naval Division Marines, according to Boswell, proved less adequate under fire than *Irresistible*'s own Marines and when 'Lieutenant Sandford and I moved inland to find why we had had no signal to advance on the fort it seemed that there was no properly organized defence for our work. Because of this we had to crawl back and then along the beach, behind a bank of seaweed.' It was perhaps this experience which reinforced Boswell's later expressed conviction that the idea that the Army was essential for the successful demolition of the Narrows' forts, was a 'hoary old myth'.

Colonel Matthews of the Plymouth Battalion, Royal Marines, went with one of the companies to Kum Kale. The Brigade Major, C.F. Jerram, observed their progress through binoculars. In a letter to a former Marine, W.J. Parnham, who became orderly to Colonel Matthews, Jerram wrote many years later:

> I spotted Turks breaking away from the windmills and it looked as if they were going to cut off Bewes' Company in the nullah[4] at the foot of the hill. I was sent ashore to tell Col. Matthews to withdraw and to stay and help him. A good deal of bullets and shrapnel going in, which frightened me into fits and I landed at the Fort where I found no one doing anything. All they knew was that Col. Matthews was somewhere out there and that there were snipers in the houses fifty yards away and if I went out there, they'd get me for sure. I hadn't time to ask why the hell they didn't get the snipers out and they didn't get me anyway. I found Col. Matthews alone – no orderly – he told me (1) to send back the Naval Demolition Party lying out on the spit, (2) get a Platoon up to protect our left flank, (3) go on and tell Maj. Bewes to retire. There were a lot of bullets; however I got to the naval party and lay down beside a seaman until I found that his idea of cover was a box of detonators. Passing the word to their officer led to a 'sauve qui peut' – in other words a complete bunk led by the officer. I yelled to him to keep behind to no effect and they left two dead men behind them. Then I went to the Platoon. Their officer was paralysed with funk and wouldn't budge. The Sergeant was wounded in the head and the men took their cue from their officer which was right and proper.

The letter continues that one young Marine agreed to come with Jerram and thus the others were induced to move. Unfortunately the volunteer was wounded and as Jerram was dressing his wound Colonel Matthews arrived to ask in no uncertain terms why his orders had not been carried out. The real answer was evaded in their agreement that Bewes' Company could escape only with the aid of covering fire and this Jerram would have to get by signal from the fort to the ships. He confessed that his journey, running like a snipe, trying desperately to avoid rifle fire, gave him more sympathy for the platoon than he had felt hitherto. Jerram added a footnote that later, as they were all embarking, the two 'dead sailors' got up and started staggering back. Two officers took a stretcher and went back for them. Colonel Matthews refused to let anyone else go and Jerram was to tell them that a boat would be sent for them. A boat from the destroyer went in after dark but, according to the letter, the crew had to be forcibly persuaded to embark upon this mission and, though each man involved was later awarded the D.C.M., the two officers who had stayed with the wounded sailors got nothing. Jerram concludes his letter with a touching recollection. When as a boy he had had fights with his older brother, he had gained the necessary courage by tightly lacing up his boots. He had found himself doing the same when being rowed into the Kum Kale shore.

 There were such occasions as this during the campaign when officers and men failed to live up to the conduct required of them, but certainly they do not seem to be numerous. 4 March was a bad day and, as for the success of larger-scale operations ashore, Robert Rhodes James points out: 'It was … a grim portent. The disembarkation of troops under fire, their deployment when landed, their handling on largely unknown beaches; all these were novel problems, not only for the men of the Plymouth Battalion, but for everyone.'[5]

As early as 2 March, Flight Lieutenant Bromet had expressed in his diary a prophetic awareness of the problems which lay ahead. 'The Germans have frightened the Turks out of their lives and brought their wonderful organization and military genius to bear to the extent of making the Dardanelles a very difficult problem for the Allies. Up to the present matters have all been our own way, but I think we shall find the Narrows somewhat difficult to pass and perhaps by that time the Germans will have produced a submarine to tackle us. They are capable of great things.'

Despite the serious damage and destruction sustained by the forts from bombardments and the landing of demolition parties, they maintained their essential function of protecting the minefields. The losses on 18 March of *Bouvet*, *Ocean* and *Irresistible* and the near-loss of *Inflexible*, each as a result of its hitting a mine, were to illustrate this all too clearly. The British North Sea trawlers used for the sweeping and their volunteer crews of fishermen have frequently been blamed for the losses, but the obvious unsuitability of the vessels for their appointed task renders criticism of the crews harsh to say the least. A.J. Marder has written that the whole idea of using these slow trawlers was a 'basic error'.[6]

Above the Suandere River, in March, there were 324 mines in ten lines, though in fact the Allies believed that there were 289 in eight lines. There were five lines of mines in the Narrows, not one, as was reported. The Kephez minefield had two fewer lines – five – than had been reported. In addition it was incorrectly conjectured that there were mines at the entrance. Twenty-one trawlers were available for sweeping, but, when working against the strong current, some of them could barely make headway and the others achieved a maximum speed of only three and a half knots. When the time necessary for assembling and manoeuvring is considered and the fact that all the work had to be done under short-range fire, it is questionable to estimate just what could have been achieved. The crews are described in the *Mitchell Report* as 'generally of poor physique with very little discipline',[7] but on 2 March Admiral Carden, having seen their performance under fire, made a general signal: 'Minesweepers are doing fine work. Their perseverance and steadiness are excellent. Much depends on them.'[8] It is scarcely surprising that their morale was eroded by the strain of sweeping at night, when they knew that the very success of their work, that is the finding and exploding of mines, would disclose them to the probing searchlights and leave them open to a concentration of shelling. On 10 March the destroyers which accompanied them failed to silence the batteries, a trawler was sunk by the mine she had exploded and heavy shell-fire resulted in two trawlers being hit while exposed in the glare of the searchlights. On the 11th, when caught by searchlights and shelling, the leading trawler turned for home and the rest followed. Admiral de Robeck reported that 'in some cases the crews appear to have no objection to being blown up by mines, though they do not seem to like working under gunfire, which is a new element in their calling'.[9] It is perhaps stating the obvious that the Admiral, who had long Royal Navy service, wrote his report from a well-armed and armoured battleship. Nevertheless his frustration was shared by officers and men in the squadron. Some, such as Midshipman William-Powlett, who had themselves felt the strain of unaccustomed danger, expressed it simply as a matter beyond the competence of crews and their morale. 'Minesweepers are too slow for sweeping. They can only do one knot against the current with their sweeps out and so they have sent for some fast sweepers.'[10] The seaplane pilot Geoffrey Bromet had no doubt about the task facing the trawlermen. 'Their job is a most arduous and dangerous one, and up to the present, although little success has rewarded their efforts, they have shown themselves most capable and absolutely chock-a-block with guts.'

By order of Admiral Carden, the trawler crews were stiffened by three Navy volunteers per vessel, but the gallantry of all concerned on 13–14 March only served to prove that the speed of the trawlers was insufficient to enable them to carry out their task.[11] Faster trawlers were requested and the French made brave efforts with their vessels. The only really effective sweeping under the special conditions of the Dardanelles was not however to be possible until after the disasters – to be described in the next chapter – of 18 March,[12] and, from almost immediately after this date, the Navy was pledged by Vice-Admiral de Robeck to a supporting rather than a leading role.

The damage suffered by the trawlers, whether with mixed crews or entirely Royal Navy crews, was severe. The *Mitchell Report* describes some of the results of the night sweeping on 13 March in which two trawlers collided and came under concentrated fire which killed the Captain and all the upper-deck hands on one. *Trawler 49* had her 'mess deck completely wrecked by a large shell, shell right through ship and out at after gallows, bunker flooded by a shell below the water line, small shell through bridge, masts and rigging shot through, boats riddled and various small damage'.[13]

Amethyst, the naval escort, suffered severely in this action too. A member of her crew, E. Weaver, wrote:

We had been ordered to go below and write letters home as well as getting some refreshment. Later at action stations all was going well, with the picket boats pulling the mines away with grappling irons, and suddenly we were the centre of searchlight glare and all hell broke loose. My gun received a direct hit and all but two of us were wounded. In the forepart of the ship, shells killed many men still in their hammocks. A watch of stokers all together in the bathroom were wiped out and the upper deck looked like a ploughed field. We got out past Cape Helles at daybreak and that was the nicest sunrise I'd ever seen.

Official sources indicate that the sweeping attempts were continued right up to 18 March, even though the plan for the attack was based on the need to reduce the forts and batteries to silence before the minefields could be completely cleared. It is a small point in view of the fact that the critical line of mines laid by the Turkish *Nousret*, which accounted for the 18 March losses, was laid on 8 March, but L.A.K. Boswell, who served in *Irresistible*, positively denied, in his recall, that there was any sweeping on the day before the attack of the area from which the bombardment took place.

Fernand Pion, an engineer and a reservist in the crew of the French minesweeper *Pioche*, described his ship as having the appearance of a powerful tug with a high bridge and drawing little water, purpose-built for its work, unlike the English North Sea trawlers, and with a gun capable of destroying the mines surfaced by its operations. The crew was well trained in the handling of the sweep and the French boats operated at a far greater speed than the British – they were capable of sweeping individually a 200-metre channel to a depth of six metres in a single sweep. Pion recalled that his Captain was summoned to Vice-Admiral de Robeck and officially informed that the English trawlers had failed and it was now up to the French. The Captain had all the machinery and engines checked thoroughly and the crew reduced to essential members to avoid unnecessary casualties. In the French sweeping operations Pion admits that during the strain of fifteen days' work up to 17 March two of their crew proved incapable of disguising the nervous state all must have experienced. They gesticulated wildly, called upon Heaven, their wives and children, banged their heads against the bulkheads, burst into tears and then had to be transferred to *Bouvet*. There they began to recover their spirits, only, by the sad irony of fate, to succumb with most of *Bouvet*'s crew to the effect of the minesweepers' failure to detect that vital line of mines off the Asiatic shore of Erenkeui Bay. Pion wrote to his mother on 2 March:

> We had our life belts on all the time and it was an unforgettable experience as the shells from batteries towards Chanak regularly straddled us and the protecting British battleship *Albion* searched for the batteries firing on us, to engage them and attempt to silence them. The French gunnery is marvellous. Don't you believe it if you hear of German telegrams reporting differently. The pigs have had the cheek to send wireless messages (one of which we have intercepted) saying that we have failed and four minesweepers and two cruisers have been sunk, which is obviously false. I hope that soon in Constantinople we shall be able to stuff their lies in their mouths with 380-mm. shells. Such a victory would have considerable influence on the course of the war as it would force Turkey to give in immediately, Russia could free the Bosporus and the Balkan peoples would all rise up with us to take their share of the oriental cake.

Beside this letter from a man obviously conscious of wider issues than the safety of his own boat, it is interesting to place the recollections of Chief Petty Officer Cave. He recalled in his memoirs of service in the cruiser *Dublin* that at 'about this time [date unstated] we took on board a group of city types, dressed to match, armed with brief cases and we left for a port away up north in Bulgaria. I managed to get a glimpse of the chart which indicated by the ship's course that the port must have been Dedeagatch. I didn't know what it was all about but by the appearance of the men's faces on their return it had not been a successful trip.' In fact the date of the return of the 'city gents' was 17 March and they had been attempting to buy Turkish withdrawal from the war. The British agents involved had been empowered to negotiate up to £4,000,000 for this aim, but the chief stumbling-blocks to successful negotiation proved to be the question of sovereignty over Constantinople and the apparently successful progress of naval operations in the Dardanelles. Evidence had come to light that the Turks were short of ammunition for their forts. A member of the well-known English trading family in Constantinople, the Whittalls, was involved in the talks and he was accompanied by a former technical adviser to the Foreign Office during the attempt to improve Anglo–Turkish relations in the summer of 1914. His name was C.G. Eady and his son-in-law, Captain G.R. Allen, has written that from the evidence of his father-in-law's diary and from the naval failure of 18 March 'it does seem remarkable that a mission which had carried matters so far successfully should have been allowed to wither ignominiously at such a moment'.[14] Another man who played a small part in the earliest Anglo–Turkish financial haggling was Captain H.N. Lyster,[15] who wrote in *The Gallipolian* of a journey made in August 1914 from London to Paris and Marseilles on a secret mission conducted by the Imperial Ottoman Bank, of which he was an employee. Only later did he learn that he had been involved in Britain offering 'Turkey a paper loan of £5,000,000 to enter the war with us or remain neutral, but Germany had offered £2,000,000 in gold and the *Goeben* did the rest'. It is tempting but fruitless to speculate on the possible consequences had either the August 1914 or the early March 1915 talks reached a happy settlement, but neither financial negotiations nor active minesweeping were to prevent the launching of the naval attack of 18 March.

Chapter 4

The Naval Assault of 18 March

The failure of the minesweeping operations led to the decision to launch another attack on the forts, but this time a far more concentrated one. Success, it was believed, would allow the clearance of the minefields to proceed without hindrance. Such a belief was, however, considerably to underestimate the threat of the batteries and particularly the mobile batteries. On the Asiatic side of the Straits, water buffalo, like those still to be seen there today, were used to move and re-site howitzer batteries at night. Dummy batteries of smoking cylinders were difficult to distinguish from the real thing in these confined, swiftly flowing waters, with fire being directed from both shores. Gone were the days, amusingly described by E.W. Bullock, a seaman in *Inflexible*, when camouflage could be painted undisturbed on one side of a vessel while long-range unanswered bombardment was being conducted from the other. Liman von Sanders, the commander of the German forces in Turkey, referring to an Allied naval bombardment on 1 March, described the work of the Turkish howitzer batteries on the heights of Erenkeui and Halil Eli:

> The batteries ... belonged to the 8th Foot Artillery Regiment commanded by Colonel Wehrle and had been detached from the First Army under my command to strengthen temporarily the artillery defences of the Dardanelles Straits. The Regiment, variously grouped on the heights of the Asiatic and European shores, gave splendid support to the artillery of the fortress and with its brave commander earned much praise. The hostile ships directed their fire not only against his batteries but against dummy positions he had constructed and frequently changed.[1]

The transfer of command of the Allied squadron from the sick Admiral Carden to Vice-Admiral de Robeck in no way interfered with the thoroughness of the preparations for the great assault. The plans are dated 15 March and are under Carden's name, though operational orders of the 17th bear de Robeck's name. They provided for the more modern ships, *Inflexible, Lord Nelson, Agamemnon* and *Queen Elizabeth*, to prepare the way by long-range bombardment for the older French ships, *Suffren, Bouvet, Gaulois* and *Charlemagne*, to bombard at closer range with support from *Triumph* and *Prince George*. It does not come within the scope of this work to describe the alternative plans and the system of reliefs or indeed the events in sequential detail but rather to look at the experience of men at the heart of the action.

A good general impression through the eyes of a midshipman in *Prince George* is conveyed by the log of A.G. Buchanan.

We were hit once on the mess deck of B2 and once on the shelter deck about twenty-one feet from A1. One of these shells burst and made a mess of everything near but no damage of any consequence was done. About a quarter of an hour after the second shell hit us, the order was passed from the foretop for A1 to stand by to man the sea boat as a Frenchman, the *Bouvet*, had struck a mine; a minute later an order was passed down 'Man the lifeboat' and then later 'Hurry up with the boat, she's gone.' This had all happened in about three minutes. Our picket boat shoved off immediately and picked up thirty-five survivors and the cutter picked up one … There were only forty-odd[2] altogether … The coxswain of our picket boat said that there were several explosions after she had gone down, apparently caused by the remaining watertight compartments giving way. Her starboard 10.8-inch gun was seen to fall overboard as she heeled over apparently badly damaged by the explosion. The *Inflexible*'s fore bridge was seen to be on fire at one time during the action, but the fire was got under when she drew out of range … As we were waiting outside for our picket boat and cutter to come up, we noticed that the *Gaulois* was much down by the head. All the destroyers raced up to her and stood by her. The *Canopus*, *Cornwallis* and a French ship also stood by. It was soon found that she was in no immediate danger of sinking … Wireless signals were picked up at about this time, stating that the *Irresistible* had struck a mine and the *Ocean* had been ordered to stand by her.

In his memoirs, E.W. Bulloch of *Inflexible* wrote:

We could hear the thunder of the guns above the engines together with the shuddering and the blast showering dust everywhere, but we had no knowledge of course of how things were going; then there was a thud which shook the ship. It was followed by the silence from our guns. Then we could hear the tread of feet on the deck, meanwhile all electric lights had failed and we lit our secondary oil lamps that gave only a dim light. The engine-room telegraphs rang half ahead and remained at that long enough for us to surmise that we were either through the Narrows or we were retiring. The matter was confirmed by a well-meaning voice shouting down the lift-shaft 'Abandon ship stations'. We were still unaware of what had happened until the engineer of the watch received from the bridge a message stating that we had been mined for'ard, and if possible we would make for Mudros and beach ourselves in shallow water.

Of the watches down below one should go to his abandon ship station and the other remain down below till the last moment. Each man tossed up with his opposite number. I won against my friend Wiggie Bennett and in my heart I felt a pang, feeling that all or none should remain down below. We were urged to get a move on as the ship was developing a list and the bows were deeper in the water also. Up we went on the various ladders, groping our way as it was total darkness on the way up. We knew our way so the only problem was the watertight door that led to the mess deck. After knocking off the clips we couldn't push it open and no wonder because we should have been pulling it. Once outside we were amazed at the shambles. First of all we could see that the mess tables and chairs had been taken for buoyancy if the men had had to go overboard, then twenty-nine had been killed in the for'ard torpedo flat by the explosion of the mine and damage by another mine had flooded the food store, thus compensating for the list we were experiencing to starboard. Some of the men were stripped to their underclothes with their lifesaving belts blown up. I noticed that one of the ship's police had a football tied to his waist and as the valve to my lifebelt was missing someone tied the end with string. Wounded were being placed into the boats. I particularly remember the Master of Arms sitting in a cutter smoking his pipe and making light of his injuries, also the Gunnery Commander being carried on a stretcher to a boat. Though he was soon to die, I heard him say 'I'm a poor specimen of humanity now'.

Inflexible did reach Mudros, and Stoker Bullock not only had a chance to survey the full extent of the damage to the ship but was one of the funeral party for the sea burial of the dead, who had already been sewn up in canvas shrouds weighted with fire bars. The bodies of those killed in the flooded torpedo flat were recovered later.

A seaman in *Lord Nelson*, G.E. Keeler, wrote in his diary for 18 March that he had seen the *Bouvet* 'turn turtle in less than two minutes'. He also recorded the difficulty of sighting the Turkish howitzer batteries and of taking on board survivors from *Irresistible*. Of *Lord Nelson* under fire, Keeler wrote, 'It was not very cheerful in the maintop with too many splinters flying around.' Keeler saw *Inflexible* taking the punishment being suffered while Stoker Bullock was below. 'Her foretop was smashed in and soon she was hit on the forebridge setting it on fire. It was a sight to see her blazing away and firing her 12-inch guns at the same time.' Keeler also saw a 'splendid piece of work' done by the destroyer flotilla as they dashed through the shells to take everyone off *Ocean*, which was flying distress signals. His final entries for the day were the cheering sight of 'Lizzie'[3] doing a bit of good to Chanak and 'Aggie'[4] with a lovely hole in her funnel knocking nearly half of it away'.

William-Powlett recorded in his diary for the same day that those who saw *Bouvet* go down 'were rather cut up. It was not a nice thing to see on our way in.' How genuinely this chronicles the feelings of someone faced by a tragedy which might soon be shared! The midshipman wrote: 'I am afraid I was not able to take my usual notes as I was too busy but I managed some and I can remember most.' He had observed the accurate Turkish gunfire on *Albion* and *Irresistible* and he made a sketch in his diary to show how the splashes sometimes obscured the whole of the ship. Regrettably the photographs he took through the gun port did not come out successfully, but he described vividly the men crowding over the listing *Irresistible* into the destroyer *Wear* and picket boats while under heavy fire. He saw *Inflexible* letting off great clouds of steam and heard her blowing her siren in distress. Volunteer cutters searched unavailingly during the night for *Irresistible* and *Ocean*, both of which had sunk. William-Powlett, as he rested on the gun-room settee, wrote in his diary that 'we were most lucky. If we had carried out the first plan we would have taken the *Ocean*'s place.'

Midshipman W.L. Berridge, aboard *Albion*, was greatly impressed by the conduct of the men on board the crippled, sinking *Irresistible*. In a letter he wrote to his parents and sister. 'All through [the shell fire] her people were waiting quietly for the destroyers to take them off. One shot fell right in the middle of the quarter deck and must have wrought awful havoc. But there was no panic, none tried to get away before ordered to. And the destroyers were wonderfully handled and saved the situation completely.' The letter concludes: 'Of other damage to the fleet I will not tell but the day was far from a victory for us. Something near our fort exploded and burst violently and I believe most of the forts stopped firing but the guns were probably intact and the Turks merely left temporarily. I hope the next show will be better.' These sentiments would no doubt have been echoed by Edward Grayken, a Marine of *Irresistible*. He had climbed the listing deck of the ship, slid over the side onto the torpedo nets, disentangled himself and was taken from the water by a picket boat which put him aboard *Ocean*. Within a very short time a not dissimilar procedure enabled him to escape from the mined *Ocean* and his rescue this time was by a destroyer.

For the French ships and their crews the drama was especially associated with the loss of *Bouvet* and the severe damage sustained by *Gaulois*. From *Vengeance*, *Bouvet* had been observed by William-Powlett to have had, in full view on deck, all her officers in full dress uniform, a band playing and numbers of sheep and cattle, as the French ship led the attack. Midshipman Seyeux, in *Gaulois*, describes in his diary for 18 March the tragically swift sinking of *Bouvet* and the prolonged strain of keeping *Gaulois* afloat. The explosion of shrapnel shells above *Queen Elizabeth* was seen as the sudden appearance of little black clouds which seemed to produce rain. When all the forts opened fire they produced an 'astonishing noise'. Blackish smoke was seen rising from the bridge of *Inflexible* and then *Gaulois* herself was hit. Men were wounded, among them a friend, and shells began falling all around them. They were hit again and a slight shock was felt throughout the ship – a more violent explosion – and they made an effort to retire. *Bouvet* turned in order to place herself behind *Suffren* and she hit a mine. A small sheaf of flame and yellowish smoke appeared from a starboard 27cm. gun turret. 'For a few seconds it continued its course then gently without an explosion it listed to starboard. The Commander clearly had had no time to stop the engines as we saw it sinking lower and lower without losing speed. A minute after seeing the sheaf of flame, before our astonished eyes, the *Bouvet* turned completely over to starboard and disappeared.' Immediately they moved towards the 'large white spot' which marked where the vessel had sunk to see if they could pick up survivors, but British motor-boats were there first, followed by a torpedo boat to help to pick up the last ones found.

Over 600 men had drowned or been killed by the explosion in that dreadful minute or so. There were sixty-six survivors. The author traced one of them, Payro Sauveur, to Marseilles. In an interview he gave an account of his escape which differed in no material points from a statement he had made to the senior surviving officer within two days of his being rescued.[5] The statement, which the author found in the French Naval Archives, recorded that he

> was sent to get spare shells for the 27-cm. port gun turret. I was in the right place for the shells when the blow came. The boat immediately listed to starboard. I was completely covered in the coal dust which came from the bunkers. I went to the signal ladder and with the second mate we climbed up. I then went up the ladder leading to the upper battery. From the bridge I got myself onto the funnel which was entering the water. Then I climbed onto the hull. I believe the second mate was trapped by the landing keel blocks and that he fell into a hatch way. From the keel I threw myself into the water. I am a very good swimmer.

The Frenchman spoke to me of the blood bursting through his ears and nose, as he was carried deeply under. He came to the surface to be rescued by a British picket or motor-boat. The officer who took the depositions in March 1915 ended his report by remarking that not a single survivor had seen any regrettable behaviour by those now living or dead.

The French battleship *Gaulois* also appeared to be doomed. Midshipman Seyeux wrote in his diary that there was no chance of reaching Tenedos. By an irony of fate one of the *Bouvet* survivors brought by an English motor-boat had only just been transferred from *Gaulois* to *Bouvet*. Inside *Gaulois* the water was rising rapidly, the dynamos had failed and there were only oil lamps giving illumination in the evening darkness as they crept towards the Rabbit Islands. The ship's company was assembled at disembarking stations and some men were taken off. Others collected chairs and tables ready for throwing into the sea if need be, for support in the water. Some partly undressed so that they would be able to swim more easily. The stokers and engineers went to their stations below with admirable *sang-froid*. The officers anxiously watched from the bridge to see if *Gaulois* would reach Mavro Island. Towing offers from *Suffren* and British ships had been refused, but when

> English officers came on board asking what help we needed, we asked for and received an anchor and divers who could examine and repair our holed keel. *Gaulois* only just reached the island in time as the rapidly constructed wooden partition which was designed to cover the yawning rent in the keel was giving way under the enormous pressure of the water. Admiral Guépratte had previously come on board to congratulate our Commander on the skilful way he was handling the ship.

Gaulois was gently beached on Mavro Island.

Rear-Admiral Lucas, in 1915 a young officer in *Gaulois*, slightly senior to Midshipman Seyeux, recalled in his memoirs the action of their Captain Biard in taking *Gaulois* immediately to the rescue of any possible survivors of *Bouvet* despite the obvious danger. Later, with half the crew off and the possibility of sinking, real, Captain Biard had asked for his best uniform and a glass of port. This was apparently to set an example of *sang-froid*, but Midshipman Seyeux, in close attendance, had not apparently understood these orders, which convinced him that his Captain was determined to poison himself rather than survive the loss of his ship. When Admiral Guépratte had visited the ship in its sad condition and was given the full ceremonial greeting appropriate to his rank, the English sailors present in the boats closely about the stricken vessel, must, considered Lucas, have been puzzled at such formality under these circumstances, but 'everyone on *Gaulois* on 18 March behaved in accordance with the great traditions of the French Navy'. Lucas himself admitted that he had been very frightened and had taken an experienced sailor with him when ordered below to search for and bring up the ship's code books at a time when it looked as if *Gaulois* would sink.[6]

The diary account of Jean Deffez, noted the similarity of the noise of the explosion of a Turkish shell hitting their deck to that of the French shells as they left the ship's guns. He made a note of the sour taste in his throat and the poisonous air from the acrid fumes of explosions, and wrote bitterly of the '*villainous Turks*' and '*criminal Boches*' who fired on the rescue work among the *Bouvet* survivors, an incident also mentioned by Sauveur in his recollections. On 20 March Deffez wrote ten long pages on the events of 18 March and confirmed his attachment to this record of his service in a revealing entry. On being ordered to prepare to abandon ship, he had gone below and in the shadowy gloom, after several attempts, found his locker and brought up to safety his diary, his wallet and a change of clothes.

In the papers of Admiral Guépratte there is abundant evidence of his personal interest in the welfare of his men. His small private diary recorded for 18 March that 'the honour of the Flag has been fully but dearly maintained. *Bouvet* struck by a mine has sunk – all on board have perished save a fraction'. Then the five surviving senior officers are named.[7] On a scrap of paper is pencilled the service career of one of the able-seamen saved from the *Bouvet*. 'Payro Sauveur. At the Dardanelles since 15 November 1914 has participated in all the actions of the 3rd Division up to 18 March. Had his position in the 27-cm. turret.' When making his recommendations after the attack, he mentioned 'Enseigne de Vaisseau de Première Classe Sagnier, a gunnery officer who showed in the action the most intelligent and ingenious zeal which he had displayed in the previous actions – a perfect *sang-froid* and an extremely valuable team spirit for getting his gun into action.' Among the same recommendations to officers and men in *Suffren* is one for a man who 'conducted himself very cheerfully under fire'. In *Gaulois*, M.E. Seyeux was one of those who 'always showed the greatest courage and calmness under fire'.

The united spirit of the Allied officers and crew, despite Guépratte's impatience with the British Admiralty for so strictly insisting upon British overall command, is reflected in the letters received by the Admiral immediately after the action of 18 March. On the day following, the Commander of *Agamemnon* wrote to express 'our deepest sympathy and sorrow with you and our brother officers and men of your squadron, in the loss and fate of so many gallant comrades'. Lieutenant L.H. Lindner in *Indefatigable*, wrote his congratulations to the French Admiral on the bombardment and his 'deep regret at the loss of so many of your brave officers and men of the *Bouvet*. My mess mates ask me to say they join in wishing you the best of luck in forthcoming operations.' From Brest, the Admiral was assured by Admiral Vergniaud that 'each day we think of you, of the brave ones who fight on those shores on such a noble mission'. If the Admiral ever doubted the warm respect in which he was held by all ranks in the British warships, those doubts must have been dispelled by a signal which was scarcely official but is, in retrospect, touchingly illustrative. Written by a British seaman, before entertainment arranged for all those not on duty, it read: 'Monsieur, I shall have great pleasure in giving a song (which I have composed) during the interval of the cinema concert if you will kindly permit me to do so. Roberts.' There is no doubt of the popularity of the French naval officers and ratings with the English naval officers who came into contact with them. *Ark Royal* seaplane pilot, Geoffrey Bromet, wrote in his diary after the 18 March attack: 'One and all were glad to see that the French squadron had been congratulated by the Vice-Admiral and also the Admiralty. Their gallant conduct and high-spirited efforts at all times have made them very popular with our fleet.'

However, for all the spirit and seamanship of the Allied squadron, the great attack had been a failure. The unswept line of mines off Erenkeui had rendered valueless the temporary silencing of some Turkish batteries and the damage to the torpedo tube gear at Kilid Bahr. In only one respect was the Turkish defence of the Narrows seriously weakened and that was in their considerable expenditure of ammunition, which was now in short supply – how short, remains a matter of debate.

Of course the significance of the damage is not to be measured solely by casualty statistics, but it is a sobering point that the number of casualties in *Bouvet* alone, with 600 lost, is ill-matched with the thirty-eight to forty-three Turkish gunners and officers killed in the bombardment. The Turkish officers interviewed in 1919 by the members of the investigating committee which produced the *Mitchell Report* testified to the maintenance of a high morale among the fort and howitzer battery gun crews. The sinking of the ships and the failure to resume the attack were of course materially important in this. The point was made that public morale was similarly influenced by Turkish victory. A Turkish naval officer affirmed that when the attack on the 18th was broken off, 'it was commonly said that the English had only gone home to tea and that they would start again as soon as they had had breakfast in the morning.'[8]

General Askir Arkayan, an observation officer with a howitzer battery on the heights above Erenkeui Bay, has written of his experiences on 18 March.

We saw a mass of ships such as we had never seen before. We were amazed, but realizing that we should be faced that day with an out and out conflict, we completed our supplies and prepared for the attack ... We knew each ship well from the lists we possessed ... The battle developed with considerable violence and at noon the French ships in the second line advanced through the first line and opened a tremendous bombardment. The batteries replied effectively. Under this fire the *Bouvet* started to withdraw, but at that moment a cloud of red and black smoke arose from the ship, which may have struck a mine. Immediately after this there was a much more violent explosion. We believed that a shell from Mejidiye had blown up the magazine. The ship heeled over at once and her crew poured into the sea. On both sides fire ceased. The destroyers in the rear hastened to save the crew. We opened fire but again firing ceased ... towards sunset the battle slackened and the ships withdrew. Just then the *Queen Elizabeth* lying off Hissarlik opened fire on my battery. She was too far away for us to reply and we withdrew the gun crews, without any damage being done. Throughout the night we prepared for the battle to be renewed on the following morning, changing battery positions and bringing up ammunition.

The well-known on-the-spot description[9] by the American newspaper correspondent, George Schreiner, was filed at the War Office with a note: 'a picturesque account of the bombardment of the Dardanelles forts on 19 March [*sic*]. It is evidently the product of a Germanophile brain garnished with great powers of imaginative description. Much of it is however undoubtedly true.' The description related that 'comparatively little damage had been done to the Turkish positions' and with regard to the morale of the defenders an intriguing point is made amidst some inconsistency. Shreiner finds the Turks in a 'rather elated frame of mind' and one cannot help but wonder if this were just what he wanted? Some Turks were building a sort of monument out of two huge steel pieces which had landed in an adjacent garden, but the 'murderous fire' on Chanak caused the many soldiers and civilians who were leaving the town to scatter hurriedly for shelter. 'But shelter there really was none. Shells were falling on the water front, and on the next street in front and behind.'

An observer of more consequence than the American was General Sir Ian Hamilton, the Commander-in-chief of the newly-constituted Mediterranean Expeditionary Force (MEF). On 16 February, it had been agreed in the War Council that the 29th Division should be dispatched to Lemnos, the island which seemed most likely to serve as a base for Gallipoli operations. Kitchener had second thoughts about the dispatch of this division of regular troops, and Churchill's changed emphasis concerning the need for troops was dramatically illustrated when he complained at the War Council meeting on 19 February that 'insufficient military support at the critical moment' might lead to failure.[10] He even announced that he would 'disclaim all responsibility if a disaster occurs in Turkey owing to insufficiency of troops'.[11] The official documentary evidence certainly invites the conclusion that the original concept was now seen to be unrealistic, or, if viewed more tolerantly, was a tempting gamble which, in its execution, might by unforeseen circumstances or checks, be subject to change, that is, expansion! On 10 March, Lord Kitchener had finally agreed to the dispatch of the 29th Division. Three days later General Sir Ian Hamilton was summoned to the War Office to be informed that he was to command the force which was to concentrate in the eastern Mediterranean to support the Navy in securing their gains. Hamilton arrived in the Aegean the day before the great assault and was able to view from within the Straits the latter half of the action.

In *Queen Elizabeth*, Vice-Admiral de Robeck conferred with the General on 22 March. They agreed on the need for a combined operation to assault and take the Gallipoli Peninsula which would enable the Narrows to be commanded from the

European side, the waters swept and thus the larger ships enabled to move through to the Marmara. So many years after the event there is still contention over this decision. Did de Robeck, confidence undermined by failure on the 18th, abdicate from exercising naval initiative; and, whoever were to have been responsible for the decision, was it to be decisively damaging to the chance of Allied success that the Turks were no longer to face a naval threat of breaking through the Narrows? In fact there is evidence, as will be seen below, that de Robeck did not completely give up all initiative in tackling the Narrows, but for those engaged in debating these issues there is a point which should not escape discussion – if and when he did, was he simply and soundly being realistic?

From 19 March to the day of the landing, the undamaged Allied ships, together with the replacements for those sunk or seriously damaged, patrolled the entrance to the Straits and the Gulf of Saros, and carried out the necessary reconnaissance of the Peninsula to prepare for the landing of troops. The minesweeping flotilla was reorganized to enable fast sweeping to be undertaken by the *Beagle* class destroyers. In addition, the bombardment of forts and howitzer batteries continued with the assistance of aeroplane observation. On one occasion, *Prince of Wales*, with two rounds of 12in shrapnel, and from a mere 1,500 yards, completely obliterated a string of camels in full career with armed riders. Eric Longley-Cook remembered his sadness at witnessing such wholesale slaughter of man and beast.

The usefulness of aerial observation is exemplified by a report from HMS *Ark Royal* of a flight in late March by Seaplane 172 (Flight Lieutenant Bromet and Lieutenant Torrington, RNVR) at an average height of 3,000 feet, with very good visibility.

> Road round Eastern end of Gulf [of Saros] has on either side of it an impassable swamp … Between Kavak River and Bulair village are four lines of traversed trenches. About one mile east of Bulair is a large camp of forty-six large square tents and six bell tents. There are two large newly dug earthworks in the neighbourhood of this camp between it and Bulair, each to hold four guns, but none were seen in place. There are numerous trenches round these two works … Forts Sultan and Napoleon did not appear to be seriously damaged. Roads all in good repair but no movement was seen on them or on anywhere else. Gun emplacement for one gun on cliff facing seaward (2 F.31). Gun emplacement for two guns in 2 D.33 flanking landing place.[12]

In considering whether to land at the Gulf of Saros, Sir Ian Hamilton must have been impressed by such a report, together with de Robeck's concern for his communications at the rear should his squadron be able to break into the Narrows. He had, it must be accepted, contrary reports on the state of defensive preparation at Bulair. They came, for example, from *Gaulois*, as is recorded in M.E. Seyeux's diary before 18 March, and from the Royal Naval Division (RND) subsequently. The thoroughness with which the Gulf was examined should not be underestimated. The *Mitchell Report* indicates that 'from 31 March to 8 April *Henri IV*, with *Agamemnon, Lord Nelson* and *Talbot*, was operating in the Gulf of Zeros [Saros]; sketches were made of all possible landing places and a few rounds were fired at Turkish works; *Agamemnon* examined Enos on the 31st and landed a party at Zeros island which brought off three Greek fishermen; boats were also sent in close to the Bulair trenches which were fired into and found unoccupied.' The use of a kite balloon by HMS *Talbot* and later both a kite balloon and a spherical observation balloon from HMS *Manica* assisted the aerial reconnaissance. From 24 March this reconnaissance was stepped up when No. 3 Squadron Royal Naval Air Service,[13] with eighteen planes, arrived at Tenedos to establish an air base to supplement the work carried out to this date by the six seaplanes attached to *Ark Royal* and the two attached to the French ship *Rabenfels*.[14] By this means and by direct naval observation, the Turkish defensive preparations, both on the Asiatic shore and on the Peninsula, were closely watched during the weeks of preparation for the combined operation.

Both contemporary evidence as well as the recollections of survivors leave no doubt that the men in the ranks and their regimental officers, as well as those in higher command, expected no easy landing. That the naval command still had every intention of getting into the Marmara is indicated by de Robeck's orders from *Queen Elizabeth* on 2 April, in which he stipulated that 'until the Military have stated their demands it is impossible to give detailed proposals of the naval co-operation ... during disembarkation the Vice-Admiral will be on board *Queen Elizabeth* [and] on the fleet proceeding through the Narrows, the Vice-Admiral will hoist his flag in *Lord Nelson* and take command of the Squadron in the Marmara'.

In his memoirs Liman von Sanders described the thoroughness of the Turkish preparations.[15] He had been appointed to organize the defence of the Dardanelles on 24 March, and so had a month for the necessary improvements, during which he strengthened the three areas which he considered possible landing places: the Gulf of Saros, the southern end of the Peninsula and the Asiatic side of the Narrows. Of great significance was his development of the mobility of his battle groups. Roads were constructed or improved, training marches insisted upon and, as far as possible, all movement took place by night. Field fortifications were constructed or strengthened, barbed wire stretched under water, landmines laid. Kannengiesser Pasha[16] acknowledged the co-operation in these preparations of Admiral von Usedom, whose base in command of the Straits themselves was at Chanak. There is in Kannengiesser's book a menacingly apt reference to the siting of 'flanking fire by machine and other guns' of the potential landing places together with wire entanglements, pits and mines and the commencement of a new road from the town of Gallipoli. This road was sheltered under the shoulder of the hilly plateau which stretches down the Straits' coast of the Peninsula to Cape Helles. When Kannengiesser wrote that 'all of us who took part in the war know how, after weeks of high tension and expectation, the final commencement of the attack was welcome as a kind of relief', it was in the knowledge of hindsight that the time for preparation had been sufficient. Nevertheless the tension and frustration had been hard to bear. It had been no less hard for the Allied troops assembling in the eastern Mediterranean.

Chapter 5

The Men of the Mediterranean Expeditionary Force

Though united in a common enterprise, the Allied force which gradually assembled in Egypt was heterogeneous in composition and character. With the English, Welsh, Scots and Irish, there were Australians and New Zealanders, some of whom were just recently out of Britain, as well as Indians, Russians, Palestinians, Senegalese, North Africans and soldiers of metropolitan France. In due course there were to be Newfoundlanders too. There was, however, further diversity in the British troops. There were Regulars in the battalions of Lancashire Fusiliers, Essex and Worcester Regiments, Dublin Fusiliers, Munster Fusiliers, Royal Fusiliers, Border Regiment, Hampshire Regiment, Royal Marines, Inniskillings, King's Own Scottish Borderers, and South Wales Borderers, and in the batteries of the Royal Field Artillery (RFA) and Royal Horse Artillery (RHA). There were Territorials like the West Riding Engineers, some of the Field Ambulance Units and the 1/5 Royal Scots. Many of the rank and file of the Royal Naval Division (RND) were in effect Kitchener Volunteers of August, September and October 1914, though there was a Brigade of regular Royal Marines within the Division. The French troops were mainly conscripts and a large percentage of the Australian and New Zealand troops had had some experience of voluntary or compulsory military training before the war.

The consequence of this was that the active-service experience of the men involved, varied from Boer War campaigning, service in India and elsewhere on imperial duty, pre-war part-time soldiering, to the precipitated, under-equipped, training from early wartime enlistment. A few gunners had experienced the first weeks of the Western Front fighting in 1914, for some in the RND there had been active service at Antwerp, and for South Wales Borderers the combined operation of Tsingtao in China, but for others previously occupied at the coal face or office desk there had been only a few short months of accelerated training. There were further differences; in physique, consequent upon conditions of work and living; in outlook, bred by different values held in communities widely separated by geography or by social distinction. The situation was made still more complicated when Gurkha, Punjabi and Sikh troops reinforced the men on the Peninsula – and it might be added that the Greeks too were represented, but by labourers, contractors and interpreters and not by a military force.

Differences of language, religious observance and sometimes food, have also to be considered, and those who focus solely on the contrast between Australian and British attitudes towards military discipline considerably over-simplify the problems of a force working in daily cooperation, in a strikingly small operational theatre, under a single commander, who was himself dependent on so many considerations beyond his control. An examination of the background of some of the English soldiers who may be taken as representative of their units will show clearly the varied material within even the Regular Army 29th Division and within the RND.

In the 29th Division, Trumpeter Lissenburg (RFA), with a family tradition of army service in India, had been at the Delhi Durbar in December 1911. In the same year B.A. McConnell had joined the Royal Inniskilling Fusiliers at Armagh depot and had served at Aldershot and in India. With approximately three years' full military service behind them, these men were among the experienced regular soldiers forming the backbone of the 29th Division which landed at Cape Helles on 25 April. Even Lissenburg and McConnell however could not match the experience of W.G. Wood, who had been in the famous 'L' Battery RHA action at Néry on the retirement from Mons in August 1914 which earned the battery three VCs.

With part-time 'Saturday-night' soldiering in the Territorial Force, G.B. Smith was mobilized from his Sheffield steel-works on 4 August to serve in the West Riding Engineers Field Company, which involved him in the *River Clyde* landing eight months later. Nevertheless his experience – once-weekly training and an annual camp – was more than that of A.E. Wilson, from a Stockton shipbuilding firm. He had joined the RND Nelson Battalion as a Kitchener Volunteer in August 1914 and found himself in action at Antwerp in the first week in October. Even Wilson's preparation for action in Gallipoli was more thorough than that of Joseph Murray (RND Hood Battalion), a Durham miner early in October 1914, who was seen off to the war in mid-October by a sobbing mother and a concertina-led station-platform sing-song from relatives and friends. 'Something had told me I should [go] and as I wished to see the world, this was my great opportunity.'[1]

Eric Wettern, who was in a family granite business, had received, as a member of the Institutions of Civil, Mechanical and Electrical Engineers, a letter dated 14 September 1914 from A.G. Lyster, the President of the Institute of Civil Engineers. The letter, having drawn attention to the desire of members 'to serve in the army now being raised', announced that an opportunity was now afforded for members to serve together in the Divisional Engineer Units of the RND. 'The terms of enlistment will be for the duration of the war but not in any case exceeding three years ... Pay is under consideration but will not be less than the Army rates.' Wettern responded to the letter and his paybook records that he was paid 2s.6d. a day, of which 1s.4d. was the special rate for Engineers. His first letter home from the RND Engineer camp at Oxney Bottom, near Dover, on 1 October 1914, gave brief first impressions. 'Under canvas, don't know anything about our duties yet – shall find out tomorrow. Shall have blue jackets uniform pro tem.' In approximately seven months Wettern would be in a dugout under shell-fire, would have definite and dangerous duties to perform and would not be clad in the much-sought-after sailor's uniform.

In contrast to the British, the French soldiers who saw service at Gallipoli had nearly all been conscripted by an annual system of class registration. By a law passed in 1913, the age of call-up was reduced from twenty-one to twenty. Of course there were regular officers for whom the Army was a career. Their task was to train the conscripts. There were also the volunteers of the Foreign Legion, and a battalion of the Legion in fact served on the Peninsula from May 1915. It should not be forgotten that there was a percentage of volunteers in the French Army as well as the older men, reservists who had been recalled to the colours. With the outbreak of war in August 1914, of three men who were to serve on the Peninsula and to whom reference will be made later, Raymond Weil, an artillery officer, would grasp the opportunity for accelerated advancement in his chosen profession, but for conscripts, Charles Thierry in the infantry, and M.A. Sylvestre in the artillery, however enthusiastically they were to play their part, their Army service was an interruption of the development of their civilian careers. Conscription secured for the French a degree of national and individual preparation for the Army well in advance of her ally, but to achieve a quality of experience to match the quantity, was no easy task. A deeper study of the varying background of the British and French troops who landed at Cape Helles and Kum Kale on 25 April would have to be carried out before valid comparisons of quality could be made, but if the 29th Division were a more homogeneous and professionally trained body of men than the French Colonial and Metropolitan Brigades, the experience of the latter as units was considerably more than that of the RND.

The social background and the degree of pre-war military training of the Australian and New Zealand soldiers in their respective expeditionary forces were richly varied, but certainly there was a unity in their spirit of loyalty to the Empire, anticipation of adventure and eagerness to prove themselves more than capable of justifying their individual and collective confidence in fulfilling any task set before them. They were proud of their identity as Australians and New Zealanders but they felt strongly the pull of imperial unity and the needs of the mother country. It is important to recognize 1914/15 Dominion attitudes towards the Empire and the widespread sense of obligation towards Britain engaged in a world war. Soon after the end of the war, a New Zealander wrote of August 1914 that 'the musterer and station owner alike forsook their flock; the bushman put away his crosscut and axe; the flax-mill hand left swamp and mill and hurried to the nearest railway station. Quiet men up on the hillside watched the train coming across country with the eagerly awaited newspapers. The strain of waiting was unendurable. With the call of Old England throbbing in their ears, they left their stock unattended in the paddocks and swelled the procession to the railway station.'[2]

Certainly more analytically, but imbued with the values of later times and with a dismissive cynicism which itself requires evaluation, the Australian historian Bill Gammage wrote in 1974 of pre-war young Australians being deliberately taught 'the virtues of patriotism and glories of race and Empire. In New South Wales State and Catholic schools, every educational influence – policy, the syllabus, text books, the school magazine, school ceremonies, and recreation – was designed to awaken in children a patriotic affection for both nation and Empire ... By 1914 most young Australians had thoroughly learnt an adherence to war, race and glory, and to two nations separated by the world.'[3] It may be appropriate to re-quote the celebrated truism that 'the past is a foreign country'.

As a direct result of Kitchener's visit to Australasia in 1910, both countries had by Parliamentary Defence Acts brought in compulsory military service for home defence, so that a large percentage of those who volunteered from August 1914 for overseas service had had experience of part-time training. These men had been to military camps, had drilled, experienced military discipline, often under the stern eye of British NCOs, and had 'fired their course' – training in marksmanship. In Australia, enlistment for overseas required candidates to be between nineteen and thirty-five years of age, of a minimum height of five feet six inches, a minimum chest measurement of thirty-four inches, and that they satisfied strict standards concerning the condition of their teeth, their feet and their general fitness. Of course of the men 'answering the call' there were some who had had no experience at all of military training, and others who had been regular soldiers in the British Army. Men beyond the age of eligibility for compulsory military service, which in Australia was twenty-six, had not done any training unless in the Australian equivalent of the British Territorial Force. For various reasons usually connected with remoteness from any recognized centre of military training, but also for reasons of independent objection to a coercive enlistment for which they could see no need, there were many who had done no military training. Recent immigrants from the British Isles, unless they were ex-regulars or territorials, were in a similar position.

With this variable factor in the recruitment and training of the 1st Australian Imperial Force (AIF) and the 1st New Zealand Expeditionary Force (NZEF), there was a more unifying factor in the considerable percentage of recent British immigrants in both forces. Gammage stated that 22.25 per cent of those Australians who embarked in the AIF during the war were born overseas and mainly in the British Isles,[4] and naturally the figure for those whose parents had been born in Britain would be dramatically higher still. Statistical evaluation of the background of the 200 Australian and New Zealander Gallipoli veterans interviewed by the present author in 1974 has not been attempted, but many seemed to have proved their manhood against vicissitude and challenge at a very early age, not least in unaccompanied teenage emigration. In so doing they had developed a sturdy independence and confidence which could be an outstanding asset in battle but which could also prove, perhaps particularly in training and in the confinement of military inactivity, potentially a problem.

Among those interviewed was one who had been a youngster disillusioned with life at a Staffordshire coalface, another who had had pre-1914 experience as a deep-sea deck hand. A timber 'bullockie' in Western Australia, a bush clearer, a kauri-gum digger in Northland, a former gamekeeper in County Durham, a New South Wales sheep-station roustabout, and an opal digger were also represented. There were men who ran away to sea and 'found themselves' in New Zealand or Australia, men whose youthful independence and determination to carve out a future for themselves were backed by their parents, men who pioneered the road, rail and telegraph system and the mapping of remote areas, men who prospected for gold and other minerals, together with those whose training and experience lay in the expanding, challenging fields of business and commerce. As they met at camps like those at Blackboy Hill, Perth, at Tahuna Park, Dunedin, Addington near Christchurch, Broadmeadows at Melbourne, Claremont near Hobart, at Randwick racecourse, Sydney, or Awapuni racecourse near Palmerston North, the equipping and training of fighting units began.

For some, like those in the Medical Corps, the training was specialized. Edney Moore, in the Australian Army Medical Corps, wrote in his diary: '18 September 1914. Biked into Concentration Camp at Brighton and was drafted into Clearing Hospital and recommended a dresser on 25 September. Wednesday 30 September. Moved camp to Claremont. Started to go into Hobart Hospital every other day for training during which time saw several operations.' More mundane is the diary of C. L. Comyns for 13 August:

> Enlisted today and proceeded to Palmerston North on 14th. Sent to camp at Trentham, Wellington. Mother was very sad at the thought but when I explained my reasons she seemed proud to understand and before we parted gave me many words of comfort and advice. In camp it is curious to see the squads in Mufti and uniform drilling. Allotted a tent, served out with equipment, belt, rifle etc. Kept very busy all day and finished very tired – 1 think with excitement. At the close of this eventful day I laid down to rest – a one day old British Soldier.

Not all the training was enjoyed and a New Zealander named Currey wrote in 1915 that he:

> learned very little at Palmerston North as most of my time was spent on fatigues, in fact I was on fatigues every Sunday I was there and have even done three days' fatigues right off ... Our NCOs coming from different parts of NZ tried to show off their good points by shouting loud and long at their men; this used to grate on the ears, especially when we were doing our best ... Some of them could not name off the parts of their gun without the aid of their hand book. When instructing their men they would bluff their way through by standing off and shouting a lot of quick commands at new men and then bully their men because they had made no progress.

While officers and men were involved at different ends of the training programme there were elementary lessons for NCOs to learn too. R.H. Harris described how 'one day we had rowed ashore and were having a picnic. One of the men came to me when the officer was temporarily absent and asked if he might go for a few minutes with his brother to see their mother who lived just up the road. On their promise to be back in ten minutes at most I let them go. We found them finally at the Three Lamps Hotel and were to regret many times thereafter that we had not left them there.'

Of course for the British troops who were not regulars of the 29th Division returning from overseas, the nature of their work in England on assembly after embodiment as a Territorial, or on enlistment in the first flood of voluntary recruitment, was kindred but for the new volunteers the most basic principles of their new life in the services had to be learned.

On occasion the inexperienced found himself with the experienced. A young Anglican chaplain, Oswyn Creighton, who had joined the New, or Kitchener, Army, wrote of his somewhat unrewarding task in the 29th Division at Leamington and Nuneaton.[5] The Division had just returned from India, and Creighton was quickly informed that 'the men are not at all religious and I would have a lot of disappointments but would always find them very civil. They did not like going to church.' However, Creighton found the men 'exceedingly smart and seasoned troops [who] have an air that there is nothing they don't know about soldiering'. Route marches with the music of their bands were regular occurrences from the end of January 1915. Creighton had some girls ejected from the gallery of Stockingford Church on Sunday, 1 January. He had asked that no ladies should be present as he wished to direct his sermon towards the importance of good behaviour towards the ladies of the locality, who 'had never had military in the place before and were naturally very excited'. On hearing ugly rumours of the conduct of troops in the late evening in the town, Creighton was one of the chaplains who carried out an inquiry patrol; it failed to disclose anything untoward. He found that most of the few who came to his voluntary services were Catholics and 'they did not sing hymns and were very loath to stand'. This attitude towards religion was not confined to the men in the ranks. 'Many of the officers are very pleasant, but I don't feel they very much care whether one exists or not. After all, why should they?'

An illustration of the extent of the involvement of the 29th Division in their local environment is provided in the recall of a former pupil at Rugby School early in 1915. 'I remember the K.O.S.B. playing the School XV at rugger with a huge crowd of fans from the school and from the regiment. The School was leading at half-time, then the K.O.S.B. brought their Pipers on to the touchline marching up and down and playing, with the result that they scored heavily during the second half and won.'

There was some trench-digging, marksmanship contests, lectures and concerts. Creighton himself secured the support of a 'coy and buxom woman who sang patriotic songs in her dressing gown and a blind man who played the concertina'. They had both been accorded a rousing reception. On 11 March, a sham battle was fought involving cyclists holding a line on one side of the River Avon, and on the following day they were reviewed by the King. From Coventry station the 12,000 men of the Division departed for Avonmouth docks. There was scarcely a dry female eye in Leamington, according to a lady who had witnessed a departure which for her remained an abidingly poignant occasion. She knew how anxiously the 29th Division casualty lists would soon be scanned by those women who had, as friends, sweethearts or warm-hearted landladies, come to know the soldiers so well. A particularly affecting example of this concerning the King's Own Scottish Borderers and their hosts in Bilton, Rugby, will be given in Chapter 17.

The training of the RND had at once to be more basic and more intensive than this. The division was formed at the outbreak of war at the specific instruction of Winston Churchill. Incorporated in it were Royal Marines, Royal Naval Volunteer

Reservists and Royal Navy officers, as well as a flood of recruits with no naval or military training. As there were insufficient ships for the men now available to crew, Churchill wished to prepare for active service a new unit which would be trained as infantry but retain naval elements in rank, uniform and procedure. He intended that 'All the men, whether sailors or marines ... will be available if required for service afloat, and it must be distinctly understood that this is the paramount claim upon them; but in the meantime they will be left to be organized for land service.'[6]

The diary and letters of Eric Wettern, a sapper in the RND, demonstrate an admirable thoroughness in practical training which would be invaluable on the Peninsula. Fitness and infantry drill were the first requirements. A letter of 7 October 1914 described a run before breakfast, parade, rifle drill, signalling, a route march and skirmishing, all in one day. 'Tonight I have just been on a night attack – twenty-five men forming an attacking party to try to get into the camp singly without being caught. Twenty-five of us were defending and we caught twenty of the attackers, five getting in.' In mid-November he moved to Walmer from Ringwould, where he had been 'cultivating a beautiful ocean wave walk which is requisite and necessary in order to avoid treading on your trousers'. The bell-bottomed trousers had been issued with little more respect to the wearer's dimensions than the round blue hat with a bow which had been handed out in identical sizes to men laboriously lined up in size order. Wettern's diary for January 1915 recorded the setting-up of wire entanglements on Kingsdown cliff and the blasting of portions of cliff to make them unscaleable. His photographs indicate the increasingly technical side of their work in demolition, digging wells and building bridges. There was still time to arrange a special dance on 5 February at the Masonic Hall, Deal, for which he pencilled in the name of Miss Dunn for the 16th and last dance, 'Valse ... Un peu d'Amour'. He left Walmer on 1 March to embark on SS *Somali*, which left Avonmouth docks the same day.

Sub-Lieutenant A.W. Tisdall (Anson Battalion, RND), who was to win the VC at the landing in April, wrote from the large camp at Blandford in Dorset on 22 February 1915, that on Wednesday 'we parade before Winston Churchill and on Thursday march off to some seaport and ship for the Mediterranean.[7] We have been promised a six-week or two-month campaign, probably fairly exciting.' Clearly Tisdall shared the common feeling of depression at Blandford because he wrote that 'the mud gets deeper and softer and the work less and less interesting, the officers get into quarrels with each other' and his observation on leading personalities still merits censorship. His last sentence made the point: 'if we do anything you will see it in the papers probably with big headlines to please Winston.' It was incidentally at Blandford that the naval uniforms were handed in for khaki, with the sole concession of a round cap with black cap ribbon and gold lettering. However, even this cap was in khaki.

The Crystal Palace was the divisional depot at which new and reserve RND battalions were trained. In addition to this, officers, NCOs and various specialists were trained for constructional work. Douglas Jerrold wrote: 'The atmosphere at the Crystal Palace was rather different: the officer's time of training there was emphatically not a period in which he learnt how to carry out orders, but what orders to give, and how to get them executed, not a period in which he learnt his drill and musketry but how to teach drill and musketry; not a period in which he was taught elementary tactics, but rather the underlying principles, knowing which he could not only solve minor tactical problems himself, but could face with a certain measure of confidence the practical business of training troops.'[8] Though this is a fair assessment of one side of the work undertaken at the Crystal Palace, B.B. Rackham (Hawke Battalion, RND) remembered the discomforts of the cold, draughty, stone-floored buildings and the spread of a serious and mysterious epidemic, which was finally traced to the prevalent habit of spitting, common to so many of the men.

H.C. Kerr remembered the Crystal Palace as the 'Glass Frigate' or 'HMS *Never Float*', and recalled in particular the tremendous efforts to create a naval atmosphere there. A ship's bell rang, no clock chimed; sentry duty was not kept, but Port and Starboard Watch were; men got shore leave and if late were reported 'adrift', though whether the fire drill of climbing down ropes from upper storeys were intended to follow naval practice or was due to the absence of more efficient safety measures was not clear. There were other RND training camps at Chatham, Betteshanger, Portsmouth, Plymouth, Portland, Gravesend, Browndown, Tavistock, Deal and Alnwick.

The Royal Scots and the West Riding Engineers had had similar training to that of the RND, but their Territorial experience was sufficient to make much of the work familiar. Returning to the Regulars, the diary of Second Lieutenant R.B. Gillett of the 2nd Battalion the Hampshire Regiment amply illustrates the less intensive pressure upon the regular during these months in England.

> 1 January: When we got to the range a gale was blowing and soon afterwards it started raining in torrents. Of course we did not fire and started home. 3 January: It is raining hard so I cancelled church parade. 12 January: We did two hours' squad drill and one of physical drill, only rifle inspection in the afternoon. 17 January: I did not go to Church Parade today so did not get up till late. I wrote a few letters in the morning. Telephoned through to Hobbs and arranged to go and have tea with him this afternoon.

It must be noted however that the diary laconically records that one element was not neglected by this battalion – regular musketry drill.

Chapter 6

En route for Egypt, Preparations and Plans for the Gallipoli Landings

The Australian and New Zealand troops were the first to leave their homeland. The New Zealanders in fact had one false start occasioned by the fear of there being insufficient naval protection for the troopships which were to join those from Australian ports. The scene for some was set by well-nigh ceremonial marching through the city centre to the docks, final quayside farewells and then a rousing, flag-waving, stirring, tear-stained departure.

A New Zealander, E.H. Honnor, admitted in his first letter home that 'a thought of home had come over him' as he left Wellington and that he realized that the parting was particularly hard on his mother, but 'after the horrors of Hartlepool and Scarborough I am proud that I will have a chance of getting a little back on them'. Less moved by the imminence of his departure was Second Lieutenant Carrington, a former Duntroon cadet. From Wellington he wrote: 'It's blowing a howling gale and is raining hard this morning [and as for farewell] there were seven speeches. Each one started by saying he wouldn't keep us long and each one kept us longer than the one before ... after the speeches about five different sorts of parsons said different sorts of prayers; at least I suppose they were different but I couldn't hear them.'

For by far the majority, the voyage was to be an entirely new experience and the interest it aroused is shown in many diaries. Sergeant A.G. Jennings of the Wellington Battalion wrote: '16 October 1914 Left Wellington harbour this morning at 6 a.m. It was a grand sight steaming out in line. The weather is perfect and there is hardly any movement on our ship. After clearing the Heads the *Minotaur* and a Japanese battleship[1] steamed ahead clearing the way while the *Psyche* and *Philomel* each led a line of five transports. We are leading our line. Had no idea the South Island was so large. The whole day we steamed through the Straits.' This diarist noticed the 'old-fashioned style of houses' he was to see in Hobart, though he thought that 'the girls do not come up to the NZ standard as regards good looks ... We had great fun in giving Hakas [war cries] and talking in Maori.'

A West Australian, E.C. Skinner, had a less satisfactory farewell from Fremantle. His letter to his sister inquired whether she had been down at the port or not.

Clarke and your humble both had good possies but we saw not a single soul we knew – the only thing I can see for it is you must have arrived at Fremantle just too late. You can imagine what a disappointment it was, especially after expecting to see you there – a very unfortunate start off, but it couldn't be helped as we knew next to nothing about the time of embarkation and if we had told friends to be there earlier nine times out of ten the boat wouldn't have sailed till late. From what the South Australian boys say (they manage things better in the East – of course that is understood) they tell us they were allowed to mix with their friends for two hours on the wharf before sailing and we were penned up like a lot of sheep.[2]

The troops leaving Brisbane received a message, 'Queensland expects every man will do his duty,' and when they temporarily disembarked at Albany in Western Australia the Queenslanders 'returned decorated with flowers', according to A.E. Joyce's diary. Some of the New Zealand troopships left Wellington on 14 October and Captain A.B. Morton, who was to leave on the 16th, watched the departure. 'It was a fine sight to see the troopships slowly draw away from the wharves, the decks and rigging crowded with khaki figures cheering and waving their farewell with bands playing good old airs ... The streets of Wellington seem deserted tonight in the absence of the hundreds of soldiers who have been in town on leave every night during the past fortnight.' Lieutenant C.S. Algie, who remembered the Boer War send-off from Auckland, noted in his diary entry for 23 September that 'there did not seem to be the same wild state of enthusiasm', but that 'there was a much more business-like air about everything. The public were considered very little on this occasion, the troops being marched aboard and kept there without the presence of any but a few civilians.' Whether the farewells were to have been well organized or not, the last sight of their homeland was an emotional moment. C.L. Comyns noted that: 'Just at sunset we passed Farewell Spit and I silently said goodbye my own, my native land. Goodbye Mother, Eilley, Doll, Friends and Wanganui. Goodbye New Zealand.'

The novelty of the experience and the sense of excitement faded during the weeks afloat. Despite attempts to hold deck sports with boxing and greasy-pole pillow fighting, endless card-playing and gambling, the monotony and the heat of the Indian Ocean took their toll. There was some seasickness at first, and later sunstroke and sore throats made for well-attended sick parades as diary after diary records that the sea was 'perfectly calm and that on board it is very very hot'.

'I am still reading Emerson and find him a little difficult – there are very few places in which he speaks in simple terms,' wrote J.R.T. Keast, who later complained that the gamblers occupied so much space that there was scarcely room to write a letter.

There was excitement and pride at the defeat of the German raider *Emden* in the Cocos Islands by the Australian cruiser *Sydney*. Many men record *Sydney* steaming off at high speed and the Japanese cruiser *Ibuki* attempting to follow but being clearly ordered back to guard the troopships. At Colombo several of the troopships took on board the prisoners from *Emden*, and one German sailor, a champion wrestler, took part in a match with the best Australian wrestler. The bout was enjoyed by as large a crowd as that which assembled at the court of King Neptune for the crossing-the-line ceremonies. Cobden Parkes, according to his diary for 13 November, had 'got ready to go before Father Neptune but only the officers went through the performance. Most of the men ran amok and water was thrown everywhere.'

Even if a transport were not carrying horses, there were likely to be bullocks and sheep on board to provide fresh meat. The smell and mess of these animals, the overcrowded canteen, the vaccinations, the physical exercises, and for some the lectures and training in, for example, signalling, were experiences to which they became accustomed. J.R.T. Keast recorded that they 'had a lecture by Dr McWay on pox. Told us what a dreadful disease it was and it is especially in Egypt. He warned all the men and gave them the best cures and preventatives he knew.' W. Thyer, a South Australian signals officer, mentioned in a letter the argument against a regular pay allowance. 'There is money aboard but owing to the heavy gambling that is continually in progress I am in accord with the policy of holding it back until prior to the landing so that some of the men will have some cash to go on with.' He may perhaps also have been in a minority in recording the excellence of a religious service and an address by their chaplain, Captain Jenkins. 'Had a nice service last night at which we sang Sankey's hymns. Was sorry when it was over.' On the SS *Arawa*, Second Lieutenant Carrington recorded in a letter that the impressive solemnity of one of their services was not increased by the Salvation Army padre being seasick during the sermon. The Australian, Thyer, wrote of the improvised unofficial games on board.

> The last night or two we have been like a mob of kids [playing trains], particularly in the section where I sleep. Get into our hammocks at the stated hour 9 p.m. and as we hang from the roof so close together that we rub sides, one case (a hard case too) acts as the engine and gets the rest of us swaying from side to side; during this performance another nut crawls along the top of us as a ticket collector at the peril of smashing his head on the ceiling. Needless to say we get into a great perspiration on the job; during the procedure we stop with a bump at various stations and yell like heathens.

Cecil Malthus[3] described how the sheer monotony of the shipboard diet of bread, stew and cheese, despite its adequacy, led to the cultivation of skill in theft by mechanical contrivance of hook and line, or by diversionary tactics. Malthus also gave an account of a potentially serious situation involving a protest over food. A similar incident on another ship bringing Australian reinforcements in May was to result in a mutiny. The whole affair is recorded in the diary of a young soldier, already a journalist and later to become a newspaper editor.

The problem, which may have originated in the refusal in April 1915 of any leave to men in Broadmeadows Camp, Victoria, developed on board the troopship *Ulysses* with grievances over the cook's illicit sale of tea. It is clear from I.T. Birtwistle's diary that there was discontent over the prices in the Soldiers' Institute canteen, the regular rigour of picket inspections which involved transit through both officers' and sergeants' messes, and the strictness and occasional stupidity of petty regulations. Even Empire Day celebrations involving the singing of the National Anthem, three cheers for the King and Empire and boos for the Kaiser failed to quench the fires of discontent. At Colombo the men were prevented from buying fresh fruit or anything else from the local vendors. A march through Colombo's steaming heat proved nearly the last straw. Leave was granted only to privileged persons – two sergeants from each company and the officers. 'Spent the day looking at Colombo from the ship, hot, perspiring, irritated. Those who have taken illegal leave have been heavily fined (privates fined £5 as well as ten days C.B. and no leave till conclusion of voyage).' With this judgement by Colonel Crouch the storm broke on the evening of 27 May.

A petition for modification of the fines attracted a large crowd of willing signatories. A jeering chant broke out parodying the Colonel's motto of 'Wipe out the Bloody Germans', which now appeared as 'Chuck the Bastard overboard'. When the officers remonstrated, the retort was, 'You treat us like dogs, won't you let us bark?' Although Crouch's presence persuaded the men to disperse, the chanting continued and efforts by the Adjutant failed to avert further trouble. A pair of Colonel Crouch's boots were taken and hidden. The canteen was closed by force by an officer and military police, who were roughly handled. One of the police was nearly thrown overboard but at the last minute hauled back and beaten up instead. The Colonel, sitting by himself in the officers' mess, became increasingly isolated. Finally the canteen was broken open and the goods looted. The guard was called out but refused to leave the guard room, and the chaplain's well-meaning diversion of having the organ played proved fruitless. The detention cells were forced open and the inmates released, the doors being flung overboard. As the evening wore on, the second-in-command, Major Smith, moved among the men and another senior officer promised attention to their grievances. The tension eased and the crisis was past. It would, however, be difficult for the 22nd Battalion to embark upon their Gallipoli service with their morale unaffected by such a prolonged experience of bad relations.

The normal grouses of life aboard a troopship received legitimate outlet in the form of newsheets. The *Clan McGillivray* had one such paper, the *Clan News*, and on board the transport *Tahiti*, bringing reinforcements from New Zealand, the *Tahitian Tatler*[4] would have needed humour no more sophisticated than the following two examples to be sure of knowing nods from its readers.

Orderly Officer (at door of Messroom): 'What Mess is this?'
Trooper McAwfull: 'I don't know, Sir, but the cook said it was stew.'
Orderly Officer: 'Any complaints, men?'
Private: 'Yessir. Taste this, Sir.'
Officer: 'H'm, rather thin and greasy, otherwise not bad soup.'
Private: 'Yessir, that is what we thought, but the cook says it's tea.'

Egypt, after a voyage of such frustrating length, seemed very attractive at first, even though the Australasian troops had expected and hoped that their destination would be England and then France. The delights of Zeitoun were similar to those of nearby Cairo, and at Mena, a few miles away, there was the stimulus even to the most philistine, of being beneath the Pyramids. In Cairo itself there were the crowded bazaars and varied entertainment, which ranged from the Zoological Gardens and Luna Park to the bawdy-houses in the notorious 'Wasser'. The eastern scents, the tram rides between the sand dunes, the gharries and the veiled women, presented an excitingly unfamiliar picture. There were so many contrasts like that between the well-dressed, wealthy Egyptian and the disturbing poverty of the deformed, dirty, ulcerated elderly or boy beggars. There was also a new sense of the colossal span of history where the edifice of 6,000 summers looked down on their tented encampment.

The journey in a troop train from Alexandria to Cairo enabled Lieutenant C.S. Algie, of the Auckland Battalion, to see something of a country 'as flat as a pancake and under cultivation. The bullock, donkey, mule and camel are the beasts of burden and hundreds of each were to be seen throughout – the ploughs are just as the ancients used, I should think. It is very hard to realize that we are in a country of such antiquity.' The great art of bartering had to be learned, and while it was possible to jump off a gharry into the sand to avoid paying, and by force of numbers or strength to escape the cheap tram fares or guide-fees to ancient monuments, payment for camel rides or photographs on camel back in front of the pyramids was difficult to avoid even if the amount were negotiable. C.L. Comyns indicated in his diary that the delicacies of barter were double-sided. 'Some of the boys obtained oranges for their identification discs, but the balance was frequently adjusted by the natives getting the cash and disappearing without giving the fruit.'

Cobden Parkes, with the 1st Battalion AIF, arrived at Mena Camp after midnight, following the train journey from Alexandria and the tram to the camp. 'Slept in coats only, on the sand. Cold as blazes. Pyramids looming over sandhills seem to overshadow everything. 9 December: Woke up at Reveille terribly stiff and cold. Went up pyramids and shown round by guide.' He climbed the Pyramids on the next two days as well and one of his party fell 'from about 100 yards from the top. Terribly injured about head but no bones broken.'

During the lengthy and increasingly tedious period spent by the men in Egypt before they moved to the island of Lemnos, the rigour of their desert training, the involvement of New Zealanders in the February defence of the canal against Turkish attack, and the infamous 'Battle of the Wasser' stand out as deserving recall. After the long sea voyage the men needed retraining for active service. The bitterly cold nights and intensely hot days had taken their toll with influenza and pneumonia. In addition to marksmanship at the Heliopolis rifle range, desert manoeuvres, sham fights and lengthy route marches had regularly to be endured, as well as full-scale military parades and a march through the native quarter of Cairo to impress the populace with the massive strength of the British Empire under arms.

The training was exhausting and not everyone appreciated its necessity. The fact that the commander of the Australian and New Zealand Division, General Godley, had his wife with him and that she was often in attendance when the troops were training make it scarcely surprising that her supposed remark at one review, that she wished to see the men 'do it again, Alex', spread like wildfire. It may of course be one of the earliest celebrated 'furphies', or latrine rumours, the truth of which can seldom be established. Cobden Parkes's diary records his personal regret at having been caught up in a collective refusal to obey an order after a very tiring route march, but for the New Zealanders, at least, there was a break in the monotony as they helped Indian troops repel a brave but futile Turkish attempt to cross the Suez Canal in strength.

Advance intelligence had warned of the approach of the Turks, and when their pontoons had been launched for the crossing during the early morning of 3 February they had been met by concentrated small-arms fire from No. 10 Platoon of the Nelson Company of the Canterbury Battalion. Morning light revealed bodies of Turks on the east side of the canal, and more New Zealand and Indian troops became involved in the action as the Turks shelled their entrenched positions with shrapnel. The battleship *Swiftsure* raced up the canal, sending a great surge of water up the sloping banks as she shelled the Turks. Several New Zealand diaries actually record seeing the masthead lookout on *Swiftsure* being shot, and in fact the first New Zealander to die as a result of a wound in action was hit in the neck during the night fighting. H.G. Hunter unconsciously illustrated the small-scale threat which had been presented when he wrote on 4 February that, having been ordered in the early morning to the canal to dig trenches and having seen *Swiftsure* deal with the Turks, 'we left and caught the train at 9 a.m. arriving in camp at 11 a.m'. Nevertheless New Zealanders had been in action. They had suffered some casualties and inflicted far more, though those who wrote home to the Nelson area describing heroic deeds in an epic encounter were the source of much derision when their letters, printed in local newspapers, found their way back to Egypt.

However, for the other New Zealand and Australian troops there was nothing much to excite their pride or interest. Tensions were beginning to be felt. The root problem lay in their remoteness from both their homeland and what they considered to be the real seat of the war, France and Belgium. Their frustration is well expressed in a rhyme then popular among the New Zealanders and recorded in H.P. Rasmussen's memoirs, which, after making uncomplimentary reference to Egypt, continues:

> Half the world we crossed to reach you;
> Hearts were light and hopes were high,
> Thinking that we came for fighting,
> But we're only 'standing by'.
>
> Sea-sickness, inoculation,
> Tropic heat and horsey smell,
> All the incidents of travel
> (Though we stood them rather well),
> Trains and transports, field manoeuvres,
> Bivouac beneath the sky,
> Fitting us for Active Service,
> Also perhaps for 'standing by'.

Jealousies between and within units were raising their heads. C.L. Comyns wrote home that if the 'constant energy expended in injuring others were concentrated in heroic efforts to better themselves, the results would be vastly different both for themselves, the world and our camp'. His diary describes fifty men leaving camp under strong escort to be sent home to New Zealand for refusing to be inoculated, for bad behaviour or for having contracted VD. Australians and New Zealanders, soon to serve in harmony under the grim conditions of the Peninsula, were increasingly involved in street brawls amongst themselves as well as in trouble with the Egyptians. For some, their upbringing and the constant exhortations of the Army Chaplains, were sufficient to ward off temptation. A.E. Joyce reported that there was a 'Church parade at 9 a.m. Address by Archdeacon Richard, his text being "Be not deceived". He spoke remarkably well. Everyone I think thought him good. We did not get the conclusion of his theory until he had finished, which was "Be not deceived. God is not mocked, for whatsoever a man soweth that shall he also reap!"'

As the encamped troops eyed each other through this period of frustration, mutual disparagement was to be expected and can be seen in a letter from New Zealander, E.H. Honnor.

> The English Territorials here have made complaints about not getting their food parcels; there are nearly twenty thousand of these fellows here, and you never saw such a miserable-looking crowd in all your life. Of course a lot of them are (on the whole) boys but the best of them look miserable; that could easily be overlooked if they behaved themselves; but there is not much between them and the Australians, and the way they go on here it is a wonder there is not a riot every night. The boys get a bit rowdy at times, and it is a good thing the blacks are either good-natured, good-tempered or afraid.

There had been a degree of trouble in Colombo during the brief stay of some of the troopships, and more rioting and looting at Christmas had led General Birdwood to write anxiously to General Bridges on 27 December about the conduct of the men: 'Unless … [each man] is doing his best to keep himself efficient he is swindling the Government which has sent him to represent it and fight for it.'[5] The Australian Minister of Defence, Senator Pearce, was to receive a letter from a Sergeant Collins in the AIF who attempted to put the matter into perspective. Pearce, a friend of the Collins family, was informed by Collins that, 'as one who knocked about with the next and saw all that was worst and best in Cairo (which at the particular time might be called a cesspool) I can conscientiously say that the conduct throughout was admirable. Events that did occur were caused and carried out by an element of undesirables who no matter when or where they happened to be would be up against law and order.'[6] General Bridges himself made an illuminating remark on 5 April in a letter to the Governor-General of Australia. 'Our men are in capital spirit – their discipline has greatly improved – orders are now given and obeyed that officers would hardly have ventured to give five months ago.'[7] An officer named Marks, in the 13th Battalion, noted in his diary that on 16 March, 'CO. withheld the men's pay, whereupon a deputation of the whole battalion marched in an orderly manner to Brigade HQ and laid its case before the Brigadier.'[8]

Certainly the behaviour of some of the bored troops in Cairo was bound to arouse antagonism. Egyptians had been thrown off trams into the sand, gharries had been commandeered, goods taken without payment. Cecil Malthus, on the very morning of the Good Friday Battle of the Wasser, had been shocked to see, 'a poor Arab boy run over by a car full of mad Australians and instantly killed'.[9] Neither official nor personal experience 1915 documents establish incontestably who or what was responsible for the riot in the Wasser. A participant, T.S. Smith, (2nd Battalion AIF), has described in detail how a visit to a brothel in the area – ironically a Turkish establishment – led to his being drugged, robbed and dumped in a water conduit. A flushing of cold water had revived him and he successfully searched for the house of his hostesses, with their large Nubian bodyguard. By butting the stomach of the Nubian with his head, so that the latter crashed through a balustrade into the courtyard below, he was able to depart with the day's takings, including presumably his own.

It seems that men fleeced as Smith had been, or possibly irate after VD infection, had banded together to wreak vengeance on a certain brothel in the main street. They had broken the doors and windows, and then thrown the furnishing of the rooms from upstairs windows into the street below. As the contents of one room included a piano, the determination of the men concerned can be estimated, and the crowd of interested sightseers grew larger. A bonfire was made of the beds, mattresses and other goods piled in the street. The blaze spread to a Greek drinking-shop or cafe, and the native fire brigade arrived. In the ensuing melee some soldiers cut the hoses, the civil police seemed, or were, unwilling seriously to intervene, and the area was not quietened even when Military Police, having been pelted with various missiles, actually fired into the crowd, killing one man and wounding others. The riot spread to Heliopolis, some miles to the north-east of Cairo, where a cafe, two shops and the camp cinema were wrecked or burned, but Lancashire Territorials with fixed bayonets in front of Shepheard's Hotel had prevented the trouble spreading further in Cairo itself.

Troops with pent-up frustrations which had been aggravated since their eager enlistment by the trial of a long voyage, the heat, training for 'standing-by' in Egypt and the restrictive regulations of Army camp life, had at last blown off steam. An example of the regulations which might be taken to symbolize the source of their impatience, however few in fact were affected by it, was a General Routine Order NZ Division of 28 December 1914: 'The engines of motor-cycles are not now to be started within a hundred yards of Divisional HQ.'[10] Whether or not rumour were to have laid this order at Lady Godley's door is not known, nor do we know whether General Godley were to have been correct in writing to the New Zealand Minister of Defence, Sir James Allan, on that Good Friday that a 'somewhat serious riot' had taken place – 'some men in the venereal hospital – it is said that they were Australians, but of this we have no proof – determined that they would get their revenge on the houses of ill fame where they had contracted the disease – demanded a refund of their money and on this being refused, the riot took place'.[11]

In any case the time for 'standing-by' was almost over. The Australian Division and the Australian and New Zealand Division were about to be put to the test of real battle. They had been rigorously trained. If it were maintained that they were not trained for what they would experience on the Gallipoli Peninsula, it might reasonably be contended that this was not possible in Egypt nor indeed anywhere else in early 1915.

On the evening of 3 April, with their equipment stacked ready for tram transport, the Mena Camp incinerators burning their rubbish and one battalion enjoying a farewell sing–song, the men awaited their route march to Cairo and train to Alexandria for embarkation. On Monday, 5 April, Gunner Brownell helped to unpitch tents and pack the wagons, but;

> a terrible sand storm started early in the morning and kept on all day hampering our work. Left Mena at 8 p.m. fully packed and equipped. Route marched to Cairo and reached station at 11 p.m. Loaded horses, guns and equipment on the troop trains and left station at 1.30 a.m. for Alexandria. While waiting to get away some of us ducked away and had supper in Cairo. Tuesday, 6 April. After travelling in train all night arrived at Alexandria Quay at 7 a.m. alongside troopship *A 17*. We unloaded the train and led the horses straight onto the boat, having them all aboard in three quarters of an hour. Some of our guns are also loaded on. Nicked off into town for a time both in morning and in afternoon. Changed into English coin *all my* money which was 6 P.T. = about 1s. 3d. Was told off for guard on the ship at 6.30 p.m.

The ship, *Atlantian*, sailed for Lemnos on Thursday, 8 April. Two New Zealand officers had selected their shipboard reading for the journey. At Ismailia station bookstall, a professor at Canterbury College had chosen Ovid and a young lawyer, had secured *La Vie Parisienne*.

The great expanse of Mudros harbour was crowded by naval vessels of all descriptions. They ranged from the huge *Queen Elizabeth* to little pinnaces and picket boats. The lines of troopships were the clearest evidence to the ordinary soldier that he was involved in a great enterprise. C.L. Comyns echoed the thoughts and indeed foreshadowed the recall of many in writing that the sight 'gave a feeling of awe and helped to show me how great was the mission we were on'. Within one day of his arrival, Comyns, in the Wellington Battalion, had had bayonet-fighting and musketry drill on board in the morning, and later he could see the Australians disembarking for a route march while 'our company practised landing in life boats and climbing ladders'. On the following day rowing exercises were made more stimulating by being organized into a race. Practice in unloading horses, route marches and a severe gale on the 20th and 21st were balanced by bathing, the distribution of a big mail and shipboard concerts.

Now they were so near in time and miles to their destination, despite a bad-weather postponement, and with official information and orders taking the place of rumour and conjecture, the tension increased. It was held in control by a general self-confidence, notwithstanding awareness that the test of battle was imminent When General Godley wrote to New Zealand on 21 April that 'there is no doubt that we have a very tough job before us'[12] he was expressing a sentiment shared by many in the ranks. An Australian, G.C. Grove, diligently copied into his diary the essence of Birdwood's order, which was displayed on the ship's notice-board, that the men were not to think themselves forgotten if they had to go without food for a few days because supply would be difficult, but were above all to remember the importance of 'concealment, covering fire, control of fire and communications'. Four days later, on the 23rd, he noted the details of a proclamation issued that the 'persons, property and religion of the villages of the Gallipoli Peninsula are to be scrupulously respected by all ranks of the Division'.

Aboard *Annaberg*, a New Zealander, L.H. Latimer, was struck by the irony of a religious address being interrupted by the appearance on deck of four grinding-stones to sharpen bayonets, and C.R. Rawlings recorded in his diary for the 24th, 'Inspection of identity discs and field dressing. Heavy marching-order parade during the afternoon.' During this last tense day of waiting, Corporal Hawke of the Canterbury Battalion 'crimed Signaller Ashley for insolence to NCO one day's C.B.', but we are not informed whether Ashley missed the historic 25th, the day of the landing. A typical New Zealander's reaction to the information that the Australians were to make the initial landing was given in a letter written on the 24th by Cecil Malthus. 'We reacted to this news with mixed feelings, in which relief was the main ingredient.'[13]

From the 3rd Brigade AIF troop transports during that same afternoon, destroyers took about 500 men of the 9th Battalion to the battleship *Queen*, 500 of the 10th to *Prince of Wales* and 500 of the 11th to *London*. The three old battleships, led by the modern *Queen Elizabeth*, with two more old battleships, *Triumph* and *Majestic*, six destroyers and the 3rd Brigade transports, slowly threaded their way through ships ringing with cheers and so out of the harbour. With the exception of *Queen Elizabeth*, bound for the Dardanelles, this force was to rendezvous off Imbros for the Anzac landing. The 2nd and 1st Brigades AIF and the troops of the Australian and New Zealand Division, who were to reinforce the initial assault, were making ready for their scheduled departure even as a religious service was being held under the guns of *Prince of Wales* as she made for Imbros. Taking a Communion Service later in the evening on one of the ships, the celebrant was relieved that the darkness prevented the men from seeing the tears drawn from him by the emotion of the momentous occasion.[14]

The French troops began leaving Marseilles on 4 March. The warships and troop transports, *Provence, Savoie, Lorraine, Charles Roux, Armand Behic, Italie* and others were given an heroic send-off. Fr Charles Roux, on board *Provence*, one of the finest French transatlantic liners, could not help but be struck by the sight of the promenade deck being transformed into stables with horses' heads thrusting through the windows of the luxury cabins occupied by the officers.[15] The men would have gladly exchanged some of the splendid columns and gilt decoration for a mattress in the great dining-room where they slept. Everywhere on deck there was the strong smell of dung; below deck, the smell of horses and of men was equally mixed. With a stop at Bizerta in Tunis, *Provence* reached Lemnos on the 15th. The troops moved later in the month to Alexandria, arriving on the 30th, three days later than the British Royal Naval Division, which had remained at Port Said. Since the beginning of December the Australians and New Zealanders had been encamped near Cairo, but the French troops, like the British 29th Division, stayed at Alexandria. Their contact with British troops led to numerous English diary references to the impression made by the colourful and striking appearance of the tall black Senegalese troops, and the Zouaves, the Chasseurs d'Afrique and the troops of metropolitan France. When the French troops were reviewed by Hamilton and the French Commander of the Corps Expeditionnaire d'Orient, Fr Roux wrote that bandsmen from all the different units were at forty-eight hours' notice called together to prepare a programme which included 'La Marseillaise, le God Save, et l'hymne Russe et La Marche Sultanieh'. 'The two generals, good horsemen, with a youthful aspect, had a degree of elegant smartness which produced a great impression.'[16]

With regard to the necessary repacking of stores which had occurred at Alexandria, Roux enigmatically wrote that, 'this time nothing is lacking and the place of each object is known'. Each ship was designated by a letter and a number printed on the bridge and replacing the ship's name. One rather amusing confusion remained. Hamilton's proclamation of 22 April, which was couched in moving as well as suitably martial phrases, began 'Soldiers of France and of the King.' The French translators were perturbed in case among the French troops *'quelques imbeciles'* feared for the health of the French Republic when they read that apparently they were soldiers of the King – which king? The formula was tactfully made more explicit in the French translation, *'Soldats de France et soldats du Roi'*.

The French artillery officer Raymond Weil, whose scientific ingenuity was to be demonstrated in the campaign,[17] found time on the day his battery awaited embarkation in Marseilles to buy 'pince-nez, china ink and a pocket Kodak'. He watched with concern as his horse, slung by the stomach, was winched on board their steamer, *Italie.* He was later to superintend the placement of two of the guns of the battery in position on deck for defence against submarine surface attack. His diary describes how at a slide-show and concert in Alexandria, when a portrait of George V was shown and the British National Anthem played, the English soldiers had stood and the French from politeness also rose from their seats. However, the English had not returned the compliment for Poincaré and 'La Marseillaise'. He noted that above the Staff HQ at Victoria College, Alexandria, there flew the English flag flanked by 'a little French flag'. Weil's meticulous habits are indicated by the fact that from the time he left France he always carried a bag containing a small flat spirit stove, methylated spirits, some medical ointments, his diary and a sketch pad. The first three articles performed admirable service on the Peninsula and the latter two provided posterity with a splendid record of personal service *'pour la Patrie'*.

Some of the French transports left Alexandria on 16 April, others remained till the 22nd. The rendezvous for the French was off the island of Skyros, but from here they sailed to Lemnos. After further rowing and disembarkation practice, the troops and stores for the assault on the Asiatic side of the Narrows at Kum Kale were accommodated in *Savoie, Carthage, Vinh-Long, Th. Mante* and *Ceylan*, these ships leaving the outer harbour of Mudros at 10 p.m. on 24 April.

Ships from England, carrying the 29th Division and the RND, began to leave Avonmouth on 1 March. On 2 March, Sapper Gillott (RND Engineers) was obviously rather sorry that his transport, *Somali*, was no longer being escorted by her guardian angels, in the form of two submarines. Already his diary shows that, 'about half troops sick and myself feeling as though I may become a friend of the fishes'. The following day he, 'fed the fishes'. His diary and that of Arthur Douglas[18] chronicle the collision drills, sighting the impressive snowy Sierra Nevadas, Gibraltar, the North African coast and Malta, where the first contact was made with their French allies: 'A large French battleship is coming in harbour. Ah! here she comes, *Leon Gambetta*. Oh what a rush we made for the ship's side! As the battleship neared us, their band played a nice selection, eventually turning on to "It's a long way to Tipperary". We cheered and cheered, and then joined in the song. The French crew lined their deck rails and stood to attention as they passed us, then they removed their caps and waved and cheered us.'[19] When the French troopship *Charles Roux* arrived in Malta the next day, more warm courtesies were exchanged. *Somali* reached Lemnos on 13 March and Sapper Gillott was predictably impressed by the sight of a 'good collection of battleships etc., *Queen Lizzie, Lord Nelson, Triumph, Majestic, Agamemnon*'. He noted, 'Asia Minor's snow-capped mountains which could be seen quite clearly looking very fine', but from the day of arrival the serious business of preparation for the landing began as 'several boats went out for practice rowing'.

An experienced Regular, Second Lieutenant Huttenbach, RHA, could not understand why the rifles were stored inaccessibly and wondered if the authorities were to fear that the men would sell them in Egypt in anticipation of easy replacements. For a Territorial like Henry Harris in the 87th Field Ambulance Brigade, the main problem of the unfamiliar life on a troopship was sleeping. 'When one got in at one side of a hammock the likelihood was that you came out the other side. When everyone was in, the hammocks were so close together that no one could get out until in the morning; a few of the hefty ones managed it. In a swell the hammocks all moved together with the ship's movement.' Another new experience for Harris was the issue of pith helmets and the length of cloth known as the puggaree to be wound round them. The King's Own Scottish Borderers, on board SS *Dongola*, were able to demonstrate their recent long service in India by assisting in this tricky task.

Enough has already been written, in the Official History and in other accounts, of the futile hope of secrecy and surprise once the Allied troops began their concentration in Egypt and were for example reviewed publicly in both Alexandria and Cairo. Other well-recorded features of this period before the landing were the widespread efforts to buy landing craft and, as has already been referenced, the thoughtless packing of stores and equipment on the boats which, with the unsuitability of Mudros as a port[20] as opposed to its excellence as a harbour, necessitated the return of the advanced units from the island of Lemnos to Alexandria for unloading and re-stowing.

Whatever confusion there may have been at a senior administrative level over this and however much the difficulty of the task ahead had been made more severe by the naval attempt – failure and consequent delay allowing intensive defensive preparations – these were matters beyond the control of the officers and men about to undertake the landings on the Peninsula, indeed probably beyond their conscious concern until just before the landing. Nevertheless, the point might be made that there were enormous and unprecedented logistical problems involved in such an enterprise. It is a sobering fact that Sir Ian Hamilton was informed of his appointment on 12 March and in under six weeks his French, Australian, New Zealand and British troops were landed according to plans the thoroughness of which, except in one aspect, is apparent to all but those using the distorting lens of hindsight.

Sapper Wettern's diary illustrated the activities of the RND Engineers before the landing. There was rowing,- not always successful – in Mudros harbour, a demonstration cruise off the northern shores of the Gallipoli Peninsula on 18 March, Morse practice, and a sail from Lemnos to Egypt, arriving on 25 March in Port Said. He found Port Said 'quite an interesting place. Ramshackle with some good shops. Very mixed lot of people.' After review practice, there was an impressive inspection by General Sir Ian Hamilton on 3 April. There was entertainment by the Hood Battalion band, sorting and arranging mobilization stores, filling and sealing four-gallon cans with fresh water and loading them into lighters. They left Port Said in SS *Ayrshire*, a much dirtier ship than SS *Somali*, and again there was a wait in Mudros harbour. For the RND Engineers the waiting was to be slightly extended. '24 April: Steamers leaving every few minutes throughout the day. No orders for us. 25 April: Harbour almost empty. Still no orders for us. Landing supposed to have started at dawn. Church parade at 10 on boat deck.'

For Second Lieutenant Gillett, 2nd Battalion Hampshire Regiment, it was fortunate that he was to transfer from the troopship *Manitou* to *Aragon* for the journey to Lemnos. *Manitou* was to have a narrow escape, described below. In Mudros harbour Gillett regularly practised rowing with the eight selected rowers of his platoon who even received a special word of praise from the General for their oarsmanship. They also practised getting down into the boats from the troopship by rope ladders and marching on the deck in full pack order.[21]

Gillett was greatly taken with a dummy battleship in the harbour. 'Large anchors painted on her side, a great number of guns on her all made of wood and two sham funnels.' It is recorded that a German submarine sank such a disguised warship and there must have been some measure of mystification, then disappointment, for the submarine commander as he saw the wooden superstructure float away. The skill with which these dummy ships had been prepared is indicated by the fact that range-finder, Cave, in *Dublin*, notified his puzzled captain that HMS *Lion* and other ships believed to be in Scapa were off their port bow in these warm Aegean waters! Gillett was also intrigued by an airship on a tramp steamer. The 2nd Battalion Hampshire Regiment was transferred on 21 April to the transport *Alaunia*, which sailed for the island of Tenedos, off which the men were moved to SS *River Clyde* on the evening of Saturday the 24th.

The *Manitou* incident on 16 April is one more of the small number of occasions when it is clear that a high standard of conduct and morale was not maintained. D.N. Meneaud Lissenburg was the trumpeter of the 97th Battery and was on duty at the time on *Manitou*. He had seen a small boat approaching rapidly and noticed that his troopship had stopped. The small boat, now clearly a gunboat flying the Greek flag, drew alongside the port side and the crew of a torpedo projector hurried to train it on *Manitou*. An officer on the gun boat, using a megaphone, challenged *Manitou*, shouting in what Lissenburg describes as a German accent. A White Ensign was spread over the side of Manitou and immediately the Turkish crescent replaced the Greek flag on the gunboat. The voice shouted, 'Three minutes to clear your decks.'

All the guns, machine guns and ammunition were stored in the hold[22] and we were totally unprepared for what was happening. I don't know how long we were in fact given but certainly I did not move. I saw the first torpedo plop into the sea and begin its journey directly under me as the gunboat was only twenty or thirty yards away. Nothing happened. We raced to look over the starboard side and there it was skimming away with its bow well out of the water like a speedboat. I hurried to the orderly room and asked the R.S.M. what I was to do. I expected to have to sound the 'Stand-to' but instead I was told that the order was every man for himself, scuttle away and find a boat. I was going below to get my lifebelt when at the stairs I was astonished to see the panic-stricken crush of men trying to get up, fighting against those trying to get down. There was chaos on the boat deck too. We had never had boat drill nor been allotted to a particular boat. Lt Beckett was however using his formidable figure to secure calm as he grasped the muzzle end of a rifle and threatened anyone who rushed at the particular boat he was supervising. I removed my boots and puttees, got into an overcrowded boat which, badly handled by our own men, capsized as it was lowered and we were all thrown into the water. Fortunately I was a good swimmer and got away from the side of the ship. The crew of the Turkish gunboat were laughing at us. Our ginger-haired doctor organized us into providing help for the non-swimmers, as did the steward, who had already survived the *Titanic* disaster. We were quite a while in the water before a warship, the *Prince George*, approached us and lowered her lifeboats to pick us up.

Three torpedoes had been fired at the *Manitou* and all had plunged too deeply to strike her at such close range. The gunboat was chased off and beached herself, which allowed the crew to escape. Lieutenant Gillett was told by an RFA officer the following day that some of the men from the *Manitou* had been killed by hatches and other material which would float, being thrown on top of them. Some officers had retired to the saloon to drink; others, like the Colonel, had led the rush overboard and had been quickly picked up. Some of the men, according to the artillery officer, had looted the officers' cabins, but others, Lissenburg was informed, had been led by a Second Lieutenant to release the horses and mules from their stalls where, sensing danger, they were struggling to get free. Fifty-one lives were lost, but the official military history relegates the affair to a footnote. There is some variation between the official naval account and that in James's *Gallipoli*, but whichever version were correct, the affair brings little credit to anyone.[23]

Of an altogether different character was the final dramatic naval event before the landing itself. On 17 April one of the new class of submarines, *E 15*, under the command of T.S. Brodie, in attempting to get through the Straits, ran aground just south of Kephez light. Brodie himself was killed by Turkish artillery fire, probably from the near-by Fort Dardanos. A Turkish artillery officer, Adel Savasman, was in the battery which fired on *E 15*, having first sighted its periscope and then hitting the conning-tower. Savasman found Brodie dead over his maps from a stomach wound. The Turkish officer helped to bury Brodie and the other dead on the beach, though the official naval history records that a more honourable burial was given later on higher Turkish authority.

In *Forlorn Hope 1915*,[24] C.G. Brodie, brother of T.S., and also in command of a submarine in these waters, wrote of his looking over *E 15* at the start of her endeavour to be the first Allied submarine into the Marmara. He found her all 'cluttered up with gear and food for three weeks patrol ... The men had been working all night, and were tired and unkempt but eager, and to my eyes very young. A few key ratings had been with T. S. [Brodie] in *D 8* [an earlier submarine] and I knew his reliance upon them. I could sense their confidence and affection for him.' Leaving *E 15* at Tenedos, C.G. Brodie fought to balance his brother's serenity and confidence against his own forebodings. The Royal Naval Air Service was to play its part by time-synchronized bombing to divert attention from *E 15*'s attempt and C.G. Brodie was to fly in one of the planes. When Brodie saw 'a slim grey straw at right angles to the line of the shore and a smaller black straw at an acute angle beside it ... I realized it was failure and for *E 15* final. I was conscious of disappointment but oddly no surprise.' The black straw was a Turkish torpedo boat attempting to salvage the submarine, in which some members of the crew had been asphyxiated. The others, having taken to the water, were to be picked up by the Turks.

De Robeck was determined that the Turks and Germans must not learn the secrets of this latest submarine and ordered her destruction. Two submarines, two destroyers and the old battleships, *Majestic* and *Triumph*, failed in their efforts to accomplish this, the Turks being fully alerted and greeting the battleships 'with such a shower of shell that it was impossible to get within 12,000 yards of their target'.[25] The fearful task was finally accomplished by a boat from each of the battleships daringly dodging the searchlights until, in being caught, they also found *E 15*, which they destroyed by torpedo. Lt-Cdr Robinson of *Vengeance* was in command of the volunteer crew of *Triumph's* boat while a similar crew from *Majestic* was under the command of Lieutenant C.H. Godwin. Godwin's boat was hit and sank just after all the men were taken off by Robinson's boat. Only one man had been lost under a storm of fire and the official naval history, not given to exaggeration, quite reasonably maintains that 'it was a gallant feat, finely executed, and one which it is pleasant to know extorted the highest admiration from the enemy'.[26]

The period spent by the 29th Division in Egypt is well chronicled in the Reverend O. Creighton's book,[27] and several diaries pay tribute to his organization of refreshment and leisure facilities at Mex, near Alexandria. Creighton persuaded the Brigade Major to part with funds sufficient to buy a large native tent, 'beautifully decorated inside and lit with a large arc lamp'. He borrowed tables and benches and then, with a sergeant and a transport wagon, regularly bought pastries, oranges, cigarettes, magazines, games and writing paper, thus providing a well-equipped recreation centre. His services were now far better attended, even by troops tired out after 'a long tiring day practising landing from boats'. Forty-six men applied for confirmation classes, which were arranged despite the difficulties of training schedules and the short time available. 'We sat in a circle on the sand just outside the big tent. The only light was the new moon and an electric torch I had to help me write the men's names down. I was greatly surprised at the regularity with which they came and the quietness with which they listened.'

Creighton's humility and sense of humour are attractive and must surely have contributed to the success of his ministry. In writing of Hamilton's inspection at Mex, Creighton described an unintended entertainment for which he was also responsible.

> It was a wonderful sight seeing them all massed together with plenty of room to manoeuvre on the stretches of smooth sand. I rode to a small hill at a distance and dismounted as I watched them. My groom had not tightened my saddle and girths and when I tried to mount again the saddle slipped round and I rolled off. The regiments at the moment were marching off in column. Imagine my dismay as I saw my horse take fright and tear off right past the Commander-in-chief and his staff, and then all among the men, nearly upsetting the column.

During the last few days before the landing, the details of MEF HQ planning and administration filtered through to junior officers and men. By now a booklet on the Turkish Army had been produced which gave detailed notes on organization, uniform, weapons, badges, etc. Soldiers were enjoined to recognize a

> country Turk of the village class to a certain extent by his dress. He wears as a rule a red fez, with a small coloured turban, a pair of very baggy bloomers of bluish cotton stuff, which are girt above the knee; a leather belt with a large pouch in front; white woollen stockings and large thick slippers ... In Constantinople itself soldiers must beware of the Europeans inhabiting the low-class districts near the docks, cinematograph-show keepers, grog-shop keepers and the hangers-on of disorderly houses.[28]

Of course before either the Turk of the village class or the hangers-on of a disorderly house in Constantinople had to be faced, there were the Turkish soldiers on the Peninsula. An Army leaflet[29] gave information for this eventuality. 'Turkish soldiers as a rule manifest their desire to surrender by holding their rifle butt upwards and by waving clothes or rags of any colour. An actual white flag should be regarded with the utmost suspicion as a Turkish soldier is unlikely to possess anything of that colour.' There followed a list of Turkish language equivalents to 'Surrender,' 'You will be well treated,' 'Throw down your rifles,' 'Hold up your hands',' 'Higher than that', etc.

It is difficult to make sound general observations on the briefings which were received by regimental officers, and, on occasion, by NCOs and men, because such briefings seem to have been so varied. R.B. Gillett affirmed categorically that he received his map of Cape Helles in March and that he marked in ink on the map further information on the defences as it was given to him.[30] The men engaged upon the feint landing demonstration in the Gulf of Saros knew their task too. According to Creighton, the officers and men of the 29th Division knew of the increasing strength of the Peninsula defences. 'Thursday, 22 April. It seems a perfectly desperate undertaking ... The aerial reconnaissance reports acres of barbed wire, labyrinths of trenches, concealed guns, maxims and howitzers everywhere. The ground is mined. In fact everything conceivable has been done. Our men have to be towed in little open boats to land in the face of all this.'[31] Major Davidson of the 89th Field Ambulance, entered for 21 April in his diary:[32] 'Marching orders were received this morning. They run as follows ...' In his summary of the plans he then gave full details of the objectives, with map references, to be gained by the first landings and the instruction that 'a hot meal is to be taken before leaving the ship'.

The *Official History* records the less than encouraging warning which every man in the 29th Division received from Hunter Weston, the Divisional Commander, that there would be 'heavy losses by bullets, by shells ... by mines and by drowning'. The conclusion is drawn that this may have been responsible for the degree of hesitancy shown on some beaches in the afternoon. 'As an example of the state of mind which this order induced, a man on X Beach went up to Brig-Gen. Marshall with a dead tortoise which he had found and said, "I've found one of these here landmines, Sir".'[33] Nevertheless, it is likely, and perhaps it was also proper, that for men in the ranks any briefing was minimal. Hunter Weston's printed address to his division certainly was widely handed-out and there were of course battalion orders on timing, equipment, anticipated deployment from the beaches, objectives, establishment of aid posts, etc as well as morale-boosting pep talks.

In a letter dated 24 April 1915, New Zealander Cecil Malthus wrote that he had, 'spent most of the week duplicating maps of the Peninsula with Fougere the Scout Corporal. It was slow, tedious work, all done by hand, but we have learnt to know the ground thoroughly and the knowledge will be invaluable if we are advancing over fresh country every day.'[34] He was not to know that for the Australians and New Zealanders the maps were not of the area where they would land, and that in any case they would not be advancing over fresh ground every day.

That no one expected an easy landing was abundantly evident as the naval and transport vessels moved towards their appointed stations, off the island of Tenedos in the case of the 29th Division and off the island of Imbros in the case of the Australian and New Zealand Army Corps. H.W. Nevinson summed up the emotions which roused men to tumultuous cheering as the ships left Mudros in their 'excitement, comradeship, the infectious joy of confronting a dangerous enterprise side by side'.[35] Many men, facing action for the first time, would in all likelihood have been anxiously wondering whether they would let themselves and their friends down – perhaps a matter of even greater moment than being wounded or worse.

On 19 April, Padre Creighton had been saddened by seeing the midshipmen at a ship's concert, some only sixteen, drinking a good deal of whisky and smoking many cigarettes during the evening. One such midshipman, G.L. Drewry, in a letter of 12 May, described to his father how he had felt burdened by his responsibilities towards the soldiers cooped below decks on *River Clyde*. 'I found myself on the bridge very sleepy with only the helmsman, steering towards the Turkish searchlights on a calm night just making headway against the current, shadowy forms of destroyers and battleships slipping past me. Visions of mines and submarines rose before me as I thought of the *two and a half* thousand men in the holds and I felt very young.'[36] Drewry was to show a courage within a few hours which earned him the Victoria Cross. Whisky and cigarettes may well have been the nervous signs of boys playing at being men, but, when the moment came, this feigned maturity stood the test.

With regard to deployment of the Allied troops in landings to command the Narrows, facilitating minesweeping and thus secure passage for the Allied warships through to the Sea of Marmara and beyond, French troops were to make a diversionary attack on the Asiatic side of the entrance to the Straits at Kum Kale. There was also to be a French demonstration off Besika Bay as if a landing were to take place there too, that is around the tip of the Asiatic coastline and a little further south. The Australians and New Zealanders were to be landed on the Gallipoli Peninsula North of the Kilid Bahr plateau near the prominent Gaba Tepe headland, where flatter land invited the prospect of a successful dash across the Peninsula, and the 29th Division was to make five separate landings at beaches designated Y, X, W, V and S around Cape Helles. In addition there was to be a demonstration offshore near the Turkish lines at Bulair, which, it was hoped, would convince the Turks that the main attack was to be launched here, from the Gulf of Saros, against the narrow isthmus of the Peninsula.

From 12 April, naval orders were issued by de Robeck, Rear-Admiral Wemyss and Rear-Admiral Thursby to deal with the organization of the combined operation of landing the troops.[37] From 13 April, military orders for the landing were issued by the MEF HQ Staff. The plans have come under criticism for the lack of co-ordination and there can be little doubt that naval and army planning staffs for such a huge combined operation should have been working closely together, not separately. Additionally, Hamilton failed to recognize that issues of planning, as distinct from command, strategic and tactical considerations, needed a large, experienced administrative staff, and to impose such a burden on his small GHQ Staff was unreasonable, unwise, and would have unfortunate consequences – imminently and later too.

The soundness of this and related criticisms, like the general underestimation of the Turk, can quite fairly be developed within the time frame of Hamilton's arrival in the Eastern Mediterranean to his removal from the scene in September, but of course not appropriately outside of that time frame. As for the strategic concept of Hamilton's operational planning, there is much to admire in the way he sought by his assault plans to prevent the Turks from concentrating their defensive resources. Moreover the geography of the Peninsula determined that he could not conform to the cardinal military principle of avoiding the dispersal of his own force. At Helles the plans were complex and in the event it was proved that there had been insufficient emphasis for command co-ordination – divisional and local – on adjacent beaches, and insufficient insistence on driving any initial surprise success towards wider gain. These observations may be reasonable but they cannot be freed totally from the charge of hindsight. Failure demands explanation and by extension blame – far easier to ladle than credit to the adversary or factors which, arguably, were beyond pre-vision. In respect of planning for the landings, it may be that, as many consider, the whole gamble, dubious at best, using resources needed elsewhere, and the gains from any success achieved, wildly exaggerated, then, almost by definition, the Commander-in-chief's overall scheme must be due the same scorn, but in fairness this is a prejudiced verdict. Before Hamilton's appointment, the gains to be achieved had been estimated, the troops allocated, an almost essential element, surprise, conceded. The naval assailants were battering at the Turkish door. A less determined defensive establishment than the Ottoman Empire, counselled and supported as it was by their new Teutonic allies, would have been committedly engaged in strengthening defence of the Narrows and the Peninsula. Somehow the invading force had to secure the Narrows of the Dardanelles to enable the warships to pass through. At Cape Helles there was no invitingly wide, deep, beach for the landing of a decisively large force. Hamilton's plan imaginatively made the best of an exceptionally difficult task.

History is usually 'captured' in the words of those who, in the end, win, but the account can be merciless in describing failure *en route*, any merit damned effectively by the lastingly remembered failure. Gallipoli and Hamilton fall neatly into such a category. Drawing attention to some of the small details in the plans demonstrates that the men were not launched 'casually' into an operation recognized by High Command as likely to be extremely hazardous. For base and flanking stations established ashore, sailors were to wear 'working suits and solar helmets dyed khaki colour by day. Night clothing, spare socks and one blanket are to be taken. Pistol, belt and fifty rounds ammunition, canteens and water bottles, two days' iron rations and first-aid dressings are to be carried.' And, in an order issued on 18 April concerning visual signalling, it is stated that every transport officer is to be supplied with six haversacks for correspondence, marked with the letter of the beach. A further example might be taken from Force Order No. 1 issued on 13 April which instructed that 'a hot meal will be issued to all troops before leaving their transports, and troops will land in marching order with pack and one day's rations and two iron rations (or three iron rations in the case of units for which this number is available on their ships)'.[38]

It is, however, in the provision for wounded at the landing that we see a serious underestimation of the task ahead. In an order dated 22 April, Rear-Admiral Wemyss instructed that at the landing 'one surgeon and two sick berth ratings are to be held in readiness to proceed to the beach at any time they may be required after 2 p.m. to attend and embark any wounded in the launches. The surgeons should carry their pocket instrument cases. The launches will, if possible, be taken to an empty transport, which will be called up for the purpose, or to a hospital ship, if ordered. Attendant ships will have to provide the towage.'[39] Hindsight is the historian's dubiously valid weapon, but one cannot but call to mind the near impossibility of obtaining medical aid for the grievously wounded in the early hours of the V and W Beach landings and the pathetic sight of unmanned cutters or whalers drifting helplessly from the shore of the Australian and New Zealand landing with their complement of dead and wounded. Indeed the inadequacy of these preparations left the late-arriving Deputy Adjutant-General, Brigadier General Woodward, and the Director of Medical Services, Surgeon-General Birrell, aghast, recognizing the under-provision. With less than a week to go, there was insufficient time to make material improvements and in any case the need to get soldiers and necessary stores and equipment ashore as quickly as possible, rather than use the ships' boats to bring the wounded off the beaches, was something on which Sir Ian Hamilton had insisted.[40] If High Command were to have assessed that the operation was going to be very difficult then that means a high rate of casualties and yet preparations to deal with such a situation were woefully inadequate.

This book is not attempting a continuous assessment of the administrative and executive planning of the MEF HQ Staff, but it is proper to point out that a picture of unrelieved incompetence by Hamilton and by his Staff simply cannot reasonably be advanced. One only has to glance at some accounts of the campaign to see that such condemnation is often the case. First World War generals and staff officers usually receive such treatment by printer's ink. However easy it may be to draw attention to blunders made or problems inadequately considered – and insufficient preparations to attend to casualties is a clear example that no one is going to defend – it should be recognized that the scale of the task of planning the landings and diversionary operations was unprecedented. When R.R. James made a comparison with the tragic failure of the 1809 Walcheren expedition, he surely did not stress sufficiently the enlarged scale of every aspect of the 1915 combined operation. However, James has been followed by those savaging even more conclusively almost every aspect of high political and military command in the Gallipoli endeavour. In the very first words of a new study, Peter Hart tells us that Gallipoli 'was a lunacy that never could have succeeded, an idiocy generated by muddled thinking'.[41] How easy to pronounce such a verdict, how difficult to put oneself into the mind of those making assessments based on incomplete knowledge, deploying limited and to some extent untested resources, all this under extreme pressure of time, changing circumstances, and under sceptical superior authorities – more particularly when such testing has never remotely been experienced by the trenchant critic.

3. Anzac Beachhead.

Chapter 7

25 April: The Landing at Anzac Cove

The intended landing area for the Anzac force was just north of the Gaba Tepe headland. The relatively flat terrain here[1] offered few natural difficulties opposing swift progress inland in an attempt to cross the Peninsula and secure Maidos on the Dardanelles side. As the assault in fact took place a full mile further north, in exceptionally broken country, the defences opposing a Gaba Tepe landing were to be untested and the physical obstacles to the actual landing were to be totally unexpected. Subsequent information has suggested that the difficulty of overcoming the defences at Gaba Tepe would certainly have counterbalanced the fact that easier terrain awaited the assault. The explanation of the inadequacy of the north-eastern sectors of the prepared maps was that this area, forbidding enough from sea level and bewildering from the air, was so broken by precipitous ridges, sudden washaways and twisting narrow valleys themselves entered by narrower, steep, contorted side-gullies, that accurate mapping in detail would have been difficult even under peacetime conditions.

Except where the bare sand and gravel clay had been exposed on steep slopes, and the thin layer of earth had been eroded, dense, scrubby vegetation with closely growing thorns still further hid the nature of the difficulties of moving inland from where the landing actually took place. Low but abrupt slopes rise immediately above the cove itself, and then to the north, seemingly castellated, gaunt canyons are set back slightly further from the beach. Even today, as afforestation is changing the sheer severity of much of the terrain, it remains a physical shock to visit the area for the first time. There is a road now leading off the Anzac–to–Eceabat (Maidos) route and it scales the spiny Sari Bair Ridge (see Map 2) giving access by side tracks to the various cemeteries, but to leave this road is to risk at best having one's clothing torn and at worst getting lost and having a serious fall. Viewing the area from the top of this main ridge, one is aware that in winning this little horseshoe of broken beachhead the Australians and New Zealanders had certainly achieved something remarkable, though nothing remotely decisive.

North of the long straight beach from Gaba Tepe is a slight headland which became known as Hell Spit. From this headland a small crescent-curved beach of about 1,000 yards in length – Anzac Cove – ends in a further headland, Ari Burnu. From a seaward approach, the immediately significant geographical objective is the Sari Bair Ridge. As it runs diagonally south-westwards towards Ari Burnu, its most significant heights separated by sudden depressions, the ridge splits into three subsidiary ridges. The first one to be faced from Anzac Cove was subsequently named MacLagan's Ridge. (Almost all the location points now to be listed are similarly under the names 'conferred' upon them during the campaign.) MacLagan's Ridge leads to Plugge's Plateau, below which lies the Ari Burnu headland. From this plateau an unscaleable razor ridge leads to the southern end of Russell's Top, from which the distinctive 'Sphinx' juts out precipitously. Russell's Top, further inland, had a seaward-side extension known as Walker's Ridge, before it reaches the saddle of the Nek and the main ridge at Baby 700. The height of none of these features is extraordinary; it is their steepness and abrupt changes of direction and slope which make this such difficult country for advancing infantry and scarcely practicable for artillery despite the later achievements of the Anzac gunners.[2]

The significance of the mapping being inadequate and therefore the need for improvisation during the assault, is well demonstrated in the British *Official History* concerning the description of First Ridge. 'It is important to note that whereas the original map indicated that troops could advance straight up First Ridge from its Southern extremity to Baby 700, in point of fact the Razor Edge made this impossible, and to get from Plugge's Plateau to Russell's Top it was necessary to climb down into the gully and up the steep slope on the other side.'[3]

The Second Ridge runs from Baby 700 to Pope's Hill, Quinn's Post, Courtney's Post, Steele's Post, to 400 Plateau, Lone Pine and Pine Ridge. Third Ridge, which became known as Gun Ridge, leads from Chunuk Bair to Scrubby Knoll and Anderson's Knoll and has a seaward spur which in fact forms the Gaba Tepe headland.

To secure the main heights of the Sari Bair Ridge, which at approximately 970 feet commanded the land on both the Aegean and the Dardanelles side, was to be the critical objective from the start to the finish of the campaign, and though a few Australians and New Zealanders and indeed a few British soldiers briefly glimpsed the gleaming Narrows from these heights, the intervening distance to Maidos, so mockingly insignificant in being less than two miles, was not to be covered by successfully advancing Allied troops.[4]

The strongest Turkish defences commanded by enfilade fire the intended landing area just north of Gaba Tepe leading to Brighton Beach. These defences on and near the Gaba Tepe headland consisted of trenches, wire entanglements, two 12cm guns and several Nordenfelt guns. There was in addition a mountain battery on Lone Pine directly to the rear of the beach. Actually in position in the Anzac Cove area, where the landing was to take place as a result of navigational error in the dark, the defences were much less significant and amounted to a few defended posts on the low hills commanding the beach north of Ari Burnu and a trench on Plugge's Plateau. There was but one battalion to guard the Gaba Tepe coastline, but in reserve there were five further battalions which awaited information concerning the precise location of the intending invaders' real threat. Further reserves at Maidos itself were available to bolster the defence of Gaba Tepe, Helles or even of the Asiatic side of the Dardanelles.

The instructions received by General Birdwood, in command of the two divisions here, were explicit.

By the time the Second Division begins to land, sufficient troops should be available to admit of a further advance. Leaving the covering force to protect the northern flank of the landing place and line of communication, an effort will be made to storm Mal Tepe, which is the centre and key to the ridge over which the Gallipoli-Maidos and Boghali-Kojadere roads run. Should the A. and NZ Army Corps succeed in securing the ridge the results should be more vital and valuable than the capture of the Kilid Bahr plateau itself.[5]

It was the task of the troops on the warships stealing through the darkness towards Imbros and then Gaba Tepe to effect a landing and secure the beachhead. They were the covering force preparing the way for the main body to land and strike for the heights with the vital road and Dardanelles shore beneath.

'I don't know my own feelings. I don't think I am afraid at any rate. It is just a mixture of excitement and wondering what it would all be like' is the diary entry of C.J. Lawless. It was written a few hours before the landing, but with the covering force was an unidentified soldier who did not survive the campaign but who recorded on the Peninsula a fine account of what he experienced.[6] He was on board HMS *London*. After a service at midnight they had all tried to get some rest.

We were called upon to fall in at 2.30 a.m., each man was given a very liberal supply of rum, and then stood by to await landing. Time 3.30. The moon just going down behind the horizon, the cliffs ashore just looming up like large grey clouds. The war boats had all stopped steaming. Sailors were everywhere, moving about very silently. Not a noise of any kind could be heard. The sea was as smooth as glass. The boats were being lowered into the water. The order came to get into the boats. Every man was in a short time seated in his respective boat, and everything was done in such a quiet manner that one would not realize that such a movement in the dark had been carried out. Each man had on his person a full pack consisting of one towel, one shirt, socks, greatcoat, cap, comforter, a change of underclothing, three sandbags rolled up and tied into the belt of the equipment at the back, three days' rations, consisting of from two to three tins preserved meat, three pounds of hard biscuits, and one emergency ration consisting of half an ounce of tea, two of sugar and an extract of beef. They also had from two to three hundred rounds of ammunition.

The boats were in four lines and a pinnace was in front of each line. They towed us [to] within a certain distance from shore, and then let us pull the rest of the way ourselves. Everything was going well, and one can marvel at the way it was carried out for quietness. But an accident happened as we were nearing shore, one of the pinnaces' funnels caught fire and sent up a flare that could be seen miles off. Then a voice rang out in the quietness 'You are going the wrong way, bear over,' but our man would not move out of his course. The voice rang out again, and then they tried to force us over by coming close alongside us. Still our man would not move out of his course so they towed us in and made the landing in the place where our boat was making for ... On nearing the shore the first thing that came to our notice was the flash of a huge searchlight. It appeared to come from Cape Helles and shortly afterwards there came a second flash from farther round the Cape. Then everything remained quiet and still again. We were fast approaching the shore and the steam pinnaces had cast us loose. Then a shot rang out in the cliff in front of us and the echo in the still of the morning travelled right along the hills. There was a pause and the battle commenced to rage ...

Our boys had to jump over the side of the boats into the water, in some places up to our armpits, our rifles were not loaded and we had to fix bayonets on getting ashore. Now we had received orders that as soon as we had all got ashore, every man was to fix bayonet and get into line, each man taking hold of the sleeve of the man next to him with his disengaged hand. But one can imagine to oneself why that was not carried out. Some men were shot getting out of the boats, others in the water and sank to rise no more, and a great number on the shore, so that the orders laid down for the line of advance could not, under the conditions that then existed, be carried out... Men of all units were mixed up, command as far as orders were concerned was lost, i.e., what to do and how to do it. There was one yell and a rush towards the cliff... shouting like demons. The value of our severe training in Egypt standing us in good stead.

The strength of the current and the difficulty of discerning accurately the coastline ahead had led to an error of navigation. Subsequent rumours of the Turks having moved the navigation buoy supposedly set by *Triumph* have not been satisfactorily substantiated. Commander Dix, on the left of the landing flotilla over which he held command, was aware of the drifting and bunching northwards. He was frustrated in his efforts to correct this, and the error was further compounded by Lieutenant Waterlow, who was responsible for guiding the tows. Waterlow, sighting Ari Burnu, identified it as Gaba Tepe and altered his course accordingly. Commander Dix took his tow across the stern of those crossing his desired correction course ahead and the sailors in his boats brought them in around Ari Burnu while the three left-hand tows were some 200 yards north. Altogether the landing was about a mile further north than had been intended.[7]

Despite the naval responsibility for the error, seen both in contemporary evidence and in retrospect, the bearing of the young midshipmen – one, Eric Bush, being not yet sixteen years of age – made a tremendous impression. G.A. Radnell was just one of many Australians who paid tribute to them. Their composure under fire, their businesslike command and authority were what those responsible for their training at Osborne and Dartmouth, the junior and senior departments of the Royal Naval College, would have expected but would nevertheless have been intensely proud to see so amply demonstrated. A New Zealander remembered the general amusement which eased the tension when a rosy-cheeked midshipman dealt with a querulous remonstration by replying that he expected to be addressed as 'Sir'. The midshipman was of course in command of his boat.

Midshipman Eric Longley-Cook had spoken similarly to an Australian officer and then, as his picket boat came under fire, a 3pdr shell came through the thin steel screen in front of his wheel, through his straddled legs and the cabin immediately behind him, to wound two sailors in the stern of his boat. On a second trip to the landing beach he was somewhat dismayed to see dark khaki bundles above the shoreline and then relieved to find that they were not bodies but merely the discarded packs of the Australians as they stormed up the beach to the higher ground. Longley-Cook wrote to his father: 'The extraordinary thing is that I didn't feel a bit funky.'

Eric Bush's admirable conduct was recorded in *Bacchante*'s 'Report of Proceedings' that is the Captain's report. 'I would especially wish to bring to your notice the two Midshipmen of this ship who were in our steamboats: Mr Eric Wheeler Bush, Royal Navy, and Mr Charles Douglas Herbert Horsfall Dixon R.N. who came to us as *only first-term cadets from* Dartmouth and who I saw repeatedly doing good work.' The father of another very young Midshipman, Aubrey Mansergh, had been so annoyed at still having to contribute to his son's Dartmouth fees, knowing that he had been in the term leaving the college early as a result of the outbreak of war, that he had written to the First Lord of the Admiralty about it. Churchill promised to look into this injustice but was 'happy to inform my father that his son had been awarded the Distinguished Service Cross for service at the Dardanelles'.

Bacchante's young ship's writer, A.H.K. Cobb, denied the privilege of taking the troops ashore, was in command of the fore transmitting room with twelve hands under him. He watched the landing and was able to describe it immediately in his log. 'We closed to within 800 yards of the shore and commenced firing at 4.30 ... on the farther ridge a splendid Turkish battery was concealed and they burst shrapnel over the landing troops absolutely unmercifully. By our heavy firing we were able to stop the battery considerably and by night we had landed some thousands who had taken the first ridge and were entrenching themselves rapidly. You could see them silhouetted on the skyline digging like sin.' Another officer on board *Bacchante*, W. O'Neill, watched the Australian effort and recorded in his log the murderous fire of the Turks 'causing many casualties, but nothing could stop these undaunted troops who simply had their bayonets fixed and made a gallant charge up the hill'.

The sudden cliffs and valleys and unexpected precipitous rises led to the development of completely unconnected fighting incidents. Men deliberately jumped feet first to slide down the gravelly sides of a miniature canyon and, with a free hand to grasp at roots, used bayonet or entrenching tool to clamber up the other side in pursuit of shadowy figures who were often using paths of escape of course unknown to the Australians. How far to advance where there seemed little or no opposition was a question some had to answer, but, as the morning wore on, when to retire if opposition increased and one's own party was small, became the critical issue. Peter Hart, in his account, is severe in his criticism of the Australian Colonel Ewen Sinclair-MacLagan in respect of his excessively cautious command of his men in this respect.[8]

Following quickly upon the landing of the covering force, came the main body, to be landed by destroyers and troopships. G.C. Grove found the beach, 'littered all over with bits of web equipment, bags of iron rations, caps, hats, rifles, ammunition lying in amongst the dead and wounded ... packs and equipment had been left all over the place in the scrub and on the side of the gully.' Grove, with the 2nd Field

Company of Engineers, was soon involved in carrying stores up the gully behind the first ridge and there they bored successfully for water.

> Troops on the way to the firing line were stopping all day to get a drink so we were working pretty hard with the pumps, having to fall flat on the ground every minute or so on account of the shrapnel shells and bullets bursting over and amongst us all the time. There were a lot of snipers about on the ridges, so when passing backwards and forwards to the beach we had to keep under cover as much as possible. Stretcher-bearers and A.M.C. passing unceasingly backwards and forwards between the beach and the firing line doing magnificent work. Guard mounted over water reserve during the night. I had the 12 to 2 a.m. shift, very dark when moon went down. Had to keep our eyes very wide open in spite of our tiredness. Did not get any rest all night on account of having to man the pumps to supply the mules and water carts with water.

Corporal J. Sinclair of the 10th Battalion, wounded at the landing, wrote from his hospital in Malta on 4 May that right up to their landing it was impossible to exaggerate 'the hospitality and kindness of the sailors of the *Prince of Wales*. ... If I ever have the chance to help any British sailor I shall do so'.[9] Sinclair admitted in his letter that from the top of the first hill 'we went after [the Turks] without much system, all the different companies mixed up ... I think the lack of system was why we missed so many snipers who lay in the bushes and were passed by our men'. Though he did not mention that their orders at every level had been to press on with all attention to speed, he was critical of Australian conduct later in this confused day. 'Then they came running in. One fellow stood up and started to explain why he had come in, with bullets falling around us thick as peas. He ought to have got down as quickly as possible. He did get down when he was ordered to. This is typical of the way the Australians acted throughout. I do not think we fully appreciated the danger we were in, any of us.'

Another letter, dated from 4 May, from a 10th Battalion man, W.J. Welch, wounded at the landing and apparently anxious to get back to the Peninsula to 'find the bloke who got in on me when I wasn't looking', wrote of the landing: 'My word, what a mix-up it was,' and G.D. Shaw in the same battalion conceded in a letter to his wife that he felt 'years older and I don't think I want to laugh very much any more'. Private Knight, more elated despite his wound, wrote of the outnumbered Turks, 'You should have seen the cowardly curs run. They scuttled out of the trenches like rabbits and we were the whippets giving chase.'[10]

The special tasks to be performed by the engineers at the landing or during the next few days were many and varied, and at least one for which they were well prepared was never accomplished. One man, D.S.M. Oakes, staggering ashore in the shallows laden with gun-cotton and demolition equipment, was with a party briefed to destroy the gun emplacement at Gaba Tepe!

Harold Bachtold was in command of the beaching and arrangement of the first pontoon for the assistance of unloading stores from lighters. The officer on the beach required so many minor adjustments to the course of the pontoon as it neared the shore that Bachtold cut short any further frustrating delay by running the joined sections ashore as he saw fit. 'It was a raft built up of barrels – the raft with us on it was towed by a destroyer about a mile, arriving at the beach about 2 o'clock in the afternoon. Directly we left our transport we had to run the gauntlet of shrapnel fire directed at us … on arrival at the beach we connected up with shore in about fifteen minutes and then handed it over to the A.M.C. who immediately commenced to use it for embarking the wounded.'

Particularly tragic had been the fate of men of the 7th Battalion in four of the boats on the left of the landing.[11] With all the rowers killed, oars lost or smashed and many of the soldiers killed or disabled, the boats had drifted helplessly just off shore, an easy target for fire from the direction of Fisherman's Hut. Among the most unforgettable of the early impressions of those who survived their first days on the Peninsula was the sight of these 7th Battalion casualties lying for several days unburied on the shoreline or in the stranded, waterlogged boats.

One letter clearly confirms that the rank and file knew that detailed plans for the landing had been made but, in the event, coping with the terrain and determined Turkish fire wrought havoc to such preparation. 'The position and routes for each battalion had been mapped out beforehand, but everything went to pot. Officers lost their way, the signallers got separated from their units, companies overlapped and got in each other's road. In the end groups of men went on and up on their own, or followed any officer they came across. We got into the wrong valley and had to re-trace and start again.' This letter, written from hospital in England in December 1915, by Private W.E. Farr of the 8th Battalion, also documents the beginnings of a withdrawal from the advanced positions taken, a retirement countermanded as will be described. Farr made critical comments about the battalion's lieutenants, reaffirmed the confusion he had described in that in his unit the men digging and firing from the line against counter-attack were often without officers or NCOs but that overall, 'the sergeants, especially those who had been in the British Army, were the mainstay'.[12]

The work of the Australian and New Zealand Engineers won an unconscious but deserved tribute in the diary of Eric Wettern who, with the 2nd Field Company RND Engineers, landed at Anzac on the 29th and found, 'several landing piers in bay at foot of cliff – crowded with stores etc. – quite a small town'. The RND Engineers were to be engaged in 'making road up shore hillside for guns – record time – got it finished by dark [on 30th] and got one gun up. Congratulated by Australians.'

Wettern had little idea of the difficulties encountered at Anzac and the recovery from the dangerous situation of the first twenty-four hours. The brigade and battalion War Diaries of the AIF provide an indication of the disintegration of the meticulous planning and the consequent strain upon the men. In official orders beforehand it is specifically stated: 'No rifle fire is to be employed until broad daylight. The bayonet only is to be used. No bugle calls to be sounded after leaving Lemnos. No bugle calls are to be sounded during the charge.' For 5 a.m. on the 25th, the War Diary of the HQ of the 3rd Infantry Brigade reads, 'Bde considerably mixed but roughly in order,' and by the 29th, 'Our men were thoroughly exhausted and their nerves shattered after ninety-six hours' continuous fighting in the trenches with little or no sleep.' The strain was not limited to the men in the ranks – one senior Australian officer was sent back to Alexandria by Bridges as he was 'quite dangerous, thinking everyone was a spy'.[13]

The capacity of the Turks, aided by the terrain, to infiltrate the newly-established positions of the Australians and New Zealanders was the source of a good deal of the morale-sapping confusion. There are numerous stories of Turks and indeed Germans in the uniforms of dead Australians, or merely unseen in the scrub or the darkness of night, shouting confusing orders to the Anzacs such as 'Don't shoot – Indian troops'. Not always was there a Captain Croly quickly to make up men's minds with, 'Shoot the bloody buggers, they're Turks'.[14] A soldier named Marks, who landed with his 13th Battalion on the 26th and fed that night on 'dead men's rations', recorded in his diary for the 27th that 'during the afternoon we were repeatedly ordered to cease fire as the British and French were coming up'.[15] Signalled messages to the same effect were received but they were found to emanate 'from spies actually in our trenches'. Then, 'the Turks heavily attacked, blowing weird calls on a bugle'. The confusion is further confirmed by a letter from General Bridges to his wife written from Anzac Cove, 'Troops had to be shoved in just as they landed which mixed units up and we never got straight for days.'[16]

In the same letter Bridges wrote that 'the Brigadiers thought that they could not hold on for another day', and there is ample evidence for this dangerous situation in Birdwood's diary and correspondence.[17] On the 29th, Birdwood wrote that his men went forward with 'too much dash for they took on more than they could manage, dashing away to the extreme spurs of the hills which were much too extended to hold … but then the most awful reaction followed', and he described how, near the beach, he had met small groups of Australians returning from the firing line convinced that they were the last of their units and had narrowly escaped being cut off.[18]

From a lower level, Cecil Malthus provides similar evidence when he wrote of a state of muddle and utter exhaustion existing everywhere and the defence of their beachhead being terribly weak. On the 26th there was an incursion into a trench held by the Canterbury Battalion by a party of Australians who had been cut off ahead of the coalescing front line. 'Now they had suddenly lost their nerve, though not immediately threatened, and working their way along the cliff top came dashing in without warning over the top of our trench … They were in a bad state with exhaustion and thirst.'[19]

Naturally only the men on the beach and near the Brigade HQs had any inkling of the seriousness of the overall tactical situation on the evening of the landing, but those involved in reversing the parapets of trenches near the beach were aware that the fearful possibility of a withdrawal under fire was being actively considered. This beach defence activity was well remembered by D.S.M. Oakes of the 1st Field Company Engineers, who had stumbled ashore with the demolition equipment for the Gaba Tepe gun emplacement, but it is right that note should be taken of the Australian Official Historian C.W. Bean's advice that the situation on the beach, with its stragglers and its wounded, should not be taken to reflect the state of morale in the firing line. However, the fact remains, an Australian brigade command request for naval evacuation, conveyed to Hamilton, was famously denied with commendation for what had been achieved and insistence to dig and dig to secure it.

In the diary of CQMS A.L. Guppy[20] of the 14th Battalion, there is a revealing entry for 25 April, written while his transport *A 31* (*Seang Choon*) stood off shore. 'At about 11 p.m. a picket boat came round and a Naval Officer shouted up to us to get boats' crews told off ready to man all boats ready to go ashore as it was expected that all troops ashore would be re-embarked. This got our blood up a bit to think that so many lives had been thrown away and the thing a failure. However about midnight the order was cancelled.'

Awaiting his time to land like Guppy was A.L. Hellman, and his diary illustrates the strain of inaction further heightened by what he could see and what he was told. '25 April 1915: Our boys are getting a terrible time. Boat after boat of wounded are being brought alongside. What an awful sight to see our boys cut about.' 27 April 1915: The sooner we get ashore the better. Let us avenge the death of our comrades. Thank God I was born a man and not a woman. I would not be out of this for anything. 28 April 1915: A lot of our men have had their tongues cut out by the Turks! We have eight prisoners on board. They are being treated as well as we are,'[21] – a marvellous illustration of tension before action breeding rumour and moral outrage.

From 4.15 a.m. according to the 3rd Infantry Brigade War Diary,[22] the first troops were being landed from the battleships and the men from the destroyers were only ten minutes behind, except for those drowned in the sad accident to a boat swamped as it drifted in too closely to the destroyer *Foxhound* when still well offshore. From 5.30 a.m. to 7.30 a.m. Australians from the 2nd and 1st Brigades were landed. There is a photograph of the HQ of the 1st Australian Division landing at 10 a.m. The first New Zealanders in the Australian and New Zealand Division were landed by 10.30 and they were from the Auckland Battalion.

From the NZ Divisional Signal Company, C.R.G. Bassett, who was in August to earn the VC, remembered being concerned at the landing when he saw lines of Australian dead, whether he would be able to 'maintain his honour' in what lay ahead. A.E. Robinson in the Auckland Battalion, far in advance of what was to be Quinn's Post, affirmed that he saw the waters of the Dardanelles, but when his companion, Private Crum, was hit and they seemed alone against heavy machine-gun fire, they made their way back. D.E. Stacey, in the same battalion, recalled that Colonel Plugge formed them up on the beach in fours to march along to the left, but before long this order was reversed, and avoiding the folly of making such a target for Turkish fire they made a much less formal move to positions on the right. W.I.K. Jennings, an officer in the Otago Battalion, had suffered the indignity of jumping into the water far too soon and having to be hauled back, while W.H. Foord, in the NZ Engineers, recalled that on their transport a good deal of time was spent in extracting the stretchers from beneath the barbed wire under which they had been stowed!

Personal experience evidence of New Zealanders at the landing consistently records the dual impact of the sight of death and, amidst death, of Australian achievement. Lieutenant Algie wrote in his diary: 'We landed on an open beach and were greeted with a sight to try the nerves of the strongest – dead, dying and wounded in all directions. The Australians who had landed at dawn had suffered heavily but performed a feat of which we were all proud in driving the enemy out of his positions at all.'

Captain A.B. Morton, with the Staff of the Australian and New Zealand Division, having mentioned in his diary for the 24th that he had 'put the finishing touch on the edge of my sword which I have decided to take with me in case it may come in useful', grimly listed over the next several pages the New Zealand killed, wounded and missing between the 25th and 30th.[23] He himself was to be killed on 3 May.

C.J. Walsh, in the Auckland Battalion, sought no disguise for his feelings. 'The Turks have got the range of this place and they pepper it. Dozens coming back wounded. Singie got shot in thigh. Lots dead … Latest news is that nearly all officers shot and extreme left wing retreating. No reinforcements and no artillery … Rifle fire continued all through night. On duty most of night. I feel very frightened. Raining slightly during night.' H.G. Hunter, in the Canterbury Battalion, having landed in the evening of the 25th, had by the 27th 'not fired a shot yet, neither have any of the rest of my platoon'. The relatively small numbers of Turks present during the first days and their skill at concealment meant that Hunter's experience in failing so far even to have seen the enemy was common.

A sergeant in the Wellington Battalion, A.G. Jennings, wrote pencilled snatches in his diary at any opportunity. 25 April: 'This is going to be serious. Boatloads of wounded Australians are coming aboard.' 27 April: 'Took a box of ammunition to our left flank and nearly got potted twice. Coming back lost my way and came across three New Zealanders lying down. Thought they were wounded and offered to help them but found they were dead.' Quite a number of men understandably recorded their distress at being unable to bring help or water to the piteously crying wounded just ahead of hurriedly makeshift entrenchments.

With far more wounded than had been estimated, there were harrowing scenes both on the beach and on the transports of untended men lying either in the sun or on overcrowded decks. For men unable to help themselves, the heat, the flies, the pain and shock effect of their wounds, as well as the sight of them, made the days from 25 April a nightmare.[24] The diary of Lieutenant-Colonel P.C. Fenwick, the New Zealand Assistant Director Medical Services, shows that,

> at one time over 400 were lying on the stones [of the beach] waiting to be moved … Violent burst of shrapnel swept over us and many wounded were hit a second time. Col. Howse was packing boats and lighters with these poor chaps as fast as possible, but the beach kept filling up again with appalling quickness … I dressed as many as I could but it was a dreadful time … At midnight I got four big horse boats which held twelve stretchers on the bottom and I packed in less severe cases along the sides, sitting, kneeling, lying – anyhow, about 120 all told.' Also on the beach, Edney Moore, in the Australian Medical Corps, noted that 'owing to boats being busy landing troops, they were unable to take the wounded off. God wasn't it an awful mix-up stooping over the men trying to help them as they lay in the scorching sun.

Eric Longley-Cook remembered his midshipman's work that day taking wounded on a huge flat-topped Greek lighter lashed to his picket boat.

> One wounded Australian had a red and black shoulder flash immediately above what was left of his arm, which was burnt black where it was not red with blood. I took this load of wounded to ship after ship, only to be waved away as they were full. Finally I took them to my own ship, *Prince of Wales*, and risking a beating for insolence secured alongside and went up to the officer of the watch, told him what had happened and that *he must* take them. All was well, the wounded were taken on board and I returned to the beach.

On board *Prince of Wales* the Australian wounded received attention, and one of the RN medical orderlies, G.F. Moseley, never forgot a soldier holding his eye in place until a naval surgeon cut the shreds which still held it. A New Zealander named Furby, himself wounded, saw amputations of fingers carried out with a table knife on board the transport *Itonus*, and another New Zealander, J.A. Fagan, who lay on a hard iron deck for his return to Alexandria, remembered not only the impossible task for two doctors on board, but the bandaged bodies washed ashore near Alexandria because of inefficient sea burials from this transport. Not all the wounded suffered from small arms or shrapnel fire. Some had spinal injuries like H.V. Hitch, who had had to make a dramatic jump down the sheer slopes of a ravine to avoid being an easy target on the skyline where he had been spotted. 'I threw my rifle down and jumped. I sailed through the air about 25 feet and landed on a slope of 1 in 1. As I jack-knifed I felt as though I had landed on a couple of bayonets.' His painful descent was not yet concluded but surely no account of the sufferings of the variously injured men could be more horrifying than that contained in a letter written by Peter Hall, in the 2nd Stationary Hospital, on 2 May, from the SS *Seang Choon* in Alexandria harbour.

> I shall not easily forget that first feeling of awe that came over me as I looked over the side of the ship, down on these boatloads of mangled human beings. As [our] infantry had not left the ship the blankets had not been sterilized – three English doctors and fifteen men none of whom had been trained for anything but general duties in a hospital trying to attend 659 wounded men, the majority of them in an awful state – it was a matter of difficulty to walk anywhere on the decks so closely were they packed. Some of these men with arms and legs all smashed up lay squeezed up against others with half their faces blown away. Men sat all night and well into the next day with congealed blood hanging from mouths unable to speak, but with an awful appeal in their eyes imploring you to bring the doctor. The doctors were doing their best but it was an impossible task to attend to so many. One man begged of me to take five sovereigns he had, just to bring the doctor to him for one minute. [One] man sat there while the doctor cut away the loose pieces of flesh and removed the shattered teeth and bone. Men [were] going for days without having broken limbs set – [there were] no proper splints.'

> For the first two days it was a common sight to find men sewn in their blankets laying [*sic*] about the deck – sewn up by men who yet had themselves to go out and face what these fellows had done.

Looking at the faces of the dead, Hall wrote that it was heart-breaking to think of those who were waiting at home for news of their menfolk. Having described the crowded mess-deck, he concluded: 'All this was someone's fault but God knows it was not ours who already had a superhuman task before us. Some day it may be fixed to somebody holding a much higher position than any of ours. Surely a want of preparation and foresight on somebody's part.'[25]

For the Turks, the exact location of the Anzac landing had come as a surprise. Major Zeki, in command of the 1st/57th Regiment, informed the post-1918 Armistice Dardanelles investigators that no special dispositions of troops had been made there because it was thought that the ground was too broken and that naval gunfire could not adequately support a landing.[26] Once it was realized that this landing was a serious threat, the readily available reinforcements were hurried up into position, but with the exhaustion of this reserve Major Zeki affirmed that the 26th had been a very critical day for the defenders.

An indication of the delicate balance between defeat and the avoidance of defeat, was given in the memoirs of Liman von Sanders, Kannengiesser Pasha and Mustapha Kemal himself.[27] At a lower level there is evidence too. Sureya Dilmen, a civilian, happened to be visiting his uncle, a captain in the 27th Infantry Regiment stationed in the Olive Grove, when news of the landing was brought to the regiment. Dilmen was given a rifle and told to come along to help fight for his fatherland and this, he recalled, he was proud to do. Captain Ozgen informed the author of the Turkish shortage of ammunition during the first days of the landing and their use of both rocks and explosive charges thrown or rolled down gullies onto troops attempting to scale them.

A remarkably interesting letter, dated 7 May, describing the landing as seen by the Turks has survived and was given to the author by its writer, General Fahrettin Altay, a Lieutenant-Colonel in 1915.[28]

> Naturally we moved up to Maidos on the afternoon of the first day of the battle, and for three or four days what anxieties we endured God alone knows! All actions devolved upon myself … above Ari Burnu there is a fairly high hill called Koja Chemen Dagh that completely overlooks the Straits. The enemy's intention was to seize this hill suddenly, but on my timely insistence, the force held in this neighbourhood arrived in time to occupy the hill before the enemy, and to force the latter into a steep, very rough and rather narrow ravine between the hill and the sea. Although three attacks were made to throw the enemy into the sea, they were foiled again by naval and machine-gun fire and by the ruggedness of the land and the enemy's defences. We suffered great losses, but those of the enemy were even greater, and he had not achieved his purpose. That he has a few troops on land is of no importance. He can land troops whenever he

likes, but his main purpose is to seize the Straits and for that great self-sacrifice is required. Of this, however, there is no sign, for the morale of his troops has sunk so low as to be beyond description, as we can see for ourselves and learn from prisoners ... These fellows will eventually have to embark their troops at Ari Burnu and remove them one of these nights. They cannot advance one step further but it will be a bit harder to chase them from Seddel Bahr.'

Thanks be to the Almighty our officers and men rushed forward with a self-sacrifice beyond description. The Germans are astonished at the bravery and self-sacrifice of our soldiers ... Only the crew of the *Nuseyri* who had been posted to some of the Arab battalions threatened to flee: but they were brought to their senses when three of them were shot.

A wounded private was being carried from the front line to the rear. I walked with him for a little, holding him by the hand. When I uncovered his face and smoothed his bloody cheeks, he sighed: 'Ah Sir, I am not grieving over my wounds, but because I cannot now see those fellows chased into the sea I am grieving. Perhaps if I could have stayed a little longer, I should have seen them.'

On the second night of the battle four thousand wounded were collected around us. The landing stages [at Maidos] were under fire from the fleet. Maidos was in flames, and shells fell on the hospital; but all the wounded were rescued except for ten or so. There were three severely wounded British prisoners, and these were burned. That a hospital should be shelled was something unheard of up till then. Later on Chanakkale was bombarded and it too was set on fire. The towns have been virtually evacuated. Gelibolu was shelled from the Gulf of Saros and a few houses burned down: later it too was evacuated. Aeroplanes twice dropped bombs near our H.Q. but only one bomb scored a hit, on the telephone tent, four unfortunate men being killed and one wounded. A splinter from a naval shell pierced my tent whilst I was away, and destroyed a basket in it.

With the orderly who is bringing this letter we have sent as a present to the Vice-Commander-in-Chief a British machine-gun, two rifles and a map. If you look at the machine-gun, which will probably be placed in a museum, you will see that I have written on it and Pasha has also signed it... I haven't any present to send you. Will you make up a small parcel of four batteries for electric torches (they are three or four piastres each), a bottle of eau de cologne, soap and a box of biscuits and send it by the orderly who brings this letter ... violent days are past and the rest is easy.

Altay's letter to his father does something to balance the picture of the Anzac landing given in Allied personal documentation. With an eye towards the morale of the recipient, that of the Anzac soldiers is described as having sunk so low as to be beyond description. The reader in Constantinople is informed of the shelling of a hospital and can draw the invited conclusion whether this had been deliberate or not. Similarly from Brisbane to Bury and Bar le Due, parents, relatives and friends would read of the Turks running away 'like cowardly curs' and of their mutilation of Allied prisoners. How universal, if ironic, that where the daily circumstance was worst, the fighting front, those who were experiencing it exercised due responsibility of hiding or inflating anything the effect of which would influence morale on the Home Front.

Nonetheless this letter from an officer of Altay's seniority contained an accurate appraisal of the general tactical and strategic situation within a fortnight of the landing, something of course far beyond the capability of the man in the ranks or the junior officer. Even if his concluding comment that 'violent days are past and the rest is easy' was obviously to reassure his father, his forecast that no further Allied advance at Anzac was possible and that the force would have to be re-embarked was an accurate prediction which would only be briefly challenged in August before being vindicated in December.

Von Sanders, now satisfied that no serious attack was intended at the Bulair lines, had committed all his reserves to Anzac and Helles. The counter-attack at Anzac, launched by Kemal Pasha with his 19th Division was decisively to wrest victory away from the Allies.

Not even the whole of First Ridge had been taken by the brave Australian and New Zealand assault. Its northern starting-point, Baby 700, a vital key, was not to be retained after its early capture despite the fact that much of Second Ridge had been won. This Second Ridge, with the northern section of First Ridge, was to form throughout the campaign the front-line zone. Isolated parties, like that led by Lieutenant Loutit of the 10th Battalion, had reached vantage-points on Third Ridge like Scrubby Knoll which enabled them to see the Dardanelles only three and a half miles away, but they had been forced to retire as the general confusion fatally delayed the sending of reinforcements to secure the vital heights reached.

On Battleship Hill and on Baby 700, similarly small parties had either been forced to retire or had been overwhelmed. The latter was the fate of Captain Peter Lalor of the 12th Battalion, while Tulloch of the 11th, having been outflanked after his successful ascent of Battleship Hill, had to withdraw when his small group was opposed by increasingly strong resistance. Lieutenant Margetts, of the 12th Battalion, twice reached the summit of Baby 700 and, 'further to the left, near the summit of the hill, where Gordon's company of the 2nd Battalion was mixed with remnants of the 11th and 12th, the line swept backwards and forwards over the summit of Baby 700 no less than five times. Each time after holding for a while, it was driven back. Almost every officer was killed or wounded, but Margetts still remained.'[29] The heroism of these men, of Major Kindon and of the Auckland and Canterbury Battalions who came up to their support on Baby 700, is inspiringly written in the Australian Official History; but the hill was lost. Without artillery support, as the Indian Mountain battery had been counter-batteried out of action, and with no Australian or New Zealand 18pdr guns in action before 6 p.m. that day,[30] the unconnected parties holding Baby 700 broke and retired at about 4.30 in the afternoon against a strong Turkish assault. The Nek was to fall in the evening, and by morning Bloody Angle too, but what was to become Quinn's Post held, and on the right, the Australian line, after bitter fighting, was forced to retire to Bolton's Ridge, a position seaward of Lone Pine, Johnston's Jolly and the crest of McLaurin's Hill. Even without Hamilton's celebrated order to dig and dig, the entrenching tool was to be every Anzac's closest ally.

Earlier in the day the Anzacs had shown their confident dash, their physical stamina and their athleticism. As the day wore on they would demonstrate their capacity to endure, grimly to hold on when faced by that most dangerously gnawing erosion of individual and collective confidence, a severe check to a consciousness of superiority. They had found that they were not, on this historic day, to stride across the Peninsula, but the Turk would learn that to check their invasion was one thing, to throw them into the sea was another. As at Helles, the scene was set for another Flanders, but in a topographical setting almost unimaginably different.

There is ample evidence that, though few of the men involved had expected easy success, the frustration of their efforts was sobering. Fortunately the effect of this depressing experience was counter-balanced by an admirable resilience and capacity to endure the grim unanticipated conditions. Against increasingly strong defences and obvious geographical disadvantage, the Australian and New Zealand troops had stormed, then defended, a beachhead and inland area which, though small, was to be so securely held that no massed Turkish counter-attack from the end of April to the evacuation in December would seriously threaten their control. An achievement in April? Certainly, yes – one giving High Command a glimpse of victory? As certainly, no.[31]

4. Cape Helles.

Chapter 8

25 April: The Landings at Cape Helles and Kum Kale

Y Beach

Of the forces assigned to launch the attack on the five chosen beaches of Cape Helles, that which landed at Y Beach involved the 1st Battalion King's Own Scottish Borderers, one company of the South Wales Borderers and the Plymouth Royal Marine Battalion. The special significance of this action is indicated by the account in the *Official History*.[1] Sir Ian Hamilton had hoped that landing at a point just west of Krithia would both threaten Turkish communications to the toe of the Peninsula and safeguard the flank of the landings around the tip of the Peninsula by providing for the establishment of a link with X Beach which would seriously threaten Turkish defence against the V and W Beach landings. An examination of the landing-site confirms the reasonable witticism published in the MEF newspaper, *Peninsula Press*, later in the campaign: 'Y Beach? – it's nothing but a bloody cliff.' The almost sheer cliffs, approaching 200 feet high, with only two narrow defiles allowing an approach to the top, had been left undefended by the Turks.

Led by the King's Own Scottish Borderers, the landing was completely unopposed. For the subsequent failure to exploit this lack of opposition, the *Official History* indicts first Colonel Matthews of the Royal Marines, the question of whose overall command was sadly decided for the most senior officer who doubted it, Colonel Koe of the Borderers, by the latter's mortal wound. Colonel Matthews, in the absence of orders confirming that he was to exploit the unopposed landing either towards X Beach or towards the apparently undefended Krithia, delayed making any decision until mid-afternoon on the 25th, when he ordered defensive entrenchment of the cliff-top 'beachhead', and furthermore failed to convey this decision to the watching ships, from which observation was hindered by the spoon-like depression of the land behind the cliff edge. The official account also indicts the lack of initiative by Sir Ian Hamilton, who had taken a special interest in the plan for an attack at Y and had invited Hunter-Weston, the Divisional Commander, to exploit it when the first indications of an unopposed landing were received. Finally the Official Historian condemned Hunter-Weston's preoccupation with events at the V and W Beaches and his lack of both tactical awareness and responsibility towards Y Beach.

The war diary of the 1st Battalion King's Own Scottish Borderers illustrates that when the Turks did come up in strength, the closeness of the fighting around their newly-entrenched position led to some of the confusion which characterises events at this landing. 'In one place a German officer walked up to our trench and said,

"You English surrender. We ten to one." He was thereupon hit on the head with a spade.' The Turks had even brought up a machine-gun on a pony. The diary frankly recorded that confusion had been caused by an order from Colonel Matthews at approximately 9.30 a.m. on the 26th that, 'the whole force would move down the coast by prolonging its right. There was some misunderstanding and this order was taken to be a command to retire.'[2]

An undated but descriptive letter, one which must have been written early in May by Pte John Lavelle, a machine-gunner in the King's Own Scottish Borderers, strikingly, has nothing to record of the first hours of the landing but then,

> at dusk the enemy began their advance on us. Their first advance was repelled easy but they no sooner got driven back but they came on again. About 9pm all seemed lost, it looked as if we had to be driven into the sea and drown or die fighting to the last. The order went down the line fix your bayonets boys their [*sic*] will be no retirement. It started to rain and the men's bolts got clagged with sand. About midnight the Turks became desperate and hurled mass after mass, sometimes they reached our trenches sometimes they were in a few yards of them. Our machine guns worked fine and never jammed once. I think if our guns had broke down it would have been all up. Me and Tom did not half zounk it into them. We managed to struggle through till dawn, how we done it we do not know every man had said his prayers hours before that. I am very sorry to say we lost nearly all our Officers, our Officers worked bravely and it was owning [*sic*] to that so many went under, we lost heavily in NCOs and men.[3]

The recollections of two men, a Marine, W.J. Parnham, and a sailor, W.G. Cave, convey some sense of the confusion of the fighting in the late afternoon of the 25th when the Turks came up in strength,[4] and shed some light on the burning issues of responsibility for the lost opportunity, an opportunity which seems still more tantalizing in the light of the adamant assertion by a third man, J.M. Johnson (Royal Marines), that in the early hours of the landing he and others had, 'strolled through Krithia and on the left shoulder of Achi Baba'.

Parnham was Colonel Matthews's orderly and throughout the action was in personal attendance on him.

> From the trawlers we got into open boats. Before dawn the ships opened up a violent bombardment and, as dawn came, our boats crept in and we were ashore. We were unexpected, surmounted the cliffs and made an advance inland, our only casualties resulting from shells dropped short by the ships. We captured some Turkish scouts and withdrew to the cliffs to take up a position. We commenced digging in when suddenly bullets from goodness knows where whizzed over us. The fire increased and we returned it but had no targets at which to fire. Then the harsher reports of hand grenades falling among us made it clear just how near the Turks were. After dark the Turks attacked in greater strength and we were driven back to the cliff edge. We were blazing away, using

ammunition brought up the cliff to us. The darkness was broken by the flashes of rifles and exploding grenades, and there was a constant crackle of small arms fire. All we had for signalling purposes was the Colonel's torch. There were awful shouts and cries. In the confusion furious complaints of 'You're firing into our backs' were mixed with the Turkish appeals to Allah. When daylight came, the ships were able to reopen fire and the Turkish attack petered out. At about dinner time we had orders to retire to the boats. It was very difficult getting the wounded down the cliffs, and the wounds from the grenades in particular were terrible. The sailors helped to get many of the wounded away using waterproof sheets. With regard to Colonel Matthews, I was with him on his quick trip round the perimeter to convey his decision about entrenchment to the C.O.s of the other units. This was at about 3 p.m. on the 25th. Next morning when we reached Colonel Koe he was being held up by two other men. The Colonel was coughing blood and was quite unable to speak. He had a dreadful stomach wound. Distressed and overcome, Colonel Matthews, without a word to the others, laid his hand gently on his shoulder and said, 'My poor fellow', and then he hurried back to our own Battalion.

Chief Petty Officer Cave, operating a range-finder from HMS *Dublin*, noticed some flashing from a dip in the cliffs and had a signalman take what was obviously a message. The message was that their CO. had been wounded the day before and needed medical attention urgently.

Capt. Kelly ordered a sick berth attendant, a whaler's crew of five, two spare hands and myself to go ashore. It took us some time to select a place to climb the cliff. The wounded man was a heavily built officer and he was in a very bad way with a stomach wound. With our patient groaning, at times delirious and only occasionally able to speak rational words, betraying by accent he was a Scot, and accompanied by another slightly wounded Scot, we made our way down, but it was exceptionally difficult with such a heavy man on such a boulder-strewn steep route. At the bottom there were boats and pinnaces ferrying wounded and unwounded off to the *Goliath* and our wounded man, who I believe died within a short time, was taken off to the old battleship.

The wounded man must surely have been Colonel Koe.

There is still dispute over whose orders had actually begun the Y Beach withdrawal. At the Dardanelles Commission inquiry, Colonel Matthews was to accept responsibility, seeing no other course but evacuation open to a force running short of ammunition and without reinforcements. A.W. Clarke (Midshipman, HMS *Implacable*), who assisted in the evacuation, remembered seeing the Colonel striding down the cliff path, swishing with his cane at the gorse which impeded him. Clarke felt sure that there was no one else to bring away from the beach.

By 11.30 a.m. on the 26th the last men had been evacuated from Y Beach. A landing begun with such promise had ended in disappointment and consequential controversy. The question whether a strategically valuable achievement at Y Beach was within the grasp of Hamilton, Hunter-Weston and Colonel Matthews himself, remains today as tantalizing as other 'might-have-beens' of the campaign.

X Beach

For the X Beach landing both the experience of the men concerned and the tactical outcome were to be more satisfactory, but not without a hint that the best advantage of initial success had not been taken. Staff planning had not allowed for the fact that the geography of the Peninsula favoured early visual communication between X and S Beaches – only two miles apart – and the joining-up of the landing forces from the two beaches, thus cutting off from Krithia the Turkish forces holding up the V and W Beach landings. As at Y Beach, the Turks did not anticipate an attack at the steep though lower cliffs just a few yards from the sandy X Beach. At this spot the 2nd Battalion Royal Fusiliers and a platoon of the Anson Battalion RND were to land. Their assault was to be supported by the 1st Battalion Border Regiment and the 1st Battalion Inniskilling Fusiliers. *Implacable* was to land the men and provide the covering bombardment. On landing, the troops were to move southwards to link up with the Lancashire Fusiliers at W Beach. *Dublin* was also to assist in the bombardment during the day.

Implacable was stationed only 500 yards offshore and the closeness of her involvement is indicated by the death, from a Turkish rifle bullet, of a surgeon on deck. Midshipman A.W. Clarke recorded in his log for 24 April:

> Entered Tenedos in the forenoon. Drew our boats from transport and also four picket boats from other ships. Prepared the boats and provisioned them. In the evening the 700 troops, the covering force, came aboard from the trawlers who had fetched them from the transports. The crews manned the transport boats and secured astern of the ship. About 10 p.m. the ship proceeded to sea for the Dardanelles, towing us in the boats astern. All the fleet followed.
>
> 25 April: As soon as daylight the boats came alongside the ship and we took the 700 aboard and in company with the ship we closed into the beach, the ship firing hard to cover us. Then the boats made a dash and we landed the first 700 men with hardly a casualty owing to the good firing of the ship[5] ... We landed troops all the forenoon with the support of the fleet. The remainder of the transports came up during the day. About 4 p.m. after we had landed the complete covering force we started to take the wounded off again.[6]

F.J. Jebens, a Second Lieutenant in the 2nd Battalion Royal Fusiliers, remembered the intensity of *Implacable*'s pre-landing bombardment, and the lack of any opposition as they landed and climbed the cliffs. Only when they moved off inland were they fired on from both a field battery near Krithia and the Turkish troops commanding the slight rise towards the right flank, where resistance was continuing to the Lancashire Fusiliers' landing on W Beach.

It was the sight of dead Fusiliers laid out on top of the cliffs which greeted the Inniskillings when they landed. B.A. McConnell has written of the strong impression this made on him when he was asked by his Inniskilling machine-gun officer to find the range of the battery firing on the Border Regiment on their left. The range he had taken was signalled to *Implacable* and McConnell saw the battery blown to the sky almost immediately. Bertie McConnell was to have the exhausting task of bringing from the beach the machine-gun ammunition boxes during a night of constant firing. With the weapon capable of firing 600 rounds to the minute, there were many journeys to undertake, each box containing 250 rounds.

X Beach was secured and, furthermore, a bayonet attack took the important Hill 114 which commanded W Beach. Nevinson[7] and others record that this attack was watched and cheered by sailors on board *Implacable*. The success did not happen early enough to prevent dreadful casualties at W Beach but it was of belated significance and relatedly was to enable Lancashire and Royal Fusiliers to outflank the Turkish defence against the V Beach assault.

But X Beach had been a searing experience for Tom Sye in the 87th Field Ambulance. 'We landed at X Beach on Sunday last under fire and in one ghastly moment for me the war had begun. I have been unable to write anything up to now, having been busy and also perhaps too horror-struck to write … I have never known it was possible to fear so acutely – I was terrified … God! When will it stop? I pray for the end with every minute that passes.' Perhaps Sye's diary is a vivid illustration that in war men are not just imprisoned by their current circumstance but sometimes additionally by the vulnerability of their nature.

S Beach

Of the five Cape Helles landings, only those on X and S Beaches could be claimed as successes in other than Pyrrhic terms. At S Beach, *Cornwallis* landed the 2nd Battalion South Wales Borderers and the 2nd London Field Company of the Royal Engineers. S Beach, with the shallow waters of Morto Bay, was dominated by the abrupt heights of the disused de Tott's battery and the beach was openly exposed to fire from Asiatic batteries. The landing was successfully made and secured, but resistance was such that there was no possibility of any breakout from the heights which surrounded the bay. The diary of Private T.S. Rees of the South Wales Borderers gave a terse description of the attack up the beach. 'Troops ready to land. Forced a landing about 7 a.m. Made a charge and took a trench. Took a hill about an hour after landing. Captured some Turks. Heavy firing all night. 26th: Enemy retiring about middle of the day and shelled by our fleet. Cannot move on, waiting for our left to come up in line.' Rees later recalled the excitement among the troops as the trawlers took them into the Straits before they were transferred to whalers and cutters which were soon under small-arms fire. Some of the wounded had to be dragged through the water from the boats to the beach and it was some time before there was sufficient organization on the beach to enable a charge to be made. Even when they had taken their immediate objectives they were constantly in danger from snipers. The snipers even troubled the covering ships. Midshipman William-Powlett of *Vengeance* recorded in his diary that on deck they were troubled all day by their 'pet sniper who hides in the cliffs and takes pot shots at people on board. We call him Rupert.'

Midshipman Tom Traill had towed boatloads of South Wales Borderers during the training preparations for the 25th. He wrote in his memoirs, 'I wish I could hear them sing again … it was a horrid thing to see those same men under fire as the small boats took them inshore at the landing.'

A particularly graphic account of the landing on S Beach is contained in *The Immortal Gamble*, which might be termed an unofficial biography of the battleship *Cornwallis*.[8] The Captain of *Cornwallis* and a number of his men, including the ship's Marines, actually landed and became engaged in stiff fighting to protect the left flank of the assault. The South Wales Borderers however were the first to be observed from the ship. 'It was an unforgettable experience to watch this well-trained battalion working its way methodically and without confusion to the top of the battery from both sides … The Marines ascending the hill watched the South Wales Borderers literally fly on ahead, line a wall at the top, place Maxim guns in position, run telephone communications down the hill and station snipers on a wall running at right angles to their position.' The Marines then joined up with the soldiers. Sailors from *Cornwallis*, having accomplished various beach tasks, joined in the attack from the beach and a trench was taken by bayonet charge. The sailors rather resented having to give up the opportunity of taking prisoners as this was properly the work of the troops. 'And all the time a battery on the Asiatic side fired on the beach below, never getting a shell inland, fairly plastering the water's edge … Some of the shells fell in shallow water, hit the bottom and rebounded again, coming out like a trout jumping.' In quite a striking revisionist judgement, Peter Hart in his book criticises the officer in command of *Cornwallis* for coming ashore when he had executive responsibilities aboard, most particularly using *Cornwallis*'s guns in sorely-needed support of the adjacent V Beach landing.[9]

The landing area thus made good here was to be taken over by the French, who, with the men from their Kum Kale diversionary landing force and the remainder of their troops, were in due course to be landed at V Beach. From here they were to move up to hold the right-hand sector of the line which was to be created out of the landing operations, until from S Beach across the Kereves Dere,[10] Achi Baba Nullah, Krithia Nullah and Gully Ravine to the Aegean, a trench-embattled no man's land had been forged which, though different in detail, bore a distressing resemblance to that from Nieuport to the Swiss frontier. So much for the hopes of politicians, the plans of generals and the gallantry of men.

V Beach

Of all the landings, that at V Beach was to hold the most striking elements of tragedy, prolonged into a grimly sustained frustration of collective and individual heroism. In the suicidal dash along the *River Clyde*'s gangways, the grim waiting for others cooped in her holds, the physical strain and danger of holding the bridging lighters together, the helpless hours of sheltering behind a life-preserving bank of shingle and the later brave rushes up past the castle to the village, all these isolated and linked dramas have combined to leave an imperishable record and ineffaceable impressions on those who survived. The most vivid and frightful overall impression was that of Commander Samson, of the RNAS. He was flying over the beach and was later to record in his memoirs that for half a mile offshore the sea was a crescent of red.

The beach itself, situated just to the west of the village of Seddel Bahr, is crescent-shaped, and the gentle slope of the enclosing land is more abrupt to the west, on the heights of which was the fort seriously damaged as early as 3 November 1914. Behind the eastern or Straits side of the crescent lay a medieval castle. The whole beach and approaches to the surrounding higher ground provided an absolutely clear field for defensive fire, with the single exception of a raised beach escarpment, the height of which the *Official History* estimates at about five feet. Photographic evidence and actual examination suggest that this may be an exaggeration.

There were strong barbed-wire entanglements along the beach and again higher up the slope, and barbed wire linked the two. There was a strong redoubt and a connected fire trench which, with the ruined castle walls, provided excellent all-round defensive fire cover for small arms, the two 3.7cm Nordenfelts (pom-poms) and machine-guns,[11] though more recently the machine-gun defence has been disputed.

There were three distinct features of the landing plan. Two platoons of the Royal Dublin Fusiliers were to land on the Straits side of the village at what had become known as the Camber. Then, by five tows of four small boats each, the 1st Battalion of the Royal Dublin Fusiliers, less one and a half companies, and one platoon of the Anson Battalion RND, were to be landed on the main beach. From the former collier, *River Clyde*, about 2,000 men, consisting of the 1st Battalion Royal Munster Fusiliers, the 2nd Battalion Hampshire Regiment (less two companies), one company of the Royal Dublin Fusiliers, one platoon Anson Battalion RND, GHQ Signal Section, the West Riding Field Company RE and three bearer sub-divisions of a field ambulance, were to debouch from specially cut holes in the side of the ship and then pass along gangways leading to lighters making a bridge to the shore. The supporting bombardment was to come from HMS *Cornwallis* and HMS *Albion*.

The *River Clyde* 'Trojan Horse' was the idea of a Commander Unwin, arising out of his anxiety over the formidable task of landing troops against well-prepared, concealed opposition. He was of course reassured and excited by the acceptance of his concept but then, as time drew on, predictably troubled by the responsibility and practical problems now fairly placed on his shoulders, in command of *River Clyde*. Would it work or had he contributed to incipient disaster?

The *Official History*[12] offers a vivid account of 25 April at Seddel Bahr, and another source, James's book,[13] mentions the Turkish use of incendiary shells which set one of the boats on fire, burning the men within her, and the dreadful details of those wounded, drowning or suffocating at the bottom of a crush of wounded and dead in boats filling with water. The exceptional initiation of the young midshipmen involved here – what one had to do and what one saw – is breath-takingly illustrated in the letters of G.L. Drewry and W.L. Berridge. On 12 May, Drewry, ordered to take over the hopper accompanying *River Clyde* for use as part of the landing bridge, wrote to his father about his task:

So I climbed over the side across the lighters into the hopper and then came an anxious time. We steered straight towards Cape Helles and in a few minutes the bombardment commenced. Dad, it was glorious! Dozens of ships, battleships, cruisers, destroyers and transports. The morning mist lay on the land which seemed to be a mass of fire and smoke as the ships raked it with shell. Straight into the sun past battleships roaring with their 12-inch, the noise was awful and the air full of powder. Shells began to fall around us thick but did not hit us. We were half a mile from the beach and we were told not yet, so we took a turn round two ships, at last we had the signal at 6 a.m. and in we dashed – Unwin on the bridge and I at the helm of the hopper with my crew of six Greeks and one sailor, Sampson.

At 6.10 the ship struck, very easily – she brought up and I shot ahead and grounded on her port bow. Then the fun began, picket boats towed lifeboats full of soldiers inshore and slipped them as the water shoaled and they rowed the rest of the way. The soldiers jumped out as the boats beached and they died almost all of them, wiped out with the boats' crews. We had a line from the stern of the hopper to the lighters and this we tried to haul in, the hardest haul I've ever tried. Then the Capt. appeared on the lighters and the steam pinnace took hold of the lighters and plucked them in until she could go no closer. Instead of joining up to the hopper the Captain decided to make the connection with a spit of rock on the other bow. Seeing this we let go our rope, and Sampson and I tried to put a brow out over the bow, the Greeks had run below and two of us could not do it, so I told him also to get out of the rain, and I jumped over the bow and waded ashore, meeting a soldier wounded in the water, we (I and another soldier from a boat) tried to carry him ashore but he was again shot in our arms, his neck in two pieces nearly, so we left him and I ran along the beach towards the spit, I threw away my revolver, coat and hat and waded out to the Captain. He was in the water with a man named Williams wading and towing the lighters towards the spit. I gave a pull for a few minutes and then climbed aboard the lighters and got the brows lowered onto the lighters. The Captain, still in the water, sang out for more rope so I went on board and brought a rope down with the help of a man called Ellard. As we reached the end of the lighters the Capt. was wading towards us carrying Williams, pulled him into the lighter and Ellard carried him on board the ship on his shoulders ... Williams was dead ...

Got a rope from the lighter to the spit and then with difficulty I hauled the Captain onto the lighter – he was nearly done and I was alone ... I stayed on the lighters and tried to keep the men going ashore but it was murder and soon the first lighter was covered with dead and wounded and the spit was awful, the sea round it for some yards was red. When they got ashore they were little better off for they were picked off, many of them before they could dig themselves in. They stopped coming and I ran on board into No. 1 [hold] and saw an awful sight, dead and dying lay around the ports where their curiosity had led them. I went up to the saloon and saw the Capt. being rubbed down. He murmured something about the third lighter so I went down again and in a few minutes a picket boat came along the starboard side and gave the reserve lighter a push that sent it as far as the hopper … with Lieut. Morse and myself on it. Just as we hit the hopper a piece of shrapnel hit me on the head knocking me down for a second or two and covering me with blood … I took a rope and swam towards the other lighters but the rope was not long enough and I was stuck in the middle. I sang out to Mid. Malleson … in the picket boat to throw me a line but he had no line except the one that had originally kept the lighters to the spit. He stood up and hauled this line in and then as I had drifted away he swam towards the lighter I had left and made it all right. Then I made for home but had a job climbing up the lighters as I was rather played out. When I got on board the Doctor dressed my head and rubbed me down. I was awfully cold. He would not let me get up and I had to lay [*sic*] down and listen to the din.

Midshipman Drewry was to be awarded the VC for his work which he had recorded as if it were a boyish adventure. He was not insensitive to the suffering of the men he saw so seriously wounded, but the newness and excitement of it all was a stronger emotion than any fears he seems to have had for his own safety. 'While the troops were going out (eight o'clock in the evening) I had a party getting wounded from the hopper and lighters and putting them on board a trawler laying [*sic*] under our quarter. An awful job, they had not been dressed at all and some of the poor souls were in an awful state. I never knew blood smelt so strong before.'[14]

W.L. Berridge, a midshipman on the covering ship *Albion*, in a letter of 22 May to his father and sister, showed that he had a clear view of events at Seddel Bahr.

The slaughter was awful and you could see them falling on the beach and in the water. They got into dead ground under a bank however and there remained for the whole day … How the Turks stood our fire I don't know. I don't mind admitting I'd have hopped it full speed … The morrow came and with it a splendid sight which very few have witnessed. The troops advanced bit by bit up the hill until near the top. It was wonderfully done and I didn't see a man fall, all the way. They advanced from cover to cover in rushes … They reached the top and took an old fort which gave them a splendid position to hold. Just as the final rush was made the main body of our troops landed on our beach came out of the village of Seddel Bahr, miraculously found a way through barbed-wire entanglements and joined hands with the rest at the top. Of course all this up to the final rush had been under cover of our fire which was of a very rapid and exact nature.[15]

With the 2nd Battalion Hampshire Regiment in a hold within *River Clyde* was Second Lieutenant R. B. Gillett. His diary does not tell us much about his service on the Peninsula. It reads: '25 April – landed. 26 April – wounded. *Caledonia* 6 p.m.' His recollections, however, fill in the picture of the coldness within the holds even though they were crowded with men, and of the scarcely perceptible slide of the boat into the sand, though they had been told to brace themselves. After complete silence, Gillett recalls the firing breaking out in a deafening roar as the bullets struck *River Clyde*. They were also being shelled from the Asiatic shore, and one shell killed men in No. 4 hold next to the one in which Gillett was incarcerated. In the afternoon some of the officers were allowed up onto the afterdeck of *River Clyde*, where they were sheltered from fire by the ship's superstructure. From here the French troops were seen attacking Kum Kale, and, in the sky, Samson's dropping of coloured flares as a guide for the naval bombardment, was also observed. Late in the afternoon they had to return to the holds and they were ordered to land just before dusk. Gillett led his platoon out along the catwalk and the sight, he recalled, was horrifying. 'The barges were piled high with dead and wounded and where the barges did not quite reach the shore, there was literally a pile of dead bodies on which you simply had to walk. The sea was red. To protect the beach against night attack we advanced through the barbed wire and took up a defensive position on the Turkish side of the wire.'

During the cold night Turkish searchlights swept the slope from the beach but the traversing machine-gun fire failed to find them. With no sleep Gillett tried to keep his men awake by passing a stream of messages along their line. He was wounded the following day in reconnoitring for an attack on the redoubt, after they had cleared the Turks out of the village. He and another officer had first climbed round the low cliffs below the Straits side of the castle in order to get into the village from the flank. A rock thrown down from the castle wall, along the line of where they were believed to be climbing, had narrowly missed them and only one of their men had been hit in the dangerous job of clearing the village, house by house.

Some awkward objects had to be carried out of *River Clyde* and down the gangways, which had taken on the aspect of a moving target at a shooting gallery. A West Riding Sapper, G.B. Smith, saw their bugler with a rifle and fixed bayonet in one hand and the cookhouse dixey in the other. He himself had detonators, explosives and a shovel. The shovel he lost in his dash down the gangway and onto the barges, with their awful cargo of dead and wounded, through and over which he had to crawl before sliding over the gunwale into the sea and finally reaching the sandbank.

Just one of the many acts of gallantry on V Beach that morning, performed in the heat of battle and without thought of reward or recognition, was that of Private Hennessy. Captain Wilson, Adjutant of the Royal Munster Fusiliers, made a report that Hennessy had displayed conspicuous gallantry in carrying three wounded men, one after the other, from the lighters where they were being fired on by snipers and machine-guns, to the *River Clyde;* and then, with Lance-Corporal Quinalt and another man, he had crawled along two lighters under heavy fire, endeavouring to throw planks across to connect them to the shore. He and Quinalt were wounded and the third man was killed.[16]

In the Reverend H.C. Foster's book there is an account by Sub-Lieutenant Perring which describes the burial on 28 April in one large grave of 213 men whose bodies had been strewn about the beach.[17] French troops who had landed on V Beach after the Kum Kale landing were left with an indelible recall of the red sand and the lines or clumps of the dead. Indeed it was this picture with *River Clyde* in the background which they chose to symbolize for them the Allied Gallipoli experience.[18] A company commander's report attached to the Royal Munster Fusiliers' War Diary states that 'there is no doubt that men were drowned owing chiefly I think to the great weight of equipment they were carrying – a full pack, 250 rounds of ammunition, and three days' rations. I know I felt it. All the officers were dressed and equipped like the men.'[19]

Among the deaths on that day was that of the Catholic Padre of the Dublins, Father Finn. He had given his Anglican colleague, the Reverend H.C. Foster, the same medal of 'Our Lady of Mount Carmel' as he had given to his men and hoped that it would bring him good fortune. Father Finn, badly wounded, had reached the sheltering sandbank but ran back to the dead and dying on the water-line to administer Extreme Unction. He was further wounded by a shrapnel shell burst but carried on his work until he collapsed and died from exhaustion and loss of blood. The Anglican wrote that Father Finn's 'death was a great grief to me, as we had become firm friends on the transport, and a great blow to his men who well-nigh worshipped him'.[20] It is interesting that in the Gallipoli service of the predominantly Catholic Dublins and Munsters at Helles and the mainly Protestant 10th Irish Division at Suvla, there seems to be no contemporary or recollected evidence of sectarian issues despite recently contentious issues, Home Rule, armed volunteers, the Curragh 'Mutiny' and just a year before the Easter Rebellion.

With regard to national rivalries, even antipathies, initially the British and French were suspicious of each other but they came to rub along well enough, and while there was some competitive rivalry, of the young bull and the old bull nature between the Australians and the British, the British being jealous too of the publicity accorded to the soldiers of the Dominions, apparently among the serving soldiers, the Irish problem had been as temporarily submerged as other dominant pre-war divisive issues of British public life, industrial disputes and class divisions.

W Beach

The slope on W Beach is appreciably greater than at V and examination discloses quite a disconcerting undertow within feet of the water-line. The implication of this may be added to the problems of burdened men, soaked and in many cases wounded, encountering the concealed barbed wire in the shallows. There were also wire entanglements and landmines above the shore-line. The encircling low cliffs, sufficiently high at either end of the little beach to dominate the shore, were strongly fortified with trenches, some evidence of which remains today. Behind the cliffs at either end of the beach, ground slightly higher than the cliffs provided the sites for further strongly defended redoubts. Barbed-wire entanglements not only protected these redoubts, but effectively cut off communication with V Beach.

The 1st Battalion of the Lancashire Fusiliers and one platoon of the Anson Battalion RND were to be landed in tows from the cruiser HMS *Euryalus*, which provided covering fire in addition to that of HMS *Swiftsure*. One company of the Lancashire Fusiliers was brought to the beach in tows from HMS *Implacable*. From *Euryalus*, six picket boats each towed four cutters. Under a mile from the beach, the six were joined by two picket boats, each towing four cutters from *Implacable*. Later in the morning, men of the Worcester, Essex and Hampshire Regiments, originally intended for the 'main-body' V-Beach landing, were to be diverted to W Beach.

One of the picket boats was under the command of a Midshipman Wilson, whose letter to his mother on 4 May gave a detailed account of what he saw of the landing. He was in the left-hand boat, No. 6, of the picket boats leaving *Euryalus*.

We got going about 4.30 and steamed slowly for the shore in line abreast gradually wheeling round to get opposite W Beach ... *Swiftsure* did a lot of firing at this time at the cliffs each side of W Beach but as it afterwards turned out she hadn't put them in the right place or at least not half enough of them. It was just getting daylight while this was going on and as it was misty it was very hard to say what W Beach was like and where exactly it was. We had only rough maps of the place and as we approached it from a totally different direction we expected, you couldn't predict what sort of reception you were going to get. We slipped about 30 yards from the beach but my boat was closer as we had come round the corner. We were nearly on the rocks and only just slipped in time. All the tows slipped alright and pulled in without fouling each other. There were two rows of barbed wire the whole length of the beach. The Turks opened fire with maxims, pompoms, rifles, just as we slipped. You could see them standing up in the trenches, which obviously had not been properly shelled. They were pouring a terrific fire down on us and it is a most extraordinary thing how any of the cutters which were open and absolutely unprotected and crammed with men survived it. The soldiers had to jump out into three feet of water and it was a most awful sight seeing them being shot down as soon as they got into the water and the wounded men must have drowned. When they got onto the beach they were held up by the barbed wire and got a tremendous lot more casualties as the Turks practically mowed them down as they moved through the gaps in the wire which they had cut.

The cliffs were successfully stormed, but Wilson had been shocked by the losses and he considered that three mistakes had been made. '1. Not shelling enough. 2. Not mounting Maxims and Q.F. guns in the picket boats. If these had had proper shields we could have fired them and done a lot of damage as we could see them plainly. It would also have encouraged the troops and drawn the fire off the soldiers onto the picket boats. 3. The men landed with their heavy equipment which got frightfully in the way while they were disembarking.'

It is interesting that young Wilson lists mistakes he considered that the Turks had made. He did not believe that they had put landmines and barbed wire in the water, as they ought to have done, and he was sure that British troops would have been able to prevent any landing at all. From this conjecture the midshipman moved on to rumour and here he was on much less sure ground: 'The Australians at Gaba Tepe got an awful hot time and saw red. They are giving no quarter and taking no prisoners. We are taking as few as possible and the French shoot everybody.'

Wilson's picket boat was later in the day used to bring the wounded off *River Clyde* and the open lighters and cutters beside her. 'There was an awful rush and some of the wounded got hit getting into the boat and squashed as well. We got about twenty in the boat and then cleared out as we were the only boat there.' Another midshipman, R.W. Moore, who had watched the landing from the masthead lookout on *Euryalus*, was to be sickened by the bloody water dripping through the shot holes in one of the cutters when it was winched aboard.

Midshipman A.M. Williams, in command of a towing boat from *Euryalus*, recalled trying not to waken the Lancashire Fusiliers when rising, lashing up and stowing his hammock in the early hours of the morning. He was to be in a steam pinnace on the right and it was, he said, a tremendous job to keep up with the other picket boats. The steel shields on the picket boats and the pinnaces protected the crews who sheltered behind them and few casualties were suffered. Later in the day he had to leave his picket boat to help in the work of landing stores. This resulted in his coxswain reporting him missing and presumed killed. The fact that in his duties he had fallen on a big round cheese and 'stank to high heaven' as a result, did not affect the warmth of his welcome when he did report back to *Euryalus*.

Able Seaman Measures, of *Euryalus*, remembered not merely helping aboard wounded from the returning cutters and sorting them out on stretchers and blankets, but taking the particulars of the dead and sewing the bodies into fire-bar-weighted hammocks for sea burial. The Reverend H.C. Foster, later in the morning of the 25th, was landed in one of the cutters which had brought back wounded. He noticed that the bottom of the boat was 'running with blood; there was blood on the oars, blood on the seats, blood all over and bits of skin here and there'.[21]

In his diary for the day of the landing, Bandsman H. Brown of the 1st Battalion Lancashire Fusiliers, in his role as a stretcher bearer, wrote that they 'disembarked under terrific fire. Plenty of our men bowled over. Picked General Hare up wounded in the leg 8am. Nearly knocked over by a sniper, same time. Worked all day on the wounded. The wounds are simply shocking. Some awful cases. We did very well indeed on the day. Buried our dead at dusk.'

One of the six Lancashire Fusiliers later to be awarded the Victoria Cross for gallantry at the landing, J.E. Grimshaw, recalled that the men were so crowded on the boats that in his boat,

it was impossible to tell who had been hit as they were prevented from falling inboard or overboard by the crush. The firing broke out all at once and the water seemed to be boiling all around us. I managed to get over the barbed wire which was in the water and then through the stuff on the beach but later when some of us got to the base of the cliff I found that my cap badge had been hit by a bullet, and my pack and water bottle riddled. One thing paramount was the effect of water and sand on your rifle mechanism and the only way to deal with this was to try and urinate on your rifle bolt. By the time we got to the top of the cliff just the remnants of the defenders had retired a couple of hundred yards. They wore a sort of balaclava helmet and a grey uniform and we saw them in the act of trying to prepare trenches. We rushed those trenches and cleared the people out. I didn't use my bayonet: just pressed the trigger. You are carrying your rifle at the trail or held in front of you.

Three accounts given by Lancashire Fusilier officers subsequently killed on Gallipoli are given in Creighton's book[22] and together they exemplify all that officers and men had to endure in driving the Turks from their well-sited trenches. An extract from Captain H.R. Clayton's letter home may be used as an example.

Men were being hit in the boats and as they splashed ashore. I got up to my waist in water, tripped over a rock and went under, got up and made for the shore and lay down by the barbed wire. There was a man there before me shouting for wire cutters. I got mine out but could not make the slightest impression. The front of the wire by now was a thick mass of men the majority of whom never moved again. The trenches on the right raked us and those above us raked our right, while trenches and machine-guns fired straight down the valley. The noise was ghastly and the sights horrible. I eventually crawled through the wire with great difficulty as my pack kept catching on the wire, and got under a small mound which actually gave us protection. The weight of our packs tired us, so that we could only gasp for breath.

Major Harold Shaw of the Lancashire Fusiliers is also extensively quoted in Creighton's book and his account is searing.

On the right of me on the cliff was a line of Turks in a trench taking pot shots at us, ditto on the left. I looked back. There was one soldier between me and the wire, and a whole row in a line on the edge of the sands. The sea behind them was absolutely crimson, and you could hear the groans through the rattle of musketry. A few were firing. I signalled to them to advance. I shouted to the soldier behind to signal, but he shouted back, 'I am shot through the chest.' I then perceived they were all hit.

On such exposed beaches as V and W, British training, discipline, loyalty to one's comrades and sheer courage, were put to the most searching test, as indeed was the renowned Turkish quality of dogged determination against adversity as the defenders faced the heavy preliminary bombardment. It was a harrowing experience for all. The British, at great topographical and tactical odds, the Turks, against far heavier shell-fire and many more men, performed with a heroism which has left an imperishable record in the heritage of their country. Lancashire Landing Cemetery and the Turkish memorial to their machine-gunner above V Beach are eloquent witnesses to the cost of such service, as indeed is the grim brevity and understatement of the Lancashire Fusiliers' War Diary entry for 5.30 a.m. on the 25th. 'Landed under heavy fire from machine guns and rifles from cliffs. Heavy casualties. Several men hit in boats and in water before getting ashore.'[23]

Diversion in the Gulf of Saros

After naval bombardment of the Bulair lines by HMS *Doris* and HMS *Dartmouth*, minesweeping activities, aeroplane reconnaissance early on the morning of the 25th, and a naval reconnaissance by HMS *Kent*, close to Karachali village, and by HMS *Canopus* towards the Bulair lines, the Royal Naval Division on the ten or eleven transports was kept waiting until dusk, when 1,200 men were embarked in the transport ships' boats. They were towed towards the shore, but according to the *Mitchell Report*, the only man to land was an officer, Bernard Freyberg, who swam ashore to light flares intended to simulate the bivouac fires of encamped troops. Of course the inactivity throughout the day must have lessened the reality of the exercise, and the Mitchell inquirers found after the war that the Turkish officers on shore had not been deceived because the transports had not been handled as if they 'really meant to land troops'.[24]

In the Hood Battalion, Joseph Murray wrote in his diary[25] for the 25 April: '10 p.m. Volunteers from RND C Coy, manned boats and we were towed into 800 yards from Turkish shore to make the Turks concentrate some of their troops to oppose us. While we were cruising about Sub-Lieut. Freyberg[26] swam ashore and ignited some fire bombs.' A. E. Wilson, of D Company, Nelson Battalion, recorded similar details in his diary. 'Proceeded to within 200 yards of shore and returned to shore without drawing any fire. Left Gulf of Saros and steamed to end of Peninsula.' Murray recorded in his book[27] that before the night operations on 25–26 April they were all issued with a new pair of canvas slippers, cardigan, a woollen cap-comforter and two bandoliers each having fifty rounds of ammunition, and plenty of hot cocoa. With regard to the amount of time spent in the boats – 'were we lost? If it was the intention to land, why didn't we? If we were to attract attention only, why not a few rounds of rapid fire? If [the rifles] were not to be used, why on earth did we bring them with us?' The Official History explained that the Hood Platoon was merely covering Freyberg's swim.[28]

Similarly ineffective seems to have been the influence of the French diversionary demonstration off Besika Bay, south of Kum Kale. The strength of the Turkish forces at Bulair, where a landing was expected, and the difficulties experienced at the Helles landings against numerically weaker opposition would suggest that anyone advocating that success was within reach from the Gulf of Saros has nothing of substance in support of the argument.[29]

Kum Kale

The purpose of the French landing at Kum Kale was to confuse the Turks as to the area of the main landing and to protect the V-beach landing from the fire of the Kum Kale battery. The 6th Colonial Regiment and a battery of 75mm guns and necessary landing stores were brought towards the Asiatic shores in *Savoie*, *Carthage*, *Vinh Long*, *Théodore Mante* and *Ceylan*. The French warships and the British *Prince George* covered the landing, and the Russian cruiser, *Askold*, added her bombardment. *Askold* had already been nicknamed 'the packet of Woodbines' by the British for her five funnels, but the chivalrous Guépratte took care that officers and men on board were given due personal recognition in his reports and recommendations. More French transports were ready to follow up the initial assault, which was largely, though not entirely, being made by Senegalese troops together with metropolitan French field-ambulance men, engineers, machine-gunners, signallers, and of course the gunners.

There were towing delays in the strong current, so that the supporting ships maintained their covering bombardment over a longer period. The earliest objectives were quickly taken, as the flat land provided little cover for defenders. The fort, the village and tomb of Achilles were soon in French hands, but in the area around the village cemetery, resistance stiffened. As more French and Turkish troops were sent into this area, confusion increased. Gondard, an officer in the Colonial Regiment, described what happened: 'Throughout the night of the 25th we had alerts but we were able to repel the Turkish attacks. In the morning the Turks waved white rags. We stopped firing and the Turks came forward. We took them prisoner and I was collecting their arms and ammunition. But in fact more and more Turks were coming up and they had not given up their arms. We found ourselves surrounded, at least those of us not in a group. I was grabbed by both arms and with a third man thrusting a gun into my back I was marched off.' Colonel Ruef's official report, quoted in the British *Official History*,[30] indicated that this confusion led to unofficial French reprisals. The French executed an officer and eight men of a group of about eighty who, apparently giving themselves up as prisoners, had been encouraged to escape during negotiations and recommence the fighting when reinforced by Turks who had not given up their arms. Colonel Ruef blamed the inadequacy of the French interpreters for the confusion which had led to this 'deplorable incident'.

The French troops had had landing practices within the harbour at Mudros, and General Albert d'Amade's official report stressed that he and Admiral Guépratte had ordered such an exercise for all troops involved. There does not seem to be general agreement among survivors of the landing on the question whether they had been told in their briefing that their landing was to be a diversion and that they were to be re-embarked, and yet Hamilton's orders to d'Amade leave no doubt about this.[31]

François Bollon, in the single European battalion of the 6th Colonial Regiment, remembered that they had practised landings in rubber or canvas boats at Lemnos but some of these boats had sunk and they were not used again. There was certainly no briefing for the men with whom Bollon landed. They did not know it was to be a diversion, but he recalled that a good many of the officers did not land with them. Bollon and his comrades had had to carry a sort of wire contraption which could be pulled out by two men like an accordion. It was not barbed wire but could be used as an obstruction against a counter-attack. In his knapsack there were twenty biscuits, two container tins, brand new boots and a body-belt, and they were wearing their capes over their uniforms. They were in tows of three cutters and not only did they make slow progress against the current but the rope towing their boat snapped and they drifted away, which caused more delay before they were rescued. Bollon remembered quite categorically being told in the boat by a sergeant that it would be better to commit suicide than be captured.

We landed after the Senegalese troops and saw some of their dead as we advanced towards the fort. We had to dig individual holes for cover and from them we made two fifty-metre dashes forward. In my section of fifteen men, the captain was killed and two men either side were both hit in the stomach and during the night asked piteously for water. They were both dead in the morning, and I seemed to be the only one alive in my section. Earlier I had heard Capt. Blanchard call out, '*Sauve qui peut*'. It was very difficult to see the Turks, and during the second day the Turks received reinforcements which enabled them to get through to within thirty metres or so of us. Then their officers were shot and soon a large number of them were surrendering but we ourselves were soon to be pulled off the shore. By the time I realized what was happening, the boats had left but fortunately I was spotted and one came back for me.

Jean Pierre Bory, on one of the troopships, wrote of the first wounded Senegalese troops being brought on board, and then of the prisoners. 'There were about four hundred I think, with five officers, two of whom were Germans. The officer prisoners were well accommodated in cabins but the ordinary soldiers were put in the hold under double sentries. They were given a large barrel of water from which to drink and dress their wounds. Some had really bad bayonet wounds.'

Perhaps over-reacting to Alan Moorehead's complimentary summary of the action,[32] R.R. James considered that 'it had been something less than the glittering triumph sometimes claimed for it',[33] but despite the lateness of the landing and the confused nature of some of the action, the French soldier had captured and held his objectives. A large body of Turks had, ultimately, been engaged after the initial landing, and there is no evidence that any of these Turks was able to serve on the Peninsula before 29 April. The V Beach landing would have been still more hard-pressed had the landing at Kum Kale not been successful, though the delay at Kum Kale was regrettable. The French had taken 500 prisoners and the severity of their

Chapter 9

Helles in April and May

The Turks had been forced to retreat by the initial determination and greater strength of the Allied assault upon Helles. They had been unable to bring reinforcements quickly from the Asiatic shore because of the Kum Kale landings and they were heavily committed to the defence of Anzac. It seems clear that at several levels of British command and indeed among the men themselves there was an unreadiness to strive urgently to profit from the Turkish withdrawal after the tremendous endeavour of the 29th Division on 25 and 26 April. The X Beach landing was linked to W Beach on the 25th and after fierce fighting Seddel Bahr village was won on the following day. It was not however until the afternoon of the 26th that the forces on V and W had made effective contact, and their positions were not linked to the S-Beach troops until 5.30 p.m. on the 27th. At this stage a continuous Allied line across the Peninsula from X to S Beaches had been established, but the Turks had been allowed to retire to organize the defence of the village of Krithia, an essential position on the approach to the strategically dominant hill, Achi Baba. At the point of closest penetration towards Krithia, the Allied line was a mere 2¼ miles from V Beach itself.

The *Official History* leaves no doubt about the tired condition of the Allied troops attempting on 28 April the task of capturing the shelled Turkish village nestling at the foot of the brooding dominance of the 700-foot hill from which there was observation of all Allied operations.[1] With the ground sloping into a saucer-like bowl rimmed by the seaward cliffs and isolated knolls near the cliffs, any attempt to advance was completely exposed. The only natural cover lay in the gullies or nullahs which ran like the spokes of a wheel-hub from the slopes of Achi Baba to the sea. The depth, steepness and tortuous bends of the four main gullies, particularly Gully Ravine and the Kereves Dere, were to be significant factors in the planning of all future offensive operations. This flat land, apart from the gullies, offered no natural cover from Turkish observation. It was to be criss-crossed from gully to gully and longitudinally linked for communication with the base areas near the beaches, by a webbed network of trenches. Now virtually obliterated, the web is documented in trench maps no less complex than those for the Western Front and even if the trenches of the Peninsula were sometimes less deep, less professionally constructed and equipped, they were in the main separated by a narrower no man's land than those of the Western Front. At Anzac the trenches were in certain sectors only five or seven yards apart, and at Helles, as the gullies became fortified, there were places where only a sandbagged barricade or an abrupt bend in a gully separated forces which would otherwise have been able, by machine-gun or sniper, devastatingly to enfilade the enemy trench, or, over the short intervening distance, lob various types of army-issue or homemade bombs into the opposing positions.

Of course this trench system was a creation of weeks and months of virtually static warfare. It was constantly being improved or elaborated, but that a form of trench fighting was conducted from the third day of the campaign is indicated in the *Official History* account of the opening of the attack on Krithia on 28 April. 'About 8 a.m ... the weary troops of the 29th Division climbed out of their trenches and plodded forward in the general direction of Krithia.'[2] The armoured cars of the RNAS, one or two of which were at least landed, though uselessly, at Cape Helles, the bicycles of some 29th Division Units[3] and the horses of the Australian reinforcements which were to get no further than Egypt, as the optimistic facade of hopes of a swiftly successful campaign, were to be forgotten in the attrition of trench warfare.

On 28 April the troops were indeed worn out after their physical and nervous exertion since the landing. The lassitude which descends after the last reserves of energy have been called upon was increased by the sun and acute shortage of water. Diary entries and letters escaping the scrutiny of the censor indicate the strain. On the 28th, South Wales Borderer Rees merely had time to record: 'French force took over our position at 2 a.m. Joined the Brigade at dawn and entrenched. General advance started after breakfast under heavy shell and rifle fire. Reinforced the Border Regiment. Got repulsed twice and then took the position again at 6 p.m. and entrenched. Joined the Battalion at 12 midnight and entrenched.'

Stretcher-bearer work at X Beach had been exhausting. Private Tomkinson of the 87th Field Ambulance snatched time to make a diary entry describing how on the night of the landing he had

tried to sleep in a sitting position, the room being scarce. Rained slightly. Turks made a desperate struggle to clear us off. Sgt Johnson killed. The Navy opened a terrific bombardment. A terrible night.

26 April, 3.30 a.m: Went out to Inniskilling trenches and brought back a wounded man. Beach covered with wounded. Firing ceased about 4.30 a.m. Things quieter till evening, when Turks began a fresh attack, got a little sleep, but was terribly cold about the feet ...

28 April: About 1.30 p.m. the wounded started pouring in from the action, a general advance having been made. About 2 p.m. went along the cliffs to assist the walking cases, got some back in a rowing boat, then brought in a stretcher-case overland. Made another journey to an old farm used as an aid post. Volunteered to go to firing line and bring in Major MacAllister of the K.O.S.B. Shrapnel was bursting all about us. He was wounded in right pelvis and had to hold his leg all the way. Capt. gave morphia. Brought in another case after a little tea. Got wringing wet, having put my jacket over wounded man. It came on to pour with rain ... Shall never forget the scene when I got back to beach. Pouring with rain! Beach littered with corpses and many very serious and were groaning. Very cold and lack of groundsheets to cover the wounded. Rain stopped about 9.30 p.m. Changed my shirt, had a cup of tea and went out about 10.30 ... Got a case, a

1. Lieutenant N.D. Holbrook (arms folded) and the crew of submarine *B 11* soon after the December 1914 exploit of torpedoing the Turkish battleship *Messudieh*. (Liddle Collection – L.S. Ormsby-Johnson)

2. HMS *Triumph* after the action of 18 March 1915, and resultant damage from a Turkish shell to a gun on the foreshelter deck. (Liddle Collection – P.P. May)

3. Despite War Council and War Office equivocation – and to say nothing of security in relation to the intended surprise nature of what might be attempted, a Private in the 29th Division has no doubt where he is going and tells his mother 'We are off to the Dardanelles'. (Liddle Collection – W.C. Moore)

4. HMS *Triumph* and damage to an officer's bathroom during the action on 18 March. (Liddle Collection – P.P. May)

5. A signal from Vice-Admiral de Robeck received in the Wardroom of the seaplane and aircraft carrier HMS *Ark Royal* after the action on 18 March, reporting the loss of the French battleship *Bouvet*. (Liddle Collection – G.R. Bromet)

6. These three young naval officers, Midshipman Lowry, Midshipman Malleson and Midshipman Russell of HMS *London*, have all been in action in the Dardanelles, most notably at the landings of the Australians on 25 April. but now, in May, it is time for a picnic near Mudros on the island of Lemnos. Their youthful faces make it difficult to credit the responsibilities of midshipmen at the landings. (Liddle Collection – E.W. Longley-Cook)

7. Commonwealth response: 24 September 1914 and Australians embark on SS *Omrah* at Brisbane, Queensland, for a destination as yet unknown to them. (Liddle Collection – A.E. Joyce)

8. This is a photograph to illustrate the upper age and experience range of some who served on the Peninsula. It is of Harry Malpas Stephenson in 1895. In 1915, as Lieutenant-Colonel, he commanded the 10th Battalion the Manchester Regiment. (Tameside Metropolitan Archives – The Manchester Regiment)

9. This French horse is photographed by its 'master', artillery officer, Raymond Weill, as it is hoisted ashore at Alexandria. (Liddle Collection – R. Weill)

10. New Zealanders search for their kitbags on disembarkation at Alexandria, December 1914. (Liddle Collection – O.L. Watson)

11. Australian bearing and physique splendidly evident on informal parade at the Pyramids. (Liddle Collection – W. McClennan)

12. Royal Naval Division Officers do not all appear to have regulation ponies for polo between training exercises in Egypt. (Liddle Collection – W.E. Bland)

13. Sharpening bayonets on board a troopship. (Tameside Metropolitan Archives – Museum of the Manchester Regiment)

14. Eve of landing at Anzac Cove: Australians aboard the battleship HMS *London*, 24 April, bound for Gallipoli. (Liddle Collection – C.F.H. Churchill)

15. Naval officers in charge of Beach Parties at the Anzac Landing, 25 April. From the left, Midshipman Marriott, Gunner Gamblen and Midshipman Haes. (Liddle Collection – HA Vetch)

16. The new Trojan Horse, SS *River Clyde*, approaching V Beach, about five minutes before beaching, and photographed from one of the Royal Navy picket boats towing in cutters and whalers filled with troops for the landing on this beach. (Liddle Collection – L.A.K. Boswell)

17. This photograph taken from the bow of *River Clyde* shows the dreadful cost in dead and wounded on the lighter ahead of her. The lighter, towed in by *River Clyde*, had been heroically lashed to the collier to assist men moving down the gangways to reach the shore avoiding deep water but they had been exposed to fire from Turkish positions undestroyed by naval shelling. Some survivors from the cutters and whalers attempting to reach the shallows, have sought the slight shelter offered by a bank of shingle just above the waterline. (Liddle Collection – W.G. Hole)

18. SS *River Clyde* viewed from the shore, its sally ports and gangways clearly evident. (Liddle Collection – John Prust)

19. SS *River Clyde* continuing to find use as a transit point. (Liddle Collection – H Wilson)

20. Captain G.N. Walford, with two other officers, rallied soldiers in Seddel Bahr village inland of the castle above V Beach, but, in their taking of the village, Walford was mortally wounded. His name was gazetted for the award of a posthumous Victoria Cross and this is the letter from His Majesty King George V expressing his regret at not being able to confer the award personally. (Liddle Collection – G.N. Walford)

BUCKINGHAM PALACE

5th October, 1915.

It is a matter of sincere regret to me that the death of Captain Garth Neville Walford deprived me of the pride of personally conferring upon him the Victoria Cross, the greatest of all Military Distinctions.

George R.I

Mrs E. Walford,
        7 Pelham Crescent,
            London,   S.W.

21. Officers of the Manchester Regiment watch the unloading of field guns at V Beach. (Tameside Metropolitan Archives – The Manchester Regiment)

22. Officers of the French 176th Infantry Regiment use camp furniture and the shade of a tree to make the most of a period of rest at Helles. (Liddle Collection – Charles Thierry)

23. Not only did the French excel with their field artillery, the famous 75s, but they brought to the Peninsula heavier artillery than was provided by the British, a key deficiency in the MEF. Here a heavy French piece is in action. (Liddle Collection – Jean Bareille)

24. French Senegalese
troops at Helles. Their
side-arm knives, as with
the Gurkha kukris,
added a special frisson
to their reputation
among the Turks. (Liddle
Collection)

25. At Helles, in the
field, the French present
Gallantry Awards. (Liddle
Collection – Jean Bareille)

26. Men of the 10th
Battalion Manchester
Regiment in the
trenches at Helles.
(Tameside Metropolitan
Archives – The Manchester
Regiment)

27. With no area at Helles free from shelling, football matches were on occasion disrupted by enemy action but here Lancashire Fusiliers challenge for the ball in an uninterrupted match. (Museum of the Lancashire Fusiliers)

28. Gurkhas at Helles. (The Gurkha Museum)

29. Indian stretcher-bearers bring a casualty down to the shore for evacuation. (Museum of the Lancashire Fusiliers)

30. A trench periscope in use at Helles. (Liddle Collection – E.F. Wettern)

31. A King's Own Scottish Borderer ready for the gas attack which never came. (Museum of the Lancashire Fusiliers)

32. Corporal Louis Coonie of the 1/4 Battalion King's Own Scottish Borderers, in a bomb bay preparing to release a catapult bomb aimed at the nearby Turkish positions. (Museum of the King's Own Scottish Borderers)

33. Cooks of the Lancashire Fusiliers. (Museum of the Lancashire Fusiliers)

34. A Turkish officer prepares to leave the Anzac sector having negotiated a truce for 24 May to bury the great number of bodies strewn in no man's land. (Liddle Collection – Mrs M. Kent)

by general Liman von Sanders and
Lt. Col. white one of our staff officers.
Seemed very queer all day with everything
so quiet no firing or anything all time.
Our men and Turks were exchanging
cigarettes and tobacco whilst some
were burying the dead. The smell was
something cruel most of the bodies
being almost totally decomposed.
The sight was most queer, men
sitting round in bunches smoking
and sharing their food with the
enemy, amidst, detd bodies,
amputated arms legs and heads
and general horrible surroundings.

35. An Australian sapper's diary of the truce. (Liddle Collection – G.C. Grove)

36. A New Zealand medical orderly with donkeys to transport non-ambulant wounded to the dressing station on the beach at Anzac. (Liddle Collection – Gibson Bishop)

37. The Commander-in-Chief, General Sir Ian Hamilton, inspects trenches at Anzac. (Liddle Collection – J.G. McNeill)

38. De-lousing – a necessity. (Liddle Collection – W.E. Chadwick)

39. Lieutenant-General Sir William Birdwood in a relaxed pose at Anzac. (John Prust)

40. One of the first burials at what later became Skew Bridge Cemetery at Helles. Padre Bewill Close takes the service. (Liddle Collection – E.F. Wettern)

41. The danger of bathing here at W Beach, as these RND medical men are – Surgeon Mayne submerged – was not just from shelling but from the effluent of the gantry-supported latrine built here to allow waste to enter the sea directly. (Liddle Collection – Cyril Mayne)

42. Yeomanry on the beach at Suvla. (Liddle Collection – H. Fellowes-Prynne)

43. The desperate shortage of water following upon the Suvla landing. (Liddle Collection – E.H. Dixon)

44. Horses landed at Suvla. (Liddle Collection)

45. South Wales Borderers attempting to wash in Suvla Bay. (Museum of the South Wales Borderers.)

46. August 21st and the crossing of the Salt Lake under shelling. In the foreground, Lieutenants Crocker and Marsden of the 3rd County of London Yeomanry. (Liddle Collection – L.G.C. Booth)

47. Officers of the Dorset, the Berks and the Bucks Yeomanry study orders for the imminent attack of the 21st August on Scimitar Hill. (Museum of the Dorset Yeomanry – Wingfield Digby Estate)

48. The sun-scorched vegetation of the Suvla plain catches fire during the attack of 21 August resulting in a terrible fate for the wounded and incapacitated, not reached by stretcher-bearers. (Liddle Collection – J.N. Mankin)

Gallipoli
August 5 1915

Dear brother,

Little enough did I think 12 months ago to-day that on the anniversary of mobilisation I should be writing you from a hole in the Gallipoli Peninsula, not having seen you for 10½ months, and to the tune of 75ᵐᵐ. guns. However you never know your luck, and I may see you in time to celebrate my 20th birthday at home, tho as things look at present, there's not much chance of that.

49. 'I may see you in time to celebrate my twentieth birthday at home, though as things look at present, there's not much chance of that' – the last letter written by Second Lieutenant Eric Duckworth of the 6th Battalion Lancashire Fusiliers. It is dated 5 August and he was killed two days later. (Liddle Collection – E. Duckworth)

50. Britain's first aircraft carrier, the converted HMS *Ark Royal*, with aeroplanes and seaplanes. Here, a Sopwith seaplane has either just been hoisted aboard or is being prepared for lowering into the sea for take-off and a reconnaissance flight. (Liddle Collection – G.R. Bromet)

51. One of the most vulnerable positions in the Anzac front-line, Quinn's Post – difficult to reach and exceptionally dangerous to hold, with the Turks just a few yards away. (Liddle Collection – A.E. Robinson)

52. New Zealander Errol Rudd operating a captured Turkish machine-gun at Hill 60 on the extreme left of the Anzac front. (Liddle Collection – O.L. Watson)

53. Sapper Wettern in his Helles dugout which he named 'the Pigstye'. (Liddle Collection – E.F. Wettern)

54. The French interrogate a captured Turk. (Liddle Collection – Raymond Weill)

55. The misery of the late November storm, then successively, flood, freezing temperatures and snow. November 28th, in the bleak Anzac sector. (Liddle Collection – WE Chadwick)

MORNING' NEWTON I SHANT NEED A COLD BATH THIS MORNING HMP. 15.

GALLIPOLI NOV-1915

56. Humour in adversity: In the freezing flood an officer decides that his servant does not need to prepare his morning cold bath for him. (Liddle Collection – J.C. Wand)

57. At Suvla: the washing has been done and the rations have come up the line to the Green Howards. It's time for a photograph before lunch. (Museum of the Green Howards)

58. Probable evacuation preparations: Green Howards prepare barbed wire entanglements. (Museum of the Green Howards)

59. Evacuation deception: Dummies made by Sappers of the Royal Naval Division in the attempt to convince the Turks that the Allies remained in strength in the trenches as in fact they were departing. (Liddle Collection – E.F. Wettern)

60. A busy scene at Suvla. Is this a stage of the evacuation of 'materiel'? (Museum of the Green Howards)

61. Allied troops leaving the Peninsula aboard HMS *Hibernia*. (Liddle Collection – C.J. Minter)

man of the Border Regt. Must have weighed fifteen stone. Got back about 2.45 a.m. ... Roused about 5.30 a.m., having got into a place that was wanted. Made a new and bigger dugout.

A letter written on 4 May by Captain Warneford Nightingale of the 1st Royal Munster Fusiliers reflects tiredness, strain and also savage satisfaction in the infliction of heavy losses among the Turks assaulting their positions. They themselves had suffered severely at the V Beach landing. 'We have got a good bit of the old Peninsula now but the last fortnight has been absolute hell! It is the only word for it. There is hardly anybody left in the Regiment – only four officers and all the best men gone too. We're no worse off than any other regiment either and of course it was all expected.' The house-to-house fighting on the 26th, the arrival of the French on the 27th and the advance on the 28th are described.

We have been in the firing line (continuously) and are all very exhausted. We never get any sleep at night as the Turks know we are waiting for more troops, and they attack us every night to try to get a victory over us before we can get help. On the night of the 1st of May we had a tremendous attack. They crept up in the dark and were in our trenches and bayonetting our men before we knew the attack had begun. We lost some trenches but recovered them all in half an hour. The attack lasted from 10.30 till dawn. The Turks attacked again and again shouting Allah! Allah! It was most exciting hearing them collecting in a dip in the hill about forty yards away waiting for their next charge. We mowed them down and only once did they get so close that we were able to bayonet them. When dawn broke, we saw them in hundreds retiring and simply mowed them down. We took 300 prisoners and could have taken 3,000 but we preferred shooting them. All the streams were running blood and the heaps of dead were a grand sight. We lost four more officers and 200 men. We now total four officers and 430 men out of our original 1,000.

The experience of the French troops on the right flank had been very nearly disastrous. In their blue uniforms, and with some in white cork hats, as soon as they were observed approaching the entrance to the Kereves Dere they were targeted by shell-fire. When the Turkish counter-attacks were hammered home from the night of 1 May, there was a real danger of their being driven into the sea at Morto Bay. Raymond Weil, an artillery officer, sent 'desperate signals to the transport *Provence* asking urgently for tugs and barges to bring our ammunition ashore because we are needing it'. The terrible confusion in the darkness at V Beach among the wounded and the stores on lighters ready for unloading made it impossible that night for the ammunition to be brought up to the French position, but somehow the infantry held on. Weil's captain was so exhausted after being without sleep for two days that he could scarcely speak. According to Weil, the ferocity of these counter-attacks was due in no small measure to the German commander of the Turkish troops exhorting them to destroy their enemy, for retirement would be the death of their religion, country and nation. There were other factors, related by Turkish veterans, as for example their bitterness against the black Senegalese soldiers with their dreadful knife (*coupe-coupe*) and the 'unfair' use by the British of flechettes, the metal darts dropped from planes on any concentration of troops.

Australian and New Zealand troops were transferred from Anzac to take part in the second attempt to seize Krithia, which had been scarcely defended, according to the *Official History*, on 25 April.[4] It had not been strongly defended when the Allies had attacked on 28 April and had not been outflanked in a battle which had merely straightened the British line by removing the indentation in its left flank. The Turks had now been considerably reinforced and were strongly entrenched in front of the village in a state of readiness against further assault. This came on 6 May.

The Australians were not thrown into the attack until 8 May and an Australian sapper, McKinlay, who was wounded early in a charge which resulted in fearful losses, remembered an English stretcher-bearer pleading successfully to come over the top with the Australians to bring in the wounded. He also saw the Australian war correspondent, Dr Bean, striding along with his walking-stick, disdainfully refusing to take cover. McKinlay and others recalled the repeated encouragement of their Colonel, 'Come along Australians', but for many New Zealanders the memory of the attack across the Helles 'Daisy Patch' is as grim as any recollection of their service on the Peninsula.[5] J.G. Gasparich stated bitterly that: 'the men had to make zigzag dashes across an open area wholly exposed to enemy rifle and machine-gun fire. I watched every single man in one party fall as he was hit so that none reached the spot where we had dug shallow cover. The grassy daisy-covered space was now a pathetic field of dead. Other lines followed and except for three men who swiftly returned to their cover the same fate awaited all who tried to reach us. I was aghast at the utterly useless and wanton waste of valuable lives.'

William Farr's letters (4th Battalion AIF) supply original evidence to the same effect. 'Nobody seemed to know what really we were to do. The officers had no instructions and some of them seemed bewildered.' Farr had criticised the performance of his officers at the Anzac landing but certainly the circumstance he described in this attack at Helles seem very largely to free from blame those in junior regimental command. When his platoon was ordered into the attack, all formation was almost immediately lost, some men crawled to get shelter from the banks of a stream which ran between the lines from Turk to Allied positions, others tried to get shelter from a rise in the ground towards Achi Baba, while others again, tried to enter Indian trenches and dugouts ahead of the assault position. 'The dust was rising from the ground with the bullets cutting into it, like it does when a thundershower comes down after a drought.'

Farr found himself seemingly alone in the open and made a dive for a dugout, already occupied by three men taking shelter. Soon he scuttled to another as shrapnel balls swept the ground smothering half-hidden men with dust and small stones. In what he called 'blind advances', dashes forward were made, past dead Turks and jettisoned Allied packs. In an advanced trench now occupied by men from other brigades and in fact two French soldiers, Farr's officer said he had no orders for them but advised them, in small groups, to make for a position still further forward. Farr did so but tripped on a puttee which had come loose and only just made it to the position before the area they had crossed was swept by explosions of shrapnel shells.

Desperately, lying prone, they deepened the shallow trench. They were now without officers or NCOs. There was rougher ground ahead offering better cover but the men were exhausted and only Farr went forward with the shelling now less severe. As he dug for cover he saw two lines of steadily walking troops moving still further forward. They were men of the Drake Battalion RND. He joined them, and when they halted to dig in, wounded came back saying there were Australians of the 8th battalion ahead, short of ammunition. Farr got an empty pack and ammunition from wounded men in the area, pressed forward again having to wade through the slimy-green corpse-obstructed stream of another nullah, keeping pack and rifle dry. As he wrote in this same letter: 'Each man had his own set of adventures', and though his were not finished, he did find his unit and the ammunition was certainly welcome.[6]

The French, still in their distinctive uniforms, suffered cruelly in this second battle for Krithia, but already the famous French 75s were winning praise from all for their accuracy and rapidity of fire. Raymond Weil, with one of these batteries, in turn paid tribute in his diary to the supporting naval gun-fire on the morning of the attack and recorded how their spirits had been raised by the arrival of both troops and munitions from the troopship *France*. At 7 p.m. on the 8th, just after watching a magnificent attack by French troops, he sadly saw the French falling like flies before a Turkish counter-attack. There were signs of panic, as the French were not protected by artillery fire during this counter-attack, but later in the evening the positions lost were regained.

British, Commonwealth and French troops had advanced against withering fire and had suffered dreadful losses. Their gains by the end of 8 May were still far short of their objective for 6 May. An ominous resemblance to Western Front conditions was appearing, though there was still one source of encouragement amidst the gloom. At this stage of the campaign the British naval support of their troops was an ever-present source of strength in materiel and in morale. On 28 April a single one of *Queen Elizabeth*'s 15in shrapnel shells with 24,000 bullets seemed entirely to wipe out a Turkish company charging British troops and the sinking of a Turkish transport by *Queen Elizabeth*'s indirect fire across the Peninsula, are incidents described in the *Official History*.[7]

The progress of the fighting could be observed from the warships without the need of telescope or field-glasses. Midshipman Clarke of *Implacable* scribbled a note on 7 May for later transfer into his log: 'The troops made a determined attack all the forenoon and succeeding in gaining a mile or so although up to date they did not capture Achi Baba as was intended. The resistance was terrific and the air was full of shells. We assisted where we could by firing.'

Two letters written within two days of each other, from men in reinforcement units, and a third letter, from a naval officer, provide significant first impressions. On 17 May, Charles Thierry of the French 176th Infantry Regiment, assured his parents that at that moment his unit was in the rear suffering few casualties. They were however always under shell-fire and that evening were moving up through the second line to the front line, so would his parents not expect any letters for a week. 'We hope to push the Turks back and then the base area will be a little quieter.' However, the concept of a quiet base area was never to exist on the Peninsula. Dugouts or strongly-built shelters were as necessary for the Divisional Commanding Officer as the trench dugout was for his men.

The second letter was written on 15 May by an English officer in a Territorial regiment, Second Lieutenant E. Duckworth, 6th Battalion Lancashire Fusiliers.

> Well, we have had two days experience in the front trenches and they are not full of the joy we anticipated when we were so bored in Cairo! In fact they were distinctly otherwise. I myself was lucky enough to come out unhurt but my platoon … [crossed out by censor] suffered somewhat through having to advance about 100 yards over open ground. I cannot go into details as regards numbers of casualties but 12 per cent only are killed out of the total of killed, wounded and missing. The enemy are very heavily entrenched on a hill which is at present our main objective to capture. They have an enormous number of machine-guns and their fire is very well controlled. Their artillery is not as heavy as we had expected and shell-fire has not cost us above a few men. However we have had our fill of war and shall not mind when it ends. I have just censored an article by the *Times* correspondent which gives you full detail and a bit more. But I expect he has to enlarge a bit in order to make a story… The men stick it quite well on the whole, though amongst the younger there was a tendency perhaps natural to hang back a bit. The fire we went through was inconceivable, like a wall of bullets. The old South African people say they never struck anything like it in the whole war.

On board HMS *Minerva*, a young naval officer, H.K.L. Shaw, had written to his family on 10 May:

> Things have quietened down a lot for us on board the ships; but not so on shore where, as Harry Lauder says, 'the cannon's death rattle' goes on day and night, by Gad! Things are fairly humming on the land and from all accounts the casualties on both sides are tremendous. The Turks and Huns having had plenty of time to prepare, have taken full advantage of all the natural advantage of their hilly country and have fairly dug themselves in; also they seem to have an enormous number of guns etc. in concealed gullies so it's going to be some job to shift them. I can assure you that all of us out here are pretty fed up with the breezy manner in which a lot of the newspaper rags have been spouting about getting to Constantinople etc. as if it was a mere walk-over.

The Allied failure in the first two battles for Krithia was not only significant in terms of the final result of the campaign but also by circumscribing the area of the Peninsula held at Cape Helles, it determined the nature of the fighting. At this stage and for the rest of the campaign the land won from the Turks was scarcely more than an enlarged beachhead. When Helles was evacuated in January 1916 the British front line was approximately four miles inland from V and W Beaches, and still another mile beyond lay battered Krithia. In May, despite the scars of shelling and lines of entrenchments, the plain in front of Krithia was still green, carpeted with flowers, rimmed by the deep blue of the sea which glistened in the morning and turned to molten gold against the rays of the setting sun. Under a clear azure sky, in the quietness between shelling, with the air as yet not strongly poisoned by cordite fumes or decaying corpses, the scene retained something of its surpassing beauty. 'Later, except for the trees and shrubs, the Peninsula, worn down by the passing of thousands of men, and the endless coming and going of transport from the beaches to the camps, became a bare sandy waste. In time it was worse than that ... The army was indeed caught between the hill and sea; it could go neither backward nor forward. The plain, for all its openness, was a prison which became a tomb.'[8]

With the defenders' morale intact, their positions well-entrenched, their numbers adequate, their artillery and small arms weapons and ammunition sufficient, there was simply no reason why the inexorable disadvantage of the attacker in 1915/17 warfare, was going to be reversed. If the defending positions were not obliterated by overwhelmingly effective artillery power, no man's land would not be crossed in effective numbers. The circumstances which made for change on the Western Front in 1918 were beyond imagination, never mind reach, on the Peninsula in May 1915.

Chapter 10

May and Early Summer at Anzac

While the prime task for the troops at Anzac during the month of May was to ensure that the area won at such cost was maintained against mass frontal attack, and that the flanks were secure, there was at no level a passive acquiescence in the stalemate. At the very beginning of the month raids on either flank indicated the aggressive spirit which remained for so long a characteristic of the defence of Anzac.

In a reconnaissance far out to the left by New Zealanders during the last days of April, a Turk had stumbled down a gully and landed helplessly in the arms of some Canterbury men. J.A. Anderson recorded that, in the tangled vegetation and difficult ground, the New Zealanders had got behind the Turkish defences and secured information from their prisoner of an enemy outpost near the Salt Lake. This post was attacked by fifty men of the Canterbury Battalion. They had been transported to Suvla by boat during the night of the 1/2 May, and the signed report by Captain Waite and Captain Cribb shows how completely successful was this well-conceived raid.[1] 'We came on a trench which was occupied by a party of Turks asleep. One Turk grasped his rifle and wakened the others, whereupon some of our men fired, killing three and wounding four others. We covered the rest of the party and disarmed them ... All arms, equipment and papers were collected and taken to the torpedo boat *Colne*. The papers were handed to General Godley on our return.' An officer and twelve Turkish soldiers had been captured, but on the right flank a raid still more dangerous, in view of the known strength of the defences, had been unsuccessful.

At dawn on 4 May, a hundred men of the 11th Battalion AIF, together with some sappers, were landed just north of the Gaba Tepe headland with the task of raiding and dismantling the fort, the main gun of which was such a danger to the Anzac beachhead. The four ship's boats, making the landing from the destroyer *Colne*, were fired on as they were just off the beach and, as the men landed, machine-guns and a 1in quick-firing gun convinced Captain Leane, who was in command of the party, that despite the shell-fire from supporting ships there was no hope of success for their mission. Under heavy fire the party was re-embarked – the originally planned escape route along the beach to Anzac, through gaps cut in the wire by a support party, was clearly too dangerous.

R.L. Jones, who was on this raid, remembered that single men had been invited to volunteer and that, on the beach, under cover from the fort, they had gathered round Captain Leane like a troop of scouts round a scoutmaster. A man had been sent to reconnoitre and he came back with the report that they had no chance of taking the fort, so a signaller flagged a message to that effect towards Anzac. The only reply was, 'Regret cannot assist. Goodbye and good luck.' The plight of the small force was then signalled to the ships off shore and the reply was that they would assist by taking the wounded off. Under a Red Cross flag this was done and the Turks did not fire. Following the successful embarkation of the wounded, the Navy, under the cover of a very heavy bombardment, sent boats in to get the Australians. 'A middle-aged sailor bearded like the one on the back of the cigarette packet was rowing in our boat towards the ship with his head erect like those of the other sailors while we were only too anxious to take cover from the fire. He called out to one and all, "The Good Lord had us in the hollow of His hand this day".' Certainly, with only six killed and eighteen wounded, the survivors had reason to feel fortunate.

The main Turkish effort to throw the invaders into the sea came on 19 May. On the 18th, RNAS reconnaissance had reported large concentrations of Turkish troops assembling behind their front line and still more reinforcements being landed on the Dardanelles shore. The massed forward movement into the attack was sighted from the Anzac positions just before 3.30 in the morning. A Turkish veteran, Captain Ozgen, asked by the writer how morale had been maintained as the successive assaults the Turks were to make were devastatingly dealt with by artillery fire from Plugge's Plateau[2] and by machine-gun and rifle fire all along the Anzac position, responded that military discipline, patriotism and religious fervour had all played their part, but he emphasized the influence of a military band concealed in a forward position which had played martial music throughout the action.

W.W. Paterson, in the 3rd Infantry Brigade, writing to his brother on 12 July, described how he was lying out in front of his trench on outpost guard when,

> I heard a murmuring and rustling ahead of me. I woke up my mates and we got ready. Presently about fifty yards in front over a sky line I saw moving figures coming towards me. We sent back word to the firing line ... In another minute a form rose up out of the low scrub about fifteen yards in front of me and started giving orders. I had him covered as he rose and although pretty nervy I do not think I missed. It seemed as if my shot was the signal, for immediately the machine-guns opened with a roar and with another roar the Turks rushed forward. We darted back for our lines and got in just as they came up in dense masses about fifty yards behind.

Paterson went to assist the short-handed machine-gunners and shared the work of firing, feeding in the belts of bullets and bringing up water, oil and ammunition. With traversing bursts they swept the front, also wiping out a party of men and mules moving to the front. Then, in broad daylight, their gun, assisted by naval shrapnel fire, caught the Turks in the open and mercilessly destroyed their retreat.

The attack provided the first opportunity to inflict heavy casualties among the Turks from positions of relative safety. 'Then they rushed to within twenty or thirty yards of our position but our lads mowed them down like grass ... our lads were as cool as if they were shooting ducks ... one poor chap died on his knees not thirty yards from our trenches and is still in the same position.'[3] A.L. Guppy wrote his diary account[4] that night of a particularly celebrated incident during the attack. 'At the entrance to the sector of our trench captured by the Turks … L/Cpl Jacka leapt over [two dead Australians] and got in among the Turks. He quickly shot three and bayonetted four more and cleared the sector.' Jacka had in fact held the position on his own for a quarter of an hour, his feat earning him the first Australian Victoria Cross award of the war.

In the Australian Medical Corps, Edney Moore must have been sufficiently aware, even during a heavy day of tending to wounded, that an outstandingly brave man had been lost when he wrote on the 19 May: 'Poor Simpson of 3rd F.A. was killed early in morning while still doing good work with the donkey.' The imperturbable manner in which this man, born in South Shields, County Durham, but enlisting in a West Australian unit, had brought wounded men down to the beach with the aid of his donkey was already growing into a legend which in doing due honour to Simpson was to symbolize the brave work done by men of all the field ambulance units. Later (in 1916), Colonel Fergusson, in command of the 21st Kohat Mountain battery, wrote of Simpson:

One Australian stretcher bearer in particular attached himself to us permanently from the very first. We called him Murphy because that is what he called all his donkeys. He always had a donkey with him which he used to work Shrapnel Valley, bringing down men wounded in the legs or any cases which could ride but not walk. He had many donkeys and men killed beside him but led a charmed life himself till 19 May. We treasured his last donkey and evacuated it safely at the end with a view to presenting it to Australia but it was stolen from our mule lines in Mudros.

Simpson was not to receive the anxious letter from his sister in England which would have told him that 'Mother has not had any word from you since she read of the landing of the Australians in the Dardanelles – of course I expect you will have had your hands full … Oh to have you home again. Home will not be complete again until you come back.'[5] By an interesting irony of fate one of the New Zealanders who did similar work to Simpson but whose name was never well-known has been commemorated in an unusual manner. Sapper Moore-Jones, the New Zealand soldier artist, was handed a photograph which was said to be of Simpson. He used it to assist in the painting of a fine work which he inscribed 'To the memory of our comrade Murphy (Simpson) killed May 1915.' The photograph was in fact of a New Zealander, Henderson, and so the features of the stalwart Simpson in the painting are those of Henderson, who had been, unknown to the photographer, the subject of his print.

The war diary of one of the New Zealand reinforcement regiments, the Auckland Mounted Rifles (landed at Anzac on the 12 May), shows that the cost to the Turks of their great offensive had been high. 19 May: 'Walker's Ridge … at about 3.30 the enemy assault our trenches in superior force but are driven off at 4.30 a.m. by gallant counter-attacks by a troop of 4th commanded by Lieut-Col James and also by a troop of 11th Squadron commanded by Lieut P. Logan. The enemy leave the ground strewn with dead and wounded.' The Australian Light Horse regiments and the New Zealand Mounted Rifle regiments, though disappointed at leaving their horses behind in Egypt and thus changing their role in accordance with their Peninsula destination, were to provide infantry reinforcement at a vital time after the frustration of the first Anzac assault and with the growing threat of reinforced Turkish counter-attacks.

Sapper G.C. Grove's diary for the day of the attack described how, 'some of the Turks had managed to get even onto the parapet of our firing trench but were driven off at the point of the bayonet and point-blank rifle fire. Several Turks taken prisoner and hundreds killed and wounded. In front of No. 4 Sap they were literally piled up in heaps.'

The problem of burying the dead of no man's land was not new but was now made far more serious by reason of number and early summer temperatures. A young New Zealand Staff Officer, J.L. Anderson, who had aptly written in his diary[6] on 5 May that, 'the whole place beggars description', was to add two days later that from a battery commanded by a Major Sykes he had seen, 'dead men which neither we nor the Turks can get at. There will have to be an armistice soon for identifying and burying.'

Both the Australian and the British *Official Histories*[7] describe in detail the first moves towards a truce to bury the dead, and the whole story is recorded in General Birdwood's diary. Local command initiative on the Australian side, in sympathy with Turkish wounded in no man's land, had been taken even before General Birdwood's request to Sir Ian Hamilton for a truce had been refused because the Turks might have used the request as propaganda. The unofficial truce, arranged locally on the evening of the 20th, had been terminated by fears that approaching darkness would enable a surprise attack to be launched by the large numbers of armed troops who appeared to be concentrating in the Turkish forward trenches. In one sector, Turkish stretcher-bearers were fired on as they moved forward in the gathering gloom without the Australians knowing of the informal negotiations. A resumption of firing effectively prevented the Turks taking advantage of General Walker's verbal invitation for a parley to discuss a cease-fire, but a written invitation to send an officer to conduct negotiations led to the Turks taking up this offer.

Many troops who were on the beach or had a view of the beach saw this officer coming along the shore from Gaba Tepe. He was helped into the sea and round the barbed wire which closed the extreme right flank of the Anzac position, blindfolded and led on a horse into the lines. Negotiations for a truce on the following day, the 24th, were successfully concluded and at least one copy survives of the Australian orders issued for the truce – in La Trobe Library, Melbourne.

The suspension of arms was to last nine hours, from 7.30 a.m. to 4.30 p.m. Parties of not more than 200 unarmed men of each side, equipped with water bottles, stretchers and picks and shovels, were to work in 1,000-metre-long areas designated after the Staff officers of either side had worked on delimiting no man's land. Arms and equipment of dead and wounded officers were to be handed over without restriction, but the bolts of the rifles of the rank and file were to be removed first. No work was to be done on trenches, saps or communication trenches or gun emplacements. A dividing line was to be marked by 200 white flag-bearers from either side and to this line the bodies were to be taken and laid respectfully in line, not in heaps, for removal and burial by men of the respective sides. To avoid any misinterpretation, rifles were to be carried to this line on stretchers and not by hand. Strict observation was to be maintained throughout, to see that there was no breach of the agreed terms by preparations for an attack under the guise of truce activities.

Naturally advantage was taken during the nine hours to survey as much as possible of enemy positions. According to the Turkish Captain Ozgen's memoirs, Lieutenant-Colonel Mustafa Kemal, who was in command of the 19th Division, had dressed as a medical orderly and by this means succeeded in viewing the Australian positions. Certainly notes and sketches containing much useful information were made by Australian officers. Whether particularly tall troops were selected for the work is difficult to establish, as indeed it is to know whether there were a serious attempt to leave equipment like bayonets sticking up in order to be used as sighting marks on particular positions. Although two Australians were shot by a sniper[8] who knew nothing of the agreement and, according to the Australian *Official History*, a Turkish howitzer on Gaba Tepe was fired, there was no incident which seriously endangered the continuation of the truce.

M.G. Butcher, in 1915 a Trooper in the 3rd Light Horse, remembered that those concerned with the no man's land activity had been ordered to be shaved and particularly smart in their appearance to impress the Turks, and he also recalled the fraternization which took place and a Turk declaring loudly, 'We are bloody silly.' Another Australian, D. Marks, noted in his dairy that he had 'exchanged coins with Turkish and German officers',[9] and certainly the period of the truce provided a quite exceptional experience. G.C. Grove observed the work of the burial parties. 'Seemed very queer all day with everything so quiet, no firing or anything all the time. Our men and Turks were exchanging cigarettes and tobacco while some were burying the dead. The smell was something cruel, most of the bodies being almost totally decomposed.'

The work of moving and burying bodies, some in a state of advanced decomposition was difficult as well as particularly unpleasant. The New Zealander, Lieutenant-Colonel Fenwick, wrote that:

> Everywhere one looked lay dead, swollen, black, hideous and over all a nauseating stench that nearly made one vomit. We exchanged cigarettes with the other officers frequently and the senior Turkish medico gave me two pieces of scented wool to put in my nostrils ... there was a narrow path absolutely blocked with dead, also a swathe of men who had fallen face down as if on parade ... The Turkish officers were charming. The Germans were rude and dictatorial and accused us of digging trenches. I lost my temper (and my German) and told them the corpses were so decomposed that they could not be lifted and our men were merely digging pits to put the awful things into.

An Australian Salvation Army Padre, McKenzie, wrote to his wife on 29 May that it had been, 'the most dreadful experience even I have had, burying people who had been dead a month. I retched and have been sleepless since … No words can describe the ghastliness.'

Of the strain of service at Quinn's Post in the Anzac front line during this period, Cecil Malthus has written graphically.[10] This post, at the top of a steep cliff, was reached by a straight staircase with the steps cut out of the cliff and reinforced with brushwood. Divided into no less than six separate commands at the head and on either side of the ladder, the position was in parts only seven yards from the Turkish parapet, with a listening post even closer, and was as ridiculously insecure as it was vital in preventing Turkish domination of the valley below the cliff. Australians and then New Zealanders had won, defended and improved these hazardous positions under constant grenade attacks, rifle fire and the threat of enemy mining explosions. The listening post was a

little timbered passage, practically below ground level, though heavily roofed with sandbags. A tiny loophole enabled us to watch the Turk's parapet a few feet away and through a manhole at the side we could crawl or lean out to throw bombs. I spent two nights in this place and both times the roof was more or less blown in and some of my companions were badly wounded … To lie cowering in the darkness of the cramped and evil-smelling pit and watch a big bomb sputtering among the corpses just against our loophole while waiting for the burst was an experience that no man could endure unmoved.

M.S. Chambers noted that even when the men became expert in throwing bombs back before they burst, speed of reaction and agility of movement were hampered by two important factors. 'The trouble was that the explosions deafened us so much that after a time we could not hear where the bombs were falling and then the strain was pretty bad. The trenches were very narrow and a man had to be careful not to get stuck when either reaching for a bomb or getting away. Wounded men lying in the bottom of the trenches were really the worst sufferers from bombs.'

There were experienced Australian miners in the 1st Field Company Engineers and one of their officers, Henry Bachtold, recorded on interview how the work of undermining the opposition positions proceeded.

From the front line every 200 or 300 feet we ran an incline tunnel. We had 8 hour shifts. I discovered that we got more done if we worked 6 hours and everybody came out for two hours and let the place cool down. Then after we had run these main tunnels perhaps 100 feet or thereabouts we connected them altogether. From that underground tunnel we probed forward then with various other kinds of tunnels. Of course the Turk was doing the same sort of thing but I decided on working with 16 foot of cover. Consequently the Turks always were above me and as soon as they were too close I used to pop them off with a mine [that is a countermine – a camouflet – to destroy the workings and the enemy digging them].

With all going well for the Australian tunnels forward,

> after the chamber had been cut out I then prepared all the explosives myself. The explosive was in square canisters, something like a gallon oil tin. I used to stack these in the form of a wall, sometimes a double wall and I drew out two tins. Unscrewed them and into one I put in the ordinary detonator into which you push a piece of fuse and crimp the thing together. Well, then the thing was to start putting a certain amount of instantaneous fuse hooked onto the detonator and that went into one of the tins and the place where it went in was carefully sealed and then as a safeguard we had electric detonators. They had two wires and the thing was to connect those wires and bring them through to an exploder. When I was satisfied that I had connected them up properly I asked the boys to pass me the sandbags. We had to build back at least 10 to 15 feet of bags, then the leads were taken to a suitable place – in this case the Battalion Headquarters.

The mine would be detonated to coincide with a local attack attempting to take possession, repair and reverse a position threatening the Anzac line.

A diary entry by a New Zealander, A.E. Gascoigne, indicates graphically conditions in front line posts close to the enemy and under which mining activity was known to be taking place. 'We are continually sapping towards the Turkish trenches in our front and have now only a few feet to go. The Australians are sapping towards the Turks' trenches and are now only ten yards away. The Turks have only to put their rifles over their trenches and shoot straight down onto our trenches. Hand bombs are being hurled every few minutes.'[11]

Courtney's Post and Johnston's Jolly were further examples of positions involving exceptional problems of intercommunication and supply as well as active defence. A consideration of the problem in these positions with regard to food, water, sanitation and men incapacitated by wounds, makes one aware of the debilitating effect of service in these sectors. As the summer heat increased, the flies massed and the maggots waxed in numbers and girth. Among the men retaining vivid recollections of these singularly dreadful conditions was J.G. Gasparich.

> The flies flew in their thousands from swollen, rotten bodies lying in the scrub. From this oozing matter where they bred so promiscuously they would move to the open latrines and so to the men themselves. They sought moisture from our ears, our noses, our eyes, our mouths. Men wrapped their heads in hessian in an endeavour to escape them until they were nearly suffocated in the heat but still the flies managed to get in. Liquid spilled on the floor was soon covered by layers of furiously struggling flies fighting to reach the dampness. You had to keep a moving hand over any morsel of food and drink in a forlorn attempt to keep the flies from entering your mouth.

Inadequate latrine facilities, unvaried and perhaps unsuitable food, were to make men already weakened in nerve and body a ready prey to enteric fever and dysentery, but the full effects of this were to be kept at bay until the supreme effort to break out of the Anzac position in August.

It should not be assumed that Australasians alone were enduring these trials at Anzac. At the landing there had been the 150 young Englishmen of the Ceylon Planters' Rifle Corps attached to the Australian and New Zealand Army Corps. In a letter of 17 May, Birdwood wrote, 'I have an excellent guard of Ceylon Planters who are such a nice lot of fellows.'[12] Also from the Indian Army there was the 7th Mountain Artillery Brigade,[13] which had been in action since 25 April. Colonel Fergusson, of the 21st Kohat Battery, wrote an account in 1916 of the astonishing heroism of Karm Singh, one of his gunners, who continued at his post despite being blinded in both eyes by shrapnel. He had kept on saying, 'Bilkul taqrah [quite fit], Sahib' to all anxious inquiries.

From August, the 1/5th, 1/6th and 2/10th Gurkhas and the 14th Sikhs, all from the 29th Indian Brigade, were to serve at Anzac, as of course were English units,[14] but the Indian Mule Cart Corps with two officers and 227 other ranks had been at the original landing. Together with the Second Indian Field Ambulance, the Indian Mule Corps, with their little carts or winding trains of mules, was to carry out a large part of the difficult, dangerous and essential work of the movement of supplies from the beach. Although an attempt was made to set up a narrow-gauge railway or tramway line, it was never of real operational value, and the Anzac supply line was largely maintained by the Indians and the six officers and 240 men of the Zion Mule Corps which also landed on 25 April.

This Jewish unit suffered eight killed and fifty-five wounded during its Gallipoli service. The men were of Russian nationality and were refugees from Palestine. The unit had been formed as recently as 23 March in Egypt, when these earnest volunteers had sworn an oath of obedience to their English commanding officer, Lieutenant-Colonel Patterson, and their appointed officers. A feature of the Zionists' work was that at every opportunity, whether at Helles or at Anzac, they rode their mules and it was not long before they were known either as the 'Allies' cavalry' or 'Ally Sloper's cavalry'. Though to the majority of the men Russian and Hebrew were their native tongues, they were commanded in English, and F.W. Parker remembered the influence the Peninsula had on one of the tenets of their faith. Parker was in charge of a supply dump and the Zionists refused on principle to carry the sides of bacon from the jetty to this store. On the arrival of a special dispensation from the Chief Rabbi allowing them to eat bacon, and of course carry it, the unit applied unsuccessfully for their previously rejected rations.

Parker also had recall of a special, perhaps unique, 'unit'. It was the task of a man named Wilson, who had been a butcher, to row from shore armed with a sort of lance, later with a butcher's knife lashed to a pole. He was clad in waterproof clothing and had to lance or slash the gaseous bloated carcasses of mules killed ashore and unsuccessfully dumped in the sea for burial, to make them sink. On return from these missions, Wilson's smell was abominable, his nickname unprintable.

Similarly unusual and linked, but less electively, with Wilson, was an experience recollected uncomfortably by A.L. Rutter. Weakened by dysentery, he had fallen from the perching poles into a latrine. Helpless in the stinking liquid 'porridge', as he was too ill even to attempt to climb the steep sides of the pit, his faint cries had, after some time, been heard. He was dragged out and thrown into the sea to get clean. Rutter was in fact a keen and not unskilled violinist. Somehow he had managed to bring his precious violin to the Peninsula and on quiet evenings before dysentery had begun to take hold of him he had played in his trench the popular airs of the day. Not surprisingly 'Turkish Patrol' was one of the most popular and on several evenings, as the notes rose into the still air, the applause of Australian troops was distinctly joined by acclaim from the Turkish trenches. Entertainment of a different kind was provided on 18 June, when A.S. Hutton saw that 'two of our chaps had a real good stand-up fight at the supports of Courtney's Post yesterday. It lasted about half an hour. There was much cheering going on.'[15]

Besides the news which arrived in out-of-date Australian and New Zealand papers, officially approved information was issued in the form of the *Peninsula Press* news-sheet which was displayed on various boards at Anzac as at Helles. A boost for morale was naturally pre-eminent in this MEF HQ publication. In a report published on 11 June, readers were informed that a Turkish prisoner had on him a copy of army orders which stated that a great deal of ammunition is being expended and 'this is proof that while the enemy is losing the terror we at first instilled in him, we ourselves are afraid'.[16] It seems little wonder that an Australian wrote on the back of a copy he sent home of the *Peninsula Press* for 22 May, 'We don't get the bad news. This is our only source of information.'

Despite the attempt to censor information coming to the troops at Anzac, and of course the Australasian newspapers themselves contained only approved news, there is little evidence that censorship was any more strict at Anzac than at Helles. While many of the letter-writers were intentionally or otherwise their own censor and some seem to show their awareness of the censor by warning the recipient that they could not give details, few of the large number of letters which remain in archival or personal preservation show traces of the blue pencil. There is no doubt of the identity of the censor most feared by B. Savage, writing from the Peninsula to his former headmaster. 'The censor will gaze with suspicion at my bulky letter, visions of stolen plans and designs may rise before his eyes, so I had better close. I hope you won't correct my letter as an essay and return it for me to rewrite as a reminder of the days when my corrections exceeded my homework in quantity.'

Both June and July saw costly diversionary attacks launched with little time for considered planning, as MEF HQ considered the secrecy of the date of the main offensives being launched at Helles must take precedence over all other factors. The losses suffered without any apparent local or overall benefit, together with the problems already mentioned, gnawed away at the physique and morale of the troops. As early as 16 June, Lieutenant-Colonel Fenwick, the Assistant Director of Medical Services, was moved to write in his journal: 'The flies are a dreadful nuisance. You have to brush them off just as you put each bit of food into your mouth, otherwise you eat flies, because they decline to leave the food, even when inside your mouth. We have no means of killing these pests.' Fenwick was in fact soon to leave the Peninsula to work in a general field hospital at Heliopolis, near Cairo, but still earlier in June a young staff officer, J.L. Anderson, noted that 'diarrhea [*sic*] is getting pretty serious here and in the congested way we are at present is likely to remain. Things may become serious. It is hard to find latrines sufficiently far enough away not to interfere with things in general and to keep them away from the wells.'[17] Anderson proceeded to criticize the lack of preparations for offsetting these problems and blamed Fenwick for this inaction.

On 7 June, Private H.V. Palmer of the Canterbury Battalion escaped the rigours of Quinn's Post for a swim, even though it was under shell-fire. 'I took shelter under an old wharf and finished my wash, being the first wash I've had for a week after laying [*sic*] in very dirty trenches and getting smothered with maggots from dead lying under our rifle points … after dinner we rested but was annoyed by small flies. We took our shirts off and had what we call a count of lice to see if there were any cowards among them [who had] left while we were under fire but they seemed to be all there. We gave them something to do in our trousers by turning them inside out to get next to the skin again.'

Even under these conditions, on the evening of 15 June Palmer's Nelson Company managed a concert, with their new Colonel giving a song and other men obliging, despite the rifle fire, with songs or recitations. By the 22nd however, Palmer was finding sleep very difficult to come by, anywhere near Quinn's. 'If you laid down in the dust you got full of lice and annoyed by flies and men walking over you and when on duty [you are] getting blown to pieces by bombs or the Turks tunnelling towards us and blowing up the trenches.' Away from the front line, fatigues on a shift basis were extremely exhausting for men whose nerves had been strained, lacked sleep and were generally debilitated. Well might another New Zealander, Sergeant Cardno, write for the 26 June, 'A big sick parade today. It's high time the men were given a spell.' On 8 July the same diarist wrote that 'the health of the troops is very bad. A rest is badly needed.'

The manner in which some officers below Staff level, like F.M. Twisleton, made critical appraisal in their letters of the conditions under which the campaign was being conducted, is interesting.

The men dress as they please and as they can, slacks, riding pants or shorts, anything does, and anything does as far as language goes … the men will risk anything for a swim, the days are hot, there is little water and unless you get into the sea you can't wash … there ought to be a first-rate canteen ship where men could get what they need in order to vary the diet. If they could get milk and rice there would be fewer men getting sick. It is a pity the powers that be stopped the daily issues of rum. A large proportion of the men have been used to a certain amount of alcohol every day, and to have it stopped means making them unstable, though they might not think so themselves … I have not yet seen a forge for sharpening picks and they should be everywhere, nor yet a grindstone. It would make things much easier if all tools were sharp.

In the same letter, this Otago Mounted Rifles officer made a pertinent observation on the way the campaign had developed. 'If the Army and Navy had stuck together Gallipoli would have fallen easily. But the Navy came and went several times and gave the Turks two months to prepare defences.'

Despite the fact that July saw no major offensive at Anzac it proved a depressingly costly month, with an alarming decline in the condition of the troops. Uncovered latrines and unburied corpses provided such a breeding ground for the large green flies that diarrhoea and dysentery caused the necessary departure from the Peninsula of many men and the weakening of almost all. Unappetizing, often unsuitable food, persistently under the assault of swarms of flies, was an aid to neither health nor morale. Bully beef which could be almost poured like treacle from its tin and rock-hard biscuits flavoured with well-nigh liquid plum or apricot jam proved memorably indigestible in their unvarying repetition. A significant additional discomfort was widespread dental decay, for the treatment of which there were completely inadequate facilities. The loss of five teeth through eating hard biscuits was recorded by G.C. Kilner. These factors, together with delayed mail, parcels with spoiled contents and a growing sense of purposelessness, eroded the spirit of men who were to be called to make one more supreme effort.

So many diaries mention a daily tragedy nearby. One recorded men excitedly rushing for the newly-arrived mail and being hit by a shrapnel shell burst, others the loss of a close friend. Gruesome details like those recorded by Sergeant Cardno are phrased in an unemotional, mechanical, detailed way: 'Lawrie was killed, blown to bits.' A.S. Hutton was still more explicit: 'One of our fellows had his brains blown out just in front of me, some of which went on his cap, some on my trousers and some on the ground.'[18]

The troops at Anzac could hardly be expected to display the confident aggression of the early weeks of the campaign, but they knew that something was afoot and that it might enable them successfully to break out of their embattled position. Their wary readiness and parsimoniously conceded optimism is expressed in Cardno's diary entry for 5 August: 'We are ready for the big move on the left. I don't know what's in store for us but I hope we pull it off.'

Chapter 11

At Sea: Disaster on the Surface, Achievement Below

Though the naval officer on board *Minerva*, H.K.L. Shaw, had quite reasonably observed on 10 May that, 'things have quietened down a lot for us on board the ships', this state of affairs was to change alarmingly within the next fortnight. On 12 May the security and confidence of naval personnel were further demonstrated by a well-conceived co-operative operation with an attack by the 6th Gurkhas. The attack secured the bluff overlooking Y Beach which had been such a thorn in the Allied left flank as Turkish snipers in concealed dugouts with bullet-proof shields effectively prevented any outflanking of Krithia. A Gurkha scout officer on board the cruiser *Talbot* assisted in the direction of heavy fire which enabled the soldiers, almost without loss, to take a position previously defended in strength. Not surprisingly the success of the attack also owed much to the special quality of the troops involved – the silent traversing of Y Beach and the climb up the steep cliffs to wait concealed in the darkness for the moment of attack, were peculiarly suited to these splendid soldiers. This 'Gurkha Bluff' success, however, was to be balanced on the following night by a loss of major importance.

The Turkish torpedo-boat destroyer *Muavenet-i-Miliet*, with a German commander and a German-reinforced crew, had used the dense banks of fog as she approached from Chanak to escape detection until the very last moment as she fired three torpedoes at *Goliath* in Morto Bay, where the old battleship was supporting the French at the Kereves Dere. *Goliath* quickly turned turtle, trapping hundreds of men below decks. She sank in about two minutes and approximately 570 of her crew were lost, some escaping the ship's plunge only to be carried away in the darkness by the swift current. The night-time isolation of troops from the supporting ships is well illustrated by the fact that several detailed diaries of French officers and men within easy day-time sight of *Goliath* make no mention of the tragedy.

An account by a surviving midshipman was published in 1916, significantly without the ship being named:[1]

Some of the midshipmen were already standing on the deck in their pyjamas ... the ship was now heeling about five degrees to starboard and I climbed up the port side. It was nearly pitch dark ... a crowd gathered along the port side 'Boat ahoy! Boat ahoy!' they yelled, but as the ship listed more and more and there was no sign or sound of any approaching vessel, the men's voices seemed to get hopeless. Inside the ship everything which was not secured was sliding about and bringing up against the bulkheads with a series of crashes ... She had heeled over to about 20 degrees, then she stopped and remained steady for a few seconds. In the momentary lull the voice of one of our officers rang out steady and clear as at 'divisions':[2] 'Keep calm men. Be British!' Then the ship started to heel rapidly again and I felt sure there was no chance of saving her. I turned to jump overboard ... Raising my arms above my head I sprang well out-board and dived. Just before I struck the water my face hit the side of the ship. It was a horrid feeling sliding on my face down the slimy side and a second later I splashed in with tremendous force, having dived about thirty feet. Just as I was rising to the surface again, a heavy body came down on top of me. I fought clear and rose rather breathless and bruised.

The midshipman swam to get clear of the suction of the sinking ship and watched her going down. He could hear objects being smashed inside the ship and saw the final 'mass of bubbles' where she had disappeared. He tried to swim towards *Cornwallis* but failed to reach her. 'Soon the shrieks of the drowning grew faint in the distance and I swam on with three others near me ... The current was very strong and of course this was a great help to those of us who were swimming.' Finally he was caught in the beam of the searchlights of HMS *Lord Nelson* and picked up by another ship's boat.

Another survivor on board had been badly bruised by drifting wreckage. Similar impressions are given by a number of men. Seaman W.H. Clarke, the only one of six men from Ramsay, Isle of Man, to survive the loss of *Goliath*, wrote to his wife: 'We were in the water about an hour and it was an awful sight to see so many men struggling. I was almost done when I got rescued. I have often heard about men singing facing death and I have now seen it in reality. We are all suffering shock as a result of the terrible sensation and I am not feeling up to the mark at the time of writing.'[3]

The log of George Keeler on board *Lord Nelson* provides an interesting indication not only of the depression caused by the loss and of the great efforts to save as many of the crew as possible, but of the acceptance that the ship's work was still to be done.

A very bad start for the day. At 1.25 this morning we lost the *Goliath*. I woke up hearing the lifeboat's crew called away. I ran up on deck but was not soon enough to catch up the lifeboat. We were soon having some of the lads aboard and were dishing out blankets or anything for them to put on ... We got about eleven officers and 100 men aboard. Three died soon after ... After saving all we could we got under way and stayed at sea all night and got into Mudros in the following afternoon. We buried the dead on the way. When we arrived in Mudros we coaled 550 tons.

Vice Admiral de Robeck wrote on the 16th to Vice Admiral Limpus at Malta dockyard: 'My most important requirements are nets and lighters to which to hang the nets and place them round these ships; when that is done we can feel some confidence that the ship will not be done down by a submarine.' Six days later he wrote to Limpus regarding the loss of *Goliath:* 'I fear poor Shelford had no sort of arrangements to meet a torpedo attack: it is all quite incomprehensible to me and am recommending a Court of Enquiry later on.'[4]

The state of tension induced by the loss and the rumour of the arrival of German U-boats were felt no less by officers and men of the Mediterranean Squadron than by the Admiralty in London. Geoffrey Bromet, the RNAS seaplane pilot, entered in his diary on 10 May: 'There is now a genuine submarine flap and *Ark Royal* has been ordered to reduce her draught to fifteen feet and find a comfortable secluded spot in Kephalo Bay where she is to remain until further orders.' The crisis was brought to a head by the sinking of the battleships *Triumph* on 25 May and *Majestic* on 27 May. *Queen Elizabeth* had already been ordered home and left on 14 May. She was to begin an undignified withdrawal of the major vessels from close Peninsula support which, while tactically and strategically justified, nevertheless is recorded and was recollected by many soldiers at Helles and Anzac in terms indicating that they had been forsaken. In retrospect, many, not unnaturally, view the period as that in which the whole fate of the expedition was decided.

In a diary account written in December 1915, an unknown petty officer in a trawler acknowledged the changed situation: '... trawlers and minesweepers should never be forgotten by the troops since the submarines drove our battleships to shelter. It was then that the Turks took advantage and brought heavy guns and bombarded the troops with such fearful loss; for six weeks from sinking HMS *Triumph* the situation changed completely; all that was on the sea was trawlers and fleet sweepers to feed the Peninsula. T.B. destroyers were kept at it and must have covered many a mile, drawing the enemy's fire etc.'[5]

It goes without saying that in the Dardanelles and on the Peninsula in mid-May 1915 only a very few individuals in senior command could have been conscious of the London-centred titanic struggle being waged by argument, influence and willpower over the future development of the now less attractive Dardanelles/Gallipoli initiative. It was being fought in the War Council, the Admiralty and the War Office – to some extent in Paris and in French and British High Command on the Western Front, and in the Australian and New Zealand governments too. More than the strategic conduct of the war was in fevered debate, what was at stake may not have been life and limb, as on the Peninsula, but, certainly for the prime movers in London, ministerial position, reputation, ambition, were all on the line.

The commander of the German submarine which produced such a fateful development was Otto Hersing. His account of the exploits of *U 21* was published in 1932.[6] He had left Wilhelmshaven on the date of the Gallipoli landings and had safely navigated his way round Scotland and through the Straits of Gibraltar. He had eluded French and British patrolling destroyers and smaller craft and at about noon on 25 May approached Gaba Tepe, where *Triumph* was sighted. Hersing wrote that, 'the English ship had been shooting into the Turkish trenches and was now having a mid-day rest. It was steaming up and down the coast at about five or six knots with torpedo nets out. All the crew were on deck and sunning themselves; only the lookouts with their binoculars were watching for a U-boat.' However, *Triumph* was also being protected by the encircling sweeps of a destroyer, which made Hersing's task more difficult. He went to a depth of sixteen metres to avoid the risk of being rammed and, though the destroyer's screws were heard overhead, the submarine remained undetected. *Triumph* was torpedoed and sank, according to Hersing, in nine minutes, but he had to remain below the surface for twenty-nine hours in all before he could surface to recharge his batteries.

The recollections of Percy May on board *Triumph* belie any atmosphere of mid-day relaxation. They were at action stations, watertight doors shut and the light guns manned. Calmness on board together with the admirable seamanship of the patrolling destroyer, *Chelmer*, ensured the rescue of all but seventy-three of her complement of more than 600. Of course the rescued men were in a shocked state despite the brave cheer which the *Official History* records their giving to *Triumph* in her last plunge, but the damaging blow to May's own physical and emotional well-being came from an unexpected source. The rescued men were crowded onto the decks of *Chelmer*. May was on the fo'castle immediately below the muzzle of a 4in gun when it blasted off at the supposed sighting of the submarine. Both his eardrums were perforated and bleeding, his hair and eyebrows were singed off and, though he was not to be invalided out of the service, the searing shock of this incident was to disturb him throughout his life.[7]

The whole drama had been played out in full view of the Anzac trench system. The Turks cheered, and Hersing was even to receive congratulatory letters from Germans who were prisoners of the Japanese after the successful Anglo-Japanese taking of Tsingtao in which *Triumph* played a notable part. A New Zealand officer, C.R. Rawlings, wrote in his diary, 'HMS *Triumph* sunk out in the roadstead by Turkish submarine about 12 o'clock. All the other warships and transports are clearing out as well.' Australian Sapper Colin Grove was in a dressing station having a septic arm and leg seen to, when,

> I was astonished to see all the vessels near, hospital ships, destroyers, battleships and transports moving about turning round and round. I began to wonder what was on. Some time later I was looking out to sea and I caught sight of a flash on the water. I called some of the chaps and they agreed with me that they could see it the second time it appeared. We watched carefully and to our astonishment at 12.7 p.m. we saw the [periscope] of a submarine appear out of the water. Almost immediately there was a splash, a report and then to our alarm and disgust a terrific explosion occurred on board the HMS *Triumph*. At once a column of water shot up into the air as high as the masthead. She listed to starboard almost immediately and gradually began to lean over more and more. I at once got my telescope on her and could see the sailors all lining the decks. A large puff of black smoke came from the funnels and then everything was clear and we knew that the fires had been drawn to avoid an explosion. Already destroyers were hurrying at full speed to the scene. From the beach could be heard the order, 'four steam pinnaces make at full speed for *Triumph*'. Within a few minutes they

were there, but by this time the doomed vessel had heeled right over on her side and turned turtle, her propellors being seen easily sticking up clear of the water. Through the telescope men could be seen floating in the water, climbing up onto the pinnaces and destroyers and lining the decks of the latter. Within a few minutes other destroyers were racing off in all directions to search for the submarine. One destroyer fired four shots at something in the water but it could not be seen whether they had hit anything. At 12.19 *Triumph* sank below the water having taken twelve minutes from the time she was hit.

U 21's work was not yet completed. Hersing's published account shows that he was off Cape Helles early on the 27th and saw a great number of small craft, 'going to and fro in front of the beach like wasps around their nest', and then the masts of a battleship lying at anchor close to the shore. He found a small gap in the defensive screen and was thus able to torpedo *Majestic*, which sank quickly with the upturned keel of the bow half remaining above water. He searched unavailingly for other major vessels and proclaimed in his memoirs that, 'the whole strong English and French fleet had taken refuge in the well-protected harbour of the Isle of Lemnos'.[8]

Majestic had immediately heeled over to port at an angle of 45 degrees and remained at this angle for a minute or two. Seaman John Edward Kelly had a narrow escape before the battleship capsized. 'Managing to reach the foc'sle, he climbed down the ship's side, and when she turned on her beam ends he crawled forward to get clear of the booms and nets in which many of the men became ensnared as they jumped overboard. He then climbed up the side of *Majestic* until he got on the upturned bottom and from there he was afterwards rescued and taken aboard a steam trawler.'[9] Remarkably, though the warship went down in about seven minutes, a total of only forty-seven of the 647 crew was lost.

Midshipmen's logs reflect a general picture of alarm and urgently undertaken security precautions consequent upon these losses. Midshipman Buchanan, in *Prince George*, noted that 'We left the harbour [Mudros] at midnight [26/27 May] for Cape Helles. We were about four miles off Cape Helles at 5 a.m. when we received a signal sending us back to Mudros. We could see the *Majestic* lying off W Beach surrounded on the seaward side by colliers to prevent a torpedo attack on her.' On the torpedoing of *Majestic*, Buchanan's ship was ordered back to search for the U-boat but finished the day at Mudros. As a way of relaxing he, 'went for a picnic in the whaler in the afternoon, found a very good sandy beach for bathing from'. Ship's writer Cobb, in *Bacchante*, was at Mudros on the 25th when news arrived of the loss of *Triumph*. 'It is a very sad show ... all the ships are coming in here helter-skelter to escape the German submarines.' He added a detail which may seem to encourage further speculation on morale but no more than that: 'Had a court of inquiry on board on the suicide of a seaman in the *Carmania* yesterday. I took shorthand notes which ought to get me 10 bob.'

A further point of ironic significance in the light of later knowledge is that on the 27th, after the sinking of *Majestic*, the cruiser *Bacchante*, steering a fast zigzag course, sailed to Bodrum in search of the submarine. Several small craft and schooners were sunk in the harbour at Bodrum and on the 29th, *Bacchante*, having failed to find *U 21*, was back in Mudros. Hersing's memoirs show us that he arrived in the neighbourhood of Bodrum on 30 May. In fact the German submarine base had been secretly prepared on the north side of the Gulf of Cos by Hans von Mohl,[10] acting on Admiral Souchon's instruction to find and establish such a base. At first, fuel and other stores came to the base by camel train. The weakness of this supply link was just one of von Mohl's problems, the most serious of which was to escape detection from prowling British and French reconnaissance patrols. Two German officers, three German ratings, a Turkish naval officer and twenty-five gendarmes lived in the ruins of an old stone tower which they shared with scorpions and snakes, but they had the satisfaction of hearing a personal account from Hersing of his successes and from another U-boat captain whose prey was probably the troopship *Royal Edward*. The base, which was useful for the larger U-boats and indispensable to the small ones with only one motor, remained operational till October, when it only just escaped detection.

An interesting sidelight on the British attempt to find this base is provided by G.W. Heath.

I was on H.M. Yacht *Beryl*. This boat had belonged to the Prince of Monaco and then to Lord Inverclyde. The Admiralty was now using it for secret service work. We had to dress in civilian clothes in all ports and as we claimed to be from the New York Yachting Squadron we flew the Stars and Stripes in or near port. We had a concealed gun for self-defence during our work of searching the Aegean for oil stores which would have given an indication of a submarine base.

There had very nearly been a further Allied disaster to add to the three British battleship sinkings,[11] – the running-aground of *Albion* off Gaba Tepe on 22 May. In a letter written on the 26th, Midshipman Berridge informed his parents that it was, 'perhaps the most trying time of our existence here'. They were well within rifle range and yet everyone went aft and they were made to 'jump about' while the engines were full astern. *Canopus*, another old battleship, and destroyers, 'beautifully handled', made repeated efforts under fire to pull *Albion* clear. The Turks, 'soon began to burst shrapnel over the quarter deck but there was no one there. They tired of this and at 8.15 started to hit us with cannon shell. Almost every shot hit and every few seconds there was an explosion and the clattering of falling splinters. One shell set the twelve-pounder cordite on fire on the port side of shelter deck. It didn't last long but we ditched all the rest outside, though it was dangerous work. At 9.11 we got off... our total casualties were one killed and nine or ten wounded. Cheap, wasn't it?' It is scarcely surprising that Berridge follows his account with a well-calculated plea to his mother. 'Mother dear! I hope you don't mind, but I smoke in moderation. You will understand what a trying life this is with submarines to add to the charms. So please forgive me. It is very soothing.'[12]

That some young officers were deeply concerned at the overall significance of the naval losses is shown in Geoffrey Bromet's diary comments on the reporting of Winston Churchill's celebrated Dundee speech, in which the First Lord had commented on the sinkings. Bromet wrote:

> It is stupid to say that ships like the *Triumph*, *Majestic* and *Goliath* can easily be spared. They cannot. It is equally false to say that our losses are necessarily great but that they were expected to be and when looking at the losses involved, we must not forget the prize for which we are contending. If these statements were made in all good faith nobody could complain, but when they come from the mouth of a man who fully expected … the navy alone to force the Dardanelles and in about three months, it is scandalous … It is wrong to tell the good people of Dundee that the Dardanelles is as good as forced when the greatest difficulties have yet to be tackled and it is grossly unfair and discouraging to Mr Tommy Atkins to suggest that his job is easy and ought any day to be accomplished.

The whale-like keel of *Majestic* off W Beach was a grim sight for soldiers wending their way down to the beach for stores. It was so near that the stronger swimmers were easily able to reach it. There was however naval news of a different character which did something to counterbalance the gloom caused by the departure of the big ships and the remaining evidence of one of the three disasters. On 30 May, Second Lieutenant Duckworth wrote home that he had, 'just heard of a fine exploit by two of our submarines in the Sea of Marmara; the Commander has got the VC. Also reported the *Goeben* sunk.' His information on *Goeben* was wrong but the Marmara intelligence was accurate, with the achievements considerable.

The *Mitchell Report* carefully examined the relative effect of attacks on Turkish communications from Constantinople by submarines, aircraft and naval bombardment, and, with the help of information supplied after the war by the Turks, the Mitchell investigators had no hesitation in declaring that, 'the limitations imposed upon the Turkish communications by the operations of the submarines nearly proved decisive'. The Turks admitted that at one period in June they had only 160 rounds of small arms ammunition per man left. 'This was due to the ships sunk by the submarines and to the fact that the land route was not yet equal to the call made upon it.'[13]

The question of how critical the Turkish shortage of ammunition was is a difficult one. Examination of a report by the German officer in command of Turkish ordnance production and supply, Admiral Pieper,[14] casts some light on this matter. It indicates the tremendous efforts made to increase production from existing factories and to convert others for munitions purposes, the introduction of skilled German labour and the use of military conscript labour, the specialization of weapons and ammunition for the particular geography of the Peninsula and the successful production, just too late for use at the Dardanelles, of flame-throwers and gas shells. It was the Allied submarines which most seriously reduced the effectiveness of the vigorous attempts by the Germans to increase Turkish munitions and arms production. Between 25 April 1915 and 3 January 1916, with the single exception of the period 8 to 12 June, there was always at least one British submarine in the Marmara. There had been losses: *AE 11* was sunk on 30 April, *E 7* was sunk at the Nagara net on 4 September, the French *Turquoise* captured on 30 October and *E 11* sunk on 6 November, but Nagara Point had been passed on twenty-seven occasions and troopships had been driven from the sea by the second half of May. By that date the Turkish troops on the Peninsula were entirely dependent for reinforcements on a five-day march from Usun Kopru after a day's train journey from Constantinople. Ammunition and similar supplies had to come by bullock cart or camel train from Usun Kopru. As the submarines also attacked railways, bridges, harbours, viaducts and all food supply vessels as well as preventing Turkish naval reply to British indirect bombardment, their work was of the utmost significance.

The nature of submarine work and living conditions at this period and the constant attempts by the Turks to strengthen their defences, as for example by the Nagara net, made the strain on submariners one that should not be forgotten in recording the striking achievements of, for example, *E 20*, in her twenty-day cruise. Diesel engines powered the submarine on the surface and worked the dynamos which produced the electricity for undersea travel. When submerged, the problem of air, fouled through over-use, was made more serious by the pollution of acid fumes from the batteries, and there was also a constant and overpowering smell of oil. These were critical factors in physical and mental endurance, which was continuously being tested by the ever-present threat of the current, shore batteries, patrolling torpedo boats, mines and nets. Small wonder that there was frustrated disappointment when at first 'blood money' to the tune of about £1,000 per man was not paid to the crew of Commander Boyle's *E 14*, which had sunk a Turkish troopship and in consequence was able to claim from the Admiralty £5 per head for every member of the enemy they had put out of action.[15]

Some of the mundane problems of submarine life are described in W.G. Carr's book *By Guess and by God*.[16]

> All boats carried soap which would lather in salt water. Bathing consisted of stripping and jumping into the water while the watch kept a sharp look-out … clothes were laundered using the steel decks as a washboard, and hung up on the jumping wires to dry … Some cooking could be done on the little electric stoves but it was impossible to keep good anything that was not hermetically sealed. Canned goods, hard tack and the blessedly ubiquitous rum were the chief items on a submarine menu. Drinking water was a luxury indulged in only when one was really thirsty.

Food and drink were not the only things demanding economy. The famous submarine commander, Nasmith, used swimmers later to recover the expensive torpedo which had missed its target, the swimmers man-handling it carefully to ease it back into its tube.

Boyle, Nasmith and other submarine commanders led their crews to staggering achievements and won renown for such prolonged operations as the one in which Nasmith sank the Turkish battleship *Barbarousse Haireddine*, destroyed the Berlin-

Baghdad railway line near the viaduct at Eskihissar, and sank four ships off the Golden Horn at Constantinople and others in the Marmara.[17] On one of these exploits, Nasmith's *E 11* saved her batteries and increased excitement on board by cruising lashed to a sailing vessel to hide her from the closer shore; on another they had to proceed submerged with a mine caught on their port hydroplane. In his official report on his passage through the Nagara net on 11 August, the commander of *E 14* gave a description which shows that, while those in command bore the added burden of responsibility, none of the crew could remain unaware of their danger.[18]

I missed the gate and hit the net. It is possible the net now extends nearly the whole way across … There was a tremendous noise, scraping, banging, tearing and rumbling and it sounded as if there were two distinct obstructions as the noise nearly ceased and then came on again and we were apparently checked twice. It took about twenty seconds to get through. I was fired at on rounding Kilid Bahr and a torpedo was fired at me from Chanak, breaking surface a few yards astern of me. A mile south-west of Chanak I scraped past a mine, but it did not check me. After I got out I found some twin electric wire round my propellers and the jumping wire; also the tops of the periscope standards, the bow and various parts of the boat were scraped and scored by wires.

The achievement of Lieutenant D'Oyley Hughes who, from *E 11* on the night of 20/21 August, swam ashore in the Gulf of Ismid, pushing a tiny raft with the necessary equipment for his demolition work on the Eskihissar railway, would be difficult to surpass in the most imaginative boys' adventure story. The *Official History*[19] describes how he found the best place to scale the cliffs, which he did armed with revolver and bayonet, a torch and whistle to hand, dragging the 16lb gun-cotton charge up with him. There was too much activity on the railway viaduct itself, as the submarine's shells had previously damaged it, and so the officer had to place his charge on the approach. His use of the fuse pistol alerted the men working on the line and with an exchange of shots he made for the coast chased by Turks. He had reached the sea when he was rewarded by a huge explosion. His urgent whistle from about 500 yards out to sea failed to disclose his whereabouts to the submarine and he had to return to shore for a rest. He swam out again as dawn was breaking, and though the submarine now came under rifle fire from the cliffs and D'Oyley Hughes returned to shore, failing to recognize her in the mist, he realized his mistake, entered the sea again and was picked up utterly exhausted. It was this August exploit of *E 11* which the *Official History*[20] shows had sunk or destroyed in twenty-nine days a 'battleship, a gunboat, six transports and an armed steamer, as well as twenty-three sailing vessels, from whose cargoes of fresh victuals and fruit [Nasmith] had been able to keep his men in good health.'

The variety of submarine activity in the Marmara is recorded in the diary of Petty Officer Stephens of *E 2*. On 13 August, *E 2* had proceeded through the Straits, getting caught in the nets but freeing herself in ten minutes, despite the detonating of a mine above them. She was pursued by a destroyer but eluded her, and at 5 a.m.

on the 14th a gunboat was sighted. 'Dived and attacked her and soon disposed of her with a torpedo from our starboard beam tube. Proceeded under engines and picked up a dhow which we burned, taking six Turks out of her. Carried on till a seaplane made us a visit. This sent us under quick enough to dodge the bomb she dropped for we heard it explode when we were under.' Meeting *E 11*, they gave Nasmith's submarine ammunition and in return received a 'bag of apples'. Another dhow was caught and burned after its crew, with the crew of the previous one, was put in the dhow's small boat. More dhows were burned and their cargoes thrown overboard.

On the 18th, a steamer was sighted and a torpedo prepared until she turned out to be 'a hospital ship so we had to let her off'. On the 20th they sank a gunboat, on the 22nd a transport, and on the 24th they shelled forts and damaged other shipping in a harbour by torpedo. Munition works at Mudania were shelled on the 27th and a railway line on the 28th. Over the next few days more dhows were burned, an aeroplane was dodged, the bottom of the sea was hit and, it will be realized, the boat had to be regularly ventilated and the batteries recharged on the surface. On 6 September *E 2* made her way over, 'to the islands which we had not visited for a few days. They must have got bold as they had not seen us lately for we got our best bag of any day up there.' Sixteen dhows were sunk on that day. However, there was to be a setback on the 7th. 'Came up at 7.40 and proceeded under engines towards Constantinople.' In the evening, with their nose into the beach, they settled down at sixty feet for the night. 'Prepared a gun-cotton charge for our 1st Lieutenant in an endeavour to damage the railway. We got on our way at 2 a.m. and made our way nearer in shore till we reached twenty feet. 1st Lieutenant went off with his charge about 3 a.m. Since then we haven't seen him. Should very much like to see him back again for he was too good to lose. We waited on the beach till well after daybreak with our conning tower awash but we had to clear out as there were destroyers about …' They went back at night to try to pick up the 1st Lieutenant but he did not turn up. Shortage of fuel, poor trim and water leaks were signs that *E 2*'s trip was approaching its end. *E 7* had failed to make its rendezvous with her and they heard on their wireless of the loss of that submarine. Stephens recorded: 'Think we must have scared pretty well everything out of the Sea of Marmara as there is nothing to get hold of anywhere.' On the 14th they went straight through the nets without difficulty and, though *E 2* was shelled by the guns of Kum Kale, they were then safely on their way to their Imbros base.

Unhappily, the general record of French submarines was not so good. French historians, Chack and Antier,[21] list the weakness of the French boats in both endurance and offensive capability and the melancholy account is not disguised. 'In these conditions, it is not surprising that four of the five French submarines which tried to force the Dardanelles – *Saphir*, *Turquoise*, *Mariotte* and *Joule* – perished there.' *Bernouilli*, the fifth, failed to find any target, but the most regrettable incident concerned *Turquoise*. This vessel had arranged a rendezvous near Rodosto with the British submarine *E 20*, but was caught in the Nagara net, ran aground and was disabled by gunfire from the nearby battery. In the interior of the boat there was complete confusion. The lighting failed and before the officers could open the sea cocks to sink the boat the Turks were on board and the crew captured. Of course the submarine made a fine prize at Constantinople, though neither the Turks nor the Germans considered her sufficiently serviceable to be used in active operations. The most significant fact however was that the commander of the *Turquoise* had failed to destroy a vital book which disclosed to the Germans the rendezvous with *E 20*. The *U 14* was hurriedly made ready to keep the rendezvous and the unsuspecting British submarine was sunk. Nevertheless the British achievements beneath the sea were undeniable and, while it is impossible accurately to estimate how near the submarine had brought the Turks to being incapable of sustaining their defence of the Peninsula, the record of leadership and of the service of the undersea sailors was superb.

Chapter 12

Helles in June and July

With the exception of the Gurkha Bluff operation, the territorial gains achieved since the second battle for Krithia (6–8 May) had been negligible. Sir Ian Hamilton, frustrated by the unwillingness of the War Office to despatch reinforcements and concerned at the increasing strength of the Turks, was tempted to believe that success in a new major attack might convince Lord Kitchener of the value of sending effective numbers of reinforcements without delay.

It is possible to admire for detail the meticulous plans for the great attack of 4 June at Helles, but even allowing for the benefit of hindsight, one cannot help but wonder whether optimism, perhaps even desperate optimism, had been allowed to obscure military reality and the scant prospect of a successful attack against well-entrenched, determined defence. There were insufficient troops for the attack, but an attack was undertaken. There was insufficient heavy artillery and insufficient high-explosive ammunition. It was completely unrealistic to expect the armoured cars to make any progress at all and none was made. Inadequate reserves were available to exploit a success, yet when a breakthrough seemed just possible, the reserves were incorrectly handled. The ruse of the cheering and bayonet-waving, combined with an artillery lull, to lure the Turks from their trenches, completely failed and for a gain in the centre of the line of between 250 and 500 yards, there were 6,500 Allied killed and wounded in the morning alone. As the French troops played a critical part in both the failure of the overall offensive and the qualified success in the centre, it would seem reasonable to deal with their experience first.

On 2 June they had received an impassioned leaflet appeal from their Commander, General Gouraud:[1] 'The moment has arrived to join with our English comrades in an assault by bayonet to capture the line of Turkish trenches which faces you and hold them against every counter-attack. Not an inch of captured land must be given up.' The soldiers were exhorted to remember that, in fighting the Turks, the hated Germans were the real enemy, and that mercy was to be granted to Turks who surrendered. The troops were encouraged to fight like their brave comrades in France, who were up against far heavier artillery than they were.

On 3 June the French orders[2] were issued. 'At 11.15 there will be a general interruption of the firing. During this interruption, which is designed to give the enemy the idea that they must man their parapets, the infantry without getting out of their trenches will show their bayonets and start cheering. At 11.30 the bombardment will restart. The infantry attack will be made at mid-day precisely.' The second part of the orders provided for the first aid post nearest to Morto Bay to be used to supervise the evacuation of the wounded to hospital ships, obviously so that the more dangerous and tiring journey down to V or W Beach would not have to be undertaken.

In the attack the next day, the French infantry were unable to make any progress on their sector. The *British Official History* made a point which would have to be couched more carefully today. 'It must be admitted, indeed, that though the French corps was brilliantly staffed and commanded, the proportion of French infantrymen was insufficient to "leaven the lump" of coloured troops who formed the bulk of the infantry rank and file, and whose conduct under heavy artillery fire again proved unreliable.'[3] The report of General Simonin,[4] the Commander of the 4th Colonial Mixed Brigade, describes how the *élan* of the French troops was destroyed by the crowding of the trenches with returned wounded, by the high parapet over which they had to climb when they were far too encumbered with heavy equipment, and finally by the totally inadequate artillery preparation.

Ironically the French 75mm bombardment did much to aid the British in their attack, even though the French artillery had not been successful in their preparation for the advance of their own troops. Charles Thierry recorded in his diary: '11 a.m. The bombardment intensifies. It is terrible. Never have I heard anything like it and we are in the reserve trenches. What a terrible noise. The ships in the Straits also join in.' Raymond Weil, with the 75mms, wrote of the frustrating need to economize in the use of ammunition. His diary is written in snatches during the day. His fear that, 'in these conditions it is not going to be sufficient – but we shall see', is ominously recorded before the bombardment even started. During the bombardment and before the infantry attack, he made no effort to hide his concern. 'I am very afraid – the fusillade of small arms and machine-gun bullets is still raging', and 'we are literally inundated with bullets'. Towards the middle of the afternoon he heard by field telephone that, 'on the English front a slight advance towards Krithia had been made, but on our front it is a disaster … our poor infantry have been scythed down by the machine-guns'. Another artilleryman, Marcel Pegard, recorded in his diary the tremendous noise of the bombardment, the constant work of feeding the guns and the frustrated waiting for an order to move forward.

On the British front, in the sector held by the 42nd Division, the attack was initially successful. The *Official History*[5] noted that the 'Turks were on the run; and the Manchester Territorials, fighting like veterans, were all in high fettle'. On 8 June, Second Lieutenant Duckworth wrote of the attack that it was preceded by

an absolutely terrific bombardment by our artillery. Fifty yards of the enemy trenches kept going into the air at a time with half a dozen lyddite shells fired in a volley, and when we got into their trenches the dead bodies were as thick as flies round a jam pot. I tell you I've seen some sights that would make you physically sick if I told you and I don't mind how soon I'm back in Rochdale … I have had two men in my platoon killed called Smith and Mudd. The latter is a particularly sad case – three little kids, eldest six and has never seen the youngest. Have written his wife and told her that if there is anything you can do for her she has only got to go [and ask] and also Mrs Smith. Smith was an awfully nice fellow.

The handwriting then makes a purposeless heavy diagonal line across the page before continuing, 'Excuse that mess but I must get my neck down. Half the parapet of my dug-out has just collapsed and a large shell-case landed in the trench two feet away. It is quite hot. Luck again.'

In the Hood Battalion, RND, Joseph Murray had taken part in what he considered a 'plucky bayonet charge. Some went for the second line but never returned. After holding the line for about an hour we were forced to retire to our firing line owing to us being under enfilade fire.' Once his section had got up to the firing line, Eric Wettern, RND Engineers, saw the dreadful destruction of the re-formed Collingwood Battalion RND: 'Whole Brig, had to retire. Rotten sight to see the retreat. Nearly a panic.'

Lieutenant Savory, of the 14th Sikhs, was concerned in a personal drama on 4 June, which was to involve his parents in that most harrowing of experiences, the receipt of the buff-coloured telegram of War Office notification of, and condolence on, the loss of a son. The first letter Savory had written after the battle was on 8 June. In this he reported that they had had some hard fighting and that the regiment had done 'awfully well'. 'It is hard to say what happened on account of the censor; but I am now Adjutant, as well as a Double Company Commander, and our mess is four strong including the doctor ... so you can draw your own conclusions as to casualties etc ... May I have some tooth powder? *Not* paste, as my orderly was killed the other day with my tin of powder on him, consequently I am now reduced to borrowing.' In a second letter, written on 11 June, Savory wrote that as Ashmead Bartlett, the war correspondent, had got away with 'exaggerated yarns of this place', he himself was going to go into more details in his account of 4 June.

> Our methods here seem to be based on a theory that all tactics are rot, and that the only way to do anything at all is to rush forward bald-headed minus supports, minus reserves and in the end probably minus a limb or two. We had our own special task to advance up a nullah (a thing one has always learned should never be done, until all the ground commanding it is first seized) against the Turks who were in a wired trench at the end and also on both sides and at the top, and their machine-guns took us in front and rear and from practically every side.'

Savory then described the suicidal attack and his own good fortune in merely getting a bayonet wound in the forehead.

> Those damned Turks mutilated some of our wounded, and fired on our stretcher-bearers and wounded, when they were trying to get back to cover ... I had the extreme satisfaction of bayonetting three Turks, only in the excitement of the moment I left it sticking in the third and ran on with only a revolver ... They are dirty, unwashed looking devils and nobody loves them: but from all accounts they are getting fed up with the war in general and the Germans in

particular: one prisoner I saw volunteered the information that he hated the Germans by spitting and saying 'Allemong' in quick succession.

Before this letter, with its mixture of frustrated cynical criticism and cheerful bloodthirstiness, reached home, his parents had been officially notified that their son had been killed in action. Savory senior wrote to the officer in command of the battalion for further details, and this letter, by a further irony, was dealt with by the son, who was now acting in command. Further telegrams and a field postcard had however by this time corrected the misinformation, and his mother had optimistically written to her son that, 'they say it is very lucky to have your death announced and to live'. Savory senior wrote with understandable feeling, 'I shall laugh about it some day. At present I am only filled with a sort of exhilaration that you live – though wounded – and a thankfulness that beats expression … Good luck to you, my dear boy. I curse the Germans and in a lesser degree the Turks! and I only hope you killed a few of *both* before they winged you. I wish I was young enough to kill one or more of each. Nothing would help me more in my present frame of mind.'

A lifetime later, his son recalled that admiration for the bravery of the Turks, notably their snipers, in no way diminished the savagery of warfare: 'I can recollect the taking and shooting of a whole batch of Turkish prisoners but I would rather not talk about that.' However, he did expand upon his experience in the assault on the Turkish trenches in the Third Battle of Krithia. 'I was young and fit and had all the bravery of the novice. I ran ahead of my men and found myself standing on the edge of a Turkish trench with a Turkish soldier down below looking at me rather surprised. So I bayoneted him. I got him through the shoulder and skewered him to the back of the trench. I can watch that chap's face today.' Knocked unconscious, Savory came to, finding his body being used as an aiming rest until the Turks disappeared and he found in the trench his dead bugler mutilated, an attempt having been made to cut off his penis.

Though it would be wrong to make general observations from these memories and the 1915 correspondence, it is nevertheless as well to be aware of the extent to which the Gallipoli experience affected the Home Front. Somehow, unlike Salonika or even Mesopotamia, the scene in 1915 and 1916 of events of considerable significance which only transiently dominated the news, the public's consciousness of Gallipoli was alert, concerned and sustained. *Hansard* and the national daily papers may be cited as evidence that at Helles, Anzac and later at Suvla, there was no, 'forgotten army'. It was scarcely surprising that Gallipoli was to figure prominently on Australian recruitment posters, and that the main attraction at 'war meetings' was a 'soldier from the Dardanelles, wounded'.[6] Though the diary entries are for concluding stages in the campaign, an English schoolgirl provides an interesting illustration of the short time lag for the release of Peninsula news and comment. The diary is clearly influenced by the direction of her parents, but on 2 November 1915, young Miss Alexander wrote that 'Mummie has heard what happened at Suvla Bay', on 6 November, that Kitchener had gone out to the Dardanelles, 'where they are doing so badly', and, as early as 9 January, that Helles had been evacuated and the 'whole expedition has been a fearful waste of men's lives, ships and money'.

Recollections of the third battle of Krithia and of the later fighting in June and July at Helles support the evidence of letters and diaries. Greville Cripps was a lieutenant attached to the Royal Dublin Fusiliers and his battalion, the combined remnants of the Royal Munster and Royal Dublin Fusiliers, attacked in support of the 14th Sikhs. Cripps was in command of four Vickers machine-guns, despite his protest of ignorance of the gun. He recalled the excellent target his men made as they were herded into the narrow defile of the gully. When the Sikhs could get no further, his men were ordered up through them and he was sent in front to search for a position for his machine-guns to give covering fire. He clambered up the side of the nullah towards the Turkish wire, the posts of which he could see. Surrounded by dead and dying Sikhs, he himself came under fire. Crawling along like a snake in front of the wire he saw that it was unbroken and immensely strong. He slithered down into the gully again, watched by the men below, and tried climbing the other side, but once more soon came under fire and found the Turks above that side too. Cripps's good fortune was that he was now separated from his men and freed from the responsibility of leading them, as the major in command now instructed, round the S-bend of the gully straight into a hail of fire. The major had decided that the men could not remain where they were. The officer who led the platoon had reached the Peninsula only the night before. 'With a yell and a roar from us all, he charged round the corner' into an uproar of fire. Later in the afternoon a single mortally wounded man crawled back, the only man in that platoon to be seen alive again.

R.M. Gale (RND Engineers, Signals Company), a sapper attached on 4 June to the French troops, saw the Senegalese troops, urged on by their officers, waving their rifles with bayonets fixed.

> The rifle fire from the Turks rose to an unbelievable intensity. There was no sound of individual shots; it was a sustained roar. Looking up one expected to see a curtain of bullets and one had the feeling that even a finger above the parapet would get hit. Then the men began to scramble over the parapet. My heart ached for them as it looked like certain death to be in the open. Almost immediately the first casualty dropped back into the trench. He was a large black man and both hands were clapped to his left thigh and the blood was spurting through his fingers. My dominant feeling was one of surprise that his blood should look exactly like mine; what colour I expected it to be I cannot say. More and more wounded came in and made their way either alone or assisted to the rear. The medical arrangements were probably situated in the support line but I can only say that I saw none at all. More casualties tumbled back. Some died as they fell; some just lay where they fell and died soon; I cannot recall any able-bodied men returning. The heat and the flies beat down.

Gale was seeing war for the first time. Later in the afternoon, white French troops were moved up for an attack, and Gale caught the eye of one fixing his bayonet, patting it and smiling at the young Englishman. 'I managed to smile back.' The vividness of his impressions remained stark over the years. Later still on that day he took a wrong turning in the trench system which led him into a different sector. 'It was difficult to make progress because the floor was covered in wounded and one of them winced fearing that he was going to be trodden on.' Gale risked a look over the parapet and saw scores of khaki-clad bodies in the burned-up grass and barbed wire. 'They lay about like dead leaves in autumn. These were the men who had travelled out on *Ivernia* with me; the rough-talking Tynesiders who had been vaccinated on board and, as I had seen for myself, had arms black and swollen. I have no doubt that many died with one arm more or less incapacitated.'

It should not be presumed that preparations for, and the experience of, a major offensive dominated every week in June and July. Indeed some troops were given a respite from their privations. Gale himself was to enjoy a spell at the rest camp on Imbros. Semaphore and heliograph practice on sunbaked hills, walks in flower-covered glens with clear streams, undisturbed sea-bathing, villages and beaches where Turkish Delight, fruit and nuts could be bought, biblical scenes of water jars being filled by veiled women at wells – these were refreshing experiences, even though the thudding of the guns at Anzac could still be heard over the twelve miles of intervening water. Back on the Peninsula, though nowhere was free from shell-fire, improvised recreation was taking place. From the first, sea-bathers had stoically ignored the desultory shell-fire and the French artilleryman, Sylvestre, recalled the fascination of the French at the English preoccupation with games of football even under such fire. *The 7th Manchester Sentry* trench news-sheet recorded the progress of the battalion football team in the Dardanelles Cup. The 7th Manchesters had beaten the 8th and 6th Manchesters and the RAMC, and none of the team had been wounded when the battalion had taken its turn in the line before the next round on the 'artillery ground' against the 10th Manchesters. This game was delayed as 'shells actually dropped right into the centre of the playing pitch and even through the goals'. The delay proved an unfortunate omen for the 7th because, 'although much better than our opponents', they were defeated 1-0.[7]

On 10 July, the RND held a sports meeting. Gale himself was unplaced in the cycle race and prevented from improving on this in the sack race, which was indefinitely postponed because of 'unsporting' Turkish shelling. That weekend also saw a church service held at dusk. Non-denominational, and accompanied by rifle and machine-gun fire, the quite emotional service closed with, 'Abide with me'. Gale enumerated in his account a list of the conspicuous absentees in his Gallipoli experience – YMCA,[8] proper canteens, shops, concerts, civilians and females. There were not even any female nurses ashore, but he did remember an occasion when the padre lectured on the antiquity of the land in which they were serving.

The stranglehold of trench warfare over the possibility of any outflanking movement or successful breakthrough naturally led to the development or improvisation of weapons and equipment suited to these conditions. The trench periscope and the rifle similarly adapted were obvious examples of this, but the close proximity of the opposing trenches led to makeshift 'factories' for jam-tin bombs and the construction of catapults, some of which, from their three-legged stance, were capable of hurling these bombs 200 yards.[9] The jam-tin bombs were made of gelignite, detonators and slow-burning fuse supplied from the RE stores on W Beach. The tin was filled to the correct weight with bullets and odd pieces of metal – usually fragments of Turkish shells, according to Royal Marine, Tom Jameson, whose company had been employed as divisional bombers. George Horridge remembered the bombs being filled with stones, the fuse lit by a cigarette. The catapults were fitted with ten or twelve lengths of rubber fixed to the top end of each arm and the other ends were fixed to a wire and canvas container suitable for holding a bomb. There was quite an intricate firing mechanism, but one which would have been recognized by Roman or medieval projectile-engine experts. The fuse had of course to be lit before the release rachet was struck and it would burn for seven seconds. Slight delay before release would ensure an explosion over a shorter range or in the air above a trench.

The jam-tin bombs were also thrown by hand. Where the trenches were particularly close, chicken wire covered them in, as a protection against such missiles. Previously, men had been killed or severely wounded attempting to throw the bombs back or shield their comrades from one about to explode. Lord Rowallan has written of his experience as a young officer on the Peninsula, 'that by taking the red cover off the instantaneous fuse, it looked very like the five-second fuse and this proved a temporarily effective deterrent to the Turks' willingness to throw back the bombs'.

Two documents in the French Military Archives at Vincennes[10] indicate the concern with which new technical developments were viewed. A letter dated 9 August to the French War Office, complete with authenticating squashed, dried Gallipoli flies, was dispatched folded round a bullet. The sender, Captain Bidoz, reported in the letter that the bullet had completely torn off the arm of a soldier and he wished to know if it was an explosive one. Earlier than this, the *Société d'Optique et de Mecanique de Haute Précision* had sent out a trench periscope for trial. Anticipating the curious soldier, the accompanying instructions were precise. 'Never attempt to take one to pieces. You will ruin it. Hold the periscope by the body with the left hand, put your eye to the eye piece and adjust the focusing ring with the right hand.'

On 18 June information was found on a dead Turk that mines were being dug under the English and Australian positions. An official order declared that mine activity could seriously affect morale and the men should be made aware of the fact that once the mines had exploded the danger had passed. One presumes that this advice took it as understood that there WAS immediate danger, as the explosion was likely to be followed up closely by an attack for the purpose of taking and commanding the crater, but after that, the men in the affected sector had no need for continued anxiety. However, there can be little doubt that to be aware of a tunnel being dug and packed with explosives beneath one's position, was bound to be unnerving. For the tunnellers, whether for mines or for communication purposes, the work could be still more unnerving. Joseph Murray has written graphically[11] of the dangers of the tunnels caving in, of an underground hand-to-hand engagement with counter-miners and of a tunnel being exploded by the Turkish counter-miners.

With 4 June as an oppressive memory and with the increasing 'refinement' yet hopelessness of trench warfare, it is little wonder that a French Secret Situation report[12] on 31 July, lamenting the loss of 500 mules in a single day from shell-fire, the fact that there was danger everywhere, no possibility of rest and a general 'diminution of military valour,' counselled the immediate abandonment of Gaba Tepe and instead an attempt to be made on the Asiatic shore. In fact, further major attacks were launched in front of Krithia on 21 June by the French and by the British on 28 June and 12 July. The French, attacking in the Kereves Dere sector, planned thoroughly for their assault and used their adequate supplies of ammunition to good effect for the preliminary bombardment. Father Charles Roux[13] wrote that they were all filled with confidence and felt sure that this time worthwhile gains would be made. Gains were made and held, but they could not be exploited. Charles Thierry was to be slightly wounded in this attack, and his diary for 21 June, scribbled as might be expected, is detailed and explicit.

> Reveille at 4 a.m. Lot of alcohol in the coffee. I didn't take it as I wanted to be calm. We left our haversacks and made our way to the reserve of the first line. At 6 a.m. an intense bombardment began. Trench mortars. It is terrible. They are replying very heavily and shells are falling less than five metres from me. At 7 a.m. we see the first bayonet attack. It is the 176th Regiment. I see them, heads down running into the smoke. They have got off quickly because of the specially placed ladders. Then a second line leaves with bayonets fixed. On the left we can see the first wounded coming back. They appear to have taken two lines of trenches. Our work consists in making a sap – a shot has hit my ladder. We get our equipment ready to make the sap. It is 3 p.m.

Later in the day the diary is recommenced. They had advanced to the Turkish first line and everywhere there were dead, dying and wounded. The French were now short of ammunition. Thierry helped a wounded Turk, who kissed his hand in thanks. The shelling began again at 6 p.m. Shrapnel balls were 'falling like rain', and some seconds after, the nearest man is hit and, 'I was hit in my left hand'. In a letter to his parents he drew a diagram of his wounded hand to assure them that, despite his departure from the Peninsula for hospital treatment at Alexandria, he had been only slightly wounded.

It was about this time that Claudius Viricel wrote that on arrival at the Peninsula he had been considerably disconcerted by two sights. The first was, perhaps predictably, a corpse. The second was the hot-tempered action of an officer, beating with his baton a soldier who had accidentally snagged and broken a field telephone wire with his rifle. First impressions of the Peninsula were all too frequently unfortunate from the time the French troops, landing at V Beach, had had to move past the lines of dead Dublins and Munsters. A later reinforcement, Lieutenant Woodworth, 7th Manchesters, arriving without full kit, was curtly informed, 'Get something out of that bloody lot', and he unwillingly selected, from a pile of blood-soaked equipment, a bullet-holed haversack.[14] One diary – that of a young draft replacement officer in the Royal Munster Fusiliers, B. S. Aitcheson – managed briefly to summarize in a single day the essence of the Peninsula. Saturday, 31st July: 'Left the beach 6 a.m. Through nullah to reserve trenches. Awfully hot. No grub. Long march. Done up. Snipers and big guns. Flies!'

The British attack from Gully Ravine on 28 June suffered from lack of supporting artillery, ammunition and bombs and the Turks were able to counter-attack with 'showers of bombs'.[15] Though Gully Spur was captured, the British casualties were heavy, and the profitless expenditure of men in attacks against strongly-held positions insufficiently destroyed by artillery was demonstrated both by the Turkish counter-attacks in the first week of July, when their losses near Gully Ravine amounted to 14,000 men, and by the Allied attack on 12 July.

The history of the 5th Gurkhas[16] describes the intensity of the Turkish counter-attack on the night of the 2/3 July.

> At 3.50 a.m. the Turks were seen to debouch from the ravine opposite the positions held by the 5th and 6th Gurkhas ... Supports were rushed up and a withering fire was opened on the densely packed mass which showed as a darker shadow against the dimly lighted background. Almost at once the guns too began to take their part in the work of destruction, and, posted as they were to a flank, did vast execution by means of enfilade fire magnificently directed. Further to add to the utter hopelessness of their task, the attackers were raked from the other side by the quick-firers belonging to one of the two destroyers which had already proved of great assistance in repelling hostile counter-attacks.

Despite their losses, the Turks massed more and more men into these attacks:

> As though determined on self-immolation, even larger and more densely packed became the columns which now swarmed into the open. They were mown down in heaps; annihilated ... Extraordinary scenes occurred in our own trenches, now so congested by the presence of the supports that many men were unable to find standing room at the parapet. Some of these overcame the difficulty by climbing onto the parados and shooting from there over the heads of their comrades in front. Others were seen to hand their rifles to their more fortunately placed friends, whose own weapons had become too hot to hold.

Before the Allied attack of 12 July, the Turks were subjected to the heaviest Allied bombardment they had suffered. On the 11th, Major General Egerton informed the 52nd Lowland Division that 'G.O.C. 8th Corps does not anticipate that there will be many Turks alive in the trenches when you enter them.' On the morning of the 12th the men were informed by the Corps Commander that 'if every man goes straight for the part of the enemy's line which is the object of his unit, the capture of the trenches is assured'.

In the event, the Turkish trenches were shallow or half-completed or even non-existent and the artillery bombardment had further reduced their protective cover. The Scottish soldiers, caught in the open by machine-gun fire, suffered terrible casualties. James Barnet (2nd Lowland Field Ambulance), in an unforgettable baptism of 'active service', helped to carry the wounded back from the advanced dressing station at Backhouse Post – ceaseless work for almost three days, two men to a stretcher. In their utter weariness it was as well that they were not reminded of training at St Ninian's, Stirling: six men to a stretcher, raising and lowering of stretchers by number.

The 52nd Division took the brunt of the fighting on 12 and 13 July in the attack known as the action of Achi Baba Nullah and these troops had only just arrived on the Peninsula. One of the Scottish Battalions, the 6th Highland Light Infantry, was, with the 1/4th Royal Scots and the 1/4th King's Own Scottish Borderers, to lose many men in July. Major C. S. Black wrote in the Battalion commemorative booklet[17] after the war, that 12 July,

> had been awful but the days that followed were hideous. On Gallipoli there were no reserves. The troops that stormed and carried a position, had to consolidate and hold on to the captured ground for days or it might be weeks afterwards. And what ground it was to hold on to during those sweltering July days! All around in the open lay our own dead, whom no one could approach to bury by day or by night, for to climb out of the trench even in the dark was to court disaster. The trenches themselves were littered with the Turkish victims of our shell-fire, in places piled on top of one another to the depth of several feet. The stench was indescribable. In one communication trench that had to be used for days until another could be cut, it was necessary to crawl on hands and knees for many yards over the reeking bodies in order to keep within shelter of the parapet. The heat was stifling both day and night; water was almost unobtainable. Turkish snipers could fire direct on to the floor of some of the trenches. It was hell!

Leaflets dropped by a German aeroplane over the French lines on 26 June made the most of the miserable conditions under which the invading troops were living. Attention was drawn to the all too obvious fact that victory seemed no nearer. The losses to German submarines and the Allied dependence upon sea-borne supplies was pointed out. 'You are exposed to certain loss from hunger and thirst.' Above all, it was claimed, 'The English, insatiable in their desire to dominate, have assured themselves of your services by expenditure from which you will not profit.' However, even under these plausible blandishments, the French troops did not respond to the Turkish invitation: 'Don't hesitate any longer … Come … Our arms are open.' Some French troops did indeed, like Marcel Pegard, blame the English, 'always with their pride', for the miserable frustration being endured, particularly as the English, in individual French consideration, were on occasion 'fighting like rabbits', but the end of July was to see the prospect, with reinforcements, of an attack to change their fortunes and raise morale. Reinforcements were at last to be available in considerable number and a new offensive was to bring fresh troops buoyant with optimism, eager to tip the scales towards an Allied victory.

Chapter 13

August Offensive: Plan, Command, Men and Endeavour at Anzac

'The big move on the left' mentioned by Sergeant Cardno in his diary for 5 August was an attempt to achieve a breakout on the left of the Anzac position, to seize the heights which commanded both sides of the Peninsula, and, with this daring venture, co-ordinate a new threat to the Turks by a landing just a little further North, at Suvla Bay.

There had been serious French protests about any move which concentrated on Anzac and ignored the Asiatic shore, even though it was clear to all concerned that a landing on the southern shores of the Dardanelles, by capturing the gun batteries there, could only be for the defence of Helles, and in particular the right-wing sector occupied by the French, rather than of material assistance to any plan for a swift victory on the Peninsula. However, Hamilton did not allow the French pressure to deflect him from what he considered the right location for the decisive blow.

The Sari Bair ridge had withstood frontal attack. The limited area held at Anzac was unsuitable as a base for the landing and deployment of large reinforcements for a further such attack. To the left of the Anzac position there were, however, three gullies which might allow a new approach up the sides of the ridge leading directly to the vital objectives of Chunuk Bair and Hill 971. If, with a limited diversionary attack by the tired troops at Helles and a major diversionary attack on the right of the Anzac position, reinforcements were secretly moved in at Anzac to be used with Australians and New Zealanders in a night attack up these gullies, an attack which itself would coincide with a landing of new troops further north at Suvla Bay where there was ample room to secure a base for them, then the campaign might still be won.

The plan was imaginative. The drive for the heights, if successful, might just have secured a key to victory; the expanse of Suvla Bay, with the Kiretch Tepe Ridge won, the separate low hills secured swiftly and the more distant 'W' Hills assaulted without delay, would have created a safe and extensive base with an almost ideal landing area from the sea for reinforcements, artillery, ammunition, food, water and an army's every need. However, clearly, and in the event decisively, the plan made demands on leadership at Anzac and more particularly at Suvla, which were not met; on complex, timed co-ordination which proved impossible to achieve given the nature of the terrain and movement in the dark at Anzac; and in relation to water supply at Suvla, which was to be disastrously mismanaged. It seems to this author that the issue of whether the troops themselves were up to the tasks they were set, is shunted down the line of significance by failure in the three areas listed above.

During the four nights before 6 August, the British 13th Division was to be landed and concealed at Anzac. This in itself was a huge problem, but it was successfully accomplished. At 5.30 in the afternoon of 6 August the Australians were to attempt a more questionable part of the plan, a concentrated and sustained attack on the right flank opposite Lone Pine to draw the Turkish reserves into this area. Immediately after dusk, New Zealanders, including Maoris troops, were to clear the low ground on the left of the Anzac position for the advance of three columns up the gullies. The columns which were to move up the right-hand gullies, the Chailak Dere and the Sazli Beit Dere, consisted of New Zealand troops and the 26th Indian Mountain Battery. They were to meet on Rhododendron Spur for a joint attack on Chunuk Bair. This attack was to coincide with frontal attacks at the Nek, Pope's and Quinn's, all designed to be mutually supportive in the strike for Chunuk Bair. The left-hand column of Australians, the 29th Indian Brigade, the 21st Indian Mountain Battery and New Zealand engineers, was to move up the Aghyl Dere to win Hill Q and Koja Chemen Tepe.

The Suvla landing was to be precisely synchronized with the Anzac movement. At 9 p.m. on the 6th, the 11th Division was to land at Nibrunesi Point, take the two isolated hillocks in the face of their attack, cross the open plain ahead of them together with the seaward ridge to the left and, if possible, the three further hillocks and the foothills below the main encircling ridge, in the clefts of which lay their later objectives, the two Anafarta villages. The 11th Division would be reinforced at dawn on the 7th by the 10th Division and two further divisions would be landed within a few days.

The planning stage of each attack held certain imponderable and perhaps critical factors. At Anzac, in the broken scrub-covered terrain, was it going to be possible to maintain both surprise and co-ordination? To move by night large bodies of men up three scarcely-reconnoitred gullies and deploy them into co-ordinated surprise attacks, was a severe challenge. Concerning Suvla, there was doubt over the accuracy of reconnaissance reports which discounted the presence of effective opposition. Furthermore, if the main encircling ridge were not taken, the newly-landed troops would be under constant observation as they suffered in the heat of the Suvla plain. At least one senior Staff officer was convinced that their IX Corps had completely inadequate artillery support to deal with any serious opposition, and, for both the Anzac and the Suvla attack, water was a major problem. If lines of supply were disrupted by heavy shelling, or if fresh water could not be made available, the troops would be in considerable difficulty.

From Nibrunesi Point the coastline forms a semi-circular bay, the northern horn of which is Suvla Point. This point is the seaward entry of the Kiretch Tepe ridge which falls precipitously to the sea and rims quite steeply the plain it encloses as it meets the Tekke Tepe ridge, itself linked to the Sari Bair ridge. Isolated hillocks and the shining, white expanse of the Salt Lake were the features of the flat Suvla plain, with its low scrub, coarse grass, few trees and some cultivated fields. The more northerly landing beach, with its soft sand and grass-tussocked dunes, was backed by Hill 10. Nibrunesi Point itself was commanded by a hill called Lala Baba. Immediately inland of Lala

Baba lay the summer-dry Salt Lake. The planners were insufficiently sure that it was dry enough to allow a direct crossing to assault the next tactical objective, which was Chocolate Hill, before Green Hill, Scimitar Hill, and the 'W' Hills, foothills to the main encircling ridge, had to be taken. The villages of Anafarta Sagir to the north and Biyuk Anafarta to the south nestled into depressions in the rising ground towards the heights above. It would be difficult to imagine a more natural amphitheatre for the enactment of the drama which lay ahead. Certainly the still-preserved dugout from which the Turkish senior officer, Mustapha Kemal – on his way to legendary status – would observe the events from the seaward top shoulder of Chunuk Bair, gave him a superb view of every Allied troop movement. Concealment was at first impossible during day-time and indeed remained so until the most determined and deep spadework had been completed.

Re-affirming that the central purpose of this book is to illustrate what it was like for the men experiencing the campaign and not to evaluate plans and decisions made by High Command – though further attention will be given to these fundamentally important matters in the Epilogue – some comment must be made here on the issues of leadership and the common charge that the troops at Suvla were simply 'not up to it'.[1]

Leadership at Anzac, below the British senior officer in command, Lieutenant-General Sir William Birdwood, involved Australian, New Zealand and now British senior officers with the reinforcements assigned to this sector. With regard to the Australians, Birdwood's insistence on the Lone Pine attack was bitterly resented by the divisional commander concerned, Major-General Harold Walker. Similarly the attack at the Nek resulting in fearful losses left a bitter legacy of recrimination against those who had ordered it and then failed to arrest its suicidal futility. However, it should not be forgotten that the Australian war correspondent, Keith Murdoch, who so roundly condemned British leadership and the British reinforcement troops in his celebrated letter, was, in a less well-known letter, as critical of Australian leadership in August. On 13 September he wrote to George Pearce, the Australian Minister of Defence, 'Monash and Hughes dashed their men against a high post here – Baby 700 and they should have known after the first line went out that the job was hopeless. It was pitiful – fine Australian heart and soul and muscle wiped out in an impossible task. Oh, there is a lot of murder through incapacity.'[2]

At Suvla, in command of IX Corps, against Sir Ian Hamilton's expressed wishes, was Sir Frederick Stopford, in post by reason of availability – he was in command at the Tower of London! – and seniority, so sadly unsuitable by age and service experience for the responsibilities he would have to exercise. Discord with regard to strategy and tactics among his Staff, some men not up to the mark as divisional and brigade commanders, most of them at that level insufficiently clear as to his task and the urgency with which it had to be undertaken because they had been inadequately briefed, such was Hamilton's concern over breaches of security, all this, and inadequate mapping, laid more than just the foundations for failure.

And the men at Suvla about to see action for the first time; how may they be fairly measured? The first British troops used at Suvla and at Anzac in August, apart from the Indian Army Gurkhas and Sikhs, were largely Kitchener volunteers.[3] Widespread criticism has implied that they were therefore raw inexperienced troops, mostly of poor physique and many of them 'mere boys'. This harsh judgement of the troops at Suvla in some contemporary evidence and historical works seems to have a triple source. First, it was clearly observed from Anzac that the landing at Suvla was not being vigorously pushed inland, second, this led to bitterly vented frustration by Australians and New Zealanders, who felt that their great efforts in April, in May and now above all, in August, had been let down, and third, of course the men at Suvla were involved in failure and that incurs blame. It might be added that the attack at Anzac failed too, but in so doing it gave no excuse for notoriety.

As viewed from Anzac, inaction at Suvla remained an abiding memory, and the Suvla veterans were left to nurse their resentment at what they considered the injustice of the charge of dithering, digging and even swimming, while Australians and New Zealanders fought unsupported. The condemnation had come with the patronizing charge that men, pale and stunted by years in mills, factories and coalmines, or stooped by office work, could hardly be expected to cope with Gallipoli.[4]

In fact, a complete cross-section of society had volunteered in Britain in August and the autumn months of 1914. If the miner dominated some units, units which incidentally were to distinguish themselves at the Battle of the Somme, the farm-worker dominated others. A generally smaller stature in regiments largely drawn from mining areas does not seem to have been a handicap in the building of a tradition like that earned for example by battalions of the Northumberland Fusiliers, but to follow the argument on size, a search among the Suffolk, Dorset and Wiltshire troops would not have revealed many pale-faced, unhealthy, bent men. The new divisions had had ten months of training and were in fact far from lacking in enthusiasm, high morale and a sense of purposeful optimism, even though it cannot be maintained that their military knowledge was sufficiently deep to cope instinctively with terrain vastly different from what they had experienced in training. They were convinced that they could complete the job bravely begun and were ready to play their part in the tipping of the scales.

The charges that they were reluctant to land,[5] though confirmed by one well-placed naval officer, were unsteady under fire, and had neither the physical adequacy nor the mental readiness for the fighting, are not conclusively established. Two points are worth bearing in mind. First, at Anzac in particular, the terrain was perhaps even more difficult and the fighting just as intense as it had been in April. Second, the recent troopship voyage had left all the new arrivals except the 11th Division with little time for proper acclimatization. For example, units which spent their time at Mudros before the landing, may well have been depressed by the low morale and poor administration there, which did little to prepare them cheerfully to accept the scorching sun, dust-laden wind and prevalent diarrhoea. Furthermore, the long, dark, cold, cooped-up, six to eight hours which the Suvla troops spent in the landing 'Beetles'[6] was hardly an ideal preparation for the launching of a vigorous drive inland.

Returning to the general question of accounting for the disappointments at Suvla; the absence of adequate briefing and informed preparedness at almost all levels of command, the incapacity of the Corps Commander and of some of his divisional and brigade commanders and their staffs to maintain an active purposeful control over the advance from the beaches, these are the key factors. When, for example, Chocolate Hill was taken by troops from different regiments and brigades now confusingly intermixed, the brigade commanders concerned were two miles away at the landing areas, far too far away in the circumstance to exercise any control.

The work of command at battalion level was also bedevilled on occasions by excessive age for military campaigning and by 'innocent' ignorance of precisely what had to be accomplished. Of course it might be said that a lack of independent initiative was shown, but who was to be expected to show it and precisely under what circumstances? Initiative which involved taking independent action in the tightly-planned organization of a major military undertaking was not to be lightly undertaken by a Regular Army or a New Army officer all too conscious of the rigid chain of command. Similarly, though there were exceptions, junior officers and NCOs in command of companies or platoons could scarcely, on the wide open plain of Suvla, take independent action with a hundred or less men in an action involving thousands. Furthermore the lack of precision or any emphasis on speed in both Corps and 11th Divisional orders reflected an influential indecision as to what could be gained by the end of the first day.

The *British Official History* explains the situation succinctly.[7] Most of the brigade and battalion commanders were well over fifty years of age and had been brought out of retirement to command this Kitchener New Army of volunteers. 'Some were men who would never have attained command in times of peace, and they lacked the power of inspiring the well-educated and enthusiastic young civilians who had flocked to the Army at the first call to arms.' The irony of this enthusiasm and dash remaining untapped because of ineffectual leadership, is increased by our knowledge that the German commander of the Turkish defence of the Suvla area was aware that his force was too small to prevent a landing. He concentrated his efforts merely to delay the forward movement of the enemy troops. His troops were instructed under no account to become cut off. He had insufficient men to maintain a forward defensive line above the shore and had to rely on independent posts on the hills, hillocks and headlands, with some short lines of entrenchments in the gaps between the strong-points.

Without machine-guns or barbed wire, beach defence was by contact mines and trip wires, but the trench digging and troop movements had been done at night and with careful concealment from Allied daylight observation. The Turkish delaying capacity at Suvla was greater than was anticipated. Stopford persuaded Hamilton to sanction IX Corps orders requiring a main concentration on securing their base, and the essence of the initial bold plan and its vital link with the Anzac flank attack, had dissolved before the first troops landed at Nibrunesi Point. Anzac and Suvla were now, in effect, to be separate undertakings and hence Robert Rhodes James's assessment that 'the Suvla landing, by itself, was an irrelevancy'.[8]

On the evening of 6 August, Australian troops opposite the Lone Pine position opened the offensive from the Anzac lines. Across open ground, they were to attack deep entrenchments, most of which were roofed with heavy pine logs. So solidly constructed was the roofing that only in isolated sectors was it possible for the Australians to pull it sufficiently clear to allow themselves to drop into the darkness below and engage in the fierce hand-to-hand bayonet fighting which distinguished this terrible attack. Most of the troops who succeeded in getting into the Turkish trenches were in fact to do so by overrunning the trench and returning along the communication saps to bomb their way into the position from the rear.

Tunnels dug from the Australian front-line trenches enabled some troops to avoid the full exposure of no man's land and break out within forty yards of the Turkish line. Attempts had been made by the artillery to destroy the wire which defended this line. The troops taking part in the attack had white calico patches stitched or pinned to their backs and wore white armlets for artillery identification. It is not possible to match with unseen material the comprehensive detailed account in the *Australian Official History*,[9] but the experiences of a few men will be related here to indicate something of the ferocity, skill and courage displayed in the attack.

T.J. McKinlay recalled that 'the noise was unbearable and as it was my first experience in a battle you can imagine my feelings and thoughts, with no time to look around but look straight and fire straight. When I swung round to get some more ammunition I caught sight of my mate George falling back with blood squirting from a large hole in his head.'[10] B.M. Johnson, suddenly faced by a Turk in the confines of a trench and unable to fire as his rifle's safety catch was on, instinctively hurled the rifle like a harpoon at his enemy. In the intensity of the bombing to defend the newly-gained position, heavy casualties were suffered and inflicted. Padre McKenzie wrote on 16 August that it was an, 'awe-inspiring sight to see the boys charge and carry the Turks' trenches ... There were many who never reached the trenches, blown to pieces with shells or riddled with machine-guns and rifles. I was in it and saw it all. Men were killed and wounded on every side of me. The 4th Battalion went in with 843 and came out with 283.'[11]

C.R. Duke, then a private in the 4th Battalion, vividly remembered the checking of equipment and then the march into the forward trench from which two-man foxholes had been dug still further forward.

The tension as we waited for the whistle was unbearable. We had some seventy or eighty yards to go and as the fire grew hotter we might have been doubling over crisp straw as this was the impression the noise of the firing made on me. We had to go straight to the third-line trench over the top of the others. I got to this trench absolutely exhausted and was regaining my breath when a big Turk came charging along being pursued by two Australians; as he passed me I shot him in the back. Immediately we met more Turks and I made an attempt to bayonet one but my bayonet stuck in his leather equipment and as he was about to shoot me, he himself was shot by a rifle fired over my shoulder. I fired at a dark head peering from around the traverse and two bombs came back in reply. I was paralysed with fear waiting for them to explode but none of us was seriously hurt. We got on to the firestep to face Turks apparently about to attack when enfilade fire hit us all, killing six and leaving two of us wounded.

From the position in the Australian line known as the Pimple, the bewildering delay was clearly observed, as the troops stood on, or ran along, the earth-covered pine roof searching for a way in, while those who inadvertently moved in front of the loopholes were of course killed. The attacking troops fired into the loopholes and through such holes as they could make in the cover. In the maze of twisting communication trenches behind the main trench, parties of men were chased, bombed or bayonetted into corners or behind bends from which they waited to fire upon the first enemy troops who appeared.

The *Australian Official History* describes how the Australians quickly learned to carry their rifles vertically around the bends to avoid giving the split-second warning of a gleaming bayonet. There is ample evidence of the extraordinary, fearless catching and returning of enemy bombs in the closely-confined fighting, and of men with a hand smashed still attempting to catch and throw the bombs back. Under these conditions there was no time for the normal practice of throwing greatcoats or partly-filled sandbags onto the smouldering-fused bombs.

L.W. Graham recalled that at the close of the action many of the dead of both sides who choked the trenches were dragged into some of the Turkish communication trenches, which were then sealed off. Two men whom he saw had bayonetted each other simultaneously and remained impaled together. A man called Keysor and another in his battalion, had particularly distinguished themselves in the bombing, which had to be done from the firestep, as the Turkish trench which they held was so deep. A piece of burning rope was used to light the home-made bombs, but in catching the Turkish bombs a number of men lost a hand.

Seven Australians earned the Victoria Cross for their bravery in this attack, which drew in all the immediate Turkish reserves, but the Australian losses had been extremely severe. In the attacks on the following day the losses were to rise again. These attacks took place against German Officer's Trench, at the Nek, at Pope's and at Quinn's. They were launched without the benefit, or result, of success at Chunuk Bair and each involved harrowingly disadvantageous circumstances for the assailant.

Against German Officer's Trench, not only was the thin roof of the underground forward trench from which the assault was to be launched in danger from the three mine explosions timed to go off before the attack, but Turkish shelling seriously disrupted the movement of the troops as they assembled. It blocked trench sections and communication passages.

In the entire campaign it is difficult, however, to select an assault more desperately futile than that at the Nek, designed to contribute to the attempt by New Zealand troops to take Chunuk Bair. With the New Zealanders far short of their objective, Australians, on Russell's Top, across a narrow open ledge where the Turks themselves had attacked on 30 June at ruinous cost, were to assault the more elevated Turkish line and its support trenches. The upward-sloping, broken, low scrub-covered ground to be crossed, varied in distance according to the positions of the opposing front-line trenches but was in the region of sixty yards except where reduced by Australian forward sapping.

On a constricted front, four lines of the 3rd Light Horse Brigade were to attack in turn. The third and fourth of the lines – each line with a specific task – were from the 10th Light Horse and they had to follow two lines which had just been wiped out virtually to a man. The intensive artillery preparation had been stopped too soon, allowing the Turks to man their forward trench in time to direct a storm of fire from their rifles and, from their slightly more elevated support trenches, by Maxim machine-guns, across the few yards separating them from the Australians.

In his fine book on the Nek, the Australian Peter Burness[12] quite reasonably puts the blame for the critical seven to eight minute hiatus between the halting of the bombardment and launching of the Light Horse assault, on a failure at Divisional level to check the synchronisation of watches. He puts forward an interesting theory on the possible origin dating from awareness at the time of negotiating the 24 May armistice to bury the dead, that Turkish time seemed to differ by eight minutes from Allied time. This, of course, is today of no more than historical interest. The failure was fundamental, though not exclusively so, to the disaster which befell the men waiting to carry out their orders.

Of the first line, most of the officers and men were killed within the first five yards of the attempt to leave their own trench. Few from the second line got much further. With the distressing wreckage of dead, dying and wounded encumbering their movement in the trench, the 10th Light Horse then took up positions on the fire-step for their assault, reaching to grasp the pegs knocked into the forward face of the trench to help haul themselves out of the deep Turkish-dug position.

The youngest man in the regiment, C.H. Williams, finding himself between the sergeant and the sergeant major, was told that there was no hope for them and that he must lie down immediately he got out of the trench. Once out, he was in fact pulled down and, with a small party which had taken similar action, he found cover in a slight dip. They stayed there until dark and then crawled back. Enie Bain was on the left in the fourth line and his brother, a sergeant major, was more to the right, but: 'I saw and heard him moving along the line calling to the men to get ready and that they would be up on Baby 700 for breakfast. Well, the right of the line did go over the top and my brother was killed. We were not ordered out of the trenches as orders to cancel the fourth-line attack in view of the massacre reached us just in time. I was soon told that my brother had been brought in dying. I didn't get to him in time and all there was left for me to do was to bury him and write to his wife.'

Two pairs of brothers were killed in the same attack. Perhaps thirty or forty yards had had to be covered, and chance, even against the curtain of fire, allowed a very small number of men to reach the enemy parapet. Those who got inside were killed, one heroically planting his signal flag to be clearly seen for a short while sticking up from the trench. A number of men crouched up against the parapet between the firing loops. They could see bayonets and brown arms above them but, until they were put out of action, they continued lobbing bombs backwards into the trench.

With nightfall a straggling number of wounded attempted to crawl laterally into cover or directly back to the Australian line past dead and dying. Failure at the Nek enabled the Turks, who had suffered few casualties, devastatingly to enfilade the

Royal Welch Fusilier attack on the right towards the Chessboard. In addition to this, the first-line Australian attack at Quinn's was as costly a failure as that suffered at the Nek. These attacks, mercifully now halted at Quinn's, had been launched without the essential, planned pre-condition of successful progress in the leftward flanking attack. There seems to be no parallel on the Peninsula to this case of men going so knowingly and fruitlessly to their deaths. To read in the *Australian Official History* the detailed, moving account of officers and men given time to be aware of the immediacy of their death, and not merely of danger, is a disturbing and humbling experience. In the attack at the Nek, and in particular for those in the second, third, and fourth lines, that comforting, if unrealistic, feeling that, 'it can't happen to me', was totally removed from the men involved. The evidence of what was about to happen to them was before their eyes. There was no wavering and every man steeled himself sufficiently for what was to be the supreme but useless sacrifice. That the attack might serve as a microcosm of the appalling futility of warfare, of trench warfare in particular, and of the burden sometimes borne by the soldier, does not rob the men of their surpassing steadfastness in the face of death. A senior officer, writing a letter of sympathy to the parents of Lieutenant W.E. Addison, killed in this offensive, wondered, 'whether a splendid death like his is not more a matter for congratulation than of condolence', and across the ocean of time which separates us from 1915, the meaning behind such an arresting sentiment can just be grasped, however reluctantly, by anyone fully aware of events at the Nek in the early morning of 7 August.[13]

The complicated and interrelated movements in the flank attack from Anzac and the resultant four-day battle, are covered with meticulous detail in the *Australian Official History* and no attempt will be made here to re-tell something already so brilliantly related. It is nevertheless possible within a general framework to be aware of the differing nature of unit experience by looking at the evidence from individuals involved in separated sectors of the attack and at various periods before its final withdrawal in the face of the Turkish counter-attack.

The assault up the Aghyl, Chailak and Sazli Beit gullies which was the key to the whole offensive, necessitated the clearing of the foothill approaches to the three chosen routes for the ascent to seize the heights. The men were as fully briefed as available information allowed and there was a sense of purpose and qualified optimism in the air which rejuvenated men drained by dysentery and privation. For 6 August, A.L. Guppy entered in his diary: 'All officers and NCOs were lined up today and General Monash told us something of what our next job is going to be. Our company officers then showed us on maps how we were to carry out our work and told us all the plans … and now at dusk we, with full water bottles and two days' rations, are awaiting orders to move. The boys are all in great spirits in the expectations of another move after the inactivity of the last weeks. It is strange the feelings that possess men on the eve of an action.'[14]

Lieutenant A.N. Oakey was to earn a Military Cross for his work directing a party of New Zealand sappers using a ship's grapnel as silently as possible to pull clear the wire entanglements at the bottom of the Chailak Dere. They came under fire from an enfilading trench but nevertheless removed five out of the six bays of timber and wire. With the Otago Mounted Rifles leading the initial attack on the foothills below the Chailak Dere was Trooper M.A. Richards. 'We moved into the creek but the Turks must have had wind of our intended attack: just as we got into the creek they opened fire … we did not fire a shot as we went out without any cartridge in our rifles. We were told to take the place with the bayonet and by jove we did in great style … two Turks came around a bush and I got them both.' His diary account shows the urgency with which the New Zealanders moved through the difficult country, having only very short rest spells before resuming the climb. In spite of this the anticipated time for the completion of this preparatory attack was two and a half hours longer than had been estimated.

Casualties had been quite heavy and, according to Sergeant Cardno, it was difficult to find and move them in the dark to the field dressing station which had been established in a captured Turkish officers' dugout. Later, as the wounded came flooding back from the heavy fighting on the 8th and 9th, the clearing stations got so crammed it became impossible to move the men down to the beach to ease the overcrowding and get medical attention for them under less hard-pressed conditions. The inadequacy of the hospital ship arrangements was regretfully recorded by Edney Moore of the Australian Army Medical Corps: 'We filled up two which are in now, immediately and so far no others have turned up. It is awful to see poor fellows who it is impossible to help here, whereas if they could be got on a hospital boat, there is no doubt many lives could be saved.'

An especially moving sound during the evening of the 6th had been that of the Maori soldiers singing, in their impressive harmony, 'Jesu Lover of my Soul', during a service in which their chaplain had spoken to them of the special way in which the good name of the Maori people lay in their keeping. Later on, the fiery 'Komate', from those same throats, was to resound from the hill that they had captured. 'The war cry mingled strangely with the cheers of the Aucklanders.'[15]

The column which was to make use of the successful capture of the foothills was also largely composed of New Zealand troops, together with men of the 26th Indian Mountain Battery. By the Sazli Beit Dere and the Chailak Dere, the infantrymen were to assault Chunuk Bair itself. It was during the night attack that a most unusual scene took place in which Turkish troops on Table Top actually helped men of the 8th Company Otago Battalion, commanded by Second Lieutenant Gibson Bishop, up the last yards, hugging and kissing some of them presumably because they were glad to surrender and escape the continued misery. From here, the New Zealanders moved up Rhododendron Spur and onto the slopes of Chunuk Bair, which was also under attack by the 10th Gurkhas. In the darkness however, the Canterbury Battalion, moving up the Sazli Beit Dere, had become lost. From that battalion a Private Hunter kept a diary: his entry for those hours of darkness is charitable in view of the tiredness and frustration all must have felt. 'Came around to the valley between No. 1 and No. 3 outpost, advanced up there for nearly a mile and then came back again. The Heads got a bit mixed.'

Hunter's diary records that the battalion got up to the head of the valley, 'just at day break' and their entry into a blind side-gully resulted in the troops on the higher slopes being unsupported for any further advance. As has been mentioned, the delay contributed to and worsened events at the Nek, Quinn's Post and other related engagements but, without his Canterbury men, the commanding officer of the New Zealand Brigade, Brigadier General Francis Johnston, fatefully held up further advance. Later he was to compound this error, but paradoxically, by sending forward just one battalion, the Auckland Battalion, together with two companies of the 2/10th Gurkhas, into the assault. Taking every advantage of the time lapse since first threatened, the Turks now had sufficient troops at a location known as the Pinnacle summarily to deal with their assailants. Command issues here, not just at Suvla, are high-lit by the commanding officer of the Wellington Battalion, Lieutenant Colonel William Malone, now refusing Johnston's order to advance, in what Malone judged to be futile wastefulness, just before orders came from on high, Major General Alexander Godley, the divisional commander, to suspend further operations.

To prepare the way for the much longer and more difficult movement of the attack up the Aghyl Dere, British troops secured the first objective. The main assaulting force consisted of Australians, New Zealanders, the 21st Indian Mountain Battery, Gurkhas and Sikhs. The timetable for this attack seemed to ignore the fact that a good deal of the ground was un-reconnoitred scrub and was likely to be extremely difficult to negotiate in the dark. Furthermore the organization of a long composite column in the broken ground was sure to be exceptionally demanding if speed, silence, and contiguity, were to be essential elements. In the event, a 'short cut' proved disastrously ill-advised and further delays, interminable halts, and fire from scattered and unseen enemies, had so seriously exhausted the troops that two Australian battalions dug in, unable to go further. It should be noted that the assaulting troops here were not fresh to the Peninsula and were in a weakened condition as a result of widespread dysentery.

The Gurkhas and Sikhs, totally unfamiliar with the ground, had, with varying degrees of delay and loss of direction, taken up position to the right of the Australians and far short of the objectives that the column had been set. Even at the planning stage, the unrealistic attempt to win Hill 971 reduced the chance of gaining and holding Chunuk Bair, the loss of which was in fact to prove decisive as Turkish reinforcements arrived here just in time to forestall an Allied local coup, which, momentarily, had some real possibility of development.

Within three days of the attack, Lieutenant Savory, of the 14th Sikhs, had written of the, 'very high country covered with dense scrub in places sometimes six feet high and, as you can imagine, perfect for defence but damned hard for the attackers ... none of us is very hard after three months of enforced inactivity in the trenches, and consequently when attacking up a very steep slope we all get so done up that we have to stop for a bit to rest.'

The frustrations of the 2/10th Gurkhas were expressed by a lieutenant who had been attached to them because his regiment, the 27th Punjabis, contained so many Muslims that it had been thought inadvisable to send it to Gallipoli. Saturday, 7 August: 'Went wrong last night and never arrived, so had to take the hill by day. Did a charge with some N. Zealanders but never arrived – so stayed out with thirty men and about thirty New Zealanders until dark and then made our way in. Got some water somehow or other. Dossed down for night in a gully. Collected some survivors from another company who came in after dark. Scott wounded and missing. Stevenson, Birkbeck, Campbell killed.'

The scrub had been so thick that it is recorded in the *History of the 5th Royal Gurkha Rifles*[16] that one man, unable to fire his rifle through it, had set an example by using his kukri to cut loopholes in the dried, prickly vegetation. It was the vicious nature of the thorns and snares of this scrub that an Australian, E.C. Skinner, referred to in a letter describing the necessity to drop quickly to the ground regardless of the discomfort, when there was need for cover or opportunity for rest. In the attack, Second Lieutenant Cosby, with some 1/5th Gurkhas, got to within 200 yards of the summit. Here, they were pinned down for the rest of the day by withering fire but managed to disengage and retire under cover of darkness.

For the Australian D. Marks[17] in the 13th Battalion, the night march had provided constant problems of co-ordination, but in all the difficulties, 'the Padre would insist upon staying at the head of the column with us. The night was fearfully dark and as we turned into the Aghyl Dere shots broke out from ridges on right and left. A platoon was detailed to clear each side, the men went in with the bayonet and nothing was heard but a few shrieks and some prisoners were immediately brought in … Our native guide and the interpreter were continually being apprehended by our covering party and stood in imminent peril of their lives.' This diary included for the same day, 7 August, an interesting reference not merely to the discovery of a number of wells with clear, cool water but a farmhouse with bees and blackberries. 'Men robbed the hives with the aid of their gas helmets', a constructive use on the Peninsula for equipment never needed for its military purpose. Among the prisoners taken by the Wellington Mounted Rifles were, 'two young fellows, their father, and his father, the latter a grey-haired patriot whose hand the son took whenever we shifted them'.[18]

On the 7th, the delayed and weakened New Zealand and Gurkha attack failed to take Chunuk Bair. The left-flank attack and the conditions it faced are described in the *British Official History*. 'The 4th Australian Brigade had not moved since dawn, and the Indian Brigade, widely scattered, had lost all cohesion. The heat of the day had been tropical, water was very scarce; and the New Army battalions, utterly unaccustomed to hill climbing and suffering acutely from thirst, had been tired out to no purpose.'[19]

When the attack was resumed on the 8th, despite strong opposition frustrating the weary Australians, the 1/6th Gurkhas, later reinforced by British troops, got to within reach of the crest of Hill Q, and New Zealand troops gained the top of Chunuk Bair. Enfilade fire severely reduced the number of British troops able to join the New Zealanders on Chunuk Bair and the latter were experiencing difficulty in digging in because of the rockiness of the ground. When the Turkish withdrawal was discontinued and their reinforcements arrived, those troops forward of the crest were almost all killed.[20]

There was a desperate urgency for adequate communications and for immediate reinforcement. Under heavy rifle fire the small figure of Corporal C.R.G. Bassett repeatedly laid out new telephone wire and repaired it as it was damaged by shell-fire. This soldier whose chest measurements had failed two medical scrutinies, and who had been so concerned on 25 April whether he would be equal to the test he was to face, was to be rewarded with the Victoria Cross for his courage during the long hours on Chunuk Bair.

The work of the Wellington Battalion in holding much of the crest until they were relieved in the evening, had been heroic. Successive short bayonet rushes were launched at the Turks to keep them at bay and the New Zealanders even had to vacate their own shallow trench when it became filled with their own dead and dying. Reinforced by the Auckland Mounted Rifles, the Wellingtons disguised their lack of ammunition, bombs and adequate support, by the sheer aggression of their defence.

On Chunuk Bair the lack of water was a desperate problem, as was the impossibility of attending to isolated wounded. These men, if unable to find or scrape any cover, were exposed there to be hit by machine-gun or rifle fire, fragments from bomb or shell explosions or by shrapnel shell balls. Few survived. The unwounded were in no continuous line but rather in isolated groups where a degree of cover had been found or laboriously dug. Short of food, water, ammunition and close companionship, as well as being under constant fire, the prolongation of intolerable strain on this height matches with a different intensity the ferocity of Lone Pine and the acceptance of death at the Nek.

There was, however, to be a final tragedy to destroy the possibility of profit from the endurance of these men and it was not to be associated with the Turkish reinforcements moving up Hill Q and Chunuk Bair, nor with the sad absence of aggressive leadership at Suvla. In the renewal of the attack on these heights on the 9th, the 1/6th Gurkhas and some supporting South Lancashires took Hill Q, or at least the saddle between it and Chunuk Bair. An officer in the South Lancashires, G.R. Mott, led his men into a charge with his hunting horn and it was not until a retirement on the same day that he discovered, 'my watch pocket had been shot through and my watch cut off the leather chain, also a small bottle of citronelle sent to me for flies, scattered to pieces ... my equipment on the right side cut away badly and my puttees ripped in two pieces'. However, in the very moment of the encouraging possibility opened up by this Gurkha and South Lancashire success, howitzer shells began bursting among them. The *Australian Official History* asserts that there is no doubt that the shelling here had come from within the Anzac position.[21] At about the same time, New Zealand troops were shelled from the same source. It was believed at the time, and is indeed recorded in diaries and letters, that the Gurkhas and New Zealanders had been shelled by the Navy and some historians have supported this view. Whatever the truth of the matter, the effect was disastrous.

The demoralizing nature of the experience was clearly illustrated in the harrowing details of an undated letter written from hospital by a New Zealand survivor, H.E.

Browne. He wrote of men flung into the air by the exploding shells, of silhouetted limbs outspread against the sky, and of a man unable to take the strain being told that he would be bayonetted if he did not shut up. 'Poor old Hughie Pringle was killed, his throat ripped by a piece [of shell] and presently there came groping past us Clutha McKenzie blinded. Young Mell Bull his jaw smashed and another unrecognizable. As they passed us their faces were covered in blood and seemed to hang in tatters … Physical fear is a strange thing. While all are more or less affected by it in a tight corner, most manage to contain it, but in some cases it causes them to lose all control over themselves.[22]

For men who had seen the Turks running before their charge, as the Gurkhas, Warwicks and South Lancashires had, and for the New Zealanders who had resisted every effort to throw them from their tenaciously-held position, this shelling led to confusion, dismay and of course recrimination. The Turks, now in greater strength, counter-attacked on the morning of the 10th and both Chunuk Bair and the Pinnacle fell into their hands. The British units holding these positions were intermixed and their numerical strength was perhaps 2,000. The attack came when not all were in position and they were overwhelmed by wave upon wave of Turks advancing with the bayonet. Advantage to the attacker was a new phenomenon on the Peninsula and the terrain held by the British gave advantage to troops able to attack in sufficient numbers from several flanks at once in this manner. Those troops who remained against the onslaught were bayonetted.

Reginald Savory witnessed the desperate, disorganised retirement from positions won by such endeavour. He later likened it to the bursting of a dam, a flood of men animated simply by sheer terror, confusion, utter weariness, men at the end of their physical tether, without unit cohesion or officers they knew.[23]

The Turks lost heavily too, especially when Captain Wallingford's New Zealand machine-guns at the Apex were able to sweep the Turks with enfilading fire as they swarmed down the slope of Chunuk Bair towards the Farm. As far as British losses were concerned, of 890 men of the 10th Hants who went into action in this engagement, 508 were killed, wounded or missing. Perhaps the most pitiful fate was that of survivors of the 5th Wiltshires, who lay between the lines for a fortnight in the Sazli Beit Dere. Water was found from a spring but was apparently supplemented by some from sympathetic Turks who knew where their foes were but neither fired on them nor took them prisoner. In an attempt to escape, some were killed by the Australians who mistook them for the enemy, and others by the Turks, who had observed their dash. Two men managed to reach the New Zealanders and one, in his weakened condition, was carried out to help to locate and rescue the five remaining survivors.[24]

August 10th did not see the end of the Allied offensive. The Suvla attacks up to and including the major attempt to advance on the 21st to take Scimitar Hill and the W Hills will be described in the next chapter. From the Anzac beachhead, on the 21st, an attempt was made to link Anzac to Suvla more securely by capturing Hill 60. This scarcely discernible rise was defended by a maze of trenches and had not been adequately photographed from the air. The composite force which attacked Hill 60 from Anzac, like the Yeomanry in their crossing of the Salt Lake on the same day and the 29th Division in its advance on the W Hills, was to suffer cruelly. Australian, New Zealand, Gurkha and British troops maintained their attack and renewed it on the 29th but the summit of the hill was not taken.

Just before one of these attacks, a New Zealander was approached by his closest friend, who, white and trembling, confided that he was afraid. The New Zealander, J.F. Rudd, did all he could to comfort his friend but the latter was sure he was soon to be killed. With final checking of ammunition and guns completed, 'I can still remember the feeling as we looked at our watches and saw the time creeping nearer to five o'clock. The whistle went and out hopped the first row of men and they fell like ninepins, then the second row went out and my friend Jack Bindon's premonition was fulfilled.'

Fear of a different kind had been experienced a fortnight or so earlier by a sixteen-year-old New Zealander, N.R. Maxwell, who had falsely stated his age in order to get to Gallipoli. Given bullet-holed, blood-stained equipment on arrival, he had ditched his rifle and fled to a side gully on 8 August. Once there, he had 'manufactured' some sapping work for himself to do. Found by an officer and ordered to get a rifle from those lying beside some corpses, the young soldier was still further unnerved by the voice of the nearest 'corpse' admonishing him, 'put that bloody rifle down, sonny, we're not all dead here'.

Conditions on Hill 60 were grim even if familiar to, 'old hands'. The bodies of Turks had to be used to make parapets at the rear of the captured trenches, which were of course facing the wrong way. Deepening the trench enabled the bodies to be covered but, as the heat aided decay, dark smudges appeared, discolouring the sandy clay. A blackened hand would show, or perhaps a foot, and fat maggots dropped from them onto the rations of the living. Further horror in the attack on Hill 60 lay in the scrub catching fire, burning wounded and setting off the grenades some of the dead and wounded had been carrying. In the close bombing work, Second Lieutenant Throssell's cool gallantry, described in the *Australian Official History*,[25] leading the defence of an exposed position, is yet another example of sustained, inspiring courage combined with the virtues of swift reactions and a practical response to each problem which faced the small party of six or more men.

With the narrow but costly failure at Hill 60, the Allied attacks on the Peninsula fronts ended. As a Gloucestershire soldier was to write to the Rector of Dyrham, 'progress is very slow but it always is a very hard job to put a man out of his home'.[26]

On 2 September the Turkish Lieutenant-Colonel Fahrettin Altay wrote to his father:

The hopes of the British have collapsed. Will they bring up fresh troops, perhaps Italian, and land them on the old beaches – or elsewhere? We are used to it and let them come if they like. In one respect it helps our soldiers, who strip all the British dead of their boots, and now have fine British boots on their own feet … When the rains begin, unpleasant as they will be in our trenches and saps, they will be far worse for the British. For they will be stuck in the marshes and swamps on the low ground, and the rain and the floods pouring down the ravines that descend from our lines will swamp them.

The accuracy of this officer's assessment of British strategic hopes is matched by that of his prediction of the winter discomforts which would bring new miseries to the Allied troops, now without prospect of doing more than holding on.

5. Suvla Bay.

Chapter 14

August Offensive: the Landing at Suvla

Towed in the dark by destroyers to within 500 yards of the shore, the new large motor lighters took the first troops, 500 to a lighter, from Imbros to their Suvla landing, 'B' Beach, a long sandy beach South of Nibrunesi Point. All went well. Fred Bradford was the 'A' Company signaller of the 6th Green Howards, which was to have the distinction of being the first New Army unit to go into an attack. It was just after 9.30 p.m. on the sixth of August. He recalled that: 'Getting ashore was not too bad. We lined up on the beach and got our orders. No firing – bayonet only. I saw Captain Morgan look at his wrist compass and point in the direction of the hill ahead [Lala Baba]. As we went towards the hill, firing broke out and I heard Turks screaming "Allah, Allah". A lot of our men were killed, including Captain Morgan. The wounded were crying out and in the darkness it was all confusion.' Nevertheless, in bitter fighting, the hill was captured by troops tired from morning training as well as from the demands of the trip from Imbros and the strain of operating in darkness. Bradford did not know that a Staff Officer of the 11th Division, Captain John Coleridge, sent out early on the morning of the 8th to report on progress and the condition of the units engaged, came upon the Green Howards, that is the 6th Yorks, and judged that, 'the battalion (now) had only five officers with it, and the men were distinctly demoralised. In my opinion the battalion wanted relief.'[1] I think we can presume that by 'wanted' his meaning was 'needed'.

Troops being landed further to the left of Nibrunesi Point, within the bay itself, 'A' Beach, were delayed by the approach of their lighters, towed by three destroyers. There were problems with the tow ropes and when the lighters attempted to make for shore under the power of their own engines, they hit sandbanks and reefs. Alerted now, the Turks opened fire on the stranded boats. It was pitch dark and at first it was judged the water was too deep for the men to disembark. With their heavy packs, cumbersome equipment and rifles, certainly many would have drowned. There were inevitable delays until in one case, a battalion's commanding officer marshalled his men for orderly disembarkation and called successfully for taller men to carry and hold a rope ashore to assist those who might otherwise have drowned. But there was further confusion as the troops, in consequence, got ashore in the wrong place.[2]

Delays from hitting the sandbanks or reefs and failing to find bearings once ashore, were affecting the movement inland of other units too, and the wide-open expanse of the area was proving in the dark as confusing as the narrower confines of Anzac had been in April. Hill 10 could not even be located, let alone taken.

At daylight, 'the position at Suvla was verging on chaos ... little of the situation was as yet known at 11th Division headquarters and nothing of it by the Corps

Commander'.[3] On the question of events at Suvla being outside the knowledge, let alone control, of the higher command, it is interesting to note the personal diary of a ship's writer on *Triad*, the armed yacht at Imbros used as de Robeck's HQ, James Luck, who was constantly engaged upon naval HQ secretarial work for the Staff, wrote on 6 August, 'if everything comes off as we expect, we ought to be well on the road to Constantinople before long. We have wonderful organization but it seems to take an awful time to set it going.' On 7 August: 'Admiral [de Robeck] has not returned from the *Chatham* as expected, therefore I conclude we are doing well and he is going to follow up.' On 8 August: 'Evidently everything is progressing swimmingly. From the signals I see we have taken Chocolate Hill.' It is little wonder that on 12 August Luck wrote, 'The Admiral seems to be anxious with regard to the situation. I wonder what is the matter?'

Something certainly had been the matter! The 10th Irish Division had landed on the morning of the 7th after yet more delays and found neither progress nor orders to encourage them. The dash and enthusiasm of the keenest troops can scarcely have remained unaffected by the experience recorded in the diary of Lieutenant Terence Verschoyle of the 5th Royal Inniskillings.

7 August: Arrived off Suvla Bay at 9 a.m. Watched bombardment by naval guns all morning. Landed via lighter at 4 p.m. Took up position on hills north side of bay. Pretty cold night.

8 August: Glorious day. Wandered to and fro along hillside all day, not firing a shot and only occasional sniping against us. Took up another line at night.

9 August:Beautiful day. Remained on hill all day moving forward about 200 yards at night and dug in.

10 August. In same position all day; a good deal of sniping going on. Kirk and self nearly strafed through excessive curiosity.

11 August: Glorious day. Still on hill. A fair amount of sniping causing odd casualties. Bathed in morning – most refreshing. A trip wire put up in front by REs.

In this fashion the diarist proceeds until he is involved in an attack on the 15th. Thus the inaction, viewed with dismay by the troops on the left at Anzac, was graphically recorded by one of the men concerned. For other men, like Corporal J.H. Tansley of the York and Lancaster Regiment, there was abundant physical exertion as well as fighting, but his diary too shows that confusion abounded.

7th: Early morning landed on Peninsula under fire. Dawn-made charge under fierce shrapnel and rifle fire. Had many narrow escapes.

8th: Made an attack. Marching all night.

9th: Made an attack then retired. 10th: Made an attack under severe rifle fire. Came back to support trench.

11th: Went to beach to reorganize. Under shrapnel fire.

British and French aerial reconnaissance, in flights on the 7th and 8th, had reported the absence of any strong opposition in face of the landing and indeed those units which had pressed forward had demonstrated the accuracy of this intelligence. The delay in pressing forward had however been too long – Turkish reinforcements, after a forced march, were arriving in strength. In the early morning of the 9th, the 6th Battalion of the East Yorkshire Regiment, after delays through lack of support, attacked up the slopes of Tekke Tepe. They were finally surrounded, after losing heavy casualties to the fire of the newly-arrived defenders who had just reached the ridge in time.[4] The wasted days at Suvla had been disastrously decisive. If the men had been denied the opportunity of securing victory, they were now to be provided with the privilege of advancing, with inadequate artillery support, across the Suvla plain against an enemy now more strongly assembled, well-emplaced and with artillery able to fire directly upon a target in full observation. All the advantages of surprise and great superiority in numbers had been frittered away and no one would pay more dearly for this than the troops who had been allowed to remain in their early positions. From 7 August they had been affected with problems which were at one and the same time the cause and the result of their inaction.

A really desperate shortage of water developed quite inexcusably at Suvla. A merchant vessel specifically converted to bring pumps, hoses, water tanks and well-drilling equipment was delayed in getting moored to the shore as were four water lighters. Water receptacles, requisitioned in vast numbers, and mules to transport them, were simply not there either. In addition, the general uncertainty as to what to do, but the need to remain alert to do it when orders came up and when that further move would be required, led to a sleeplessness which worsened the exhaustion produced by the heat, lack of water, digging, marching and counter-marching. It is well-documented that men made irresponsible by their acute thirst, cut for their immediate benefit the hoses filling the water tanks when at last hoses and tanks were in place. There had been a complete failure to transport and distribute the necessary water swiftly, to dig for water with sufficient urgency, or to locate, test and defend the known wells. This resulted in dreadful privation. Verschoyle recalled that on the left flank none of them would ever forget the water supply maintained by the destroyer *Grampus* during their scorching experience on the Kiretch Tepe ridge. General Stopford wrote somewhat ingenuously to Hamilton on the 10th that the lack of water was one of the main reasons for the failure of his men to make the anticipated advance inland, thus rightly condemning the administrative planning of his own Staff as well as the inaction of the divisional and brigade Staffs. Though the lack of an adequate supply was felt most cruelly in the central area inland of the beach, flat and fully exposed to the sun, there is abundant contemporary and recollected evidence that real thirst had been a new and savage experience for almost all the men in the first days of the landing.

Two Territorial divisions, the 53rd Division, landed on the 9th, and the 54th, on the following day, were to be thrown directly into the fray just as Turkish reinforcements had also arrived, and with Turkish artillery sited in their incomparably commanding position, the prospect of a successful general advance across the Suvla plain had been dramatically reduced. Furthermore, the attack, when launched, would be totally without the element of surprise and even without unequivocally clear objectives. There was a further irony in that Sir Ian Hamilton, his focus being on the breakout from Anzac, learning to his fury of what seemed to him inexplicable lack of progress at Suvla, landed there to confer with Stopford and then ordered re-direction of the urgent move forward he had required. This caused further delay as new assembly areas had to be reached, new orders drafted and, not least significant, objectives narrowly held, would now have to be conceded. The subsequent regaining of these re-defended geographical features would cost many more lives.

E.D. Wolton, an officer with the 1/5th Battalion of the Suffolk Regiment in the 54th Division, wrote of their advance at 4 p.m. on the 12th:

> The enemy were not surprised but we were, as no battle orders had been given and we were literally flung into action unprepared at a minute's notice. Our own colonel, Colonel Armes, told us verbally at the commencement of the action that we were to advance a mile to drive out snipers! No physical objective was given, so in consequence our line of attack was disjointed and irregular depending upon the character of the terrain and the measure of the local opposition. It was for this reason that whole detachments of our brigade were wiped out piecemeal.

As early as the 9th, the increasing intensity of the firing through the dry scrub had started bush fires which sent aloft billowing clouds of black smoke, hiding the awful tragedies contained within the heart of the swift-spreading fire. Of the attack on the 21st, C.W. Brand wrote six days later:

> We trudged forward for over two and a half miles, over a mile of which was swept by shrapnel fire, the shells falling all round us and men falling in every direction. The hills in the distance were just huge crackling mounds of rifle fire while here and there the sharp insistent rapping of the machine-guns was heard. The ground was covered in places with dry gorse and stunted trees which caught fire and crackled fiercely. Many of the wounded had crawled under these bushes, thinking in a frenzy of pain that they would afford protection, instead of which the fires spread and they were found burnt to death, sometimes past all recognition by the stretcher-bearers.

C.F. Mayne, a surgeon-lieutenant with these stretcher-bearers, remembered the frantic efforts with spades to beat out the flames threatening to engulf men still alive. Unburied, blackened, charred corpses and the loathsome, swollen, decomposition of other bodies in clearly recognizable units, imprinted ineffaceable memories for many.

Of the attack on the 21st, J.C. Dart, a signaller in the 10th Irish Division, wrote: 'Mounted Brigades walked across plain in most orderly fashion but suffered severely'. He was easily able to distinguish them because of the sun reflecting on the small metal shapes[5] cut from biscuit tins and strung round the men's necks to dangle on their backs as assistance to naval observation for supporting fire. H.F. Prynne has described how, advancing at a steady pace in artillery formation, they had broken into the double as they passed through the fire, and E.L. Hutchings of the 10th Battalion Middlesex Regiment which took part in the attack on the 10th, recalled the 'wall' of high explosive and shrapnel fire as they crossed the Salt Lake, which seemed endless, before the final dash to the foot of Chocolate Hill. Impeded by his entrenching tool as he scrambled up the hill, foolishly he threw it away. Frequently during the next few days he regretted his impatient jettisoning of equipment which would have provided him with the means of shovelling shallow cover for which he desperately scraped with hands and bayonet.

The bitterness felt by men conscious of the mismanagement from which they were suffering was scorchingly expressed by an officer in the 6th East Yorks, Lieutenant Eric Halse.

> Result of the attack: nil. We lost another 200 men and seven officers out of eleven. It is a scandalous wicked shame. If things had been properly managed we could have had a ridge of hills (which was the idea of our landing) at half the cost. Now we are no further forward than the day we landed and yet we are losing men and have suffered so much. Oh it is wicked and somebody ought to be made to suffer for all the mistakes. I can't express all I want to, it is beyond me, but if I live to get home I shall just say what I think.[6]

In such a major attack as that of the 21st, the toll could be ruinous to a battalion's effectiveness, but, day to day, there was another morale-sapping scourge. Snipers now seemed able to inflict losses as disturbing as those inflicted during the early weeks at Helles and Anzac. There were some trees at Suvla and they provided good cover for the snipers, some painted green and black to represent foliage and branches. A woman sniper had been caught at Helles, but a still more extraordinary sight was recorded in the Suvla diary of Lieutenant Lindberg of the 8th Northumberland Fusiliers: 'Sniping in trees hard at work again. We brought down three. Another was painted to represent a pig.' Casualties in Lindberg's Company included more than half the officers but these losses were not all from enemy action – dysentery and sunstroke claimed some, including Lindberg himself by the 16th.

The attacks made with great courage on 9, 10, 12, 15 and 21 August had failed to secure significant advantage. The high hopes for Suvla were sunk in all too familiar stalemate. The Corps Commander, Stopford, was superseded on the 15th, and the failure of the Anzac/Suvla assault led to the termination of Hamilton's command of the MEF, though his removal was not effected until October. For the surviving regimental officers and men of the 11th, 10th, 53rd and 54th Divisions, their punishment for failure was to remain in the stagnation and discomfort of the late summer heat at Suvla and, with the exception of the 10th Division, drafted to Salonika in October, to await winter conditions.

Three further and final aspects of the August offensive deserve mention. Of least significance was the profitless and nearly disastrous landing in the Gulf of Saros of 350 undisciplined Greek irregular troops under two French officers. The landing was from the destroyers, *Minerva* and *Jed*. It does seem scarcely likely that so small a number of untrained troops could have carried out any useful diversionary activity. According to the *Mitchell Report*[7] it was difficult to get the men into the warships' boats for the landing, still more so to persuade them to leave them, and quite impossible to control them in the face of strong opposition ashore. With forty-six killed, wounded and missing, they were withdrawn after an operation which was unfairly taxing for all concerned.

The second matter for mention is of a different order of importance; naval support for the Suvla landing and the attack from Anzac. It was provided by cruisers, destroyers and monitors. It is perhaps worth noting that no battleships were used and, at Suvla certainly, their guns might have made up for the deficiency in field artillery though the smoke and hanging plumes of earthy dust and sand of the bombardment itself and the unanticipatedly gloomy atmospheric conditions, made identification of targets fiendishly difficult. Nevertheless, troops crossing the Suvla plain testify to the encouragement they received from the naval gunfire. It was far less easy to give naval support to the Anzac attack, though consistently determined efforts to that end were undertaken by *Bacchante*, *Grafton*, *Endymion* and other vessels. Certainly the searchlight work and shelling of the Old No. 3 Post by *Colne* was a vital factor in assisting the clearance of the foothills before the Anzac night attack could be launched.

The third aspect of the August offensive deserving notice is the diversionary attack at Helles. This attack, which was meant to draw away from Anzac the potential Turkish reserves, was to begin on the evening of the 6th and continue in a second stage on the 7th, in order that the maximum benefit could be obtained by the available garrison and field artillery working with the support of the Navy. The supply of high-explosive shells was still far below what was necessary, and the Turkish counter-bombardment caused many casualties in the crowded assault trenches, where the attacking troops waited a full seven hours before zero hour of 3.50 p.m.

The small gains initially made were lost in counter-attacks and the renewed British attack the following day had a similar result. Casualties were heavy, with over 3,300 killed, wounded and missing for little, if any, material effect on the Turkish defence of Anzac. The 29th Division on the 6th, and the 42nd Division on the 7th, distinguished themselves in the Battle of the Vineyard in front of Krithia but, as the history of the 42nd Division records[8] of the Manchesters, 'losses were grievous, the attacking lines being mown down by the enemy's machine-guns'.

The tragic futility at Helles, paralleled by the diversionary assaults on the right flank of the Anzac front, serve for many in their judgement as a conclusive indictment of High Command. Certainly these truly dreadful losses reaffirm the ruinous price to be paid in the prevailing conditions of warfare, 1915–17, by the side under a strategic requirement to attack. Politicians demand success from their generals on whatever enterprise they are set and military success cannot be won by inaction. It is entirely appropriate that when plans to attack lead to costly failure condemnation is brought to bear, but searching for a way out of attritional warfare in 1915 was at that stage of the war not hampered by a lack of imagination but because the problem was beyond imagination – only the critical weakening of an opponent's will and capacity to continue the struggle would bring the opportunity to exploit greater human and material resources and the employment of co-ordinated refined military tactics, and thus defeat an exhausted opponent. Emphatically this was not the case with the Ottoman Empire in August 1915.

Chapter 15

Troopships and Hospital Ships

For most of the reinforcements packed in the troopships *en route* for the Peninsula, the voyage, though not without considerable discomfort in the foetid atmosphere of the lower decks and the apprehension of submarine attack, was the most thrilling experience of their lives. Volunteers to a man as far as the British were concerned, with an infectious, boyish confidence, many were fascinated by the sights in Valletta harbour in Malta, the oriental smells at Alexandria, as much a part of the scene as the domes and minarets, the small boats laden with fruit and souvenirs for which haggling became a necessary talent.

Many letters deal with the fundamental problem of *mal de mer*, more frequently referred to as 'feeding the fishes'. An RAMC private, Stanley Parker-Bird, wrote with frank disdain for the sufferings of others: 'I am happy to be able to say that although nearly all the fellows have been very much indisposed, I have not been affected in the slightest… I am enjoying the trip immensely and only wish it were to be for a few more weeks, for it is really grand to lie on the deck and do nothing. Now that the boys are getting well again we are arranging for concerts and deck sports so we shall spin the time out very well.' There were injections against cholera and typhoid to be endured, but once in Alexandria and Mustapha Camp, unless the men moved straight on to Mudros or the Peninsula, there was sea-bathing and trips into Alexandria, where the YMCA provided tea, bread and butter and three fried eggs for a very small outlay.

There were, however, other sights and scenes in Alexandria which, attracting some men, profoundly shocked others. Of Cairo, Sergeant Morris wrote his immediate impression in a notebook to accompany his diary.

While I was in Mena Camp I paid a visit one Sunday afternoon to the vilest place on earth, the Wazza [Wasser] bazaar. As I went through the narrow streets and dirty lanes, I was almost overcome with the vile scenes and nauseating smells. Leaning from the windows of their dens were women of every nationality – excepting English and American – who pestered the passer by with their solicitations: 'British Tommee very good, very nice, my house very clean. Come on, come in.' Besides the houses of the prostitutes there are also the 'show houses'. In here native women arrayed in the gaudy finery of the East sit in disgusting positions, or dance some vile form of native dance which is nothing more or less than a series of immoral antics. I was sickened and pained to think that human beings would descend so low as to yield their members, servants to iniquity in such a form.

For those encamped at Mudros awaiting transportation to the Peninsula, there were none of the temptations – or repulsions – of Egypt. J.C. Attwood, on landing from his troopship, spent two nights without groundsheet, blankets or tent, and for a good deal longer had no easy access to washing, shaving or drinking water. He remained convinced that it was this absence of organization which made so many men ready prey to the dysentery widespread on the Peninsula itself.

Eric Wolton, of the 1/5th Battalion of the Suffolk Regiment, journeyed east in the huge liner *Aquitania*, which carried about 7,000 men. Thankfully, his deck (C) had access to the fresh air. As the lights of Merseyside faded and amid thoughts of what would happen to the three Wolton brothers on board and sadness at leaving relatives and friends, he felt above all satisfaction that at last, 'we were to share the hardships and dangers that our own comrades had borne for so many months'. Nevertheless, Wolton also recalled the chastening interchange with a troopship of Australians returning to Gallipoli. The new troops cheerfully yelled 'No!' to the Australian chant 'Are we downhearted?' and thus left themselves open to the rejoinder, 'Then you bloody soon will be'.

Not all the ships arrived safely. One of the distinctive features of the Cape Helles monument is the rows of names of men who never reached Gallipoli but were drowned in the torpedoing of the *Royal Edward*,[1] which sank in the Eastern Mediterranean on 13 August with a loss of over 850 lives. A.T. Fraser,[2] in the Border Regiment, was in a deck chair on the afterdeck starboard side when suddenly dozens of men ran past him from port to starboard. The explosion came before he had time to ask what was the matter.

> The ship had no escort and we had not been ordered to have our life-belts with us. The hundreds on deck ran below to get their life-belts and hundreds below would have met them on the way up. I shared a cabin accessible from the deck I was on and I raced there to get my life-belt and ran to my lifeboat station which was on the starboard side. As the men arrived they fell in in two ranks. Already the ship was listing and this prevented our boats from being lowered, so we were ordered to jump for it. I saw no panic, but of course one can imagine what was happening on the inside stairs. I swam away from the ship and turned to see the funnels leaning towards me. When they reached the sea, all the soot was belched out, there was a loud whoosh and the ship sank. No explosion, no surge. So I was alone. The little waves were such that in the trough you saw nothing, on the crest you saw a few yards. The water was warm. I wondered if there were sharks.

Fraser found some wood to rest on and he was joined by a seaman, an older man who had twice previously been torpedoed. This brought the young Scot confidence. An upturned *Royal Edward* lifeboat was to provide seventeen of the survivors with a little more security though in what Fraser calls a half-hourly recurring turbulence, the boat turned over, offering them conventional but completely water-logged accommodation every alternate half-hour but at least providing them with something to do. There was no singing and little conversation. From the first ship that passed a voice hailed the scattered men and promised to signal for help. The vessel could not stop, as it had high explosives for Lemnos.[3] Some of the men became depressed and showed unwillingness to clamber back in the lifeboat when it overturned, but on each occasion all were persuaded. Finally the hospital ship *Soudan* arrived to pick them up in her lifeboats, and at two o'clock Fraser was safely aboard her after just under five hours in the sea. He remembered that, 'a large number of men lost their false teeth as we were constantly sick in the sea–and these men were sent back to England. We, the younger ones, were clothed and kitted and were on another ship three days later for Gallipoli.'

The inexperience of fifteen-year-old James Houston (2nd Lowland Field Ambulance) led him to strip himself of all his clothes once he reached an upturned collapsible boat. Naked and shivering, he waited for rescue as drowned men floated by, their legs out of the water, the body below supported by an incorrectly worn life-belt. John Crighton (87th Field Ambulance Reinforcements) put to good effect the advice he had been given by his father who had been torpedoed earlier in the war. He dived immediately into the sea, swam well away from the ship and then alternately swam and trod water till he was rescued.

On 2 September, the transport *Southland*, carrying Australian troops for the Peninsula, was torpedoed within sight of Strati Island, forty miles south of Lemnos. Some men were killed in the explosion of the torpedo striking the ship, but nearly all the soldiers and crew were rescued by ships which came up in support, and a skeleton crew of sailors and volunteers from the soldiers kept the ship afloat and guided her safely into Mudros harbour.

For many men the journey was to be made in the reverse direction, to hospitals in Egypt, Malta, Gibraltar or Britain. Their stay on the Peninsula had been cut short by wounds or by dysentery, and their voyage was made in hospital ships. After the discomforts of the Peninsula, these men were often overwhelmed by the sheer luxury of a bed and clean white sheets and by the attention of the British, Australian or New Zealand nurses, who, in retrospect, seem to have been uniformly beautiful in their angelic ministrations. S.B. French, who was at Suvla, recalled the two hospital ships anchored off shore.

> Both were of course painted brilliant white with a red cross marked on the side. One was the *Roselart Castle*. At night, on duty in the trenches, one gazed out to sea and there were the two great ships brilliantly lit from stem to stern. It always brought a lump to my throat. I eventually finished up on the *Roselart Castle* with a flesh wound plus enteric and dysentery. You can imagine my reaction once again to lie in a bunk with clean sheets after weeks of living like a savage. We naturally needed some cleaning up. Socks came off almost taking the skin with them and of course we were full of lice.

For the wounded, the journey from shore to ship was uncomfortable and sometimes even hazardous. James Barnet (2nd Lowland Field Ambulance) recorded that, 'stretcher cases had to be loaded on to the ship's boats with the thwarts boarded over.

These were then towed out by a picket boat with two of us in charge. On arrival at the hospital ship, a cage or box with openings for stretcher handles on two sides, and a rope from each corner, would be lowered. We had the task of loading each stretcher, mindful all the time of our boat's bumping against the ship's side and the rise and fall of our respective levels.'

The work of nursing wounded or sick cases in Egypt and on board hospital ships, was arduous and could be dangerous. This is clearly recorded in the diary of Sister Speedy from New Zealand. At the Deaconess Hospital in Alexandria during August, 'there was no such thing as getting off duty. It was a case of go on from 7 a.m. till 11 p.m., 12 or 1 a.m. and perhaps 2 a.m'. In September the diary notes the death of Miss Smailes, Miss Chadwick and Sister Hawken from dysentery, Sister Griffiths in an ambulance crash at a level crossing, Miss Rockell after an operation, and then, on 1 November 1915, 'ten of the 36 sisters are missing believed drowned' in the torpedoing of the *Marquette* on its way to Salonika. There are, however, far more entries dealing with the bravery of her patients with severe wounds or weakening dysentery.

R.B. Gillett, wounded in the first week of the landing and transported in the hospital ship *Delta*, remembered that the engines were stopped at intervals and one offered up a prayer for the unknown casualty who had not survived his wounds and was being committed to the deep. Charles Mackintosh, badly frostbitten at Suvla, was filled with self-disgust at the black liquid coming out of his blistered feet if they encountered the deck as he crawled on hands and knees to the latrine from his shipboard bed.

A nurse, later Mrs G.A. Hale, was on the medical staff appointed to the liner *Aquitania*, used at the end of the campaign as a hospital ship. The vessel took on board many of the frostbite cases.

Each man was allotted a cot before arrival on board so there was no overcrowding, but in the Bay of Biscay there was a terrible storm in which the plate-glass windows on the upper deck were smashed and the seas poured in. On the lower decks where the patients' cots were stapled to the floor, the violence of the storm wrenched many of the staples out. One odd thing I recollect very clearly was that practically nobody was seasick. I am still stirred today by the poignant memory of the ship's little chapel, crowded with staff and a few ambulant patients, with the sound of their voices singing, 'Eternal Father strong to save' with all the fervour and gratitude they could muster.

The contemporary account of Corporal C.R.S. Saunders showed how fortunate he was to experience life aboard a hospital ship.

An order came around that a man was wanted to accompany Second Lieutenant Wedgwood Benn MP, who was being invalided away with jaundice. I applied for the post and obtained it. That was about the luckiest thing I have done since the war started. We boarded the hospital ship *Valdivia*. What a treat it was to be amongst the light and warmth of this spotlessly clean ship. They gave me sleeping quarters with the hospital orderlies and I was given some food. I remember devouring piles of bread and butter, cheese, cakes and a lovely hot cup of cocoa. How I slept and how bad I felt the next day. I think I slept the next two days right off. Recovering, I visited my officer, but he was so well attended to by the nurses that there was absolutely nothing for me to do.

On 5 October, a War Office circular memorandum was issued to Medical Officers and nurses on hospital ships and ambulance carriers.

It has been brought to the notice of Sir Ian Hamilton that, here and there, on Hospital Ships and Ambulance Carriers, Medical Officers and Nurses have allowed themselves to become too seriously impressed by the stories of young officers and men who have come on board sick or wounded. It is natural under the circumstances that these tales should be over-coloured; it is natural also that contact with so much suffering should incline the listeners to sympathy; but it is certain also that, whether from the standpoint of the individual sick or of the military operations as a whole, such enervating influences should be resisted. All grades and degrees of the medical staff must make it a point of professional honour to maintain a hearty tone of optimism calculated to raise rather than lower the confidence and courage of the fighting men who have been temporarily committed to their charge.[4]

On board the hospital ship *Delta*, Private C.D. Selsby kept a diary which gives an account of his experience from his embarkation as a casualty through sickness. '15 October. Had a good hot bath and then went to bed. The first time for about three months. Had a fair night's rest but aching all over.' Selsby enjoyed his Bovril, custard, sweets, bread, butter and marmalade and cocoa, the books and cigarettes provided and the Chaplain's administration of Holy Communion. He found the ward very hot and stifling but was too weak to stay on deck. His entry for 19 October reported '30 dead on board of dysentery'. The wound card attached to him read, 'Persistent diarrhoea', which seems inadequate in conveying the degree of debility suffered by victims of the 1915 'Turkey Trot'. Selsby was to survive and to reach Queen Mary's Military Hospital at Whalley in Lancashire in time for the Christmas celebrations, which included a denominational service, a cinema exhibition, Clayton le Moors prize band, a 'Grand Concert', where appropriately a Mr Critchley sang 'The Crown' and 'There's only one England', but above all, a Christmas dinner. The menu card shows each of the items ticked off by the young soldier: soup, roast beef and Yorkshire pudding, roast pork and savoury and apple sauce (unticked), boiled potatoes, vegetables, plum pudding, brandy sauce, mince pies and dessert, beside which Selsby pencilled in, 'bananas, oranges and apples'.

A good deal less pleasant were the professional reactions to some of the makeshift hospital ship arrangements recorded in the diary of Naval Surgeon Lorimer.

30 June 1915: When I got to the *Saturnia* I found the whole ship packed with wounded, lying about anywhere, no order, nor anybody in charge apparently. The wounds had not been looked at for 48 hours at least, and in that climate were in an awful state, live maggots in many... The other naval surgeons who had arrived were all working independently as there was nobody to give instructions. The M.O. of ship was at dinner when I wanted to report for duty and had apparently chucked his hand in. It made one ashamed of the medical organization of the Army.

The Dardanelles Commission Report noted that the arrangements for dealing with the transport of the wounded were, until August, in a very unsatisfactory state and that the, 'terrible story of the *Saturnia* [was] a most extraordinary indication of the absence of organization'.[5]

Some left the Peninsula during the campaign for reasons other than wounds or disease. According to a document in the French Military Archives at Vincennes,[6] the French General Bailloud communicated to the French War Minister on 9 July that reports from the Colonel commanding the depot at Mudros stated that a certain number of officers recently arrived from France had not the physical aptitude or morale for service in the Orient. One had to be evacuated within a few days of his arrival. The Colonel considered that some of these men had come having been, 'attracted by the mirage of a trip to the Orient', and Bailloud asked that the next batch should be more carefully examined. Hamilton was to have something of the same problem with leadership of, and within, IX Corps at Suvla.

Chapter 16

The Dead

H.C. Foster, Oswyn Creighton and Ernest Raymond[1] have all written of their experiences as padres on the Peninsula and of their attempt, under adverse conditions, to give decent Christian burial to the killed, among them men with whom they had breakfasted that day or had exchanged a regular word. Foster relates that the question of the burial of the Turks led to a conference of chaplains at which after, 'quite an animated debate, it was agreed that no Mohammedan should be buried without a short service in which the Lord's Prayer should form a part'.[2] In his published diary[3] Creighton gave an indication of how, soon after the landings, cemeteries were established and other places were designated as such. On 11 May, 'when we got to the cemetery at six, it was to find he had been buried some hours before ... so I just said a few prayers over the grave, and went with the two majors to see about a piece of ground being railed off as a Lancashire Fusilier burying place, where some day a memorial might be erected above the beach where they made their famous landing.' It is clear that some units had the opportunity and concern to arrange and record meticulously the burial of their men. Such a unit was the RND Engineers, who took photographs and drew plans of the wooden cross – marked graves and accordingly were able to compare the positions with those in the Official War Grave cemeteries which were developed from the makeshift ones of active service.

For many, particularly at Anzac and in the tangled scrub of Gully Ravine, or in the wider open Suvla plain, with its shallow gullies leading from the amphitheatre of the Kiretch Tepe, Tekke Tepe and Sari Bair ridge, there could be no known grave. Human remains are still being uncovered at Anzac, where the author in 1972 saw the newly-discovered bones of six men, and found the skull of another at the mouth of Gully Ravine. Of those killed or wounded and then burned to death in the August scrub fires in the Suvla attack and perhaps some of those drowned or frozen to death in the storm and frost of late November, no identifiable remains would be recovered, so that the post-war headstone merely commemorates their death and not the immediate presence of their remains. Lance-Corporal Tait, of the Northumberland Fusiliers, was killed in August at Suvla, though his wife was informed in September that he had been 'wounded' and in October that he was 'wounded and missing'. In March of the following year, there came two contradictory accounts of how he had been killed. In May 1916 she was warned that in accepting an Army pension instead of an Army separation allowance, 'this must not be taken as any proof of the death of your husband'. It is scarcely surprising that for long after the war Mrs Tait could not accept that her husband had been killed.

A good deal has been written about the so called, 'lost army of Gallipoli', the Sandringham Company of the 5th Royal Norfolk Regiment, which disappeared seemingly without trace in an attack in August. The mystery may in fact have been solved four years later when a War Graves unit found a grave containing 180 men of whom 122 were Royal Norfolks, but sinister rumours were reported that the men had all been shot in the head. Then the watch of the commanding officer, Captain Beck, turned up in a Constantinople shop window, was bought and returned to the Beck family.[4] The disappearance of so many men and the reported manner in which they had been killed, have made this a special case with Stephen Chambers' splendid book on Suvla the most recent attempt to address the issue.[5]

Acceptance of death and of wounds was simply the reality of service in any military campaign and it is this accommodation to prevailing circumstance which from the diary records would seem a more accurate analysis of the soldier's attitude to death than the common idea that he became 'hardened to it'. The latter implies an insensitive coarsened brutality which goes well with the theatrical bravado implied in the familiar stories of shaking hands with the stiff hand protruding from a trench wall or parapet of which a body formed a part. The diary of Eric Wettern unconsciously provides perhaps a truer reflection of the soldier's attitude to death.

23 June: Section III party caught by shrapnel on mule track returning from work in the evening. Nunn and Mason killed outright. Ledbrook and Serg. Goodwin wounded. Bad day for our section. Nunn and Mason in new cemetery in evening. Everybody upset.

24 June: Sorting out Nunn's kit. Busy till late with various correspondence. Treacle for tea.

25 June: Mail in. Still no papers. Got rice from Frenchmen. Ledbrook died from wounds – funeral in evening in new cemetery next to Nunn and Mason.

12 July: Webster killed by shrapnel in comm. trench – just starting out to work. Bombardment continued all day … huge mail in evening. Got my parcels at last. One in bits. Supper party with Murphy, Dixon, Thomas and Harris – rice, pineapple and coffee. Webster's funeral after dark-next to Nunn and Mason.

18 July: Feeling rotten. Stayed in dugout and slept all day. Kept off grub. W.C. with seat to it near incinerator! Great luxury. Patronized it all day.

A letter which has come into the public domain ninety-eight years after it was written touchingly undermines the seemingly reasonable presumption that with so much death around one and dealing out death to the enemy, the necessarily protective growth of a thick, hardened skin must virtually calcify emotional reaction. Intriguingly, the letter is not written to a family member but to the writer's landlord and landlady at his billet near Rugby where the King's Own Scottish Borderers had trained and made friendships before departure for the Dardanelles:

It is with deep sorrow the news I have to relate to you in this letter. John and Tom have both been killed in action. John as you know was wounded on the 4th of June but he was allright [*sic*] again and rejoined the regiment when we were resting the day previous to going into the trenches and he got killed in a bayonet charge on the 28th of June and John my dearest pal on earth fell mortally wounded through the head on the morning of 5th July and died sixteen hours later on the hospital ship. I never got such a shock in my life, his gun [machine-gun] was next to mine and I was up seeing him when we were told the enemy was preparing for an attack so I had to go back to my own gun again and no sooner had I got back when the message came down the line that he was wounded so I went to see him but he was unconscious [*sic*] and I had very little hope for him he had wrot [*sic*] a letter to you but was all covered in blood so I could not send it on. I tell you it is a terrible war.[6]

There is predictable but sad irony in that the letter-writer John Lavelle's death was soon to be personally recorded too. It was in the diary of his Company Commander, Captain A.M. Shaw, on 5 July:

Turks advanced in mass over sky-line at 3.40 a.m. I have three machine-guns and with them and with rifle fire we cut them to pieces ... I called attention of machine-gunner to about 20 Turks, he got up to fire and immediately fell back in my arms with the top of his head split by a bullet which expanded ... Poor Lavelle – the best machine-gunner in the regiment. A sniper got him. Spent my day trying to locate the sniper. Saw wounded sniper whom the men presently shot, he crying on Allah as they all do.[7]

It was a fortunate sniper who, on detection, escaped alive.

Just as it may be assumed that many held onto some measure of support from the belief that somehow their luck would hold – 'it won't happen to me' – there are many stories of men having a premonition of approaching, even imminent, death and of this premonition being fulfilled. It is idle to deny that men feared death, though still more they may have feared disfiguring wounds or a wound involving the loss of their manhood. Naturally in open conversation many would affect a devil-may-care attitude, and the pessimist was always the butt of fun, sometimes a perverse source of encouragement, but occasionally in letters home, despite sincere attempt to shield the reality of war from anxious families, the writer's awareness of the proximity of death breaks through. B.H.A. Eames wrote the briefest of letters home after the attack of 21 August at Suvla. 'My dear Mother, a short note to tell you we have been into action. We took part in a very big battle last Saturday and Sunday and am sorry to say the regiment lost very heavily. I came through alright, but I can tell you it was very hell. Am very fit. I cannot say much due to the censor. Much love to all, Basil.'

The letters of Second Lieutenant Duckworth, who was killed on 7 August, are filled with a thinly-disguised preoccupation with death. On 15 July he wrote, 'Mother says, "quite a lot of officers lost". Figures may interest you. Twenty-eight officers left

Cairo with the Company and four of these are left.' On 25 July: 'Was interested to read about Grandpa's will in the paper. It was the first I heard about it. I seem to get a watch after Dad's death – by which token I hope it is a long time before I get it – but I was thinking that if he sent me the watch now and he took it after my death it might be a fairer arrangement under the present crisis! However, we'll hope not.' On 29 July: 'Fifty-one weeks now since we mobilized and three months since we landed here, and we seem as far away from seeing home as ever. However, I hope the powers that be will be moved to pity for the remnants of this miserable Division and send a tug boat for them ... Life is a daily misery and there is no news ... Afraid this letter isn't very cheery but St Peter himself would be a crank under these conditions and I'm no Job.' 4 August: 'I should like to see Rochdale again. However we must hope for the best.'

Eric Duckworth's last letter was written to his mother on 5 August, two days before he was killed. 'Little enough did I think twelve months ago today that on the anniversary of mobilization I should be writing you from a hole in the Gallipoli Peninsula, not having seen you for ten and a half months, and to the tune of 75mm guns. However you never know your luck, and I may see you in time to celebrate my twentieth birthday at home, though as things look at present, there's not much chance of that.'

Chapter 17

Routine and Discipline

It is undoubtedly true that soldiers on the Peninsula, borne down by dysentery, nervous and physical debility, long periods of enervating boredom and shorter periods of intense strain, were supported by more than individual qualities and the undoubted strength of fellowship moulded out of the demanding conditions. The common denominator which did much to keep men going was Army routine. The significance of what might seem less than noteworthy, General Routine Orders,[1] illustrates that while in some matters, for example dress, there had to be flexible adaptability, in others the structure of Army life demanded regulation. Proper attention to administrative procedure, to the listing of stores and equipment, to the formalities of relationship between ranks and suchlike matters, helped to prevent sloppiness and irresponsibility, and did much to provide the individual and the unit with a solid basis for ordered, purposeful, morale-sustaining activity.

It is easy in the light of changed circumstance today to ridicule many of the orders solemnly issued in 1915. Some of them deserve such treatment, but one is then left with still less to answer the challenging question of how the men of the MEF 'stuck it' and 'stuck it' so well.

A brief selection of General Routine Orders makes the point clearly and still allows the 'raising of eyebrows' today:

139 QJVI.G. 11.5.15. Postal. The Postmaster General has arranged for the free delivery in all parts of the British Empire of unpaid or insufficiently paid letters from the Mediterranean Expeditionary Force.

179 QJVI.G. 20.5.15. Curtain Flaps for Caps. The issue of a curtain flap for caps at the rate of one per man is approved. Units will submit indents accordingly.

315 QJVI.G. 28.6.15. Equipment. The waist belt belonging to the web or bandolier equipment is only to be used for the purpose for which it is issued. It is not to be worn as a belt for keeping up the trousers.

37 QJVI.G. 10.4.15. Disposal of kits of Officers and Other Ranks who are deceased, missing, prisoners of war, sick or wounded … A sword if sent with kit should be so secured that it cannot fall out in transit.

122 A.G. 7.5.15. Salutes. With reference to Standing Orders, Section 5(h), an impression seems to be prevalent among the troops that on active service the paying of compliments is suspended and considerable slackness has been

observed in the matter of saluting. Officers commanding units will bring this matter to the notice of their men and it must be clearly understood that except when actually employed in active operations, any relaxation in this respect will be met by suitable disciplinary action.

The following daily rates of pay are authorized:

Officer Ranking as 2nd Lt.	7/6
Honorary Chaplain	Nil
Corporal	2/-
Man	1/-

Of many letters and diaries which nicely exemplify general routine and mental preoccupation outside the brief times of actual assault or defensive action, two may suffice, both written in early July. First there is the letter of Pte David Harper of the 1st/4th Battalion King's Own Scottish Borderers, sitting in the bottom of a trench where, 'the flies are a terrible pest'. He stresses that

this is my last piece of paper – I am hoping some comes my way soon or else the letters must cease and I would not like that to happen. I have not had a parcel yet but am hoping some comes my way. We now get a weekly issue of cigarettes and matches so don't bother sending any of them. What would go high now is a sweetie such as acid drops or black balls, something like that for the thirst. I believe parcels under 3lbs come out quite reasonable – quite a lot of our chaps have already got them. One Duns chap had a cake last night and not a scratch on it – by jingo, but it made our teeth water. We get our issue of rum about every night – just a tablespoon full. We get lime juice instead – it is supposed to keep the blood right, and it would take something of the kind too. We have lived on almost nothing else but bully beef since ever we landed and now the look of it is enough. Of course we have ham [for] our breakfast and always cook it ourselves. This morning we had two eggs each which they say came off a Turkish Transport which we captured – we of course means our fleet.

Harper continued with a weather report on the heat, heavy dew, rain, thunder and lightning displays at night, and then interestingly, 'We go about continually with our respirators slung over our shoulder – I think they are afraid of Mr Turk using gas.' He is encouraged by seeing so many Allied aeroplanes in the sky, eight on one day, and described a Taube dropping two bombs – 'What a splutter' he recorded dismissively. He would like to be giving a hand in the work at home and enquires about family and friends joining the forces. He tells his mother not to be anxious for him as he is 'A 1', and not to send any clothes as he doesn't need them, but simply 'that sweetie or anything tasty'.[2]

The second example is that of RND Sapper, Eric Wettern, whose letter provides a light-hearted but fair indication of life and routine on the Peninsula.

Our company is at last enjoying a much needed 'rest' after about two months of firing line work. It is about time too. The rest consists in working one day in four, on communication work etc., so it's quite worth having. It doesn't affect me however as I am still with Smith looking after the roll books and the letters and doing all sorts of awful jobs ... and I really was getting fed up with wielding the shove and pickel all the time. Asiatic Annie is trying to give us shocks again and has plonked about eight big 'uns round about since I started this letter ... on a Sunday evening too!

The last few weeks we have spent in sapping, mainly in front of our lines. It is a funny job and you don't want to put your head out and admire the scenery. It is apt to be exciting especially at night and if there happen to be any Turks messing around with bombs. It is also very monotonous – barring the bomb part of it. A Turkish gentleman came over the top of one of our saps one dark night. He gave our chaps a bit of a shock as they didn't know whether the rest of the Turkish Army was coming too and wondered whether they should stay and see. One or two just tickled him with their bayonets a bit and then it turned out that he was tired of the Army and had strolled over to us for a bit of a rest ...

The scrapping now is quite different from what it was at first and I should imagine it is now very similar to Flanders. The trenches in some places are only a few yards apart and our firing and reserve and communication trenches are an absolute maze. There must be miles and miles of trench now – a large proportion of which we can proudly look upon as our work. The difficulty we were soon up against was place names. We went as long as we could with names like the Pink Farm ... but they are all ruins and have a knack of gradually disappearing as people pinch the stones to improve their dugouts – and we as the odd job merchants have started a special stencilling and name board department and it will soon be possible to issue a directory. We have already got Oxford St and Clapham Junction and Romanos and Piccadilly Circus. You can get a drink at Romanos but they only keep one sort and you have to bring your own bucket and a piece of rope. Some genius has by the way labelled our camp Walmer Castle ...

I am not wanting anything in the clothes line at present but could do with the following – small tube of ink tablets for fountain pen, carbolic soap, a few letter cards, Gibbs shaving stick. As to luxuries anything in the grub line is always welcome, cocoa and milk powder and tablets ... they don't make compressed whisky cubes do they? I have lately taken to fancy cooking as a pastime. Our official diet is meat, bread or biscuit, bacon, tea, jam, cheese, potatoes, with occasional rum, lime juice and onions, and we get jolly sick of it (and from it) at times. So I have rigged up a kitchen range of my own and go in for occasional variations such as coffee, boiled rice, toast, Welsh rarebit, and that is about the extent of my repertoire at present. Oh, I forgot bread and milk. The coffee and rice we swop from the French for jam and the Nestles we can occasionally buy when anyone happens to be going to the canteen which isn't very often as it is a long way off and a fearful wait in the queue when you get there ... We get an occasional Taube dropping bombs, but he can't hit a ten acre field, and anyway he never stops very long. I wish he would stop a minute or two longer just once. I rather fancy though that we are up to that game about fifty times to their once.

On the Peninsula many of the crimes which would normally be expected to lead to courts martial simply could not be committed. Absence without leave and drunkenness might well be ranked as achievements under Peninsula conditions, but of course various field punishments, including the degrading No. 1 F.P., in which the prisoner was tied spread-eagled to a gunwheel for a predetermined period and which was soon to be discontinued, did have to be served. Among the General Routine Orders there is a record of a commutation of death sentences for cowardice on five men from the 1st Munster Fusiliers and one from the 4th Battalion the Worcestershire Regiment. The Orders state that, 'the General Commanding, seeing how gallantly the force was advancing against the enemy, felt convinced that he might yet spare those who had been condemned without thereby endangering the lives of their comrades'.[3]

In the period between Christmas 1915 and the Helles evacuation, Sid Blythman, a former private in the Wiltshire Regiment, claimed that his sergeant was shot at Y Gully by a firing squad after a court-martial sentence. It seems that three British soldiers were executed following court-martial death sentences during the Gallipoli Campaign. One of those tragic figures was a sergeant in the Wiltshire Regiment.

At Vincennes, documentation is available concerning the French disciplinary record on the Peninsula. The details range from the ultimate severity of the death penalty in certain cases to the bizarre instance of the report by Sous-Lieutenant Castel that a certain, 'Marechal des Logis was surprised by Trooper Parra at the moment when, in full light of day, he was embracing Trooper M__'.[4] This took place in mid-August, but on 10 April, even before the French troops landed, a Jean Fischer was sentenced for desertion in the face of the enemy to twenty years' detention, military degradation and – in a somewhat mystifying rubbing of salt into his wounds – ten years without leave.[5] In the previous month an Algerian soldier was sentenced to three years' imprisonment for outrageous offences against a superior officer, the details not specified.

Between 11 and 13 December 1915, a Senegalese soldier was charged and condemned to death for leaving his post in the face of the enemy, by means of self-mutilation. General Brulard considered but rejected commutation of the death sentence, and in the previous month, there was no reprieve for Tirailleur Bedary Xarka Tamboura of the 57th Colonial Regiment. Lest an unfair general impression be given of an unwarranted degree of harshness in the French Expeditionary Force in comparison with its ally, it may be added that the Vincennes Archives also show General Bailloud writing to the Minister of War on 15 September: 'A Senegalese soldier named Bakary has been killed and his son (15) wounded ... could you see he is, after recovery, put in a school for the children of soldiers.' Bailloud, it seems, may have been particularly attached to his Senegalese troops and he denied vigorously the implication of a French War Office inquiry in August that it might be against the racial customs of these troops to take prisoners.[6]

It is a point worthy of note that there is an almost total absence of references to field punishments on the Peninsula in the recollections of several hundred British veterans and that there is a parallel absence in Peninsula diaries. For the Western Front this is not the case, despite the fact that special punishment camps like the Bull Ring at Etaples[7] could be kept well away from the front-line. It may well be that the Peninsula imposed its own discipline, but the whole question of comparing over two Fronts, crime, indiscipline and their consequences, is one which would need carefully chosen indices before sound observations could be put forward. In any case, it could be added, there are so many variable factors that such an exercise might have but limited value. Accepting this, the personal evidence cited above, or rather the absence of evidence on the subject, suggests that the geography of the Peninsula and the stubbornness of the Turk produced a situation 'conducive' to the maintenance of discipline.

Chapter 18

Prisoners of the Turks

Twenty-one French soldiers were taken prisoner at Kum Kale and one of them, from the 6th Regiment of Mixed Colonial Infantry, Marius Gondard, wrote an account of his journey into captivity and his experiences as a Turkish prisoner of war. They were first taken to Chanak before crossing the Narrows and marching to the town of Gallipoli. From there they were taken by steamer to Constantinople and then to Afion Karahissar in Asia Minor, where they found already installed the surviving ten members of the crew of the French submarine *Saphir*. Later they were joined by thirteen soldiers taken at Helles and Anzac, and some French Marines. Later still, the full complement of the French submarines *Mariotte* and *Turquoise* were to increase the Gallic predominance over the British at Afion Karahissar, until some of the British victims of the surrender at Kut in Mesopotamia arrived in the summer of 1916. In 1915 the crews of the submarines *E 15* and *AE 2* were to add to the British and Australian contingents, but, in fact, the camp was mainly occupied by Russians.

The food was mainly chick-peas and crushed wheat with very occasional and tiny pieces of mutton. It was scarcely sufficient, but the intervention of the American Ambassador obtained some money for each of the prisoners which enabled them to augment their meagre diet. When some of the prisoners were moved to a camp at Sivas, four Frenchmen escaped and got back to France via Russia – north to Archangel, a fine achievement, and thence to England and across the Channel.

In January 1916, the 'other ranks' prisoners at Afion Karahissar suffered a cruelly cold railway journey to Belemidik camp, where they worked on the construction of the railway to Baghdad. Under the direction of Greek and Swiss engineers, tunnels were to be dug through the Taurus mountains. At this camp, accommodation and supervision conditions improved and enough money was earned to buy food in the camp shops. The prisoners even had facilities to cook for themselves. Nevertheless the climate was unhealthy; typhus and dysentery claimed many victims, especially among the Russians, despite the work of an Armenian doctor, Boyadjian, whose medical training had been at Montpellier in France.

Sports were arranged during Easter 1918 and Gondard won the long jump. The French came first, second and third in the obstacle race, won the three-legged race, and naturally won the frog-hopping race.[1] Australian victories in the egg-and-spoon race, the hundred yards and the veterans race emphasized the British failure to secure more than the tug of war, for which single event, alas, there was no prize. However, the English tended to win the football and rugby matches, so a particularly strong Australian always used to play for the French in order to even things up.

Among the papers kept by Gondard was a sheet of camp regulations which stated that anyone who tried to escape would be treated with the utmost severity and to stop an escape attempt a sentry would be obliged to use his weapon. It is pleasant to see from another document enumerating the provisions of an agreement between France and Turkey on the repatriation of prisoners, that the French were prepared to exchange two Turks for every Frenchman.

A man from the 4th Battalion the Worcester Regiment, captured in front of Krithia on 6 August, Private L. Moore, had been badly wounded in the attack. He was taken by bullock cart to Constantinople, and by reason of the severity of his wounds from an exploding grenade, this journey proved a nightmare. Moreover, he and his fellow prisoners suffered the indignity of a humiliating parade through the streets. He needed prolonged hospital treatment in the city and watched from his ward window the movement of shipping on the Golden Horn as he slowly recovered. He later worked on a section of the Constantinople-Baghdad railway as a German engineer's servant, and this brought privileges which considerably eased the conditions of his captivity.

Fascinating evidence survives of the captivity experience of an officer in the same battalion. Leonard Stone was wounded and captured but on recovery and in transit through Constantinople he escaped with a companion. They were on the loose for some days before recapture. Not only does Stone's 'police mugshot' photograph survive but also minuscule written notes exchanged in the civil prison toilet by the two men, held separately, arranging co-ordination of the details of their escape, in readiness for interrogation.

Another Worcester Regiment prisoner, S.F. Lawrance, reported that many died through the conditions of work in a tunnel on the Constantinople-Baghdad railway line, but, as he was employed as a saddler, he worked in the open air and furthermore, with others, had the opportunity to steal eggs and even chickens. According to Lawrance, there was no systematic brutality and in fact a reasonable relationship existed between the prisoners and those officers and guards who had fought in the war, but not with the elderly reservists. Lawrance received parcels of tins of meat and other food from the Lord Mayor's fund in Birmingham, the regimental fund and a Mrs Digby Bell. Most parcels were shared, though Lawrance, who admired the Australians in other ways, said that they were reluctant to share and one kept his bread with him wherever he went, even to the toilet in the corner of the room.

An Australian, captured by what appeared to have been a ruse at Anzac during the evening of the day of the April landing, wrote and published an account of his experience. R.F. Lushington, in *A Prisoner with the Turks, 1915–18*, described how he was on the same steamer as the twenty-one Frenchmen captured at Kum Kale and he felt the shame of captivity. He suffered from the normal, accepted Turkish practice whereby Turkish officers beat their soldiers, who promptly behaved in the same fashion towards their prisoners. They were the first Allied soldiers to reach the Turkish capital, though their entry was a triumph for the Turks rather than the invaders. They were inspected by Liman von Sanders, who added to the seemingly consistent efforts to subvert the solidarity existing between the British and the

French by expatiating on the sad manner in which the French had become the dupes of the English.

They left by rail for Afion Karahissar, the sailors from *AE 2* clothed in Turkish soldiers' greatcoats, fezes and Turkish slippers. Lushington's account confirms the bad conditions described by Gondard. Stone-breaking was the main activity and the men grew weaker and weaker on the starvation diet until the American Ambassador's visit brought tinned foods, blankets and clothes.

Lushington's next camp was Changri, which they reached by marches, first to Angora and on again north-westwards. The marching was very taxing and on some days began at sunrise and lasted till eight or nine in the evening, the men 'lapping up water from the hoof prints of cattle which had been standing in wet ground'. Conditions at Changri were grim, though Lushington does mention games of rugby. A prisoner would attempt to avoid manual labour by describing his trade or profession as 'goalkeeper', 'golf caddy' or 'diver'. A train journey and a march brought them to Belemidik for the railway construction work previously mentioned, which consisted of pushing trolley-loads of stones, carrying timber or hauling it up the steep hillside. Occasionally, through weakness or by design, they allowed the logs to career down the slope out of control, to be lost in the river below. Unlike Gondard, Lushington mentioned only German overseers and engineers, and there is no reference to Greeks or Swiss. The Germans celebrated with gusto the news they received of Jutland, and the Allied soldiers, oppressed by bad news filtering through from several fronts, did their best to counter this with lusty singing of the National Anthem.

In August 1916, Lushington and two others escaped, climbed to the summit of the mountain range and made for Adana and the sea. Their freedom lasted thirteen days. They had almost reached the sea when they were captured, having travelled on foot nearly 150 miles. A filthy, crowded civilian prison with chained murderers and bastinadoed civilian prisoners was to be their reward. Dysentery secured Lushington a merciful transfer to hospital, where he met and was horrified by the condition of emaciated, exhausted British and Indian prisoners who had marched from surrendered Kut. They were tended by an American doctor and an Arab Christian doctor, and the work of these two men saved the lives of many, though the daily death toll was heavy.

A further spell of civilian imprisonment and then rail transfer to Afion Karahissar brought Lushington to a camp undergoing the legendary regime of the commander, Maslum Bey. Prisoners were flogged, their illnesses neglected and their parcels ransacked. Lushington's ordeal had not ended, because he was to suffer harsh contracted labour to a German civilian, the unfulfilled possibility of an exchange of prisoners of war and grim conditions at camps at Ada Bazar and San Stephano. His book reminds one that to ignore the travail of captivity for the soldier taken on the Peninsula is to provide an incomplete picture of the Gallipoli experience.[2]

Chapter 19

Support from the Air

The seaplane support from the converted carrier *Ark Royal*, which had been active since the last days of February, was in April reinforced by No. 3 Squadron RNAS under the command of C.R. Samson, who had established an aerodrome on the island of Tenedos. In the early summer, Turkish positions and troop movements were regularly harassed by bombs and bundles of flechettes, the small winged steel darts which veteran Turks, on interview, still vehemently resented, though their aircraft were using the same rather ineffectual weapon on the Allied positions. Ships and even submarines were bombed and torpedo attacks were made with the Short floatplanes operating from the newly-arrived carrier *Ben-My-Chree*. The *Mitchell Report*[1] fully details the successful work of attacking Turkish communications by air: 112lb bombs were used to attack the vital Maritza River railway bridge at Usun Kopru in November and in the same month Ferijik railway junction and Dedeagatch railway station were more successfully damaged, hindering Turkish communications through Bulgaria.

The Turkish sea supply bases and camps and the roads were also bombed, and a Turkish War Office report described the panic among civilian workers caused by these raids. A Turkish captain told the Mitchell inquirers: 'On one occasion he saw a bomb burst among a party of twenty soldiers, resulting in fifteen killed and one wounded.' The destruction of a flour store in Gallipoli town is likely to have affected bread rations to the Turkish troops defending the Peninsula. The French paid particular attention to store dumps near Kum Kale. A Turkish major admitted that Allied aeroplane attacks had necessitated the moving by night of nearly all supplies and troops towards Anzac and Helles. Bomb and flechette attacks dispersed convoys, wrecked carts, killed camels and caused long delays.

The French regularly bombed the important Soghanli Dere rest camp on the southern shore of the Peninsula, and the white Turkish tents had to be camouflaged, but the troops were finally forced to shelter from these attacks by living in dugouts or caves in the hills, so that it became a rest camp in name only.

Of course the most important work of the aeroplanes was reconnaissance and spotting for naval gunfire. That this was not always developed to good effect was recalled by Rear-Admiral Delaye, who flew as an observer in a Maurice Farman from the French aerodrome at Tenedos. An entry in his log book shows that in sighting an enemy submarine on 27 May he had almost certainly spotted the *U 21*, which, having sunk *Triumph* on the 25th, had that very morning secured further prey in the form of *Majestic* at Cape Helles. His report, however, did not lead to the destruction of *U 21*, as she was not re-located after Delaye's reconnaissance. The admiral also recollected reporting that he saw almost no opposition facing the British landing at Suvla of 7–9 August while on patrol over the area during those three days.[2]

Delaye described the perfect flying conditions over the Peninsula till the late autumn. It was possible to fly at any time of the day and every day. His reports had quite often to be made personally to General Bailloud, the 72-year-old commander of the French force on the departure of d'Amade. The General's Chief of Staff, Colonel Girodon, had on one particular occasion warned him not to speak too loudly in case he disturbed the General, who was very tired. At the precise moment of this warning both men were startled to hear Bailloud calling out in full voice, 'Long live love and potatoes'.

Delaye was involved in co-operation with one of the newly-arrived British monitors, the high trajectory of whose shells was to prove better at searching out Turkish ravine-sheltered gun positions than the flatter-trajectory gunfire of the other warships, and the captain and the French aviators worked closely together. Delaye remembered the English naval officer as always being short of supplies, including even ink for his reports. Delaye's commiseration that his paper work would thus be reduced brought the sad rejoinder that he always had a plentiful supply of pencils. Though he observed the fire of the English monitor, of *Suffren*, *Charlemagne*, *Republique* and various other ships, Delaye's machine was on only one occasion opposed by an enemy aircraft. The Frenchman fired on his aerial adversary but no real combat took place. In fact, the German Tauben,[3] so frequently mentioned in soldiers' diaries, were never able, either by number or by individual effectiveness, seriously to inconvenience the Allied troops beyond their normal hardships. The German bombs were only of 20lb weight, many were duds and none caused serious destruction, though eight men were wounded and five officers killed by them during the campaign.

The French squadron (98T), under the command of Captain Cesari, had established itself on 1 May on the south coast of Tenedos, with the agreement of Commander Samson. The ground was flat and did not have to be specially prepared, but official documents show that at the end of August a certain Hafouz Ibrahim had still not received any 'compensation for the loss of grain in the fields used by the French'.[4]

A report[5] shows that by 16 May two aircraft were assisting artillery observation, getting orders and necessary servicing from the makeshift landing ground above W Beach at Cape Helles. Two more machines were photographing the Turkish trenches opposite the French as well as patrolling Erenkeui Bay, two were on general reconnaissance and one on bombing duties. By the end of September, the French had eighteen aeroplanes – Maurice Farmans – flying from Tenedos, and eight pilots for them. There was a large ground staff of eighty-four, but twenty-four were detached elsewhere.

Though flying conditions and visibility were so good, there were problems for the airmen in their work. The Peninsula had few easily distinguishable geographical or man-made features, and the maps were insufficiently detailed and accurate. The thick scrub afforded easy concealment and the terrain at Anzac, as aerial photographs amply confirm, was as confusing from the air as it was from the ground. The improvised Turkish anti-aircraft fire became more effective, and during the campaign successfully brought down five planes, while another was brought down by machine-gun fire. As the *Mitchell Report*[6] points out, there were further difficulties: 'observers were untrained, wireless telegraphy gear was not perfect, the aeroplanes were not fitted for carrying wireless transmission and the majority of fittings required had to be made locally'. The seaplanes of the *Ark Royal* did have wireless telegraphy and, though sets were later installed in the land-based planes, there were serious deficiencies in their quality.

A French army signaller, Emile Malcailloz, recalled an example of the sort of thing that could go wrong with these early experiments with morse-coded messages. Unable to distinguish the messages he was supposed to be receiving because an English ship was transmitting during a period allocated to the French, he used the agreed emergency signal for 'shut up' to clear the air for his message. A day or so later indignant British naval inquiries tracked down the source of a terse signal to their flagship. The unfortunate Malcailloz was summoned for questioning, but the inquiry was fully satisfied with his explanation and goodwill was restored.

A site was selected for the airfield at Helles as early as 30 April, but it was always under Turkish observation. Machines did not as a rule remain overnight there but flew back to Tenedos, having been based in pairs at Helles for work during the day. From 29 June, Turkish shelling prevented even this use of the ground at Helles and landings were made only in an emergency. As an indication of the problem, a dummy aeroplane here attracted 650 shells in October!

The final landing at Cape Helles was made by Second Lieutenant F.D.H. Bremner,[7] from the squadron based at Imbros. He had arrived at Imbros particularly well-prepared, with letters of introduction to distinguished Greeks, written by an acquaintance of his family who was able in truth to point out that the young Bremner was a 'friend of the Prince of Wales'. Bremner was medically well-prepared too, with a leather wallet in a waterproof case which contained doses of Savory and Moore's chlorodyne, morphine, quinine sulphate, calomel, cocoa extract and essence of ginger.

The difficulty of flying in January is indicated by an entry in Bremner's log for the third of the month. 'We had one or two very bad bumps in places. Quite calm at 8,000. We had to give up owing to clouds getting too bad to see the target. Very badly blown about when near the ground so pancaked the last ten feet down. Got caught in a gust which gave me a bit of leeway so landed rather heavily on the back wheel.' On 6 January, Bremner wrote, 'towards the end Archie made some very good shooting. For the first time I did not mind a bit, even when the bursts were very close.'

While spotting for the monitor HMS *Earl of Peterborough* on 8 January, though his engine was stuttering badly, he flew to investigate something noticed by his observer to the north of Krithia and, on returning, their plane was

attacked by a Hun who came up unobserved behind and slightly above me. Did not know he was there till he started firing and even then did not realize at once what it was. As soon as I did realize I attempted to turn left to bring my Lewis to bear on him and just caught a glimpse of him over my left shoulder. He then disappeared behind me and again fired a few rounds, and apparently made a big right-handed sweep and made off in the direction of Chanak. He was too fast and nippy for me to bring my gun to bear on him, and the whole thing only lasted about thirty seconds!

Bremner described in this letter how he had attempted to follow, but finding his engine revs had dropped, realized that he had been hit and, with no hope of reaching Imbros, made for Helles aerodrome. He can scarcely have been a welcome guest, because the last stages of the evacuation were under way. The plane was pushed into a dugout but would not go right in and of course the Turks were by now shelling it. With some mechanics, and using a pick, shovel and sledgehammer, they smashed the plane, as he was not, for obvious reasons, allowed to burn it. He left the Peninsula from a pier at W Beach aboard a lighter at 1.30 a.m. on the 9th to board the second-last ship to leave the bay, the armed boarding steamer *Partridge*. In his letter home on 11 January, Bremner understandably had to conclude, 'That is a full account of what happened up to five o'clock. After that I cannot say what happened, you will probably understand the reason why from the papers before you get this letter', and continued with an account of the first RNAS hockey match on Imbros during that afternoon.

The British aerodrome at Tenedos had been made by Greek labour, rental being paid for the ground and compensation for the vines which had to be dug up. The large Farman biplanes were landed in packing cases and, in an operation which seems almost from Ancient Egypt, the cases were hauled on rollers by the labourers and sailors up the slope from the shore and along the road to the new aerodrome.

On Imbros there were two aerodromes. One, near the harbour, provided such a dangerous take-off because of its proximity to cliffs and consequent air currents, that a move was made to Kephalo Point, which was constructed by Turkish prisoners. This second aerodrome was appropriately known as Kephalo Marsh because it was so near to the island's Salt Lake that in wet weather it could not be used.

Though there were also aerodromes on Mitylene and on Rabbit Island, the Imbros aerodromes, eleven to sixteen miles distant from the three Peninsula fronts and in immediate proximity to MEF GHQ on the island itself, were obviously to have considerable advantages over the others.

Of the seven types of machine used by the RNAS, only the Maurice Farmans and the B.E.2s were able to do useful work continuously, though the wooden packing cases in which some of the aircraft had been brought did provide living accommodation for the men on Tenedos, the officers living in a small house and in tents. There is no doubt that the French squadron at Tenedos was far better equipped in every way, particularly with regard to spare parts, transport, workshop machinery, hangars and trained personnel. The arrival in July of six Nieuports, two more high-powered Maurice Farmans and four Henri Farmans considerably improved the British strength, but the Maurice Farman pusher-type biplane with a 80h.p., 100h.p. or 110h.p. Renault engine, provided the backbone of the land-based aeroplane work in the Dardanelles.[8]

The outstanding personality in the MEF's field of aviation was undoubtedly the short, stocky, bearded and somewhat irascible Commander Samson. Bremner remembered how the Commander's fury and voice were roused and his language debased by the sight of unauthorized personnel walking on the landing strip at Kephalo. Samson's Standing Orders are quoted in the *Official History*[9] and they reflect the image of a man of efficiency and aggression. That sound practical common sense was another factor, is also apparent. Pilots were always to be armed with a revolver or pistol, observers were always to carry a rifle. Pilots and observers were to familiarize themselves with the photos of Turkish men of war described in the *World's Fighting Ships* – 'This book is in the office'. 'Don't make wild statements … a small accurate report is worth pages of rhetoric giving no real information. If an enemy aeroplane is sighted attack it, reporting you are doing so if spotting. Don't try to do what is termed by some people, "Stunt flying". This is not wanted for war and is not conduct required of an officer.'

In his contemporary private papers,[10] Samson's confidence is always evident. On 19 April, having hit a howitzer with a bomb, his notes record: 'I was very pleased with myself, especially the first gun, as it was the result of a careful sighting shot.' 25 April was a, 'wonderful sight and I will never forget it', but he was far from devoid of compassion as the 'corpses on the beaches and the blood in the water were sights that made you feel rather rotten sitting up there aloft with nothing to do except spotting the ship's fire'. His notes for 25 April make compelling reading. 'The water was simply whipped into foam by the shells and bullets … the *Q.E.* was putting salvo after salvo into the town … you could, from the air, trace the tracks of the shells passing through the houses before they burst.' Samson's fame spread. An Australian with the 10th Battalion wrote to a friend as early as 19 May: 'We have the best English and French flyers here. One named Samson the Germans have offered £6,000 [for] dead or alive.'[11] The death in a take–off crash of an officer named Collett clearly affected Samson deeply. 'He was burnt to death. His loss was a terrible loss to the squadron and I lost a great friend, he was absolutely irreplaceable. Chief Petty Officer Keogh, Jones and Robins displayed remarkable bravery in attempting to save him.' The tributes he paid to his men are paralleled by his admiration for those of his machines with Renault engines, 'which always [went] splendidly'.

By 11 November, No. 3 Squadron, which had averaged seven pilots, had flown 143,000 miles and dropped 205 large and 543 small bombs on the Turks. For the next month or so they would be faced by severe cold and many more flying clothes had to be worn. Samson wrote in his notes that he wished the so-called flying organizers in England could have a taste of this.

He made it a rule, 'whenever possible that if anybody bombed my aerodrome, we always returned the visit immediately and gave them worse than they gave us'.[12] No. 3 Squadron was imbued with a spirit of determination reflected in their achievements and it is certainly tantalizing to consider what might have happened had Samson achieved complete success in bombing a staff car which was, as appears from later evidence, carrying Kemal. Yet another imponderable in the alluring but fruitless game of considering when, if ever, victory were to have lain within reach of the Allies.

Soberingly, one can pass to the evidence of the log of Reginald Portal for actuality rather than potential. As a sub-lieutenant in *Bacchante*, Portal had already served at the Anzac and Suvla landings. He became an RNAS observer in January 1916, flying from Imbros. His log for that month and for February makes an unintentionally ironic comment on the futility of the Gallipoli endeavour as his reconnaissance flights over Suvla, Anzac and Helles allow him to observe the Turks taking up the long-held Allied positions. 'Tried to locate gun firing from Hunter Weston Hill. Ceased fire before we arrived.'

One pilot was singled out for the supreme award of the Victoria Cross. On a raid to destroy the railway supply route from Bulgaria at Ferijik Junction, one plane was damaged and had to land in Bulgarian territory. The pilot, Flight Sub-Lieutenant Smylie, set fire to his plane but, on seeing Lieutenant Davies preparing to land beside the burning plane, exploded the bomb still on his plane with pistol fire in order that it should not damage the plane preparing to land. Davies, though surprised by the explosion, nevertheless landed and as Bulgarian troops approached, Smylie was squeezed under the engine cowl to 'crouch on all fours between the rudder bar and the engine bearers with his head bumping on the oil tank'.[13] Davies took off successfully and the two men arrived safely in Imbros. In his contemporary notes for 19 November, Commander Samson wrote: 'one of the very finest feats of aeroplane warfare was carried out today by Davies … Davies already has the D.S.O. which he has earned twenty times over since. He should get the VC for this. We all think he deserves it.'[14]

Vice-Admiral Bell-Davies wrote engagingly in his memoirs of his time in the Dardanelles,[15] when, 'by a terrific fluke I landed a 100-lb. bomb right on the [German] hangar. The French squadron was just behind me and saw the bomb burst, so my reputation as a bomb-aimer soared with them.' He described the yellow fog through which on occasion landings had to be made at Cape Helles when the prevailing north-east winds blew the dust off the dried-up, over-trodden, pulverised Peninsula. 'At the landing ground one had to turn without being blown over and taxi hastily downwind to the spot behind the mound before the Turkish shells arrived.' At the time of the Suvla landing he was told by the Flag Commander, Alexander Ramsey, that, 'your rotten old aeroplanes will be no bloody good anyway',[16] but his reconnaissance over Suvla, like Delaye's, showed the absence of strong opposition in the first days of the new landing.

The memoir included a description of creature comforts at Imbros – an aeroplane packing case divided into three rooms.

The two end rooms we fitted with bunks and used as sleeping cabins; doors connected with the middle room which we used as a sitting room. Wash basins were made out of petrol cans fitted on hinged brackets which shot the dirty water outside. Windows were made from the glass of old photographic plates. We improved the oil-drum stove by building a proper fireplace in our sitting room with fire blocks and fire clay looted or rather salved from the old colliers which had been sunk to form a breakwater for the small-craft anchorage in

Kephalo Bay. For fire bars we used tappet rods from wrecked Gnome engines. In fact we were as well housed as possible to face a Gallipoli winter.

The work of the men operating and observing from the kite balloons moored from *Manica* and *Hector*[17] must not be neglected. *Manica* had previously been involved in manure-carrying in the Manchester Ship Canal,[18] but quickly achieved distinction on 26 April in spotting for the successful sinking by *Queen Elizabeth* of a Turkish transport seven miles from the British battleship. The only trained observer in the kite balloon section was Squadron Commander J.D. Mackworth, but, as kite balloons could stay up all day, an observer, trained or not, could sight a target and remain in continuous observation of it. He was in constant telephone communication with the ship to which the balloon was tethered. The advantages for naval gunfire of this form of observation over aeroplanes was considerable but there were disadvantages too – the balloon could not be used on windy days, reached no great height and was vulnerable to air attack – and indeed submarine attack, because it could be operated only from a specially fitted and slow-moving ship. An official report pointed out a potentially disastrous problem for the *Manica*: 'A large shell bursting near the full gas tubes below decks showed that it was running an unnecessary risk of total destruction to the ship to keep them on board, and the gas-making and compressing plant was transferred to the tug, *Rescue*.'

A Submarine Scout airship was also operated, first from Mudros and later from Imbros. It was at Imbros that the slow seaplane carrier *Ark Royal*, with its hangar for ten planes, had to be based from the time of the submarine scare rather than at its original base of operations, Tenedos. The diary of Flight Lieutenant G.R. Bromet chronicled both the tribulations and the less frequent but hard-earned achievements of *Ark Royal*'s seaplanes and aeroplanes. On 17 February, the day *Ark Royal* arrived at Tenedos, Bromet's seaplane was the only one of three to carry out a wireless trial patrol successfully. He reached 3,500 feet in twenty-six minutes and a maximum height of 4,500 feet. 'Before returning to base we dropped two bombs – one at Kum Kalessi which found its mark and one at Seddel Bahr which fell short. The enemy opened fire on us with field guns, rifles and machine-guns, but only managed to hit us seven times … The flight lasted for 1 hour 15 minutes.'

On 19 February, he was spotting for HMS *Cornwallis*, but the ship had ceased firing by the time he had reached the necessary ceiling. In a later patrol on the same day, lack of fuel forced him down before he could spot for *Inflexible*. When all the ships were ordered to fire at the same time, spotting was impossible. In recording his admiration for the, 'plucky and wise' manner in which the Turkish gunners in the forts reserved their fire until the ships were within range, Bromet 'nevertheless considered that had our seaplanes been given the opportunity of controlling the gunfire of each individual ship it is quite certain that by 5 p.m. the Turks would have had no guns left'.

When the naval shelling was resumed on the 25th the sea was too rough for the seaplanes to take off, though Captain Kilner in Seaplane 136 did succeed in making a useful reconnaissance on the following day. Great care was needed in the handling of the seaplanes, as 'new machines and spares would take six weeks to arrive from England'. On 4 March an inlet valve rocker broke, piercing the propeller and the port float. Unable to climb higher than 2,000 feet and getting too close to Turkish troops at Yeni Shehr, Seaplane 172 came under small-arms fire and 'collected twenty-eight bullet holes, which served the silly old bitch right for refusing to climb to a safe height'. The following day, 27 February, Bromet recorded that Seaplane 808 had spiralled and nose-dived into the sea. Astonishingly both the pilot, Flight Lieutenant Garnet, and the observer, Flight Commander Williamson, were rescued, Garnet holding the injured Williamson's head above water until the destroyer *Usk* arrived. In Seaplane 922, which took off immediately afterwards, Flight Lieutenant Douglas was shot in the calf and had to land, but a later flight, using searchlight communication from the *Ark Royal* and reply by wireless, successfully spotted for *Queen Elizabeth*.

Bromet was very conscious of his dependence on the efforts of his mechanics: 'C.P.O. Finbow worked solidly on a difficult and annoying job for sixteen hours and I cannot praise him or Air Mechanic Somner too highly for their painstaking and successful work and for their cheery optimism throughout.'

The resentment felt by the seaplane pilots at the restrictions placed on their work and the consequent underestimation of their potential, are revealed in numerous entries in Bromet's diary. 'The great interest taken by the Air Department in land machines is all very well but some of us would like to see a more intelligent interest taken in seaplanes.' In September, not long before he left the Dardanelles, he made the point more strongly:

> People laugh at seaplanes and ask what use are they. Why? Because they have only experienced and been able to compare the work done by *Ark Royal* (whose hard work had to be carried out with seven seaplanes of an inferior quality and with no spares) and Cmdr Samson's squadron (whose aerodrome we built and had ready when he arrived) of ten or more land machines supplemented by new ones when necessary. I allow that as things have worked out aeroplanes can do the Peninsular work better than we can, but one must not forget that the naval front extends from Enos right down to Smyrna and that had the campaign gone as it was expected to go, aeroplanes would have been of little use owing to the necessarily rapid changes of aerodrome.

As he was leaving the Peninsula in the first week of October, Bromet wrote that he had thoroughly enjoyed his eight months in the Aegean, but, 'of course we only see the fun of war. The disgusting realities of the trenches do not touch us, although I have smelt them even in the air at 3 or 4,000 feet and seen the red fringe along the Helles shore.'

It should perhaps be mentioned that Bromet had not always been so removed from close contact with danger. On 28 March, *Ark Royal* had been bombed by a German biplane, and Bromet confided to his diary that, 'it is most disconcerting to have bombs dropped on one … I think one feels absolutely helpless when being attacked from above; I certainly did today after seeing the first bomb drop and when the second one exploded about twenty feet away from me I began to wonder where one might take shelter in the case of a future attack.' Fortunately for Bromet and *Ark Royal* there was a general truth in a rhyme the seaplane pilot was to record during the campaign:

> There's a game that some play for the whole of the day
> Of dropping a bomb from the air,
> And men grin with delight if they drop it aright,
> A contingency only too rare.

For a final memory of *Ark Royal* we may turn to J.J. Teasdale, in 1915 a chief mechanic on board the carrier. He remembered that motor-boats had on occasion to traverse the chosen sea track to roughen it sufficiently for seaplane take-off. He also recalled seeing from *Ark Royal*, at the time when the ship was based at Imbros, red-tabbed staff officers commuting each morning and evening to and from the Peninsula armed for war with their briefcases.

A faster carrier, *Ben-My-Chree*, arrived at the Dardanelles on 12 July after conversion from use as a Liverpool-Isle of Man passenger ferry. Unlike *Ark Royal*, which had steam-driven hoists to winch the planes from their hangar in the hold, *Ben-My-Chree* had an upper-deck hangar aft, with a good testing and repair workshop. On 12 August, Flight Commander C.H.K. Edmonds, in a Short seaplane from the carrier, scored a perfect torpedo hit on a large Turkish transport lying off Bulair, where the ship had already been damaged, probably by *E 14*. Though the ship was in water too shallow for sinking, Edmond's torpedo success, from only fifteen feet above sea level, was the first of its kind in the war. In his flight report, Edmonds wrote that, as he looked backwards, 'I observed the track of the torpedo, which struck the ship abreast the mainmast, the starboard side. The explosion sent a column of water and large fragments of the ship almost as high as the masthead ... she appeared to have settled down a little by the stern when I ceased watching her.'[19] The Official Historian[20] considered that *Ben-My-Chree* was particularly valuable as a mobile self-contained air unit, but not the least of her achievements was one which could not have been anticipated, for the carrier rescued 694 troops and 121 crew from the torpedoed *Southland*, thirty miles from Mudros on 2 September.

It is perhaps appropriate that a final incident concerning the air war in this arena should concern Commander Samson. His log for 6 August recorded that he was engaged in dropping propaganda pamphlets. J.J. Teasdale has remarked that it was generally known in *Ark Royal* and on the island of Imbros that Samson was so disgusted at having to fulfil this function that he dropped bombs on the soldiers picking up the leaflets. This curious story cannot be substantiated but, if it were true, the persuasive value of propaganda material designed to influence soldiers defending their homeland, must have been still more limited on that particular occasion.[21]

Chapter 20

Autumn Stagnation and the Onset of Winter

From September, at Anzac in particular, the nature of the campaign changed. With an increasing readiness to live and let live above ground, the opposing forces dug deeply underground, defensively for dugouts and communication tunnels, offensively for mining activity.

Concerning Helles, there is intriguing evidence in the diary and memory of Eric Wettern of an isolated tree with flags on it denoting an exceptionally quiet sector on the right, once held by the French and later by the Royal Naval Division. At Anzac, where the trenches were in closer proximity, messages, cigarettes, jam, and the less popular bully beef were exchanged simply by lobbing them across the narrow no man's land. To quite a marked extent the attitude towards the Turk had changed too. The judgement expressed in a letter, dated 13 September, from a wounded soldier in which he expressed admiration of the Turk who 'is a very fine soldier indeed and any one who thinks otherwise can be convinced by going out to Gallipoli for a week' is paralleled in many letters and diaries.

As offensive operations diminished, health and living conditions naturally dominated other recorded considerations. On 20 September, Padre McKenzie wrote that he was infuriated that parcels and clothing were lost to the 'thousands of thieves among the orderlies and soldiers who steal the parcels and help themselves'. More serious was the general condition of the troops, in particular those at Anzac. A table of Gallipoli casualties and statistics in the *Official Medical History* shows that, while 47,803 British and Commonwealth troops were admitted into hospital with wounds, 128,708 were admitted as 'sick'.[1] Of the latter, nearly 50,000 were cases of dysentery, diarrhoea and enteric fever. Dysentery and related illnesses had become a serious problem in July and conditions after the August battles guaranteed the spreading of the disease.

At Helles, Anzac and Suvla, weakened men, in growing numbers, dragged themselves pathetically to the latrines and, with adequate hygienic facilities impossible to achieve there for an obvious host of reasons, the problem increased daily. 'Passing slime and blood'[2] is a pathetic entry typical of diaries from all three fronts. J.G. Gasparich felt that,

my whole alimentary tract was on fire and was periodically being torn from me. I was sent over to Imbros and housed in a great marquee with dozens of others in like state. We slept on the ground and were fed stew and tea which only made matters worse. We were forced by the sickness to visit the latrines every hour or so, each visit being made in agony. Some men were so weak that they crawled to the latrines and stayed there until they died. In the hospital ship to Alexandria the latrines were totally inadequate and there were long queues of men in desperation and in pain as they waited at the over-crowded toilets. The Mohammedan-style squatting-toilets in a Cairo hospital adapted from an army barracks provided the final refinement to our torture.

The New Zealander, Captain T.R. Ritchie,[3] in his evidence to the Dardanelles Commission, affirmed that the saltiness and stringiness of the Fray Bentos corned beef, the insufficiency of condensed milk, the lack of arrowroot, the inadequate purification of the water and the absence of castor oil had all helped to further the disease, but, even more than the insanitary latrines, the fly menace was the greatest evil. 'We had the ordinary open latrines. The space in Monash Gully which was not under fire was very limited and it was very difficult getting sites for latrines. What I wanted to introduce was the pan system. We introduced it at Headquarters itself and it worked very well but we could not get the pans – in one case Capt. Home of the Wellington Bn fixed up latrines with a box cover over them so that no flies could get in.'

The experience of using the primitive latrines is recalled by F.C. Sillar, who contracted dysentery when in the front line at Helles early in November. 'I was compelled to go every ten minutes from my duty post to the latrine, which was formed in a short side trench leading back from the line. Here there were three buckets covered by wooden box lids with extremely sharp edges. Just behind this latrine we had a trench mortar firing about every two minutes. The Turkish equivalent kept firing to find and destroy our mortar. Shells were falling all around and some in the latrine space itself.' Sillar must have visited his less than peaceful haven many times during his four-day stint in the line. Incidentally the many photographs of troops bathing at W Beach do not always show the large wooden structure built out from the cliffs into the sea. This structure was one answer to the problem of waste disposal, as it enabled men to perform their natural functions directly into the sea. The photographs show no, 'Beach unsafe for Bathing' signs!

During the week ending 5 September, 7.5 per cent of the troops at Anzac were evacuated sick, while only 1.7 per cent of those at Suvla had fallen victim and 5.1 per cent of those at Helles. While these figures do provide an ironic comment on the much-abused physique and general fitness of the New Army men at Suvla,[4] it is undeniable that the geography of Anzac imposed special problems, not just concerning the nature of the fighting, but for the, 'circumstances of existence'. For regimental medical officers, platoon commanders, NCOs and the individual soldier himself, maintaining an adequate state of health – body and mind – was an essential yet virtually unachievable objective.

Some of the Anzac troops were given a much-needed rest at Lemnos, but those who remained, together with the replacements, were now heavily committed to digging deep dugouts against winter conditions and the anticipated increased supplies of enemy ammunition. The supplies came from the German-directed

Turkish armament factories, as well as from the Central Powers through Bulgaria to Turkey once the full effect of Bulgaria's entry into the war on 6 September was felt.

In the absence of any heavy fighting, Anzac was a hive of activity in September and October. The work force building roads, piers and jetties on the beaches was augmented by Maltese and Egyptian labour and experiments were being carried out, unsuccessfully, with a narrow-gauge railway. In the front-line areas, more sophisticated trench periscopes, telescopic-sighted rifles, silencers, catapults and individual stalking[5] in no man's land, increasingly became the norm. One refinement used on all three Gallipoli sectors was the steel plate firmly wedged into a section of a parapet. A spring-clipped shutter covered the observation and firing aperture for sniping at the opposition. A photograph of the surface of one such plate, pitted by bullet marks after a short period of service, indicates both the need for such defence and the nerve needed to look and fire through the aperture.[6]

A network of deep intercommunicating dugouts, as well as mine tunnels, was being moled underground. The mining was difficult and dangerous work. In the shortage of candles, slush lamps, consisting of a lit wick, in oil or fat, gave out dim light in the hot, shadowed, dusty galleries in which perspiring lamp-blacked faces paused anxiously in their own digging to listen for any sound of similar Turkish activity. When such sounds were identified, the danger signal was silence, denoting the enemy's readiness to fire his explosive charge. If one side were to break into the other's tunnel, hastily-erected sandbag barricades provided cover to prepare charges to blow up the enemy tunnel while 'sentries' fired into the blackness beyond the barrier.

There was extensive mining activity at Helles too, well described in Joe Murray's *Gallipoli as I Saw It*. It was desperately dangerous work wherever it were undertaken. The Australian, A.L. Rutter, retained throughout his life the speech impediment caused by the explosion in the tunnel in which he was working, and original letters and diaries document the admiration widely felt for those men who braved the poisonous fumes in the tunnels to rescue comrades who were overcome by these gases.

Leading from a position known as the 'Western Birdcage' on the extreme left of the Helles front line was a tunnel which burrowed its way beneath no man's land towards the Turkish front line. The 7th Manchesters had been busily engaged in clearing the spoil from the tunnel. The prone soldier dragged it towards him in a half-filled sandbag, eased it past his body and pushed it backwards towards the next man. It was hot, tiring, work in such confined space. Funnel-shaped air chimneys brought some light onto the work and by this illumination, aided by a candle, F.T.K. Woodworth used to read the *Strand Magazine* in periods of inactivity during a two-hour stint. When this particular tunnel was found and 'blown' by the Turks, twenty-eight men were killed.

The capacity of a man in the ranks for vivid, verbal imagery at such a scene was recalled by Ivor Birtwistle. As the bodies of sappers and those who had attempted a rescue were laid side by side just below where Birtwistle was sitting, the evening sun neared the sea horizon beyond them, colouring the whole setting with gold, scarlet, pink and mauve. Across the purple sea lay the still darker island masses of Imbros and

Samothrace. A man nudged him and said, looking towards the heart of the sunset, 'It looks as if those chaps had rushed into heaven in a hurry and had forgotten to shut the door'.

Except for a few tear-gas grenades at Anzac, gas was one refinement of war not used on the Peninsula, despite the wise precaution of issuing many troops with primitive gas helmets or hoods. Some units had to wear them for training periods and photographs of these exercises testify to the awareness of the danger of a surprise gas attack. A temporary but unprofitable diversion was provided for soldiers of both sides by the target of migratory flights of geese, ducks and swallows, but on all three fronts the autumn was a period of relative quiescence, except underground.

Raymond Weil, at Helles, suffering from fever despite doses of quinine, confided in his diary for 29 September that it would suit him quite well if he were evacuated straight to France. Many of the French troops at Helles, though not the Senegalese, the North Africans nor the artillery units, were in fact evacuated at the beginning of October and sent to assist the Serbs in their unavailing attempt to stem invasion by the Central Powers. In the same month, the 10th Irish Division was sent from Suvla to Salonika for an Allied attempt to open a different backdoor, through Bulgaria, into the Austro-Hungarian element of the Dual Alliance, the one through the Dardanelles and the Ottoman Empire, now manifestly shut against the heaviest battering.

At Helles on 1 October, the RND Engineers Signal Company's trench magazine, *Fag Ends*, inquired, 'How long are we likely to occupy our new dugouts?' and, 'Whether the Post Office will allow Xmas puddings to be sent to the Dardanelles at a reduced rate?' In the absence of intensive military activity such questions, jocular or more serious, became a preoccupation. Though the RND sappers had construction work to do, Eric Wettern's diary for September and October records days off, walks to the French lines, a concert in a dressing station, canteen committee meetings, a raffle, taking photos, and an occasional 'shrapnel for lunch'.

During these quieter periods it was natural that the soldier became still more aware of the distance which separated him from family and friends at home. It was not just by the receipt of letters that this distance could be diminished, but in the writing of letters that the terraced house or the country village could be brought closer. The letters of a Tasmanian gunner, Sergeant Alf Clennett, illustrate this point. Full of tenderly expressed understanding of the strain upon his mother, who had three boys serving on the Peninsula, Clennett unconsciously paints with imaginative insight the continuation of everyday life in an island still affectionately known today as 'Tassy' and mentioned in all the sergeant's letters. He expresses surprise and pleasure at the sale for a good price of 'Beauty', a horse, 'getting well on towards her allotted span'. He feels regret that his ninety-year-old grandfather could not deliver his normal supply of fresh eggs to the grandsons on the Peninsula and also that his grandfather's fence is not available for firewood. To his sister he writes to say how much he would like to be badgering them in the kitchen when they are making cakes and scones.

Isn't it splendid the way the people shelled out on Australia Day? It is rather wonderful how they keep it up when times are so bad, but what a long way behind Launceston is. The Hobart people will crow about their victory this time, won't they? I notice South beat North at football too, another bang in the eye … I am glad Guy had done pretty well with the apples and sheep and cattle. I suppose he will be spraying again before this reaches you and I wouldn't mind giving him a hand again if this scrap was over… Thanks very much for sending us the violets, it is nice to see a flower again. I suppose the flowers are all out at home, how different to things here … the photo of our [dogs] is very nice too. It is nice to see them all again. Monty evidently wanted to wag his tail at me … I suppose you had quite a lively time with the Archdeacon when he was down. I can just imagine I can hear his grand old laugh.

For Sergeant Clennett, briefly visiting the rest camp at Mudros, the enjoyment of visiting some of the large naval vessels moored in the harbour would have been gladly exchanged for, 'a trip round the old bay at home'. These letters, though laden to an unusual degree with wistful homesickness, are illustrative of many sent from the Peninsula at this period – seldom written in a manner to betray low morale but bearing a consistently recurring theme: 'How different things must look at home from this desolate place.' As early as 22 May, Merseysider Tom Sye was confiding in his diary:

I have been indulging in a few daydreams … always my solace is in future anticipations – of days to come when, decently dressed, I shall again enjoy the luxuries of congenial companions and good food served up daintily. Again at times I derive joy from looking back. Little vignettes present themselves to my mind's eye – Betws-y-Coed, peaceful and beautiful; Douglas with its Port Jack and its wonderful summer days; Blackpool with its lights and thousand joys … little memories of nights of stars and gladness, of a room lit only by the flickering firelight and the shadows dancing over the walls where we two have sat and talked and dreamed the nights away.

In the autumn and winter, men newly arriving on the Peninsula, like J.M.L. Bogle, were struck by the lack of activity compared with the heroic deeds of which they had read: 'Our men seem to do so much less shooting than the Turks and … seem dog tired and worn out.' Within a day of his arrival at Helles, Bombardier Brown, who had served in France, was to write: 'Am posted to 66th Brigade HQ Staff and everything seems alright, in fact I could not have done better. Food simply grand, much better than we ever got in France and not half so much work to do.'

At Suvla, one of the day's sights was a horseman or a motorbike rider running the gauntlet of the desultory shelling which threatened his route to Anzac and back with dispatches. With water supplies now properly provided and deeper entrenchments in use, life was less dangerous, but now boredom and a sense of purposelessness, for the healthy, were an erosion of morale, though not of course to such a dangerous degree as the effects of dysentery. J.C. Dart's diary entry for 3 September is a fair reflection of a general picture. 'Feeling fed up. Had a wash in a biscuit tin. Felt much refreshed.

No mail, no tobacco. Sand blowing all over the place. Consequently we are all feeling down in the mouth.' When Newfoundland troops were landed as reinforcements at Suvla Bay, their enthusiasm led them to scramble for the shrapnel balls or hot fragments of shell which had exploded over their heads. However, the problem of digging temporary dugouts in the fine, powdery sand near the beach soon took the edge off their keenness.

In fact the Peninsula held for its prisoners one last terrible trial, made no less severe by an awareness that it would have to be faced. So concerned were the War Office and the MEF HQ about the problems of a harsh winter that an official meteorologist had been appointed. Neither he nor other experts accurately predicted the earliness of the winter storm, and its intensity found the troops completely unprepared. The prescient Lieutenant Carrington had written home on 15 August for warm woollen clothing, a balaclava cap and an oilskin sou'wester. On 7 September he noted that the weather was getting chilly and, 'such things as bronchitis and tonsillitis are flying around'. He concluded with a statement the ironic significance of which he could not of course appreciate: 'Most people will go away during the winter for some reason or another so don't get alarmed.'

In early October, storms damaged landing stages and small craft. At the end of the month, the landing facilities at each sector suffered again. Some of the winter stores and protective clothing had not yet arrived and one consignment had been returned in error to Mudros. There were further gales in November and then, from the early evening of 26 November, the War Diary of the 86th Brigade, 29th Division,[7] serving at Suvla, illustrated the terrible experience befalling those in that sector and to some extent those at Anzac.

1900. Very severe thunderstorm with very strong gale and torrents of rain.

2000. All telephone communication was cut off and all dugouts flooded out.

2100. Reported to Bde HQs that all trenches were flooded, water had come in as though it had been a tidal wave, that many men must have been drowned, and few had been able to save their rifles and equipment. The men were standing up to their knees in water, behind the parados of the trenches.

Next morning, under great difficulty, some rations were brought up for the men. They huddled together to try to get warm. 'A great deal of shrapnel was fired during the day, chiefly at parties of men who were given permission to leave the trenches, all in various states of exhaustion, to go to the ambulances. It was not expected that many of these men reached their destination and it is feared that a great number of men died from exposure.' Towards evening the weather got worse, developing into a blizzard with intense cold, and men were still struggling down to the ambulances in large numbers. The condition of the men still in the trenches grew worse as the blizzard continued throughout the night of the 27th/28th. The following day it remained intensely cold. On the 30th it is recorded that, 'a number of trench boots were received. These are to prevent the men from getting frozen feet.'

The storm, flooding, blizzard and freezing temperatures were to result in 280 deaths and 16,000 cases of frostbite and exposure. At Helles, even allowing for Eric Wettern's gift for understatement, the conditions were not too harsh. 'The Pig Sty [his dugout] let a few drops of water in but nothing much. Pretty cool alone in Pig Sty. Anxious moments but no serious trouble.' At Anzac, the deep, well-constructed dugouts provided some protection and the lie of the land carried the water quickly down to the sea. Many Australians were seeing snow for the first time and were only prevented from admiring the white-mantled beauty of the scene by the intense cold. Some, like Private Craven, made ice cream out of snow and condensed milk and there was even some snowballing. New Zealander, J.G. Gasparich, shed his soaked greatcoat and remembered that it stood as a frozen, empty, stiff-standing sentinel for several days, while an Australian, 17th Battalion officer, Basil Holmes, remembered how the snow enabled better sighting of slight glimpses of Turks in their trenches or of their shadows.

For the Indian troops and for those moving on lower ground at Anzac, the miseries of Suvla were shared. Sapper Clifton of the 1st Field Company, New Zealand Engineers, described in a letter[8] having to go down from Rhododendron Ridge to collect fifteen mules and then lead them to Hill 60. It was pitch dark, bitterly cold, the wind blowing, so that the night was to become an experience that he would never forget. On the beach everything was in confusion and everywhere there was deep slush. The necessary ropes were almost frozen and gear had to be loaded and roped in the dark. Soon the party got split up. Carrying full packs, extra blankets and sheets, and rifles, they stumbled along in the dark. One man never arrived at his destination and frozen stragglers staggered in to fight for a place in the crowd of men around a small brazier.

'Turks walk about on top of trenches. Very few shots exchanged. Rain and snow at night. Men in awful state, some dying from exposure.' This diary entry of Private W. Clark accurately summarised conditions at Suvla on the 27th of November. It is not true to say that there was no firing, as Turks and British stamped about outside their trenches trying to avoid the flood and generate some warmth, but there was very little and in certain sectors none at all. An exception must be quoted: 'The Turks apparently fared even worse than we did and were so cold that they got out of their trenches and walked about to keep warm, whereupon we shot as many as possible, poor devils', recorded Lieutenant Savory of the 14th Sikhs. Perhaps surprisingly, his men had not been so badly affected by the late November conditions as had the Gurkhas. The history of the 10th Princess Mary's Own Gurkha Rifles[9] related that the 2nd Battalion had 447 cases of frostbite. 'All these had to be evacuated, ten of the other ranks died and most of the others had to be invalided out of the service, many of them maimed for life.'

Newly appointed to command the 1st Battalion the 5th Gurkha Rifles, Colonel Arthur Basil Tillard recorded in his diary for 26 November that they had endured 'the most awful day'. The heavy rain had seeped into his dugout, soaking the blankets. The officers' dugouts and the men's trenches were flooded, the sides caving in as he inspected them. In a nicely conventional touch towards evening, he had left his dugout to wash for dinner. He got to bed 'eventually' but it became 'beastly cold'. The men were using their mess tins to bail out their trenches. A Turk tried to surrender to them but a sentry shot him before the enemy soldier's intention became clear. He had only been wounded and created (moaned?) all day. Someone went to look for him but he had crawled away. 'A truly awful night.' At about midnight he went round the lines again, finding the 'wretched men nearly frozen, though they are really in the cleanest place in the whole area but it's wickedly cold with a gale blowing from the NE. I felt so sorry for the poor little devils.'[10]

Down in the Suvla plain the flood had raced along the deres and into the trench system as a raging torrent carrying corpses of men and mules and every imaginable article of equipment. The well-known defensive block in a gully, the Highland Barricade, was swept away by the Azmak Dere, but by great good fortune a corporal of the Fife and Forfar Yeomanry, A.G. Brown, while surveying the flood, was sufficiently quick to grasp a floating box which proved to be from Fortnum and Mason. The contents included spirits, which helped his small party to keep alive. His blond-moustached sergeant had however been sniped through the head getting out of the trench and his face stared up at them from its tomb of frozen flood water for several days as they moved about the trench on its iced footing.

Soaked, sleep-deprived and then numbed by cold, their situation in trench systems making it exceptionally difficult to manage the bodily movement generating warmth to keep frostbite at bay, men slid into a zone from which neither external aid nor any internal reserves of self-preservation could reach. Charles Mackintosh was in the front-line trenches at Suvla just behind an advanced post known as Warwick Castle. His experience may be taken as illustrative of the suffering of many. He and his men were flooded out of their trenches when the torrent raced through, but they had managed to salvage some blankets and when the flood waters subsided below the firestep they clambered back in and endeavoured to keep warm. In the morning, Mackintosh saw a fellow officer, in trenches full of water, shot as he clambered on top to consider where a drainage channel should be dug. Soon after this, cries for help came from the communication trench winding towards Warwick Castle. The trench was blocked with mud where it entered the main front-line trench so that the only way to help the unseen sufferer was over the top of the trench in full exposure to the Turks. 'I got out of the trench feeling as if the guns of the entire Turkish Army were turned on me and slithered over to where the head and shoulders of a man were showing over the mud in the communication trench.' Mackintosh, finding every effort to tug the man clear prove futile, finally managed to get him out by dragging soaking sandbags to dump into piles in front and behind him, so that by standing on them directly above him he finally pulled him clear.

Utterly exhausted and unable to face the dixey of rice which he was offered, as it clearly contained some of the remains of one of the men who had been killed in bringing it forward, Mackintosh now had to face the increasing cold which followed upon the storm. He shared a dugout with a fellow officer who rocked and moaned throughout the night and in the morning the blizzard drowned almost every other sound, forcing snow down the throat of any mouth attempting to shout. One of his unfortunate companions appeared to be trying to sing, giving rise to Mackintosh's admiration. The singing seemed to change to snoring and then silence. When a corporal stretched across his officer to lift and force the body of the silent singer over the parapet, Mackintosh's protest was that of a man already losing full consciousness. He had taken off his boots so that he could wrap his puttees round his swollen feet and, finding that he could not walk, had crawled on his hands and knees towards a fire which was surrounded by Worcester Regiment officers. They gave him blackcurrant tea. He was carried down to the beach and after a further day there, spent listening to the pained protests of a badly wounded man every time a warship sent salvoes over their heads, he was stretchered off the Peninsula.

As one of the serious frostbite cases, Mackintosh's Gallipoli service was now over. It was December and the final drama was approaching. Out of the suffering at Anzac and Suvla with all the attendant disorganization, it seems scarcely credible that within eighteen days every soldier would have been safely evacuated in an operation which compels admiration at every stage of planning and every level of execution.

Chapter 21

The Evacuation

Though the full Cabinet did not finally authorize the evacuation of Anzac and Suvla until a meeting on 7 December, detailed planning had begun on 22 November. On the Peninsula, rumours had for some time bruited the likelihood of such a move. For many, the November storm seemed to make the evacuation more necessary and yet more difficult. At Anzac, it was obvious to the man in the ranks that if the Turks attacked while the withdrawal was taking place, succeeding in commanding the heights immediately above the beaches, devastating losses could be suffered. This would in due course be an important unit and individual self-discipline factor in meticulous adherence to the elaborate deception plans being drawn up.

Some general impressions of the plan's execution do stand out from the wealth of contemporary and recollected evidence. On the one hand there was a general readiness to admit that the troops and their leaders had shot their bolt, that their continued presence and the suffering being endured, were to no obvious purpose; on the other hand, there was an unwillingness to accept defeat. Dead comrades were being left behind with the 'endeavour' not successfully accomplished. The soldier was not prepared to concede that he had been defeated: outweighed by the combined forces of geography and climate and well matched by the Turks, yes, but not defeated, not thrown off the Peninsula, would be an fair summary of his attitude, judging from the evidence of letters, diaries and recollections. At the same time, he was conscious that to leave the field before the end of a match constituted defeat and, while most would be content to leave the varied privations of the Peninsula far behind them, the implication of evacuation was a bitter pill. Naturally the increased activity, its unusual nature, the heightened tension and a sense of purpose, all did something to disguise the taste.

With the centre of the Turkish line at Anzac, that is the Nek, only 800 yards from North, or Ocean, Beach, and within 300 yards of direct observation of the beach, the soldier least aware of anything other than his immediate needs can scarcely have been ignorant of the difficulty of getting off the Peninsula without a battle to hold the beach. Such a battle would clearly be fought at an overwhelming disadvantage, and to slip away silently from a position less than ten yards from Turks whose conversation could be heard, seemed unrealistically optimistic.

The sick were evacuated first and then most of the field ambulance men; gunners went with their guns. This whittling down of the Anzac garrison, intended to appear as preparation for a reduced winter establishment, was done at night. The actual sequence of events at Anzac as they were noticed by the ranks could scarcely be better described than in the diary of New Zealander, C.J. Walsh, though some of the detailed activities, like the making of dummy soldiers remembered by J.F. Rudd or the better-known water-operated rifles in the thinly-held front line on the last night, find no mention.

Thursday, 9 December 1915: Nothing of any interest going on. All companies on usual fatigues sapping, tunnelling etc. and making H.E. shelters. We used to call them funk holes but HQ objected and wanted them called H.E. shelters.

Friday, 10 December 1915: All the morning the *Endymion*, *Doris* and *Bacchante* and a couple of monitors were pounding shell in as hard as they could go somewhere near Lone Pine. [This was because of the Allied fear of what the Turkish batteries might do to the embarkation piers.]

Saturday, 11 December 1915: Got first butter issue since leaving Egypt. Drew canteen stores. Very funny. Cigarette issue. Plenty of rumours floating round. Some of the artillery shipped away somewhere. Seems to be something doing. No more stores to be landed. A lot being sent away. All the sick sent away.

Sunday, 12 December 1915: General rumours that we are going to evacuate all positions here. No outgoing mail allowed.

Monday, 13 December 1915: Very heavy bombardment by both enemy and our side this morning. According to the latest 'latrine' [rumour] the Allies are all going to quit and go home. 10th Light Horse, Otago Battalion and Field Ambulance all going away tonight. Auckland Battalion taken over 220 more yards of trench. Paul and I put in another phone this afternoon. It certainly looks as though we are going to evacuate. No more reinforcements or returned sick are to join up here. I'd like to know something. Lot of artillery, Gurkhas, Sikhs and Australians got away late.

Tuesday, 14 December 1915: Heard that good things were to be had on the beach, got loaded up with jam and cheese and also a bag of cabbage and onions. Everything points to a complete evacuation. Railway being torn up. From our bivvy we can see about ten transports near Williams' Pier at 8.30 p.m. All lists for embarkation been made out.

Wednesday, 15 December 1915: Got orders through that no bivvies are to be disturbed and all roofs are to be intact. On the beach the authorities are tipping out rum and whisky in Mule Gully and a terrible lot of rum etc. was tipped out and formed a pool. All hands were there with jam tins, dixies [sic] etc. lapping it up. Have just received final orders for HQ Signals. For last twenty-four hours seven men to remain to man phones and for last few hours I think it is going to be rather nervy. Password for tonight is Corkscrew.

Thursday, 16 December 1915: Our HQ signals orders cancelled. Only two men are to stay and man the phones, Sgt Calame and myself. All barges busy getting troops off. The last ones to go are Walker's Ridge, Quinn's and Courtney's and all are to be heavily mined. Very busy at Williams' Pier. Password Strawberry.

Friday, 17 December 1915: Just got orders through that all arrangements to be postponed twenty-four hours. Password Havelock. Very bright moonlight. Can see shipping as clear as day.

Saturday, 18 December 1915: On 3 a.m. to 6 a.m. watch this morning. Went out about 5 a.m. to waken officers and saw a great glare in the direction of Anzac. Evidently the heads burning all stores etc. Seems fairly cheeky though.[1] Four aeroplanes up at once, evidently reconnoitring. At 9 p.m. most of the boys got away. Everything going satisfactorily – only occasional burst of fire disturbing the night. Turks been working hard all day improving fire trench. Password Malta. We are leaving everything as they stand. Our funk holes or at least H.E. shelters, once our pride and joy, are now half filled with all sorts of rubbish, empty bully tins, old socks, burnt paper, broken helios etc, Burnt all our intelligence department stuff such as old messages etc.

Sunday, 19 December 1915: Last night all went well without a hitch. About twelve o'clock the nasty-tempered brutes of Turks started lobbing shells all over the place. Got orders to get into our funk holes. No damage done. Had a wash and clean up to celebrate what we fondly hope is our last day on Gallipoli. I'll feel quite at ease when I see the shores of Anzac fade away over the horizon. Things very quiet. Turks working hard on the defences. Am keeping the last two messages sent by Col. Plugge during Gallipoli campaign. 9 p.m. Report 'All quiet'. Password Cucumber. All the afternoon and tonight they are pouring it in somewhere evidently at Cape Helles. 10 p.m. Report 'All quiet'. 11 p.m. Report 'Everything normal'. Midnight report 'Situation quite normal.'

Monday, 20 December 1915: Just had a tin of Maconochies, some cocoa and a nip of Northern Cream. I feel goodo now. Got word through to commence withdrawal. We cut off at 1.52. I waited for Paul and we got our gear and bashed things about a bit and started for Williams' Pier. Got there and aboard the lighter at 2.30 a.m. Started to have a sleep and some Lieut-Col. stood on my face. Woke up and shook him up. Left pier and was put aboard Prince Abbas, left at 4.30 p.m. As we left, Suvla Bay was a mass of flames. Guns blown up on Walker's Ridge.[2]

In the last week of November a brilliant, though demanding, exercise was the 'silent stunt'. This nerve-racking experience was well-remembered by Australian Basil Holmes. In order to accustom the Turks to the quietness of an evacuation, all firing was to cease from the Anzac lines from 6 p.m. on 24 November to midnight on the 27th. The troops had to wait about in the trenches to deal with inquisitive Turks who crossed no man's land. Such parties did come and even threw bombs into the Australian positions without reply, but in Holmes's sector one Turk had actually jumped down into the trench and had been bayonetted and his comrades bombed out. In those days of waiting to get off the Peninsula, the only matching time of tension was the feeling of nervousness Holmes experienced as he turned his back on the Turk and descended the winding paths to the beach for evacuation.

The paths had been marked with flour and direction changes shown by candles or shaded lanterns set into the sides of the trenches. Where the front lines were particularly close, the trench had been floored with torn blankets, boots had to be bound with sacking and metal accoutrements similarly silenced. Even the boards of the piers had been covered and hard ground paths broken up to make a less resounding surface.

The preparations were tried in rehearsal. Other means of deception such as carrying empty boxes back up to the heights, as if supplies were still being brought ashore, were remembered by men engaged in this work, such as C.J. Arnold. Mines were laid in carefully selected positions and rifles with an improvised self-acting mechanism were set up in nearly all sectors. A line was attached to the trigger of the rifle and then to an empty can suspended in a position which would cause it to apply pressure to the trigger when the can had been filled with water to a certain level. This was achieved by means of a second can, positioned above it and pierced with holes through which water dripped into the trigger-attached can. The key to all the preparations was to deceive the Turks with normality. On the very day of departure, D. Marks of the Australian 13th Battalion, noted accurately in his diary, 'Everything normal'.[3] The Turks were still out wiring, which was of course to the advantage of their enemy and the embarkation was, 'very smooth and uneventful'. For some, the tension showed in privately confided nervousness. 'Should the Turks attack us tonight,' reflected M.E. Pearce, in his diary, 'it will be almost certain death for all of us remaining on the Peninsula, however they will pay very dearly as we are ready for them.'[4]

The path to the beach for a New Zealander, M. S. Galloway, led him beside some recently tended graves, near enough to read with a pang of anguish the name of a friend and fine Wellington rugby player whose splendid try in his last match in New Zealand provided an instant poignant recall. J.G. Gasparich remembered the eerie echoing of his footsteps on an uncovered or unbroken path and then a sudden unnerving wail from the Turkish trenches, which their state of tension translated into a sign of an imminent attack.

In the event of a major engagement during the evacuation, two fully-equipped casualty clearing stations were to be left to cope with the seriously wounded who could not have been evacuated. Though the *Australian Official History*[5] mentioned that it was hoped that the Turks would allow both the wounded and the medical personnel to be collected on the day following, there is a letter from General Monash to his wife and daughter which implies that these men would be taken prisoner but that he had 'every confidence that in such an eventuality the Turks will play the game'.[6] In the event, no casualties or medical men had to be left, but a gramophone and note were waiting for the Turks in one of the casualty clearing stations – the record ready for playing was of course 'Turkish Patrol'.

The last troops to leave Suvla and Anzac were to see the dark silhouette of their areas of occupation lit up by burning stores and mine explosions. It is perhaps not altogether surprising that some of these troops were a little the worse for wear as a result of their unwillingness to waste all the rum which, 'officially', had been poured away.

The destruction of stores had not just been limited to rum, bully beef and ammunition. Those guns which had not been evacuated were so methodically destroyed that it was hoped they would not serve even as war trophies.[7] The need for secrecy meant that much could not be destroyed and had to be left to the Turks, but with a cricket match being played on the beach and normal troop and mule movements maintained till the last, deception had been brilliantly successful. The preparations had been meticulous and they had been responsibly executed to the last detail. Nevertheless the inestimable value of fine weather and a calm sea, which was to be even more critical to Britain twenty-five years later at Dunkirk, perhaps led the thoughtful soldier or sailor to reflections similar to Birdwood's diary entry for 20 December that he was, 'grateful to Almighty God for the wonderful weather given us'.[8] On the last two nights, 20,000 troops had been evacuated with but two men wounded.

At Suvla there were huge dumps of stores to be destroyed because they could not be re-embarked without drawing attention to such activity. Blankets and bayonets, boots and water bottles, socks and woollen gloves, tarpaulin sheets and even motorcycles were remorselessly thrown on the fire heaps, while near Kangaroo Pier, on another funeral pyre, were a full fortnight's rations for 40,000 men.[9] The preparations and procedure were the same as at Anzac, but there was considerable advantage at Suvla in the greater distance between the front lines and the absence of major underground mining activity. Every gun, even those firing the normal amount of ammunition during the evening of the 19th, was evacuated and only on the Kiretch Tepe Ridge was there any delay in the orderly progress of men to the beaches. Despite this delay there was not a single casualty and every soldier was safely embarked.

With booby traps and contact mines laid both in front of them and behind them, Signaller Fred Bradford had waited anxiously for the call 'G' which would order their withdrawal. He and his small party, waiting in the eerie darkness of the wide-open plain, actually began to fear that they had been forgotten when at last the call came through. 'I could never describe the feeling of relief when that signal came.' Andrew Brown, checking his sector, had casually kicked at what appeared to be a pile of rubbish in his way and had found it was their cook, scarcely conscious, hugging a rum jar. Private C.J. Bygrave had had to organize the pulling of a log of wood on two cartwheels to the front line to replace a gun being evacuated.

P.J. Gething, an officer in the 9th Warwicks, remembered that two nights before the evacuation, all the kit which could be carried in one's packs and haversack, was sent to the beach. This included officers' valises, so they were left with just what they stood up in.

I never saw my valise again. The men took a delight in slashing the sandbags as we destroyed all we could in our trenches. The only thing we left was the earthenware jug in which we had kept our water cool during the hot days. We left it for the Turks, hoping it would serve them as well as it had served us. Sentimental soldiers that we were. I felt terribly lonely but there was too much for us to do to brood over this. We had to show ourselves all we could, draw water for the whole battalion, light and keep going all the cookhouse fires. After dark I had twenty-five men and we had to keep fire coming from as many firing bays as possible. I put a box of ammunition in the cookhouse fire hoping it would last till after we had gone. On our way to the beach I remember above all, the silence. Only heavy breathing and the occasional stumble of padded feet could be heard.

The booby traps were not all of a metallic nature. An officer named Rathbone, of the 6th Loyal North Lancs, confessed to the author, with some degree of embarrassment, that his unit left in a large container a lethal mixture of rum and paraffin designed to have a discomfortingly explosive effect of its own when the Turks drank to their victory. It may in fact be wondered whether this potent mixture were not more likely than an excess of marmalade[10] to have caused the reputed single Turkish fatality in the gorging of the edible stores left after the evacuations.

With complete success at Anzac and Suvla, it must have seemed to those at Helles that they could scarcely expect to be so fortunate. Their diversionary bombardment and local attacks had helped to distract the Turks on 19 and 20 December, but the Turks, with increasing supplies of ammunition, were now able to concentrate their attention solely on Helles.

The Senegalese troops had all been withdrawn by 22 December and the final decision to withdraw the whole force came six days later, though plans were already being prepared for this expected eventuality. As at Suvla, Turkish observation of the entire area made concealment of the preparations as difficult as it was vital. Furthermore, in terms of 'Gallipoli-distance', it was quite a time-consuming journey for the front-line troops, who had to wend their way through the maze of trenches to the evacuation beaches. If this front line were to be attacked during the evacuation of units in the rear or immediately after the vacation of the forward trenches, a successful rearguard action would have been extremely difficult.

The French Colonial Brigade left the Peninsula on the second and third of January, but the French batteries remained. The French stores, added to those of the British, presented an enormous problem, the only answer to which had to be destruction. Sadly this was the fate of many of the mules which had shared the suffering and labour of Peninsula service, to deserve a better end than the slaughter which now awaited them.

The carrying-out of a smooth withdrawal was also hampered by heavy Turkish shelling and an attack on the left of the line, but British naval gunfire must have done something to convince the Turks that there was no weakening in determination to hold on. Evacuation rehearsals took place and tremendous efforts had gone into making the piers at W Beach and the floating bridge at V Beach sufficiently secure for the embarkation of nearly 17,000 men and thirty-seven guns during the night of 8/9 January. Increasingly heavy seas, bringing damage to the piers and bridge and grounding a lighter, meant that there were always problems to be solved, such as the need for some troops awaiting evacuation from Gully Beach to march to W Beach. As the last troops got away, a thunderous roar from the main ammunition dump signalled to the Turks that they were too late and that the well-nigh impossible had been achieved.

Royal Marine W.C. Williamson was in a privileged position during the last hours on the Peninsula, as he had to hand messages to the officer commanding the withdrawal, outlining details of unit progress at each stage.

The officers sat in silence round a table with a candle in a bottle as their only light. The G.O.C. Embarkation read each message silently and passed it round. With the final message in, the Corps Chief of Staff, Brigadier-General Street, merely announced that we had better leave now, handed me two attaché cases and picked up my rifle which he himself carried. When we got to the rowing boat awaiting us, I could not help but be amused that a Staff Officer, eyeing the considerable swell on the sea, began to give instructions to the naval Warrant Officer in charge of the boat, manned as it was by seamen of the Royal Navy.

Midshipman Traill of *Lord Nelson* had the task of searching for stragglers. Not relishing a cold dark swim ashore, he had truly astonishing good fortune when a ten-foot-long, flat-bottomed, carpeted Turkish pleasure punt bumped against his cutter and allowed an easy transfer for a dry examination of the coast. The punt, held on a line by the crew of the cutter, drifted against a breakwater in Morto Bay and Traill, revolver in hand, wandered along the beach calling, 'Anybody about?' and hoping the reply would not be in Turkish. After some time, the explosion of the ammunition dump at the very point of the Peninsula convinced him that his search for lost and bewildered troops was no longer necessary. It was for him at the time a sobering thought, and subsequently, something he recalled with sardonic amusement, that he was probably alone in presenting the continued Allied challenge to Constantinople. He quickly made his way back to the moored punt and so to the safety of the cutter.

On the Peninsula, soldiers had looted from the dumps, shirts, vests and pants far in excess of their needs, remembered T.S.W. Jarvis. They were forced to jettison their surplus requirements on the long tiresome trail to the piers, as they were too much of an encumbrance. Philip Gething, fresh from the Suvla evacuation, experienced the heavy Turkish bombardment of the 7th and, sheltering from the shrapnel balls, picked some of them up still hot from the shell burst. As much to raise his own morale as those of his men, he played marbles with them. He and his men were fortunate to be on the Gully Beach lighter which did get away on the night of the 8th, so that they did not have to endure the physical and nervous strain of the march to W Beach.

A.C. Pawson, evacuated on the 4th, wrote emphatically in his diary that he didn't care, 'if I never see the Peninsula again – and I fancy all of us on board feel the same'.

but Eric Wettern's unit, the Royal Naval Division, 2nd Field Company, Engineers, was engaged with a continued close acquaintance with the terrain which had been its home since the last week in April.

5 January: Carrying stuff for barricades. Turks apparently spotted something and plonked a few big 'uns round about making a mess of trenches in two or three places. Had to get night working party from Howes to shift the muck. With Stout fixing up barricades got most of the work done.

6th: Completing barricade arrangements. Fixed up everything to drop in instantly. Rehearsals with Rugg.

7th: General rehearsal at 2. Attack by Turks on Fusilier Bluff preceded by bombardment of whole line. Shrapnel and Annie[11] in our sector. I went up to tie white tape on crinolines[12] and got a bit of it coming back. Rest of company left, leaving only ten of us. Part of firing line went off.

8th: Hoods on our left moved out very quickly… straw down and muffled feet … 23.45: All moved out. We put down crinolines in front line … we put down umbrellas[13] and crinolines at Supports … Waited for Dumezil and bomb people at Ligne de Repli barricade. Further wait at Post 11 for Thompson. Then all down to Post 15. Eski. Longish wait for Blake. Barricaded road. Put gear on, proceeded down. Very quiet. Few French left round Camp des Oliviers. Via Cypresses to F.U.P. at Seddel Bahr – then in fours – slow progress over beached French warship on to destroyer *Grasshopper*. Like sardines, on board before 0300. Few dud shells from Annie. Out to sea. Bonfires started 0400 on all beaches and Turks started shelling like blazes and sending up red flares. Fine to watch it from a distance.

This diarist, Eric Wettern, wrote to his brother on 15 January: 'I expect you are feeling fairly disgusted at home at our magnificent bunk from Gallipoli … As a matter of fact we aren't exactly sorry to leave dear old Gallipoli. I think we could have stuck it all right, though it was getting a bit warm, but I suppose they thought we should never do any good by staying there.'

However, one person did feel that the soldiers' efforts deserved appreciation. A West Australian schoolgirl sent a present of a notepad to, 'a wounded Anzac soldier'. She thanked him for his, 'kindness in going to the front. I am glad to hear that you soldiers have tried [your] very best to fight for the King and Country. I wish you will get better and go to fight again', but she added with unaffected sincerity, 'I hope the war will end soon'.[14] As the Gallipoli soldier continued his war service, if fortune were to favour him, for almost three more years on the Western Front, or in Mesopotamia, Salonika, Egypt or Palestine, he would echo and re-echo the schoolgirl's sentiment – 'I hope the war will end soon'. In so doing he would unconsciously mock the high hopes entertained for the campaign in which he had first been associated.

Epilogue: The Responsibility of Naval and Military Command

An examination of the leadership of Vice-Admiral John de Robeck and General Sir Ian Hamilton from March 1915 when they took up their positions of supreme command, to the collapse of the August offensive, must take into consideration factors outside their control. If it were shown that, from the start, the scales were weighed against them both by events prior to their appointment and by pressures from independent sources beyond their influence, then the significance of misjudgements which may reasonably be attributed to them, must surely be lessened. Indeed, if it were judged that a successful outcome to their leadership challenge were beyond achievement, then how critical were any errors of command taken in pursuit of the unreachable?

The Gallipoli conception, its likelihood of success and the attendant consequences of victory, from 1915 to the present day, have sometimes been viewed as through the telescope of an amateur astronomer who reports on what he would like to see rather than what he actually sees. Peter Hart in his recent book, *Gallipoli*, is emphatically guiltless of such a charge with his castigation of the 'lunacy' of the whole affair but in the case of both de Robeck and Hamilton, events prior to their appointments considerably reduced the chances of success attending their best endeavour. For de Robeck, there are arguments in defence of his supposedly pusillanimous failure to attack the Narrows again, immediately or subsequently, following upon the failure of the assault on 18 March. In the case of Sir Ian, there are exculpatory arguments too, despite the weight of criticism of his command. However, as this work is not least a tribute to those over whom the Admiral, the General and their Staffs exercised sway, the question of errors in command must be considered.

Certainly as far as the MEF is concerned, there was a philosophy of command seriously open to question, an unjustified reliance on subordinates, and then issues which allow for different interpretation but largely remain as negative factors in overall assessment; the underestimating of the Turks and an incapacity to inspire the men under his command, devoted though most of his GHQ staff were to Hamilton, with one notable exception.

With Vice-Admiral Sackville Carden's final breakdown in health on 16 March, de Robeck, as he had been concerned with all the planning for the great assault in the immediate offing, was given full responsibility for it, but only one day before it was to be launched. In the attack he lost three battleships, had three more seriously damaged and suffered grievous casualties, largely as a result of the sinking of the *Bouvet*. The hard evidence to him was of Turkish preparedness and of the ineffectiveness of the

Allied shelling and minesweeping. He was not even sure whether his losses were to have been from land-fired torpedoes or from drifting mines. He knew nothing, on the evening of the 18th, of the subsequently reported depletion of Turkish ammunition, nor of any supposed panic in Constantinople. Even as he assured the Admiralty of his intention to resume the attack, he doubted the wisdom of such a decision. He had the newly-appointed Commander of the MEF with him ready jointly to undertake a mission now so clearly fraught with difficulty. For all his Chief of Staff's persistence in advocating renewed aggressive naval operations – and Roger Keyes was to continue provoking alarm in senior naval circles kindred to that of the First Lord of the Admiralty in both naval and political zones – there were strong arguments for awaiting the arrival of the MEF.

With the support of naval guns, soldiers could be landed in strength to destroy the guns of the forts defending the minefields and hold the forts and heights above them to allow the mines to be swept undisturbed. De Robeck had scanty evidence in support of any contention that a resumption of the offensive would not be equally costly and indeed lead to the arrival of a damaged fleet, weakened in numbers, into the Marmara to face *Goeben*, *Breslau* and the Turkish fleet. A fear for the security of his supply line would also appear to be entirely reasonable.

In his book on Gallipoli, Sir Roger Keyes wrote that his examination of the Narrows after the action left him with a 'most indelible impression that we are in the presence of a beaten foe'.[1] That this examination had taken place in darkness from the deck of a single destroyer surely limits its credibility. Similarly, when Keyes wrote that 'it only remained to us to organize a proper sweeping force and devise some means of dealing with drifting mines to reap the fruits of our efforts',[2] the problem of matching this sort of appraisal with harsher reality invites sympathy for de Robeck. A.J. Marder, though sympathetic towards the school of thought which regretted the failure to renew the naval attack, accepted that Keyes was never one to see beyond the immediate next step and that his judgement was clouded by his 'eagerness to get at the enemy'.[3]

The charge made against de Robeck is that he refused to be convinced that the organization of the new *Beagle* class destroyer sweeping force gave him an opportunity to clear a sufficiently wide channel to allow his ships to approach the inner forts and reduce them completely to ruins at close range. It is maintained that this could have been done early in April and without any troop involvement. In de Robeck's agreement at the 22 March conference with Hamilton and Birdwood on *Queen Elizabeth* that the Navy would await Army readiness for a combined operation, his detractors see the decisive subordination of the Navy's role. This persuasive argument gathers some strength as we see neither on 25 April, nor in early May, nor indeed in August, any serious attempt to force the Narrows. The Navy's acceptance of the role of transporting, supplying and covering with gunfire the operations of the troops, is seen by de Robeck's critics as the seal upon his failure to secure success by the obvious and most economical means. Peter Hart is unequivocal in seeing 'no hope for a naval attack on 19 March'; Liddell Hart is more cautious, considering criticism of the changed role of the Navy, a 'moot point',[4] but in any case the War Council on

27 March supported the decision taken at the conference on *Queen Elizabeth*. The caution shown by de Robeck may be compared on a lesser scale with that consistently maintained by Jellicoe with the Grand Fleet. The sheer weight of responsibility at this level of command and the additional competing pressures upon him of the First Lord of the Admiralty and the First Sea Lord must certainly be kept in mind. If the failure to renew the attack were to have deprived the Navy of an opportunity for Nelsonian victory, if the scurrying back to Mudros of the big ships after *U 21*'s exploits, were to appear undignified, de Robeck's assessments were based on realistic appraisal. His doubts about the soundness of Keyes's alluring picture were crystallized in discussion with Hamilton and Birdwood. In this way he came to the decision that the MEF must be the essential striking force of a combined operation to secure the Narrows and open the way to Constantinople for the Naval Squadron.

A brief word may be added on the manner in which the Navy fulfilled the role chosen by de Robeck. As there was no overall command structure, however much goodwill there was within the two separate elements of the combined force, the lack of any experience in working together was made more serious by there being no ultimate authority. De Robeck can scarcely be held responsible for this, but the handling of such problems as wounded and water supply would have been considerably improved under such a structure. As early as 20 May in a letter to Vice-Admiral Limpus, Vice-Admiral Wemyss stressed the difficulties and disagreements over inter-service cooperation. He severely criticized the inadequacy of the army medical arrangements and the decision of the GHQ Staff in refusing to be based on the Peninsula, but he saw the root of the problem as the Admiralty. 'The light-hearted way in which they allowed this tremendous operation to be undertaken with no means beyond those which could be provided by the ships of the Fleet and thereby curtailing their effective use, is nothing less than criminal.'[5]

Other reservations have been expressed about the naval performance at the Dardanelles, one being that the bombardment at the April landings was from too great a distance to achieve the object of neutralising the Turkish defence. Whatever their orders, some commanders of the old battleships notably disregarded such caution and came close inshore in their attempt effectively to blast resistance away but this did not occur at the two vital landings, V and W Beaches. However, only the high trajectory shelling of monitors – none there in April – really had the capacity to destroy the low profile well-dug positions from which Turkish defence was maintained.

The success of the British and Australian submarines could be advanced in support of the case for naval effectiveness in the area, so dramatically influential as they were in hampering Turkish re-supply to the Peninsula of men, munitions and war materials, but in considering naval performance in relation to the direct fulfilment of an accepted support role, what can be said? In fact, several well-planned, small-scale, military operations were successful because of close-support by warships, and the supreme achievement of inter-service co-operation was of course, ironically, the administrative and executive handling of the evacuations.

For Sir Ian Hamilton, the millstones around his neck from the outset, and the subsequent externally imposed limitations on his freedom of action, proved heavy burdens. He and his Staff had an incredibly short time to prepare an operation unprecedented in nature and scale. His army was scattered, his knowledge and experience of the Turks and of their land were negligible. There was a constantly pressing need for speed on the one hand waging damaging war with the need for thoroughness, on the other. His force had insufficient troops, was short, above all, in artillery and its ammunition, and in engineers. The cutters and whalers from which his men were to land on a defended shore had no protection against the fire of the defenders. He was jealously prevented from having the newly-developed protected landing craft until the landing at Suvla and the whole venture was never whole-heartedly backed. With the War Council divided and Kitchener, by personal conviction and increasingly demanding circumstance on the Western Front, under anti-Gallipoli pressure, Hamilton's endowment had crippling clauses which were likely to limit any chance of realization. Overshadowing many of these factors, increasing their in-built disadvantage, was the time-lag after 18 March or indeed from late February, when the Navy had demonstrated beyond doubt Allied commitment to the Dardanelles. The Turks were given time to make defensive preparations. The essential factor of surprise in a combined operation had been conceded, though it has to be admitted that secrecy of troop movements in the Eastern Mediterranean would always have been difficult to achieve.

It has been claimed that despite the haste over Hamilton's appointment and despatch to the Dardanelles, he demonstrated no realistic appraisal of the task he was accepting. He did not demand sight of any studies of the task he was facing. Only the campaign's most recent historian, Peter Hart, considers that he had access to adequate cartographic resources and War Office Intelligence to assist him in his planning, though Hart considers that 'the prevailing military culture was such that Hamilton could not make the entirely reasonable demand for a set of fully evaluated combined operations plans conditional to his accepting command of the MEF'.[6] More of this later but should he have required a serious appraisal of resources available to him in relation to what was needed for France? Military and political disappointment over Neuve Chapelle on the very day of Hamilton's departure to take up his command, and the developing explanation for the failure of this first major British offensive, along the lines of shell shortage, were soon to fester into scandal. Should Hamilton have hesitated before accepting and argued over the size of the force he was to command? In putting forward such a question, surely there is some measure of unreality here too? Which professional soldier is going summarily to conclude his career by turning down the chance of a supreme command at a time of national need?

Yes, at this stage of the war it was apparent to senior soldiers that there were not enough trained men yet to turn stalemate on the Western Front into breakthrough and not enough field and heavy artillery with their ammunition for the Western Front, never mind a new land campaign, but what was the invited new appointee as Commander-in-Chief to do or say about this? 'No I cannot accept this post until you have got available for me all I judge I need'? In the long-run, and after someone else's failure, that might have earned the rejectionist a footnote in military history, but in

March 1915 there was a war on, a declared need for him, and an opportunity to end a fine career with a triumph.

It had been said that the Allied plans underestimated the defensive fighting qualities of the Turks, and Hamilton's maintained optimism, in view of his failure to achieve victory quickly, has been seen by some as evidence of his being out of touch with reality. In effect, 'Some more troops, some more and bigger guns and I can get this job done' – not of course a direct quotation – indicates that he, no more than any senior commander at this time, had no real answer to the terrible 1915, (and continuing), dilemma of the force committed to attacking the well-entrenched, armed and determined defender. He shares with the War Council culpability in this respect – underestimating defensive fire-power, and underestimating the Turk.

In a recent biography of Hamilton, the author, John Philip Jones, almost cruelly quotes Hamilton's own words dismissively dealing with the sound 1899 predictions of the Pole, Ivan Bloch, concerning the future of modern war with the overwhelming advantage weaponry had now given the entrenched defender: 'all that trash written by Monsieur Bloch before 1904 about zones of fire across which no living being could pass, heralded nothing but disaster. War is essentially the triumph, not of a chassepot over a needle-gun, not a line of men behind wire entanglements and fire-swept zones over men exposing themselves in the open, but of one will over another weaker will.'[7]

These words were published in 1910 in a small book recommending conscription. It is not much of an excuse that on the great issue of conscription he was to be proved right, but Hamilton is far from alone in living to regret his words. If he were in fact still seriously to underestimate the advantage held by the defender in 1915, he had few illusions about the difficulty of his assignment, and his Special Force Order to the troops before the April landings, for all its eloquence, is no lyrical appeal for glory without sacrifice.

However, the evidence is there of Hamilton's persistence with frontal attacks at Helles against an enemy well dug-in, armed, ammunitioned and in sound morale, and the reverse side of the good coin of Hamilton's optimism is revealed too in his almost apologetic request for reinforcements. In the small numbers for which he asked may be seen one of the reasons for their arrival in relatively small number and too late for his enormous task. There were other reasons too, fundamental reasons, as recent commentators chorus – the troops were simply needed for France.

The influence of his loyalty to Kitchener, amounting almost to awe, was just one of the inherent difficulties consequent upon his appointment. Hamilton never allowed his immediate, on the spot, knowledge and responsibility for the campaign to redress the imbalance of this relationship with Kitchener forged during the later stages of the Second Boer War. With the taciturn Kitchener operating from the War Office as if he were Commander-in-Chief rather than Minister of State for War, Hamilton's admiration for his old South African War Commander-in-Chief, compromised Sir Ian from the start.

As Commander-in-Chief, MEF, Hamilton was in a position to influence critical elements within the campaign; adequate reconnaissance for a wise choice of landing beaches, the degree of supervision he would exercise over his subordinate commanders in order to maintain co-ordination between them and thus the best chance of success with the overall plan being complex – something true of both April and August – flexibility within his broad strategy to meet any initial check and the placement of reinforcements accordingly, the decision as to where to launch a new offensive with major reinforcements and the personal influence he was to exercise throughout his force. For the choice of his Staff and the efficiency of its work he must also accept some responsibility. Though each of these areas will receive some consideration there were factors which embrace all these issues and which do much to explain Hamilton's failure to wrest achievement out of the morass of problems.

By training and predilection Hamilton believed in conferring real responsibility on his Staff and subordinate commanders. He exuded confidence in the likelihood of their success. He lacked the capacity and had not the intention to lead the expedition at every stage of its planning and execution. This was against his philosophy of command. To give subordinates free rein if they were of outstanding ability in administration, tactical appreciation or in leading men, is essential under large-scale campaign conditions; but if these men were ill-chosen and proved defective, the Commander-in-Chief must swiftly interpose his authority. In the MEF there proved to be too many commanders of poor quality in times of critical significance, most particularly in August, and Hamilton's system of devolution was cruelly exposed.

The choice of landing areas was limited by the size of his force, the rocky coastline, small beaches and the inbuilt task of aiding the Navy in capturing the Narrows. In fact, Kitchener's instructions to him on 13 March 'strongly deprecated' the occupation of the Asiatic shore.[8] For such reasons, separately or together, the Asiatic shore of the Dardanelles or the mainland itself were out of the question. It should be remembered that the Allied force of four British divisions and one French was 'actually inferior in strength to the enemy in a situation where the inherent preponderance of defensive over offensive power was multiplied by the natural difficulties of the terrain'.[9]

The landing had to be made on the Peninsula, but on the Aegean side for adequate protection from the Turkish forts of the Narrows. If the Gulf of Saros at Bulair were to look geographically inviting, it was also the most obvious place for a landing to be expected. However, a landing here would be of little assistance to the Navy, as cutting the narrow neck of the Peninsula did not immediately threaten the forts of the Narrows, which could still be supplied by sea. The same could be said for Birdwood's initial preference for Enos. There were further disadvantages, such as the difficulty of co-operation here with the Navy, the strength of the Turkish defensive preparations and the fact that, in the movement towards the forts of the Narrows, the rear of the landing force would be exposed to attack from reinforcements dispatched by sea or land from Constantinople.

Some of these disadvantages, notably the distance from the Narrows and the question of naval co-operation, removed Suvla Bay from consideration at this time. Hamilton, appreciating the danger of the dispersal of his forces, nevertheless decided that the key to the problem remained the Narrows. He chose therefore five beaches at Helles which would disperse and perhaps confuse the Turks. Quite reasonably he assessed that they would be heavily committed to defending the area north of

Gaba Tepe. This area offered a relatively short crossing of the Peninsula nearer to the vital Narrows than Suvla offered and of course far nearer than Bulair. To confuse the Turks still further, a diversionary landing on the Asiatic shore was to be carried out and two further diversions, one at Bulair, threatened. There is imagination and logic in such an assessment, which was made from as thorough an aerial and naval reconnaissance as was possible. The smallness of the beaches was another argument for the dispersal of his forces and the only point which might be made is that the difficulties of co-ordinating several separate landings would be a major problem. However, to get a large force ashore as quickly as possible at Helles made the use of several beaches essential.

Robert Rhodes James made the point that Hamilton's Staff did not know of Cunliffe Owen's detailed memorandum on the Dardanelles defences and that, in mapping, the Staff was hopelessly unprepared. The point has been made that Peter Hart takes issue with this and it may be wondered how Hamilton could insist on having intelligence information that he did not know existed: to have refused to act without adequate briefing material would have cost the expedition invaluable time even if it were not to have cost him his position. Hamilton's own reconnaissance and the information available to him resulted in plans acceptable to Birdwood, though the Australian Official Historian maintained that in retrospect the only chance of success which Hamilton had with such a force was to throw it suddenly from Gaba Tepe at the Narrows and trust to surprise to carry it through before the enemy could be reinforced.[10] Again the phrase 'in retrospect' reduces for the author of this book the legitimacy of the point being made and when one accepts that the supporting effect of the naval gunfire at Helles was overestimated, only the April and May experience would prove this.

At the Helles landings there is little doubt that devolved command demonstrated its disadvantage. The officer bearing the responsibility, Hunter-Weston, allowed himself, however understandably, to become preoccupied with his two main landings at V and W Beaches. Consequently he lacked awareness of the opportunity being afforded to exploit the Y-beach landing by diverting troops intended for V and W to Y Beach. He also failed to urge the exploitation of success at X Beach to threaten outflanking the Turks at W Beach and making every effort to strike across the narrow tip of the Peninsula to link with the men earning success at S Beach The failure to capitalize on the lack of initial opposition at Y and to insist on the vigorous pursuit of a link between S and X certainly contributed to the heavy casualties at V and W and to the loss of any chance of an early capture of Krithia and attempt to seize the dominant hill position of Achi Baba. The 29th Divisional Commander could have made such decisions, but committed, as he chose to be, at the tip of the Peninsula, he saw no such opportunity. Hamilton saw Y Beach from *Queen Elizabeth* and later in the morning sent a message to Hunter-Weston suggesting the sending of troops to reinforce those at Y. Hunter-Weston was not disposed to alter the original plans and Hamilton refrained from making such an order over the Divisional Commander's head. This was a decision well within his compass and an opportunity was lost.

Hamilton must also accept a serious measure of responsibility for the woefully inadequate preparations for the wounded both on 25/26 April and in August and with the water shortage intimately associated with the Suvla tragedy. Here critical judgement is on unquestionable ground with wounded men paying the penalty for Hamilton's virtual disregard of his administrative staff and ruinous over-reliance on his small GHQ Staff.

His GHQ Staff was equipped neither in competence nor number to cope with the volume and complexity of administrative problems. It was simply folly to leave his administrative Staff in Egypt, as remote in miles as they were low in the General's esteem, and the G.H.Q Staff, in the exercise of almost total sway over organizational matters, made serious errors through sheer lack of experience. Some of the errors were to be exposed officially. The Dardanelles Commission, set up in 1916 to investigate every aspect of the concept and execution of the campaign, was to enquire searchingly into the provisions for wounded and unsurprisingly found the attempt of the GHQ Staff to prepare plans for the evacuation of wounded without reference to the Director of Medical Services ill-advised.[11] With masterly understatement the Commission reported that 'the greater part of the sufferings of the wounded in the first days after the landing seem to us to have been inevitable, but there seems to have been some want of organization in the control of the boats and barges carrying wounded to the hospital ships and transports, which occasioned delay in their embarkation'.[12]

The use of the first reinforcements to strengthen the attack on Krithia rather than reinforce Anzac seems reasonable in view of Hamilton's decision that Helles must be the concentrated heart of his attack and that the small beachhead at Anzac was unsuitable at that stage to take large-scale reinforcements and deploy them for attack. The casualties sustained in the frontal assaults at Krithia were grimly depressing, yet knowledge of the parallel costly failures in France – Aubers Ridge, Festubert – demonstrates that criticism of Hamilton or Hunter-Weston must take into consideration the total failure to that date of finding an answer to trench warfare deadlock.

For the August offensive, however, Hamilton designed an imaginative concept, switching concentration from Helles to the left of the Anzac positions, in co-ordination with a new landing at Suvla and merely requiring diversionary offensive at Helles and on the right at Anzac. Hamilton had hoped for much more than was achieved at Suvla, but a secure base for supplies and reinforcements was established and the fact that his scheme did get men, though fleetingly, on heights which overlooked the Dardanelles as well as the Aegean, suggests that the plan held some merit though its flaws were to decree that bravery in the assault at Anzac was matched by that of the defender and moreover, here and at Suvla, the Turk was better led. The assault on the left at Anzac demanded a high degree of co-ordinated efficiency and physical effort from drained Australasian and Indian troops and inexperienced British troops, together with new Indian troops also unfamiliar with the terrain. This burden was made heavier by the failure at Suvla to attack vigorously and profit from the initial surprise and numerically weaker Turkish defence. The Dardanelles Commission Report,[13] Major-General Fuller's verdict,[14] and most subsequent accounts consider the plan faulty because of the weakened physical condition of some of the men and the 'half-trained state' of the others, but some historians consider this challenging plan the campaign's single example of realistic daring, offering hope of success. Nevertheless, whatever merits or demerits the plan contained, the defeat of the August offensive maintained the previous pattern of the inefficiency of subordinate commanders, and Hamilton failing to intervene in time to put things right. Ironically the Dardanelles Commission Report considered that 'Sir Frederick Stopford's difficulties were increased by the intervention of Sir Ian Hamilton'.[15]

Hamilton had had little alternative to accepting Stopford[16] as commander of IX Corps, though he had asked for Lieutenant-General Rawlinson or Major-General Byng. He had still less opportunity to object beforehand to the appointment of the sadly ineffective divisional commanders, Major-General Frederick Hammersley[17] and Major-General John Lindley[18] or the brigade commander, Brigadier-General William Sitwell.[19] The system of appointment and seniority stands condemned by their promotion as it does in the case of other elderly generals with neither the physical endurance nor the recent service experience to command in the field in a modern war. It might be added here that Major-General Alexander Godley's command of the Anzac attack, and the performance of some of his senior subordinates as has been mentioned, also left something to be desired. However, Hamilton was Commander-in-Chief, with the overall responsibility that entails. His Chief of Staff, Major-General Walter Braithwaite, he had chosen himself, and Braithwaite too, was in awe of Kitchener. This left little scope for judgement independent of what was expected from the War Office concerning command issues at stake on the Peninsula. If Sir Douglas Haig, in due course, were going to be ill-served in France by the excessive loyalty of his Chief of Intelligence, Brigadier-General John Charteris, shielding uncomfortable realities from the Commander-in-Chief, then perhaps there might be a parallel with Braithwaite not being the man Hamilton needed.

Sir Ian's passion for secrecy, which led to the under-briefing of almost all concerned, his pliant acceptance of Stopford's objections to the immediate drive for Chocolate Hill and the W Hills, and his delay before insisting on vigorous attack at Suvla, seem hard to credit when so much hung on taking advantage of the initiative before Turkish reinforcements came up in strength. He was in a position to see his plans pursued with determination and he chose fatally to dally while they were being ruined irretrievably by feeble leadership. This was carrying devolution of authority to a degree of absurdity. All defence of the Commander-in-Chief, like sandcastles before the tide, is washed away by events at Suvla. In his final instructions to Stopford, Hamilton had stressed that the main objective was to secure Suvla Bay and long ago J.F.C. Fuller pronounced a magisterial verdict which still stands: 'this insistence that the landing was the objective was the greatest error of all, and the root cause of the eventual disaster: for in itself it was a means and not an end.'[20] Undeniably he had waited long for his reinforcements and he had suffered from less than loyal support from official quarters. He had been further undermined in the Press, but his fate was justifiably, even if sadly, sealed by Suvla.

Hamilton, for all his attractive personal attributes, his professional experience and ability, had failed to lift the performance of his low-standard generals, inspiring no drive from them and none of his own optimistic enthusiasm. It is given to few in overall command of large forces to have the magnetism to inspire in a personal way subordinate leaders and their men. Hamilton did not achieve this distinction. To the men of the MEF, he was a distant, shadowy figure – not one indeed attracting ridicule, or the venom felt for some – but certainly not held in warm affection or awe. It is clear that he visited the Peninsula on numerous occasions from his Imbros HQ and that he toured areas of the trench systems, but he remained for most, as might perhaps have been expected, as remote as Imbros, visible but without impact.

It is tempting for the Gallipoli historian to look for parallels in terms of arguably flawed strategic concepts and then their unsuccessful management in practice, even with an awareness that no precise parallels can be identified. However, with a plea for some latitude in respect of a parallel, and focussing on a kinship of gamble, execution and cost of failure – however measured – we don't have to dig too deeply into the past. Errors of strategy and the difficulty of their being worked through, do not just disfigure the past. Today, less than a hundred years after the Dardanelles venture was launched to bring a speedier, victorious end to the Great War, it is intriguing to speculate on how, in cost-benefit terms, intervention in Afghanistan as a means of winning the war against the threat of militant Islam, will be assessed. As with Gallipoli, I suspect that going there in the first place will attract the greater scorn with politicians in the stocks rather than those charged with doing their bidding.

As the Gallipoli concept, planning and execution continue to be examined, the compelling lure of its debatable mysteries is unlikely to lose its influence. In so many ways, a mystery it remains. From time to time authoritative accounts are written clearly demonstrating one case or another but will anyone familiar with the 1915 harrowing evidence, satisfactorily account for the pride with which the veteran of W Beach, or of Quinn's Post, or the crossing of the Suvla Plain, affirmed that he was glad to have been there? A struggle fit to rank with any ancient epic had been fought on a singularly dramatic stage and perhaps in a strangely timeless way – men pitted against each other – for all the 'refinement' of modern warfare. If distance perhaps lent some enchantment in the forging of such a conclusion, I don't think that it was by removing sensitivity and replacing it with vainglory, just that the man who had been there knew that he had been tried and tested and had passed the test – but of course he also knew that he had been lucky and so many had not.

Notes

Introduction

1. Greenwell, *An Infant in Arms*, p. 46.
2. Technically, Australians in New Guinea and the New Zealanders in Samoa could claim to have been on active service before the Expeditionary Forces left Australasia, and the Nelson Company of the New Zealand Canterbury Battalion was in action on the Suez Canal in February.
3. Gammage, *The Broken Years*, p. 277.

Prologue

1. Lord Grey of Fallodon, *Twenty Five Years*, vol. 1, pp. 71–2, quoted in Cassar, *Kitchener's War*.
2. Cassar, *Kitchener's War*, pp. 125–6.
3. Reginald, Viscount Esher, *The Tragedy of Lord Kitchener*, p. 106.
4. Marder, *Fear God and Dread Nought*, vol. 3, p. 140.
5. A.J.P Taylor's chapter, p. 17 in *Churchill: Four Faces and the Man*.
6. National Archives, Cab. 22/1 3623.
7. Lloyd George, *A Diary of Francis Stevenson*, p. 50, ed. A.J.P. Taylor.
8. In March 1915 the British government conceded Russian rights to Constantinople.
9. Cassar, *The French and the Dardanelles*, p. 2 of Introduction.
10. Chack and Antier, *Histoire maritime*, vol. 2, p. 142.
11. National Archives, WO/106/1462 2099.
12. National Archives, WO/106/1463 2099.
13. Gilbert, *Winston S. Churchill*, vol. 3, p. 220n.
14. National Archives, Cab. 22/1 3623.
15. Marder, *Fear God and Dread Nought*, vol. 3, p. 91.
16. National Archives Cab. 22/1 3623.
17. Bartlett, *The Uncensored Dardanelles*, p. 14.
18. H.W. Nevinson, *The Dardanelles Campaign*, p. vii.
19. Fortescue, *What of the Dardanelles?*, p. 23.
20. Fuller, *Decisive Battles of the Western World*, vol. 3, p. 235.
21. Marder, *From the Dardanelles to Oran*, p. 32. See also the correspondence of Captain L.A.K. Boswell with Peter Liddle in the Liddle Collection (Correspondence): 'The naval attack was a sound operation of war which failed for one reason only – that nobody until 19 March had seen how to deal with the mines. The Army is entirely irrelevant and only an enormous red herring.'
22. Morgenthau, *Secrets of the Bosporus*, p. 128.
23. French Military Archives, Vincennes (C.E.O. 1 Bureau 20 N 15).
24. Fuller, *Decisive Battles of the Western World*, vol. 3, p. 238.
25. Guinn, *British Strategy and Politics 1914–18*, p. 61.
26. Hart, *Gallipoli*, p. 17.
27. There are some who see the dividend of the 1915 investment being collected not in the First World War but in the success of the superbly planned and unified combined operation of the Normandy D-Day landings. According to Mrs G. Shields, Sir Ian Hamilton's private secretary

in 1916–17, the General himself believed this. It must however be pointed out that Britain's 1940 Norwegian expedition provided an embarrassing parallel in failure with Gallipoli; this suggests that the lessons of the 1915 failure still needed re-learning twenty-five years later.

Chapter 1

All personal experience documentation not end-noted can be found in the Liddle Collection (hereafter LC), Brotherton Library, University of Leeds.

1. McLaughlin, *The Escape of the Goeben.*
2. Ibid., p. 72
3. *The Tenedos Times*, original issues LC and published version, p. 63, LC.
4. National Archives, ADM 137, vol. 881.
5. Ibid.
6. Ibid.
7. *Mitchell Report*, p. 25, LC.
8. Guépratte Papers, Copies held in LC.
9. Ibid.
10. Commander Holbrook told the author that he had a crew of twelve, which included an extra coxswain as the hydroplanes were too stiff to be operated by one man.
11. *Official History: Naval Operations*, vol. 2, pp. 72–3.
12. Nearly all the crew was saved, because she sank in shallow water. Holes were cut in the keel from which the trapped men escaped. Ten officers and twenty-seven men had been killed.
13. Guépratte Papers, LC.
14. *Histoire maritime de la Première Guerre Mondiale*, vol. 2, p. 250.
15. *Saphir* was in fact refloated by the Turks and seen in Constantinople by French POWs, according to Maître Gondard, taken prisoner at Kum Kale, 26 April 1915, LC.
16. National Archives ADM 137, vol. 382.
17. Guépratte Papers, LC.
18. National Archives ADM 137, vol. 382 Captain Coode was in command of the British destroyers maintaining a watch over the Dardanelles.

Chapter 2

1. National Archives, Cab. 22/1 3623.
2. National Archives, W.O. 159 1/1 xi 3173.
3. Letters, Kitchener to Churchill, 2 January 1915, quoted in Churchill, *World Crisis*, Mentor Edition, vol. 1, p. 362.
4. National Archives, Cab. 22/1 3623.
5. Once serious naval losses were incurred and the necessity for major troop involvement was grudgingly accepted, disenchantment would split this unanimity, with significant influence on the chances of success for what had become an increasingly complex combined operation.
6. Hankey's notes on the conclusions to the 8 January War Council meeting, National Archives, Cab. 22/1 3623.
7. Hankey's notes on the 9 February War Council meeting, National Archives, Cab. 22/1 3623.
8. Chack and Antier, *Histoire maritime*, vol. 2, p. 143.
9. Tsingtao was the port of Kiaochow, the German protectorate on the Chinese Yellow Sea coast. In September 1914 British troops landed near the port and with Japanese forces laid successful siege to it.
10. Stewart and Peshall, *The Immortal Gamble*, p. 11.
11. It is a point of some interest that these troops, the South Wales Borderers at Tsingtao, would later be landed by the *Cornwallis* at S Beach on 25 April 1915.
12. Price, *With the Fleet in the Dardanelles*, pp. 12–13.
13. *Mitchell Report*, p. 37, LC.

Chapter 3

1. *Mitchell Report*, p. 38.
2. Stewart and Peshall, *The Immortal Gamble*, p. 21.
3. The first machine crashed through breaking her propeller while in the air, the second was fired on by rifles and the pilot wounded so that he had to return, and the third found that spotting was difficult on Fort 13 because the slope of the Kilid Bahr plateau was too steep.
4. A dry river gulley.
5. James, *Gallipoli*, p. 45.
6. A 'basic error was the conception that slow minesweeping trawlers could clear a passage up to and through the Narrows to enable the fleet to reach the Marmara', Marder, *From the Dardanelles to Oran*, p. 2.
7. *Mitchell Report*, p. 51.
8. *Official History: Naval Operations*, vol. 2, p. 169.
9. *Official History: Naval Operations*, vol. 2, p. 207.
10. After the bombardment of 5 March he recorded: 'It is simply beastly for the first time to sit there in cold blood to be shot at and not know where from. We were stopped and continually these salvoes would come over eight at a time and every one seemed coming straight for you … I did not like the idea of going in [to bombard] again. I felt very helpless and longed to go home. It was not the kind of fighting I expected to get.'
11. R.N. picket boats had been used against the Kephez minefield as early as 8 March.
12. From 4 April *Beagle* class destroyers became operational as minesweepers.
13. *Mitchell Report*, p. 57.
14. Captain C.R.G. Allen, 'A Ghost from Gallipoli', *Royal United Services Institute Journal*, May 1963, p. 138.
15. *The Gallipolian*, Autumn 1973, pp. 9–11.

Chapter 4

1. Sanders, *Five Years in Turkey*, pp. 54–5.
2. In fact there were sixty-six.
3. HMS *Queen Elizabeth*, firing 15in shells.
4. HMS *Agamemnon*.
5. The *Bouvet* file in the French Navy Archives and LC.
6. These books were handed for safety to a British vessel and among the Guépratte Papers is an acknowledgement of their safe return.
7. That Guépratte evaluated his officers carefully is indicated by notes he made on 15 October 1914 in which he deplores the nonchalance affected by his officers and reminds them that the men must be inspired by example as well as precept.
8. *Mitchell Report*, p. 86, evidence of Lieutenant-Commander Raaf. The *Mitchell Report* considered that this officer's main objective seemed to be to please, and no weight can be attached to his opinions.
9. National Archives W.O. 106/1465 2099.
10. Hankey's notes to the War Council meeting of 19 February (National Archives Cab. 22/1 262).
11. Ibid.
12. Original Flight Report, LC.
13. Of this squadron, the Director of Military Aeronautics in the War Office, Lieutenant-Colonel Brancker, had written to Hamilton in March: 'For offensive work and bomb dropping you will find them excellent but if you want to get efficient results from their reconnaissance you will have to keep a tight hand on them as they have very few ideas on the subject' (Hamilton Papers, Centre for Military Archives, King's College, London).
14. The *Mitchell Report*, p. 94, gives a figure of eighty bombs dropped by Allied aeroplanes between 19 March and 24 April.
15. Sanders, *Five Years in Turkey*, pp. 57–62.

16. Kannengiesser, *The Campaign in Gallipoli*, p. 94ff. In 1915 Colonel Kannengiesser was in command of the Turkish XVI Army Corps.

Chapter 5
1. Murray, *Gallipoli As I Saw It*, p. 19>
2. Waite, *The New Zealanders at Gallipoli*, p. 2.
3. Gammage, *The Broken Years*, pp. 2–3.
4. Ibid, Appendix 1, p. 281.
5. Creighton, *With the 29th Division in Gallipoli*, Chapter 1.
6. Memorandum of 16 August to the First and Second Sea Lords, quoted in Gilbert, *Winston S. Churchill*, vol. 3, pp. 47–8.
7. A 29th Division NCO, W.C. Moore, posted a card on 13 March with the plain unvarnished message: 'We are leaving for the Dardanelles on Tuesday.' Five days later the Governor General of Malta wrote to Vice-Admiral Limpus at the Malta dockyard: 'My daughter and a Miss Baring suggest raising a fund for the sailors and soldiers in the Dardanelles. – I personally don't think such a fund necessary but if you and Mrs Limpus think otherwise then nothing easier.'
8. Jerrold, *With the Royal Naval Division*, p. 45.

Chapter 6
1. Battleship is an error. *Ibuki* was a cruiser.
2. Skinner was in fact with later reinforcements.
3. Malthus, *Anzac: A Retrospect*, pp. 19–21.
4. Issue of 17 July, LC.
5. Lord Birdwood Collection, Australia War Memorial, Canberra.
6. Letter of Sergeant R.M. Collins, Box 940/1 MS 8 133La Trobe Library, Melbourne
7. Papers of Lord Novar, National Archives, Canberra.
8. D Marks, diary, Mitchell Library, Sydney.
9. Malthus, *Anzac: A Retrospect*, p. 33.
10. Australian and New Zealand Division, General Routine Orders, New Zealand National Archives, Wellington.
11. Ibid.
12. Sir James A. Wilson Papers, Alexander Turnbull Library, Wellington.
13. Malthus, *Anzac: A Retrospect*, p. 43.
14. Canon M. Andrews. See his *Canon's Folly* and LC.
15. Roux, *L'Expedition des Dardanelles*, p. 90.
16. Father Charles Roux adds a footnote concerning the piquancy of French troops being reviewed by the English officer commanding a joint expeditionary force against the Turks so near to Aboukir Bay, where Nelson had beaten the French in 1798 and on the shores of which Napoleon had beaten the Sultan's army in 1799.
17. Weil had been concerned in early wireless experiments and, in 1917, was to design and put into practice a system of co-ordinated anti-aircraft defence for Paris. This system was later introduced into other cities facing German air attack.
18. Douglas, *My Diary 1915: Walmer to the Dardanelles*.
19. Ibid, p. 8.
20. Because of the lack of fresh water in large quantities and a complete absence of piers and jetties. The *Official History: Gallipoli*, vol. 2, p. 95, makes the point that the harbour was so huge that 'even in a moderate breeze the sea rapidly became too rough for small boats'. This is supported in many diary accounts of men who had spent long exhausting hours attempting to row back to their ships after having been ashore.
21. See also Creighton, *With the 29th Division in Gallipoli*, p. 38. 'All kinds of boat drill has been going on. The men are not much good at rowing, and the boats are very heavy and cumbersome. But they are as a rule towed in strings of five or six by a steam pinnace.'

22. Note the precautions of Lieutenant Weil on board the French troopship.
23. *Official History: Gallipoli*, vol. 1, p. 140n. *Official History: Naval Operations*, vol. 2, pp. 300–1; James, *Gallipoli*, p. 91.
24. Brodie, *Forlorn Hope*, p. 37ff.
25. *Official History: Naval Operations*, vol. 2, p 302.
26. Ibid, p. 304.
27. Creighton, *With the 29th Division in Gallipoli*, Chapter 3.
28. *Notes on the Turkish Army 1915*, p. 18, LC.
29. A.A.C. Intelligence Staff, *Surrender of Turkish Troops*, Imperial War Museum.
30. This map is in the Liddle Collection
31. Creighton, *With the 29th Division in Gallipoli*, p. 42.
32. Davidson, *The Incomparable 29th and the River Clyde*.
33. *Official History: Gallipoli*, vol. 2, n. 1, p. 254.
34. Malthus, *Anzac: A Retrospect*, p. 42.
35. Nevinson, *The Dardanelles Campaign*, p. 90.
36. G.L. Drewry, letter 12 May, Imperial War Museum.
37. Given in full in the *Mitchell Report*, pp. 107ff.
38. *Mitchell Report*, p. 134.
39. Ibid, p. 121.
40. See *Official History: Gallipoli*, vol. I, pp. 145–6.
41. Hart, *Gallipoli*, p. vii.

Chapter 7

1. Both north and south of this area the terrain was higher and more broken.
2. Naturally the names used to describe this and the other ridges were acquired during the campaign, but to write more accurately of 'First Ridge', for instance, is to convey so much less than to use the names of the well-remembered and well-recorded individuality of the features of the Anzac landscape.
3. *Official History: Gallipoli*, vol. I, p. 168.
4. Had Mal Tepe itself been taken, the distance was a mere one and a quarter miles to the Dardanelles, and directly beneath this height lay the sole land supply route to the Turks defending Helles.
5. Instructions for G.O.C. Australian and New Zealand Army Corps from General Headquarters, 13 April 1915, quoted in the *Mitchell Report*, p. 137.
6. The soldier, mortally wounded in August, had given this account to R.A. Nicholas, a private in the Hospital Transport Corps.
7. It seems unreasonable to attach any weight to the theory that Admiral Thursby, the naval officer in command of the Anzac landing, had at the last moment given different orders to Lieutenant Waterlow which instructed him to set course for Hell Spit. See James, *Gallipoli*, pp. 105–6.
8. Hart, *Gallipoli*, pp. 88–9.
9. Letter, 4 May, by Cpl J. Sinclair, 10th Bn AIF, in file of 10th Bn AIF unofficial letters, South Australia State Library
10. G.D. Shaw and Pte Knight, undated letters from same source as for note 9.
11. For the sad story of these men of the 7th Battalion and the brave efforts to rescue survivors see the *Official History of Australia in the War of 1914-18*, vol. 1, pp. 325ff.
12. *Journal of the New South Wales Military History Society*, vol. xxvi no. 2 (March/April 1991).
13. Lord Novar Papers, Bridges, letter to Mrs Bridges, 5 May 1915, Australian National Library, Canberra.
14. See Belford, *Legs Eleven*. The *Official History of Australia in the War 1914-18*, vol. 1, p. 470, discounts the theory of the Turks cunningly adopting such ruses by the actual use of spies and attributes the reality of the situation to rumour, mistakes and confusion.

15. D. Marks, diary, Mitchell Library, Sydney.
16. Lord Novar Papers, Bridges, letter to Mrs Bridges, 5 May 1915, Australian National Library, Canberra.
17. Lord Birdwood Collection, diary and letter, Australian War Memorial, Canberra.
18. Ibid.
19. Malthus, *Anzac: A Retrospect*, pp. 49–50.
20. CQMS A. L. Guppy, diary, Australian War Memorial, Canberra.
21. A.L. Hellman, diary, Mitchell Library, Sydney
22. *Official History of Australia in the War of 1914–18*, vol. 1, p. 267, gives the time of landing at 4.30 a.m., with the men from the destroyers 20 minutes later.
23. The breakdown of these figures into killed, wounded and missing is not given because there are some inaccuracies: 661 names from the Auckland, Canterbury and Wellington Battalions are listed, and for example H.V. Palmer of the Nelson Company, Canterbury Battalion, is listed as killed. He was still alive in June 1974.
24. For further details of the clearing of the wounded see *Official History of Australia in the War of 1914–18*, vol. 1, Chapter 25.
25. Peter Hall, letter 2 May, Mitchell Library, Sydney
26. *Mitchell Report*, pp. 167–9.
27. Von Sanders, *Five Years in Turkey*, p. 57; Kannengiesser, *The Campaign of Gallipoli*, p. 98. See also *Gallipoli Memoirs of Mustapha Kemal*, translated typescript, and *Ataturk Memoirs of the Anafarta Battles*, pp. 4–10, both Imperial War Museum.
28. Translation of this letter was by Major T. Verschoyle, scholar and Gallipoli veteran.
29. *Official History of Australia in the War of 1914–18*, vol. 1, p. 299.
30. *Bacchante* concentrated on attempting to silence the Turkish enfilading fire from Gaba Tepe
31. For a graphic description of the evacuation issue during the night of 25/26 April, see the Australian Official History, vol. 1, pp. 457–63.

Chapter 8

1. *Official History: Gallipoli*, vol. 1, pp. 204–15.
2. National Archives W.O. 95 4311 XK 976.
3. John Lavelle undated letter, Museum of the King's Own Scottish Borderers, Berwick.
4. 'Shortly after 4 p.m. a Turkish field gun was brought into action between Krithia and Gully Ravine, and at 5.40 p.m. there developed the first of a series of attacks which continued through the night' (*Official History: Gallipoli*, vol. 2, p. 207).
5. The *Official History* gives a figure of only twelve Turkish defenders in the entrenchment near the top of the cliff, and this is the figure given in the *Mitchell Report*.
6. Midshipman Clarke recorded for the 26th that 'soon after 8 a.m. all our boats were ordered to Y Beach to re-embark all the troops from there as they had to evacuate the place … we spent the night landing French troops on V Beach without any opposition.'
7. Nevinson, *The Dardanelles Campaign*, pp. 105–6.
8. Stewart and Peshall, *The Immortal Gamble*, pp. 75ff.
9. Hart, *Gallipoli*, pp. 131–2.
10. 'Dere' is a Turkish word meaning the same as 'nullah', that is a dry river gully.
11. *Official History: Gallipoli*, vol. 1, p. 231. It should be noted that the Turkish sources denied having machine-guns in their defences at W Beach and assert that two of the four machine-guns at V Beach had been destroyed by the preliminary naval bombardment. See *Official History: Gallipoli*, vol. 1, p. 221n.
12. Ibid, pp. 232ff.
13. James, *Gallipoli*, pp. 121ff.
14. G.L. Drewry, letter 12 May, Imperial War Museum.
15. W.L. Berridge, letter 22 May, Imperial War Museum.
16. War Diary and Reports of the Royal Munster Fusiliers, National Archives, W.O. 95 4310 XK 976.

17. Foster, *At Antwerp and in the Dardanelles*, pp. 85–7.
18. On the cover of the Triennial bulletin of the French Dardanelles Veterans Association.
19. War Diary and Reports of Royal Munster Fusiliers, National Archives W.O. 95 4310 XK 976.
20. Foster, *At Antwerp and in the Dardanelles*, p. 84.
21. Ibid, p. 90.
22. Creighton, *With the 29th Division in Gallipoli*, pp. 57–62.
23. Lancashire Fusiliers' War Diary, 25 April 1915, National Archives W.O. 95 4310 XK 976.
24. *Mitchell Report*, p. 178.
25. Murray, *Gallipoli as I Saw It*, pp. 54–5.
26. Freyberg was in fact a Lieutenant-Commander.
27. Murray, *Gallipoli as I Saw It*, pp. 54–5.
28. *Official History: Gallipoli*, vol. 1, p. 164.
29. Ibid, pp. 255–6.
30. *Official History: Gallipoli*, vol. 1, pp. 261–2; taken from the French official account, vol. 8, Annexes I, No. 99.
31. French Military Archives C.E.O. 2QN 27, Ordre de L'Armée No. 1: 'Le debarquement près de Koum Kaleh est consideré comme une diversion.'
32. Moorehead, *Gallipoli*, p. 150.
33. James, *Gallipoli*, p. 126.

Chapter 9

1. *Official History: Gallipoli*, vol. 1, pp. 288ff.
2. Ibid, p 288.
3. Tom Jameson of the cyclist company Royal Marines has written that some cycles were loaded onto two barges for the landing. One drifted away never to be seen again, the other beached at Cape Helles. A.W. Clarke of *Implacable* recalled seeing bicycles strapped to the backs of some of the French troops he saw landing at V Beach on the night of 26/27 April and J.D. Creighton proudly wrote that he did much of his 87th Field Ambulance wounded and sick report deliveries by bicycle. The *Official History* (vol. 2, p. 50) records that an attempt to use armoured cars in the third battle for Krithia was a complete failure.
4. *Official History: Gallipoli*, vol. 1, p. 291.
5. Malthus, *Anzac: A Retrospect*, p. 70.
6. Letters from War Hospital, Epsom, Surrey, quoted in *Dispatch, Journal of the New South Wales Military Historical Association*, vol. xxvi, no. 2, March/April 1991
7. *Official History: Gallipoli*, pp. 292 and 282–3.
8. Jerrold, *With the Royal Naval Division*, p. 113.

Chapter 10

1. War Diary of Canterbury Battalion, Report of Raid on Nibrunesi Point Observation Station, New Zealand National Archives, Wellington.
2. See report by Brig.-General C.M. Wagstaff of action on the night of 18/19 May, Mitchell Library, Sydney.
3. Lock, *The Fighting 10th*, p. 45, quoting a letter dated 20 May by Lieutenant-Colonel S.P. Weir.
4. CQMS A.L. Guppy diary, Australian War Memorial, Canberra.
5. Letters of John Simpson Kirkpatrick, (749/80/7), Australian War Memorial, Canberra.
6. J.L. Anderson, diary, Christchurch Public Library, Christchurch, New Zealand.
7. *Official History of Australia in the War of 1914-1918*, vol. 2, pp. 164, *Official History: Gallipoli*, vol. 2, pp. 20ff. The Birdwood diaries are held at Canberra in the Australian War Memorial.
8. New Zealand and Australian Division War Diary, New Zealand National Archives, Wellington. This war diary shows that during the truce both sides levelled accusations against the other of illegal activities.
9. D. Marks, diary, Mitchell Library, Sydney.
10. Malthus, *Anzac: A Retrospect*, Chapter 5.

11. A.E. Gascoigne, diary for 18 May. He was to be killed on 20 May. Alexander Turnbull Library, Wellington, New Zealand.
12. Lord Birdwood Papers, Australian War Memorial.
13. 21st and 26th Batteries.
14. Units of the RND also landed at Anzac on 25 April 1915 and during the next few days before being transferred to Helles. See *Australian Official History*, vol. 1, p. 281.
15. A.S. Hutton, diary, (D 4975), The State Library, Adelaide, South Australia.
16. *Peninsula Press*, 11 June 1915, LC.
17. J.L. Anderson, diary for 9 June, Christchurch Library, New Zealand.
18. A.S. Hutton, diary, 29 May, The State Library, Adelaide, South Australia (D 4975).

Chapter 11

1. *From Dartmouth to the Dardanelles, A Midshipman's Log Edited by his Mother*, pp. 152ff.
2. Inspection on board ship.
3. Seaman W.H. Clarke, letter published in Isle of Man newspaper, *Mona's Herald*, 9 June 1915.
4. Vice-Admiral Sir Arthur Limpus Papers, correspondence, National Maritime Museum.
5. 'The Work of a Trawler in the Aegean Sea', *Naval Review*, vol. 6 (1918).
6. Hersing, *U 21 Rettet die Dardanellen*, pp. 46ff.
7. Captain J. Savile Metcalf RN has written to the author that later in 1915 Commander Egerton of *Triumph* had told him of the sinking as follows: 'I shouted for my bugler and there was no reply. "Where's the bloody bugler?" I called again. At that moment the bugler jumped through the door from the Shelter Deck dressed only in the lanyard of his bugle. At my order he sounded the charge, threw his bugle as far as he could into the sea and dived after it.' Commander Egerton also recorded seeing a Chinese steward clinging to a slowly turning propeller when the ship had turned turtle.
8. Hersing, *U 21*. Nothing is mentioned of his sinking the dummy battleship HMS *Tiger*. It was after this sinking that de Robeck wrote of the elderly skipper: 'Old Willy Forbes who is now nearly seventy behaved splendidly and the old man wants another job out here but thinks he had better go home and see his wife and get some new clothes.'
9. Seaman J.E. Kelly, letter in Isle of Man newspaper, *Mona's Herald*, 9 June 1915.
10. Hans von Mohl, article in *Deutsch-Africaner* (Pretoria, 1930), and memoirs in LC.
11. The private diary of Midshipman William-Powlett records a near-miss by a torpedo fired at *Vengeance* on the morning of the attack on the *Triumph*, but Hersing makes no mention of this unsuccessful attack in his book.
12. W.L. Berridge, letter, Imperial War Museum.
13. *Mitchell Report*, p. 211.
14. Report of Konteradmiral Waldemar Pieper, LC.
15. Carr, *By Guess and by God*, p. 28. The claim was at first denied by the Admiralty Prize Court on the grounds that the troopship was only defensively armed, but was carried on appeal to the Privy Council and the full amount awarded to officers and men.
16. Op cit, p. 40.
17. These four sinkings were still, in 1972, marked by buoys off Istanbul.
18. *Mitchell Report*, p. 201.
19. *Official History: Naval Operations*, vol. 3, pp. 115ff.
20. Op cit, p 118.
21. Chack and Antier, *Histoire maritime de la Première Guerre Mondiale*, vol. 2, pp. 242ff.

Chapter 12

1. French Military Archives, Vincennes (C.E.O. 20N 27 and 28), Ordre General No. 43.
2. French Military Archives, Vincennes (C.E.O. 20N 27 and 28).
3. *Official History: Gallipoli*, vol. 2, p. 47.
4. French Military Archives, Vincennes (C.E.O. 20 N 27 and 28), Compte-Rendu du Géneral Simonin du Combat le 4 Juin.

5. *Official History: Gallipoli*, vol. 2, p. 49.
6. For example, poster for the meeting at the Roseville Hall, Sydney on 23 September 1915, Mitchell Library, Sydney.
7. *The 7th Manchester Sentry*, 1 March 1916, LC. With Manchester Regiment teams contesting the Peninsula Cup in 1915 perhaps it cannot be just coincidence that a century later it is teams from the same city which dominate the English Football Premier League.
8. There was in fact a YMCA tent at Anzac in the late autumn and there is some evidence that a Congregationalist padre provided piano entertainment there.
9. This estimate given by Captain Corbett Williamson of the range of the catapults is a good deal less than that of Major-General Tom Jameson. In addition to the catapults there were 3.7in trench mortars, Garland mortars and Hales grenades.
10. French Military Archives, Vincennes, C.E.O., Premier Bureau 20 N 15.
11. Murray, *Gallipoli as I Saw It*.
12. French Military Archives, Vincennes (T.O.E. 16 N 1940).
13. Roux, *L'Expédition des Dardanelles*, p. 154.
14. The haversack is in the Liddle Collection.
15. *Official History: Gallipoli*, vol. 2, p. 90.
16. *History of the 5th Royal Gurkha Rifles*, pp. 242–3.
17. Black, *The Book of the Sixth Highland Light Infantry*.

Chapter 13

1. 'They are merely a lot of childlike youths without strength to endure or brains to improve their condition' was the opinion of the Australian war correspondent K.A. Murdoch, writing to the Australian Prime Minister (Fisher) in a letter of 23 September (typescript copy in the K.A. Murdoch papers, Australian National Archives, Canberra, M5 2823 42.7).
2. K.A. Murdoch Papers, Ms 2823 42.17.
3. The 53rd and 54th Divisions were Territorial Force units and a brigade of the Regular Army's 29th Division, was moved to Suvla from Helles on 17 August.
4. This charge was made by a number of Australian veterans interviewed and there was abundant evidence in letters and diaries of Australian troops of judgement made along similar lines.
5. See E. Bush, *Bless Our Ship*, and the same author's *Gallipoli*, pp. 243 and 246: 'They made a poor showing – no dash and a certain amount of talking. Indeed a handful who obviously had the wind up looked as if they were afraid to land.' Eric Bush's judgement of the men he landed is made clear by the tone of a further comment: 'they trickled out [of the lighters]. As there appeared to be no opposition they formed up on the foreshore and then had the shock of their lives, for a whole string of mines exploded right and left of them and there were many casualties.'
6. The landing craft were known as 'Beetles' because the hoists of the landing ramp stuck up from the general squat outline like antennae.
7. *Official History: Gallipoli*, vol. 2, p. 140
8. James, *Gallipoli*, p. 246
9. *Official History of Australia in the War of 1914–1918*, vol. 2, p. 497.
10. T.J. McKinlay letter, Mitchell Library, Sydney.
11. The figures for the 4th Battalion given in the *Official History of Australia in the War of 1914–1918* show 474 losses out of 742 attackers. 3rd Battalion losses were even heavier (see vol. 2, p. 566).
12. *The Nek: A Gallipoli Tragedy*, by Peter Burness, an exceptionally good book, takes the reader into the social scene of the 3rd Light Horse Brigade, documenting personal relationships and with disturbing realism the rivalries, even animosities which, in one instance, actually conspired to prevent a limitation of the developing tragedy. Burness is also harrowingly good on the clogging of movement in the jumping-off trench and the forward sapping as dead and wounded fell or crawled back in while the next line was readying for their assault. The psychological impact of this scarcely needed the author's excellent writing.

13. W.E. Anderson papers, letter, Australian War Memorial, Canberra.
14. CQMS A.L. Guppy diary, Australian War Memorial, Canberra.
15. H.E. Browne, undated letter, Alexander Turnbull Library, Wellington (Misc. M.S. 1196)
16. *History of the 5th Royal Gurkha Rifles*, p. 313.
17. D. Marks diary, Mitchell Library, Sydney.
18. H.E. Browne undated letter, Alexander Turnbull Library, Wellington (Misc. M.S. 1196).
19. *Official History: Gallipoli*, vol. 2, p 208.
20. According to the *Official History of Australia in the War of 1914-1918*, vol. 2, p 674, a Turkish sergeant narrowly prevented the killing of eleven wounded New Zealanders captured in their forward trench. There is also evidence of a German officer stopping a similar atrocity during these attacks on the Sari Bair ridge (see p. 662).
21. Ibid., vol. 2, p. 695.
22. H.E. Browne undated letter, Alexander Turnbull Library, Wellington, (Misc. MS 1196).
23. R. Savory, 'Some Gallipoli Memories', *The Gallipolian*, no. 18 (1975), p. 13.
24. *Official History: Gallipoli*, vol. 2, p. 714 note, and W.G. Bavin, *Swindon's War Record*, John Drew, Swindon, 1922, p. 306.
25. *Official History of Australia in the War of 1914-1918*, vol. 2, p. 758ff.
26. Letter of George Moss, 21 September 1915, Blathwayte Papers, Gloucestershire County Record Office.

Chapter 14

1. Chambers, *Suvla, August Offensive*, p. 68.
2. The Navy had not wished to land troops inside Suvla Bay because of the shallowness of the water, but it was requested by IX Corps in order that Chocolate and Green Hills could be approached from the north-west, where they were believed to be less strongly defended than from the south-west.
3. *Official History: Gallipoli*, vol. 2, pp. 244–5.
4. Their capture and execution are described in Wyrall, *The East Yorkshire Regiment in the Great War*, pp. 102ff.
5. These metal patches, as mentioned earlier, worn for the diversionary attack at Helles on the 6th and 7th, led to the grimly inaccurate report that the Turkish front line 'must' be captured as British troops were there. The patches were shining but the men were dead.
6. Chambers, *Suvla: August Offensive*, p. 168.
7. *Official History: Gallipoli*, vol. 2, p. 260.
8. Gibbon, *The 42nd East Lancashire Division 1914-18*, p. 44.

Chapter 15

1. A more distant tragedy, but one related to Gallipoli, was that of the accident to the troop train at Gretna in which so many Royal Scots bound for the Peninsula were killed.
2. Mr Fraser wrote that only those detailed for duties inside the ship were allowed to remain below decks after breakfast and there were probably 200 on those duties, plus 200 crew.
3. A New Zealander, C. McBeath, on board the troopship *Alnwick Castle*, recalled his ship passing the sinking *Royal Edward* without stopping.
4. The papers of Vice-Admiral Limpus, National Maritime Museum.
5. Dardanelles Commission Report, Part 2, p. 95.
6. French Military Archives, Vincennes, C.E.O., Premier Bureau 20 N 15.

Chapter 16

1. Foster, *At Antwerp and in the Dardanelles*; Creighton, *With the 29th Division*; Raymond, *The Story of My Days*.
2. Foster, *At Antwerp and in the Dardanelles*, p. 115.
3. Creighton, *With the 29th Division*, pp. 88ff.

4. *The Gallipolian*, No. 13 (1973) and No. 14 (1974).
5. A report in the Australian *Sun-Herald*, 29 July 1973, described a cloud seen above the troops and puts forward the possibility that this was an unidentified flying object, but see Stephen Chambers' *Suvla: August Offensive*, pp. 115–23, for a more reasoned examination of this sad episode.
6. Pte John Lavelle, letter, King's Own Scottish Borderers Museum, Berwick.
7. Captain A.M. Shaw, diary, King's Own Scottish Borderers Museum, Berwick.

Chapter 17

1. MEF Official Papers, General Routine Orders, LC.
2. Pte David Harper letter. Sadly this was in fact Harper's last letter. He was killed in the KOSB attack on 12 July. Museum of the King's Own Scottish Borderers, Berwick.
3. MEF Official Papers (G.R.O. 131 A.G. 9, May 1915), LC. The charge had been 'behaving in such a manner as to show cowardice before the enemy'.
4. French Military Archives, Vincennes (T.E.O. 20 N 17).
5. Ibid (T.E.O. 20 N 14).
6. Ibid (T.E.O. 20 N 14).
7. The Bull Ring was also a major training camp.

Chapter 18

1. *Course de grenouilles.*
2. A most unusual account of POW experience in Turkey is Group Captain C.W. Hill's *The Spook and the Commandant*, William Kimber, 1975.

Chapter 19

1. *Mitchell Report*, pp. 206ff.
2. The same evidence is recorded in Bell-Davies, *Sailor in the Air*.
3. The *Mitchell Report*, p. 513, gives the types of aircraft as Gotha, Rumpler and later Albatros, all tractor biplanes, Taube was a generic name for German monoplanes.
4. French Military Archives, Vincennes (C.E.O. 20 N 27 and 28).
5. Ibid.
6. *Mitchell Report*, p. 503.
7. Log, Imperial War Museum, and further material, LC.
8. *The Official History of the War in the Air*, vol. 2, p. 519.
9. Ibid, pp. 27–8.
10. Papers of Air Commodore C.R. Samson (D.2, Papers concerning the *Official History of the War in the Air*, Dardanelles, pp. 12, 14), Imperial War Museum.
11. South Australian State Archives, 10th Battalion AIF unofficial letters (P.R.F. 272/9).
12. Samson, *Fights and Flights*, p. 229.
13. Bell-Davies, *Sailor in the Air*, p. 135.
14. Papers of Air Commodore Samson (D.2, Papers concerning the *Official History of the War in the Air*, The Dardanelles Attack on Maritza Bridge, p. 15), Imperial War Museum
15. Bell-Davies, *Sailor in the Air*, p. 122.
16. Ibid, p, 127,
17. *Hector* arrived at the Peninsula in July.
18. *The Official History of the War in the Air*, vol. 2, p. 33.
19. Roskill, ed., *The Royal Naval Air Service 1914-18*, p. 222.
20. *The Official History of the War in the Air*, vol. 2, p. 56.
21. For the mismanagement of the seaplanes attached to *Ark Royal*, see Marder, *From the Dardanelles to Oran*, pp. 7–11. Marder uses the unpublished memoirs of Group Captain H. A. Williamson, Second-in-Command and Senior Flying Officer in *Ark Royal*. These papers are held in Churchill College, Cambridge.

Chapter 20

1. *Official Medical History*, p. 203.
2. A.S. Hutton, diary, 28 August 1915, South Australian State Library (D 4975).
3. T.R. Ritchie, Evidence to the Dardanelles Commission, Alexander Turnbull Library, Wellington (Misc. M.S. 1428).
4. Of course some of the new British troops were at Anzac.
5. *Official History of Australia in the War of 1914-18*, vol. 2, p. 812.
6. Hypnosis was used successfully to cure the shell shock affecting a young Australian after narrow escapes while working from one of these bulletproof shields. See Moore, *The Thin Yellow Line*, p. 97.
7. National Archives, W.O. 95 4310 XK 976.
8. Sapper E.C. Clifton, diary, Alexander Turnbull Library, Wellington.
9. Mullaly, *Bugle and Kukri*, p. 108, see bibliography. An interesting comparison and contrast is contained in the *History of the 5th Royal Gurkha Rifles*, p. 268.
10. Colonel A. B. Tillard, diary, The Gurkha Museum, Winchester.

Chapter 21

1. This fire had been started accidentally and caused great anxiety because it was exactly the sort of obvious activity which it was hoped to avoid.
2. In fact this was a very big mine which was judged by veteran Turks on interview by the author as being an unsporting farewell gesture.
3. D. Marks, diary, Mitchell Library, Sydney.
4. M.E. Pearce, diary, Mitchell Library, Sydney.
5. *Official History of Australia in the War of 1914-18*, vol. 2, p 880.
6. Brigadier-General John Monash, letters to wife and daughter, December, 1915, La Trobe Library, Melbourne (MS 9456).
7. Nevertheless in the Liddle Collection there is an unpublished Turkish photograph of Turkish officers and men proudly assembled beside the barrel of one of the few big Allied guns at Anzac.
8. Lord Novar Papers, correspondence from General Birdwood, Australian War Memorial, Canberra
9. *Official History, Gallipoli*, vol. 2, p. 453.
10. See James, *Gallipoli*, p. 347n.
11. 'Asiatic Annie', the Turkish gun firing across the Straits.
12. A 'crinoline' was a long pole with cross bars at each end, the whole construction wrapped round with barbed wire, and set ready to fall into and block saps and communication trenches.
13. An 'umbrella' was a smaller version of a 'crinoline'.
14. Letter by Lily Fagence, 20 April 1916, to R.A. Nicholas (LC). It is pleasing to know that in the 1970s, through the aid of a Perth (W.A.) newspaper, the Anzac veteran was able to meet the writer of the schoolgirl letter.

Epilogue

1. Keyes, *The Fight for Gallipoli*, p. 69.
2. Ibid.
3. Marder, *From the Dardanelles to Oran*, p. 23.
4. Hart, *Gallipoli*, p. 44, Liddell Hart, *A History of the World War*, p. 186.
5. Letter with Vice-Admiral Sir Arthur Limpus papers, National Maritime Museum.
6. Hart, *Gallipoli*, p. 63.
7. John Philip Jones, *Johnny - The Legend and Tragedy of Sir Ian Hamilton*, p. 172, quoting Hamilton on Compulsory Service, pp. 121–2.
8. Hamilton, *The Happy Warrior*, p. 282.
9. Liddell Hart, *A History of the World War*, p. 186.

10. *Official History of Australia in the War of 1914-18*, vol. I, p. 604.
11. See the *Dardanelles Commission Report*, Part II, General Conclusions, No. 25.
12. See the *Dardanelles Commission Report*, Part II, General Conclusions, No. 26.
13. See the *Dardanelles Commission Report*, Part II, General Conclusions, No. 6.
14. Fuller, *Decisive Battles of the Western World*, vol. 3, p. 247.
15. See the *Dardanelles Commission Report*, Part II, General Conclusions, No. 8.
16. Lieut-General Hon. Sir F. Stopford.
17. Major-General F. Hammersley, 11th Division.
18. Major-General Hon. J.E. Lindley, 53rd Division.
19. Brigadier-General W.H. Sitwell, 34th Brigade.
20. Fuller, *Decisive Battles of the Western World*, vol. 3, p. 248.

Bibliography

(Place of publication is London unless otherwise stated.)

Official Histories
The Official History of the Great War: Military Operations, Gallipoli, vols. 1 and 2, Brig.-Gen. C.F. Aspinall-Oglander, Heinemann, 1929, 1932.
The Official History of the Great War: Naval Operations, vols. 1 and 2, Sir Julian S. Corbett, Longmans Green, 1921, 1923.
General History of Medical Services in the Great War, vol. 4, Sir W. Macpherson and T. Mitchell, HMSO, 1924.
The Official History of the Great War: Casualties and Medical Statistics, Maj. T.J. Mitchell and Miss G.M. Smith, HMSO, 1932.
The Official History of the War in the Air, vol. 2, H.A. Jones, Clarendon Press, Oxford, 1928.
Sir Ian Hamilton's Despatches from the Dardanelles, George Newnes, undated.
The Official History of Australia in the War of 1914-18, vols. 1 and 2, C.E.W. Bean, Angus and Robertson, Sydney, 1921, 1924.
The New Zealanders at Gallipoli, Maj. F. Waite, Whitcombe and Tombs, Auckland, 1919.

Early Histories and Appreciations
Adcock, A. St John, *Australasia Triumphant*, Simpkin, Marshall and Hamilton, Sydney, 1916.
Bartlett, E. Ashmead, *The Uncensored Dardanelles*, Hutchinson, 1928.
Callwell, Maj.-Gen. Sir C.E., *The Dardanelles*, Constable, 1924.
Cavill, H.W., *Imperishable Anzacs*, William Brooks, Sydney, 1916.
Dardanelles and Their Story, The, 'By the author of *The Real Kaiser*', A. Melrose Ltd, 1915.
Fortescue, Granville, *What of the Dardanelles?* , Hodder and Stoughton, 1915.
Head, Lieut-Col. C.O., *A Glance at Gallipoli*, Eyre and Spottiswoode, 1931.
Herbert, A. P., *The Secret Battle*, Methuen, 1919.
Keyes, Admiral of the Fleet Sir Roger, *The Fight for Gallipoli*, Eyre and Spottiswoode, 1941.
Masefield, John, *Gallipoli*, Heinemann, 1916.
Mitchell Report, The, Report on the Enemy Defence of the Dardanelles Straits, The Dardanelles Committee, 1921.
Morley, Sir James Headlam, *Studies in Diplomatic History*, Methuen, 1930.
Moseley, S.A., *The Truth about the Dardanelles*, Cassell, 1916.
Nevinson, H.W., *The Dardanelles Campaign*, Nisbet, 1918.
North, John, *The Fading Vision*, Faber and Faber, 1936.
Story of the Anzacs, The, James Ingram and Son, Melbourne, 1917.
Wemyss, Admiral of the Fleet Lord Wester, *The Navy in the Dardanelles Campaign*, Hodder and Stoughton, 1924.
Wilkinson, N., *The Dardanelles: Colour Sketches from Gallipoli*, Longmans, 1916.

Later and Recent Histories
Burness, Peter, *The Nek: A Gallipoli Tragedy*, Pen and Sword, 2013.
Bush, Eric, *Gallipoli*, Allen and Unwin, 1975.
Cassar, G.H., *The French and the Dardanelles*, Allen and Unwin, 1971.

Chambers, Stephen, *Suvla: August Offensive*, Pen and Sword, 2011.
Forrest, Michael, *The Defence of the Dardanelles: From Bombards to Battleships*, Pen and Sword, 2012.
Hart, Peter, *Gallipoli*, Profile Books, 2011.
Hickey, Michael, *Gallipoli*, John Murray, 1995.
James, R.R., *Gallipoli*, Batsford, 1965.
Liddle, H. Peter, *Gallipoli 1915: Pens, Pencils and Cameras at War*, Brassey's, 1985.
McLaughlin, R., *The Escape of the Goeben*, Seeley Service, 1974.
Marder, A.J., *From the Dardanelles to Oran*, Oxford University Press, 1974.
Moorehead, Alan, *Gallipoli*, Hamish Hamilton, 1956.
Pearl, Cyril, *Anzac Newsreel*, Ure Smith, Sydney, and A.H. and A.W. Reed, Wellington, 1963.

Memoirs and Published Diaries
Aston, Sir George, *The Secret Service*, Faber and Faber, 1930.
Beaverbrook, Lord, *Politicians and the War*, Butterworth, 1928, 1932.
Fisher, Admiral of the Fleet Lord, *Memories*, Hodder and Stoughton, 1919.
Grey of Fallodon, Lord, *Twenty-Five Years*, Hodder and Stoughton, 1925.
Hamilton, Sir Ian, *Gallipoli Diary*, Arnold, 1920.
Lloyd George, David, *War Diaries*, Nicholas and Watson, 1933.
Robertson, Sir William, *Soldiers and Statesmen*, Cassell, 1926.
Sazanov, Serge, *The Fateful Years 1909–1916*, Cape, 1928.
Scott, C.P., *The Political Diaries 1911–1928*, ed. T. Wilson, Collins, 1970.
Taylor, A.J.P., ed., *Lloyd George: A Diary of Frances Stevenson*, Hutchinson, 1971.

Biographies
Bean, C.E.W., *Two Men I Knew: William Bridges and Brudenell White, Founders of the AIF*, Angus and Robertson, Sydney, 1957.
Best, Geoffrey, *Churchill, A Study in Greatness*, The Hambledon Press, 2001.
Cassar, George H., *Kitchener's War, British Strategy from 1914 to 1916*, Brassey's Inc., Washington, D.C., 2004.
——, *Asquith as War Leader*, The Hambledon Press, 1994.
Clifford, Colin, *The Asquiths*, John Murray, 2002.
Esher, Reginald Viscount, *The Tragedy of Lord Kitchener*, Murray, 1921.
Germains, V.W., *The Tragedy of Winston Churchill*, Hurst and Blackett, 1931.
Gilbert, M., *Winston S. Churchill*, vol. 3, Heinemann, 1971.
Hamilton, I.B.M., *The Happy Warrior, Gen. Sir Ian Hamilton*, Cassell, 1966.
Higgins, T., *Winston Churchill and the Dardanelles*, Heinemann, 1964.
Jones, John Philip, *Johnny: the Legend and Tragedy of General Sir Ian Hamilton*, Pen and Sword, 2012.
Magnus, P., *Kitchener: Portrait of an Imperialist*, Murray, 1958.
Marder, A.J., ed., *Fear God and Dread Nought* (Correspondence of Admiral Fisher, vol. 3), Cape, 1959.
Oglander, C.A., *Roger Keyes*, Hogarth, 1951.
Robbins, K., *Sir Edward Grey*, Cassell, 1970.
Roskill, S., *Hankey: Man of Secrets*, vol. 1, Collins, 1970.
Taylor, A.J.P., et al, *Churchill: Four Faces and the Man*, Allen Lane, 1969.

General, Military and Naval History
Bean, C.E.W., *Anzac to Amiens*, Halstead Press, Sydney, 1946.
Bird, Sir W.D., *The Direction of War*, Cambridge University Press, 1925.
Chambers, F.P., *The War Behind the War*, Faber and Faber, 1939.
Chatterton, E. Keble, *Seas of Adventure*, Hurst and Blackett, 1936.

Churchill, W.S., *The World Crisis*, Thornton and Butterworth, 1923.

Forrest, Michael, *The Defence of the Dardanelles: From Bombards to Battleships*, Pen and Sword, 2012.

Fuller, Maj.-Gen. J.F.C, *The Decisive Battles of the Western World*, vol. 3, Eyre and Spottiswoode, 1956.

Gammage, Bill, *The Broken Years: Australian Soldiers in the Great War*, Australian National University Press, Canberra, 1974.

Guinn, P., *British Strategy and Politics*, Clarendon Press, Oxford, 1965.

Hankey, Lord, *The Supreme Command*, vols. 1 and 2, Allen and Unwin, 1961.

Howard, M., *The Continental Commitment*, Penguin Books, 1974.

Liddell Hart, B., *A History of the World War*, Faber and Faber, 1930.

Marder, A. J., *From the Dreadnought to Scapa Flow*, vol. 2, Oxford University Press, 1965.

Moore, W., *The Thin Yellow Line*, Leo Cooper, 1974.

Robson, L.L., *The First AIF*, Melbourne University Press, 1970.

Woodward, Sir L., *Great Britain and the War of 1914-18*, Butler and Tanner, Frome and London, 1967.

Turkish and German Accounts

Armstrong, H.C, *Grey Wolf*, Arthur Barker, 1932.

Benoist-Mechin, J., *Mustapha Kemal*, Albin-Michel, Paris, 1954.

Castle, W.T.F., *Grand Turk*, Hutchinson, 1943.

Fewster, Kevin, Basarin, Vecihi, and Basarin, Hatice Hurmuz, *Gallipoli: The Turkish Story*, Allen and Unwin, 1985 and 2013.

Hersing, Korvettenkapitän Otto, *U 21 Rettet die Dardanellen*, Hase and Koehler, Leipzig, 1932.

History of Turkish Operations in the World War, Military Publication 1338, Istanbul, 1921 (French tr., Capt. M. Larcher, 1924).

Kannengiesser Pasha, *The Campaign in Gallipoli*, Hutchinson, 1927.

Morgenthau, Henry, *Secrets of the Bosporus*, *c.* 1920.

Sanders, Liman von, *Five Years in Turkey*, U.S. Naval Institute, Annapolis, 1927.

French Accounts

Bayle, X. Torau, *La Campagne des Dardanelles*, Chiron, Paris, 1920.

Chack, P., and Antier, Jean-Jacques, *Histoire maritime de la Première Guerre Mondiale*, vol. 2, *Méditerranee*, France-Empire, Paris, 1970.

David, Robert, *Le Drame ignoré de l'armée d'orient*, Plon, Paris, 1927.

Delage, E., *The Tragedy of the Dardanelles*, Butler and Tanner, 1932.

Ducasse, A., *Balkans 1914-18*, Robert Laffont, Paris, 1964.

Faurie, Capitaine, *La Guerre Joyeuse*, privately published, n.d.

Gouin, G., *L'Armée d'orient des Dardanelles au Danube*, Rotogravure S.A., Geneva, 1931.

Peandeleu, Dr, *Aux Dardanelles a Lemnos*, Imprimerie du Patronage Saint Pierre, Nice, 1920.

Roux, Fr Charles, *L'Expedition des Dardanelles*, Armand Colin, Paris, 1920.

Stienon, Charles, *L'Expedition des Dardanelles*, Châpelot, Paris, 1916.

Testis, *L'Expedition des Dardanelles*, Payot, Paris, 1917.

Uncensored Letters from the Dardanelles, by a French Medical Officer, Heinemann, 1916.

L'Illustration and *Le Miroir* for 1915.

Unit Histories

Belford, W.C, *Legs Eleven* (History of the 11th Bn AIF), Imperial Printing Company, Perth, 1940.

Black, Major C.S., *The Book of the Sixth Highland Light Infantry*, n.d.

Boinovvski, L., ed., *Tasmania's War Record 1914-18*, J. Walch, Hobart, 1925.

Burrows, J.W., *Essex Units in the War 1914–18*, vol. 1, *1st Bn The Essex Regiment*, J.H. Burrows, Southend, *c.* 1924.

Burton, 2nd Lieut O.E., *The Auckland Regiment NZEF 1914–18*, Whitcombe and Tombs, Auckland, 1922.

Byrne, A.E., *Official History of the Otago Regiment in the Great War*, J. Wilkie, Dunedin, n.d.

Carew, T., *The Royal Norfolk Regiment*, Hamish Hamilton, 1967.

Collett, Col. H.B., *The 28th: A Record of War Service with the AIF*, Perth, 1922.

Cooper, Maj. B., *The (Tenth) Irish Division in Gallipoli*, Herbert Jenkins, 1918.

Cowan, James, *The Maoris in the Great War*, Whitcombe and Tombs, Auckland, 1926.

Creighton, Rev. O., *With the 29th Division in Gallipoli*, Longmans, 1916.

Crutchley, C. E., ed., *Machine Gunner 1914–18*, Mercury Press, Northampton, 1973.

Davidson, G., *The Incomparable 29th and the River Clyde*, J. G. Bisset, Aberdeen, 1919.

Fergusson, Capt. D., *The History of the Canterbury Regiment NZEF*, Whitcombe and Tombs, Auckland, 1921.

Geary, Lieut S., *The Collingwood Battalion, Royal Naval Division*, F.J. Parsons, Hastings, 1920.

Gibbon, F.P., *The 42nd East Lancashire Division 1914–18*, Country Life, 1920.

Gorman, Capt. E., *With the 22nd: A History of the 22nd Battalion, AIF*, H.H. Champion, Melbourne, 1919.

Greenwell, G.H., *An Infant in Arms*, Penguin Press, 1972.

Hammond, E.W., *History of the 11th Light Horse Regiment*, William Brooks, Brisbane, 1942.

History of the 5th Royal Gurkha Rifles, privately published, Gale and Polden, Aldershot, 1929.

History of the Old 2/4 Battalion, City of London Regiment, Royal Fusiliers, Westminster Press, 1919.

Hurst, C.B., *With the Manchesters in the East*, Manchester University Press, 1918.

Jerrold, D., *The Hawke Battalion*, Benn, 1925.

——, *With the Royal Naval Division*, Hutchinson, 1923.

Johnson, Lieut-Col. R.M., *The 29th Divisional Artillery War Record and Honours Book*, RA Institution, 1921.

Kahan, H.J., *The 28th Battalion AIF*, privately published, Perth, 1969.

Kingsford, C.L., *The Story of the Royal Warwickshire Regiment*, George Newnes, 1921.

Lock, C.R.L., *The Fighting 10th*, Webb and Son, Adelaide, 1936.

Longmore, Capt. G, *The Old Sixteenth: Being a Record of the 16th Bn AIF during the Great War 1914–18*, Perth, probably 1921.

MacKenzie, Lieut-Col. K.W., *The Story of the 17th Battalion AIF in the Great War*, Chipping Newspapers, Sydney, 1946.

Midwinter, C., *Memoirs of the 32nd Field Ambulance, 10th Irish Division*, privately published, 1933.

Mullaly, Col. B.R., *Bugle and Kukri: The Story of the 10th Princess Mary's Own Gurkha Rifles*, Blackwood, Edinburgh, 1957.

Newton, L.W., *The Story of the 12th*, J. Walch, Hobart, 1925.

Olden, Lieut-Col. A.C.N., *Westralian Cavalry in the War (The Story of the 10th Light Horse)*, Alexander McCubbin, Melbourne, n.d.

Patterson, Lieut-Col. H., *With the Zionists in Gallipoli*, Hutchinson, 1916.

Roskill, S.W., ed., *The Naval Air Service 1914-18*, Navy Records Society, 1969.

Stout, T., *With the Royal Division Engineers*, privately published, 1930.

Third East Anglian Field Ambulance 1914-1919, Wyman, n.d.

Thompson, C.W., Maj.-Gen., *Records of the Dorset Yeomanry 1914-19*, F. Bennet, Sherborne, 1921.

With the Royal Naval Division: A Souvenir, W.H. Smith, 1915.

Wren, E., *Randwick to Hargicourt (History of the 3rd Battalion AIF)* , R.G. McDonald, Sydney, 1935.

Wyrall, E., *The East Yorkshire Regiment in the Great War 1914-18*, Harrison, 1918.

Zion Mule Corps, The, Israeli War Veterans' Association pamphlet, 1965.

Personal Accounts: The Army

Allanson, Lieut-Col. C, *Diary*, privately published, n.d.

Andrews, M., *Canon's Folly*, Michael Joseph, 1974.

Behrend, A., *Make Me a Soldier*, Eyre and Spottiswoode, 1961.

Benson, Sir Irving, *The Man with the Donkey*, Hodder and Stoughton, 1965.

Blackledge, W.J., and Digger Craven, *Peninsula of Death*, Samson Low, n.d.

Condliffe, J.B., *Te Rangi Hiroa: The Life of Sir Peter Buck*, Whitcombe and Tombs, Christchurch, 1971.

Cutlack, F.M. ed., *The Monash Letters: The War Letters of General Monash*, Angus and Robertson, Sydney, 1934.

Darlington, Sir Henry, *Letters from Helles*, Longmans, 1936.

*Douglas, A., *My Diary 1915: Walmer to the Dardanelles*, privately published, n.d.

Eades, F., ed., *The War Diary and Letters of Corporal Tom Eades 1915–17*, Cambridge Aids to Learning, 1973.

Edmonds, H.J., *Norman Dewhust M.C.* , H.J. Edmonds, Brussels, 1968.

Ewing, W., *From Gallipoli to Baghdad*, Hodder and Stoughton, 1918.

*Foster, Rev. H.C, *At Antwerp and in the Dardanelles*, Mills and Boon, 1918.

Graham, Maj. J.G., *Gallipoli Diary*, Allen and Unwin, 1918.

Hand-Newton, C.T., *A Physician in Peace and War*, N M. Peryer, Christchurch, 1967.

Hargrave, J., *The Suvla Bay Landing*, Macdonald, 1964.

Herbert, The Hon. Aubrey, *Mons, Anzac and Kut*, Hutchinson, *c.* 1930.

Lushington, R.F., *A Prisoner with the Turks, 1913-1918*, Simpkin, Marshall, Hamilton and Kent, 1923.

McCustra, Trooper L., *Gallipoli Days and Nights*, Hodder and Stoughton, 1916.

Mackenzie, Compton, *Gallipoli Memories*, Cassell, 1929.

Malthus, Cecil, *Anzac: A Retrospect*, Whitcombe and Tombs, Christchurch, 1965.

*Murray, J., *Gallipoli As I Saw It*, William Kimber, 1965.

Raymond, Ernest, *The Story of My Days*, Cassell, 1968.

*Sparrow, G., and McBean Ross, J.N., *On Four Fronts with the Royal Naval Division*, Hodder and Stoughton, 1918.

Stevens, K.M., *Maungatapere: A History and Reminiscence*, The Advocate, Whangarei, New Zealand, n.d.

Teichman, Capt. O., *The Diary of a Yeomanry M.O.*, Fisher Unwin, 1921.

Watkins, G., *Lost Endeavour*, privately published, 1968.

* soldiering accounts by sailors

Personal Accounts: The Navy and Royal Naval Air Service

Bell-Davies, Vice-Admiral Richard, *Sailor in the Air*, Peter Davies, 1967.

Brodie, C.G., *Forlorn Hope 1915*, Frederick Books, 1956.

Bush, Capt. E.W., *Bless Our Ship*, Allen and Unwin, 1958.

Carr, W.G., *By Guess and by God*, Hutchinson, 1930.

From Dartmouth to the Dardanelles: A Midshipman's Log, ed. by his mother, Heinemann, 1916.

Godfrey, Admiral, J.H., *The Naval Memoirs*, vol. 2, 1915–19, privately published, 1964.

Halpern, P.G., ed., *The Keyes Papers, vol. 1, 1914-18*, Navy Records Society, 1972.

Lockyer, Capt. H.G, *The Tragedy of the Battle of the Beaches*, privately published, revised edn 1936.

Price, W.H., *With the Fleet in the Dardanelles*, Andrew Melrose, 1915.

Samson, Air Commodore C.R., *Fights and Flights*, Benn, 1930.

Shankland, Peter, and Hunter, Anthony, *Dardanelles Patrol*, Collins, 1964.

Stewart, A.T., and Peshall, C.J.E., *The Immortal Gamble*, A.C. Black, 1917.

Journal Articles, Commemorative Publications, Veterans' Bulletins

Allen, Capt. C.R.G., 'A Ghost from Gallipoli', *Journal of the Royal United Services Institute*, May 1963.

Anon., 'The Work of a Trawler in the Aegean Sea', *Naval Review*, vol. 6, 1918.

Auphan, P., 'Un Cinquantenaire: L'Expedition des Dardanelles', *Écrits de Paris*, April 1965.

'Australians at Gallipoli, The', *Australian Journal of Science*, vol. 32, no. 9, 1970.

'Battle for the Dardanelles, 18 March 1915', *La Mer*, 1915.

Boswell, Capt. L.A.K., 'The Immortal Gamble', *Journal of the Royal United Services Institute*, January 1965

Carcopino, G., 'Les Français a l'assaut des Dardanelles', *Historama*, 238, September 1971.

'Dardanelles, Les', *Provence Marseille Magazine*, 193, 13 April 1965.

Farmer, Lieut-Col. H.M., 'The Gallipoli Campaign 1915 from the Point of View of a Regimental Officer', lecture reprinted in *Journal of the Royal United Services Institute*, November 1923.

'Forcement des Dardanelles, Le', *Revue Maritime*, 237, 1966.

MacMunn, Lieut-Gen. Sir George, 'The Lines of Communication in the Dardanelles', *Army Quarterly*, April 1930.

Mohl, Korvettenkäpitan Hans von, 'Auf U-Boots – Vorposten in Kleinasien', *Der Deutsch-Afrikaner*, Pretoria, 1930.

Smith, Capt. B.H., RN, 'Dardanelles Details', *Naval Review*, vol. 24, 1936.

Striedinger, Col. O., 'Cape Helles – A Retrospect', *R.A.S.C. Quarterly*, vol. 12, 1924.

Trumpener, U., 'Liman von Sanders and the German Ottoman Alliance', *J.C.H.*, vol. 1, no. 4, 1966.

Williams, Dr Orlo, 'The Evacuation of the Dardanelles', *National Review*, 1920.

Gallipolian, The, Journal of the Gallipoli Association 1969 to date.

Newspapers and Trench News Sheets

Various national and local daily newspapers, 1915–16.

1915 Navy news sheets: *The Aquatint*, *The Tenedos Times*, *The Tahitian Tatler*, *The Akabarbarian*, *The Clan (MacGillivray) News*.

1915 Army news sheets: *The Dardanelles Driveller*, *The Peninsular Press*, *The 7th Manchester Sentry*, *The Anzac Book*, 1916.

Unpublished Sources

1. From the Liddle Collection, Brotherton Library, University of Leeds

A list of the men who have material relating to their Gallipoli experience, the material being collected by the author and now in the Liddle Collection available for research. From this material the author's earlier book, *Men of Gallipoli*, was drawn. The 1915 rank and unit of the men are given when known.

The nature of the material is indicated by the following abbreviations; Diaries,[D]; Letters[L]; Photographs,[P]; Various papers,[VP]; Books,[B]; Souvenir objects,[O]; Recollections in manuscript,[RM]; Recollections in typescript,[RT]; Tape-recorded recollections,[RR].

British
Aitcheson, B.S., 2nd Lieut, Royal Munster Fusiliers:[D, VP, O]
Ashcroft, G., Pte, 87th Bde Fld Amb.:[P, RR]
Attwood, J.C. Sgt, 2nd Royal Fusiliers, 86th Bde, 29th Div:[R, RT]
Auger, E., Sgt, RAMC Fld Amb., London Mounted Brigade:[P, O, RM], and Spr Moore-Jones prints
Aumonier, W.W., Pte, RAMC, 3 East Anglian Fld Amb. 161st Bde, 54th Div.:[RT]
Austin, J., Pte, 6th Green Howards, 11th Div.:[RR]
Baillie, J.S., Harland & Wolf 1914, building dummy battleships:[RR]
Barnes, H., Spr, RE, 39th Bde, 13th Div.:[RM, RT]
Barnet, J., Pte, 2nd Lowland Fld Amb. RAMC, 52nd Div.:[VP, RM], and photos of Pte Handyside of same unit
Bartlett, Captain R.N.O. 6th Bn East Lancs:[L]
Batcheller, R.A., West Kent Yeomanry:[B, RM, RR]
Bates, R.B., Cpl, 1/3rd Welsh Field Ambulance (T), 159 Bde, 53rd Div.:[O]
Battersby, W.:[RM, RT]
Bennett, J.B., Pte, 1/3rd East Anglian Fld Amb. RAMC, 54th Div.:[RT]
Bentham, Wing Cdr J., Sub-Lieut, RNVR, Hood Bn RND:[D, VP, P, RR]
Bialeck, S., 1/5th Royal Scots:[RM]
Bird, W. Parker, L/Cpl, RAMC, 29th Div.:[D, O, VP, L, P, RR]
Blackmore, W.C., Pte, RMLI RM Bde, 29th Div.:[RM]
Blythman, S.W., Pte, Wiltshire Rgt:[RM, RR]
Bogle, Col. J.M.L., M.C, 1/2nd Fld Coy RE, 42nd Div.:[D]
Boon, W.H., Stoker, Petty Officer, HMS *Prince of Wales*:[RM]
Booth, L.G.C, Lieut, 3rd County of London Yeomanry:[P, VP]
Boswell, Capt. L.A.K., RN, Midshipman, HMS *Irresistible* and HMS *Queen Elizabeth*:[B, RT, RR, P, VP]
Bradford, F., L/Cpl, 6th Yorks, 11th Div:[RM, RR, B]
Brand, C.W., Tpr, London Yeomanry:[L, RT]
Brayley, Capt. C.E.W., Pte, RAMC 40th Fld Amb.:[L]
Bremner, Flt Cdr F.D.H., RNAS No. 2 Wing:[P, RR, O, VP, L]
Bromet, Air Vice Marshal Sir Geoffrey, Sub–Lieut, RNAS, HMS *Ark Royal*:[D, P, VP, maps, RR]
Brown, A., Gnr, RFA:[D]
Brown, Lieut-Col. A.G., Cpl, 1st Fife and Forfar Yeomanry:[RM, RR, P]
Brown, A., Pte 1st Bn Lancashire Fusiliers:[D]

Broughton, R., RND Signal Coy:[RT]
Buchanan, Cdr, A.G., Midshipman, HMS *Prince George*:[P, D]
Bullock, E.W., HMS *Inflexible*:[RT]
Burgess, W., Pte, RMLI:[RM]
Burrows, Cdr, E. Allison, RNR, Assist. Paymaster RN., HMS *Partridge*:[P, L, RT]
Bush, Capt. E., DSO**, DSC, Midshipman, HMS *Bacchante*:[B, RR]
Bygrave, C.J., Cpl, RFA 55th Bde, 10th Div.:[RM]
Calvert, J.J., Seaman, Collingwood Bn RND:[O]
Calvert, J.S., Sgt, RE, IX Corps:[O]
Campbell, Colonel I, Major 2nd Lovat Scouts:[RT]
Carr, J., Pte, W. Yorks. Rgt:[RR]
Carter, B.W., Warrant Officer, 4th Norfolk Rgt, 54th Div.:[RM]
Cave, W. G., Chief Petty Officer, HMS *Dublin*:[RM, P, O]
Chadwick, J., Cpl, R. Monmouth RE, 29th Div.:[RM]
Chainey, H.G., Sgt, RAMC 3rd East Anglian Fld Amb., 54th Div.:[L]
Chapman, H. S., Pte/Bandsman, 7th Essex Rgt, 54th Div.:[P, RT]
Chapman, J., Sgt, RFA, 11th Div.:[RR]
Childerley, F., Pte, 54th Cyclist Coy:[VP, RM]
Churchill, Capt. C.F.H., Midshipman, HMS *London*:[RM]
Clark, W., Pte, 3rd London Rgt, Royal Fusiliers:[RM, D, P, B]
Clarke, H.F.M., Pte, 2/10th Bn, Middlesex Rgt:[RT]
Clarke, Capt. A.W., DSO, RN, Midshipman, HMS *Implacable* and SS *Arcadian*:[D, P, RM, RT, RR]
Coan, T.H., Pte, 1/3rd East Lancs. Fld Amb., 42nd Div.:[VP, RM]
Cobb, A.H.K., Paymaster Sub-Lieut, HMS *Bacchante*:[D, RR, VP]
Cockell, R.A., Spr, RND Eng., 1st Fld Coy:[D, VP, RR]
Collingridge, Brig. H.V., 2nd Lieut, 1/6th Gurkha Rifles:[L]
Common, J., Pte, KOSB:[VP]
Constable, W. Briggs, 2nd Lieut, RFA:[RT]
Cook, Col. R., Surrey Yeomanry:[P, RT, RR]
Cooper, T., Stoker, RN:[RR]
Coppard, E.G., Sig., RE Signals:[RT]
Cory, R., Leading Seaman, Drake Bn RND:[RM, maps]
Cosby, Brig. N.R.C., 2nd Lieut, 1/5th Royal Gurkha Rifles:[B, RT]
Cragg, W., PO, Armoured Car Div, RN:[RM]
Crighton, J.D., Pte, 87th Fld Amb., 29th Div.:[RT]
Cripps, Major P.G.H., MC, Lieut, attached R. Dublin Fusiliers, 29th Div.:[RT]
Cunningham, D.Y., Stoker, HMD *Andrina*, Submarine Patrol Trawler Section:[P, RR]
Curdie, J., Sgt, Highland Light Infantry, 157th Bde, 52nd Div.:[VP, RR]
Dart, J.C., Sgt, RE 10th Div. Sig. Coy:[D, map, RT]
Davey, F.W., Spr, RND Engineers 1st Fld Coy:[RM, L, D, P]
Dixon, E.H.:[P]
Dominey, C.V., Pte, ASC, attached 29th Div.:[VP, RT, RR]
Downes, A.L., L/Cpl, Warwickshire Yeomanry:[RR]
Drage, Cdr C., Midshipman, HMS *London*:[P, RR]
Duckworth, E., 2nd Lieut, 6th Bn Lancashire Fusiliers (TF)[Letters and related papers]
Duke, H.J.W., Pte, ASC, 29th Div.:[RR]
Duke, W.J., RND:[O, B]
Durnford, W., Pte, 2nd Bn Royal Fusiliers:[RM]
Eames, B.H.A., Sgt, Queen's Own Dorset Yeomanry, 10th Div.:[L, RM]
Edmondson, J.R., Notts and Sherwood Rangers, 2nd Mtd Div.:[RM]
Edmunds, T.H., L/Cpl, RE Signals, 9th Army Corps:[P, D, RT]
Evans, E.J., Stoker Petty Officer, HMS *Jed*:[RR]

Evans, H.:[RR]
Ewart, Cdr H. S. L., RN, Midshipman, HMS *Glory*:[O, VP, RR]
Faill, W., Gnr, RFA:[RR]
Falconer, J.A.B., HMS *Talbot*:[D, P]
Fell, E.P., L/Cpl 1st Essex Regt, 29th Div.:[L]
Fergusson, Col. A.C, 21st Indian Mountain Battery:[RT]
Finch, H., Pte, 87th Fld Amb., 29th Div:[RM, RR, D]
Fitch, J.D., Seaman, RNVR, Drake Bn RND:[VP, RM]
Forster, Lieut-Cdr J.C, Hood Bn RND:[RT]
Francey, W., Piper, 1/6th Highland Light Infantry:[RM]
Fraser, A.T., Sgt, 1st Border Rgt, 29th Div.:[RM, D, VP]
Fraser, J. E., Seaman, RND:[VP, RR]
French, S.B., Lieut, 3rd London Yeomanry, 2nd Mtd Div.:[RT, RR]
Gale, R.M., Spr, 2nd Naval Bde, RND Engineers:[P, D, VP, B, D]
Galloway, Lieut-Gen. Sir Alexander, 2nd Lieut, KOSB:[VP, RR]
Garrish, O., WO2, Sig. Sgt Maj., City of London Yeomanry, 2nd Mtd Div.:[RM, RR, B]
Geal, A.J., Pte, 2nd Bn Hampshire Rgt, 29th Div.:[VP]
Gething, Lieut-Col. P.J., 9 Royal Warwick Regt, 39th Bde, 13th Div.:[RM, RR]
Gillett, Capt. R.B., 2nd Bn Hants. Rgt, 29th Div.:[P, D, RM, RR, map]
Gillott, A., Spr, RND Engineers:[D, VP]
Goldingham, A. K., HMS *Prince of Wales*:[P, RT]
Gowans, Maj. H.J., Lt, HLI:[P]
Gray, J., RNAS:[RR]
Grayken, E., HMS *Irresistible* and Monitor *M30*:[RM]
Grimshaw, Lieut-Col. J.E., VC, Pte, 1st Bn Lancs. Fusiliers, 29th Div.:[RR]
Haigh, Lieut-Col. J., 1st Royal Inniskilling Fusiliers, 29th Div.:[O, D, RT, RR]
Hale, Mrs G.A., nurse on hospital ship *Aquitania*:[RM]
Hall, S.A., Sgt, 1st Lancs. Fusiliers, 29th Div.:[RM]
Hamilton, Mrs M.: [photos and books of her RN husband]
Hammond, G.H., Sgt, attached Royal Warwicks Reg.:[D]
Harding, Field-Marshal, Lord, 2nd Lieut, County of London Yeomanry:[RR]
Hargreaves, Cdr W.D.R., Midshipman, HMS *Sapphire*:[RM]
Harris, E., HMS *Lord Nelson*: [RM]
Harris, E.S., Pte, 2/1st Bn London Rgt, Royal Fusiliers:[RT, VP]
Harris, H., RAMC, 1st West Lancs, Fld Amb.:[RT]
Harrison, W., L/Cpl, 5th Manchester Rgt:[VP, RR]
Hart, N., Lieut, Gurkha Rifles:[L]
Hartshorne, Lieut-Col. N.H., MC, S. Staffs. Rgt, 11th Div.:[P, RT]
Hazlewood, A,, Pte, 87th Fld Amb., 29th Div.:[D, RM]
Heath, G. W., Sick Berth CPO, HMS *Beryl* and GHQ:[VP, L, RT]
Henson, W. T., CPO, HMS *Agamemnon* and HMS *Swiftsure*:[RM, P]
Hepworth, C.R, Gnr, RFA:[RM]
Hibberd, A.S., MBE, 2nd Lieut, 5th Dorset Yeomanry:[RM, RR]
Hibbs, J., Pte, Royal Newfoundland Rgt:[RT]
Hicks, G., Sgt, Royal Newfoundland Rgt:[RT]
Holbrook, Cdr N.D., VC, RN, Lieut-Cdr, HM Submarine *B 11*:[RR, VP]
Hole, Maj., 2nd Lieut, Royal 1st Devon Yeomanry:[RR, VP, P, B, maps]
Hole, C. A., Pte, 1/7th Essex Rgt, 54th Div.:[L]
Holvey, F.G., Seaman, HMS *Cornwall*:[P, RM]
Hooper, Capt. J., RNR Officer, Armed Merchant Cruiser, *Sarnia*:[RR]
Hope, Capt. G., Captain of HMS *Queen Elizabeth*:[VP]
Horridge, Major G.B., 1/5th Lancs. Fusiliers, 125th Bde, 42nd Div.:[maps, RM, RR]

Houston, J.S., Pte, 2nd Lowland Fld Amb. RAMC:[P, RM, VP]
Hunnam, H.E., Dvr, 14th Siege Battery, RGA:[D, RR]
Hutchings, Major E.L., L/Cpl, 2/10th Middlesex Rgt:[RM, RR]
Huttenbach, Col. N. H., 2nd Lieut, RFA RHA:[RM, RR]
Jameson, Maj.-Gen. T., officer in RM, RND:[P, RM]
Jarvis, Major T.S.W., 2nd Lieut, 6th Manchesters:[RM]
Jebens, Major F.J., 2nd Royal Fusiliers, 29th Div.:[RR]
Johns, P.V.:[RM]
Johnson, J.M., Pte, RMLI (Plymouth Bn.):[RM, RR]
Jones, C, Pte, 87th Fld Amb., 29th Div.:[RM]
Jordan, T.C, Cpl, 2nd SW Borderers, 29th Div.:[RR]
Kay, T., Spr, R.E:[RM]
Keeler, G. E., Seaman, HMS *Lord Nelson*:[D]
Keogh, W., Sherwood Foresters:[RM, RR]
Kerr, H. C, MM, Petty Officer, Hawke Bn RND:[RM]
Kettles, A., Cpl, Scottish Horse Fld Amb.:[P]
King, F.H., Pte, RAMC, 29th Div.:[RM]
King, W. F., Sgt, RE 29th Div.:[P, RM]
Laidlaw, Lieut-Col. R.F.E., Acting Capt., 1st Royal Munster Fusiliers, 29th Div.:[P, RT]
Lamb, D. J., Gnr, RGA, 4th Highland Mtd Bde, 29th Div.:[B, RM, RR]
Lane, W. O., Sgt, RAPC, HQ 29th Div.:[RM]
Lawrance, S.F., Pte, 4th Bn Worcester Rgt, 29th Div.:[RR]
Lawrence, Lieut-Col. L. B., Cpl and AQMS, 5th Royal Inniskilling Fusiliers, 10th Div.:[RR]
Ledger, G. C, Pte, RAMC, 11th Div.:[RR]
Lee, Capt. A. B., 3rd Officer, HMT *S29*:[RR, O]
Lightfoot, Brig., 2nd Lieut, Middlesex Rgt:[RM, P]
Lindberg, Lieut-Col. C.H, 2nd Lieut, 8th Northumberland Fusiliers, 11th Div.:[L, RM, RR]
Lines, W.P., RQMS, 6th Bn Royal Welch Fusiliers:[RM]
Lissenburg, Capt. D.N. Meneaud, Trmptr, Sig., RFA 97th Bty, 147th Bde, 29th Div.:[RT, RR, P]
Livingstone, W., Colour Sgt, Fife and Forfar Yeomanry:[RT]
Lloyd, Mrs B.:[husband's Gallipoli POW souvenir]
Longley-Cook, Vice-Admiral E.W. Midshipman, HMS *Prince of Wales*:[D, L, RM, VP, P, RR]
Lorimer, Dr. ship's surgeon:[P, D]
Lowe, E.A.H., 2nd Lieut, Dorset Yeomanry:[P, RM]
Luck, J. E., 3rd Writer RN, HMS *Lord Nelson* and HMS *Triad*:[D, P, VP, RM, RR]
Lugg, W.W., MM, Gnr, RFA, 58th Bde, 11th Div.:[RM, RR]
Lynden-Bell, Major-General Sir Arthur, Staff Officer to General Munro:[RT]
Lyster, Capt. H.N, MC, 3rd City of London, Royal Fusiliers:[RT, RR]
McConnell, B.A., L/Cpl, 1st Royal Inniskilling Fusiliers, 29th Div.:[O, RM, RR]
Mackintosh, C., 2nd Lieut, 9th Warwicks Rgt, 39th Bde, 13 Div.:[RM, RR, B]
McPherson, A., Lancs. Fusiliers and ASC:[RM]
Mankin, Capt. J., Tpr, 3rd County of London Yeomanry:[B, P, RM, maps, O]
Mann, W.S., RND:[RM]
Mansergh, Vice Admiral Sir Aubrey, DSC, Midshipman HMS *Queen*:[RM, RR]
May, P.P., Leading Seaman HMS *Triumph* and HMS *Lydiard*:[P, RT, RR]
Mayne, C.F., Surgeon Lieut, RN, RND 2nd Fld Amb.:[RR]
Mead, Maj. W.G., Cpl, RE Signals, 9th Army Corps HQ:[RT, RR]
Measures, E.C, Able Seaman, HMS *Euryalus*:[RR]
Metcalf, Capt. J. Savile, Midshipman, HMS *Triumph*:[RT]
Millar, W., Pte, 2/1st City of London Royal Fusiliers:[D]
Millard, R.F., Lieut, Border Rgt, 29th Div.:[VP, B]
Minter, C.J.:[P]

Monaghan, H., Fld Amb., 29th Div.:[RM]

Moore, L., Pte, 4th Worcester Rgt, 29th Div.:[RM, RR]

Moore, R.E., Tpr, Suffolk Yeomanry, 54th Div.:[P, RR]

Moore, Capt. R. W., Ship's Writer, HMS *Euryalus*:[RT]

Moore, W. C., MSM, Bty Sgt Maj., RFA 26th Fld Bty, 17th Bde:[P, RT]

Morgan, R.E., Sgt, 7th Royal Welch Fusiliers, 158th Bde, 53rd Div.:[RM]

Morris, Canon A., Sgt, Scottish Horse Yeomanry:[D, VP]

Moseley, G.F., CPO, Med., RN, HMS *Prince of Wales*:[D, RR]

Mott, Maj. G.R., 6/3rd South Lancs. Rgt, 13th Div.:[D, RR]

Moulds, H., Spr, RE Signals:[D, RR]

Moyle, S.J., Leading Seaman, Drake Bn RND:[RM]

Murray, J., Pte, 4th KOSB:[RM]

Murray, J., Leading Seaman, Hood Bn RND:[D, VP, RT, RR]

Murray, J.N.C., Pte, Lovat Scouts:[RM]

Murrie, R.A., Pte, Royal Scots, 29th Div.:[RR]

Nathan, Lord:[photographs of his father's Yeomanry service at Suvla]

Nevinson, H.K.B., 2nd Lieut, Manchester Rgt:[VP, L, P]

Newman, I.H., Spr, 496 Fld Coy (Kent) RE:[O]

Newstead, J., Pte, 6th Yorks.:[RR]

Nightingall, C. W., Tpr, Surrey QMR Yeomanry, 29th Div.:[L, RT]

Noon, M.J., Eng. Sub-Lieut, HMFM *Princess Ina*:[O, VP, RR]

Ollive, L.H., Spr, RE Signals, 29th Div.:[VP, RM, RR]

O'Neill, W., RNR, HMS *Bacchante*:[D]

Oren, B., L/Cpl, West Riding Fid Coy, RE, 29th Div.:[RR]

Osborne, N.:[RM]

Palmer, R., Lieut, RE:[VP, maps, P]

Parker, H.G., MM, Sgt, RE Signals, 54th Div.:[RM, RT, RR]

Parnham, W. J., RM Plymouth Bn:[D, RM (including letter of Gallipoli recollections from Lieut-Col. C.F. Jerram, DSO)]

Pawson, H.A.C., 2nd Lieut, Sherwood Rangers:[D]

Penwarden, Flying Officer H.G., Cpl, 1st Royal Devon Yeomanry:[RM, P, VP]

Peterson, H., Pte, 87th Fld Amb., 29th Div.:[RM]

Pickthall, A.P., Pte, 87th Fld Amb., 29th Div.:[RM, P, L, D, VP]

Pilling, A., Pte, 6th Lancs. Fusiliers, 42nd Div.:[RM]

Pilling, H., Pte, 6th Lancs. Fusiliers, 42nd Div.:[RM]

Pippet, B.C., Ldg Seaman, Hawke Bn RND:[RM]

Pope, S.A., Kent Yeomanry:[RM]

Portal, Admiral Sir Reginald, DSC, Lieut, HMS *Bacchante*:[P, RR]

Powell-Price, Lieut-Col. the Rev. E., MC, Capt., 7th Royal Welch Fusiliers, 53rd Div.:[RM, RR]

Prynne, Maj. H. Fellowes, Cpl, 2nd County of London Yeomanry:[RT, P, RR]

Pyne, Lieut-Col. W.M, officer RE:[L]

Rackham, Brig. B.B., MC, officer Hawke Bn RND:[VP, B, RR]

Rathbone, Brig. R., Lieut, 6th Royal N. Lancs. Rgt, 38th Bde, 13th Div.:[RT, RM]

Raymond, Ernest, Capt, R.A.C. Ch.D. C.F., 126th Bde, 42nd Div.:[RT]

Reay, W., RND Medical Unit,:[D, B]

Rees, T., Pte, 2nd Bn South Wales Borderers:[D, RM, RR]

Richards, I., Dvr, RE, 29th Div.:[RR]

Richardson, R., RND:[RR]

Rix, Reverend W.E. Congregationalist Padre:[P]

Robson, E., Pte, 6th Yorks.:[RR]

Rogers, Col. C. Woodes, 9th Royal Warwicks. Rgt, 13th Div.:[O, RM, RR]

Rosamond, G.M., Cpl, 3/1st E. Anglian Div. Cyclist Coy, 54th Div.:[RM]

Rowallan, Lord, MC, officer in Ayrshire Yeomanry:[RT]

Russell, Col. T., MC:[B]

Ruthven, F., Pte, RAMC, London Mtd Bde Fld Amb:[RR]

Salisbury, J. V., Pte, Hawke Bn Medical Unit, RND:[D, VP, P, O, RR]

Sanders, Col. R.A., North Devon Yeomanry:[D]

Saunders, C.R.S., Cpl, Middlesex Yeomanry:[D, maps, O]

Savage, B., Cpl, Sig. Coy RND Engineers:[L, maps, VP]

Savory, Lieut-Gen. Sir Reginald, DSO, MC, Lieut, 14th Sikhs, 29th Inf. Bde:[VP, L, RT, RR]

Scarse, A. R., Pte, 1/4th Norfolk Rgt:[RM, VP, P, O]

Selsby, C.D., Pte, 4th Suffolk Rgt and RAMC 1/4* EA Fld Amb., 54th Div.:[P, D, L, VP]

Shaw, Lieutenant-Commander H.K.L., officer, HMS *Minerva*:[L]

Shephard, G.A., Sgt, Dorset Yeomanry, S. Mid. Mtd Bde:[O, VP, B, RM, RR]

Shepherd, P.A., MC, Lieut, RNVR, RND Howe Bn,:[D, VP, RR]

Shewen, Lieut-Col. D.G., Lieut, attached 2/10th Gurkhas:[D, RM, RR]

Shields, Mrs E., 1916–17, Secretary to Sir Ian Hamilton and literary executrix:[RR]

Siese, O.H.V., Sgt, RAMC, 2nd Welsh Fld Amb. 63rd Div.:[O, VP, RT]

Siller, F.C., Sub-Lieut, Nelson Bn, RND:[RT, L, P, RR]

Simpson, J., Pte, 9th West Yorks. Rgt, 11th Div.:[RM]

Skelton, E.W., Pte, RM Plymouth Bn:[VP, RM]

Smith, C.M.M., Tpr, Suffolk Yeomanry, Eastern Mtd, Bde:[P, RT]

Smith, E.J., Signal Boy, HMS *Euryalus*:[RR]

Smith, G. B., MSM, Spr and L/Cpl, RE, 29th Div., West Riding Fld Coy:[P, RT, RR]

Spofforth, A.A., Spr, RND Eng., 3rd Fld Coy:[RM]

Spong, A.S., Sgt, Royal Fusiliers:[RR]

Sproule, J., Pte, 6th Yorks., 11th Div.:[RR]

Steele, C., Pte, 8th Bn Lancs. Fusiliers, 125th Bde, 42nd Div.:[RM]

Stephens, Petty Officer, Submarine *E 2*:[D]

Stone, J. L., 2nd Lieutenant, 4th Battalion Worcester Regiment:[D, P, VP, RR, RT]

Stoner, B., Pte, 87th Fld Amb., 29th Div.:[VP]

Sye, T.B., Pte, 87th Fld Amb., 29th Div.:[D, VP, O, RR]

Tait, A., L/Cpl. 8th Bn Northumberland Fusiliers:[Letters and papers concerning his death]

Tansley, J.H., Cpl, York and Lancaster Rgt:[RM, map, D, VP]

Tate, Capt. H., Midshipman, HMS *Implacable*:[RR, B, D, P]

Tatham, J., Pte, 87th Fld Amb., 29th Div.:[RR]

Taylor, H, Spr, RE Signals, IX Army Corps:[P, D, RR]

Teasdale, Sqd.-Ldr J.J., HMS *Ark Royal*, Chief Mechanic, RNAS:[RT, RR]

Telfer, J., L/Cpl, RE Signals Section:[D, RM, RR]

Thomson, T., Pte, 3rd Lowland Fld Amb.:[RT]

Thuillier, Lieut-Col. H.S., 10th Hvy Bty, RA, 11th Div.:[RT, RT]

Timms, G., Pte Essex Regiment:[D]

Tisdall, A.W., VC, Sub-Lieut, Anson Bn RND:[L]

Tolley, J.W., Pte, 39th Fld Amb., RAMC, 38th Bde, 13th Div.:[RM]

Tomkinson, C.R., Pte, 87th Fld Amb., 29th Div.:[D]

Traill, Air Vice Marshal T., DFC, Midshipman, HMS *Lord Nelson*:[map, RT, RR]

Traynor, F.W., RAMC, 11th CCS, 29th Div.:[VP, RT, RM, RR]

Trotman, C.L., Able Seaman, Drake Bn RND:[RM]

Turnbull, W., Pte, 1/4th K.O.S.B.:[RM, VP]

Turner, H.H., Pte, A/QM, Portsmouth Bn RM, RND:[RT, RM]

Tysall, Capt. E., Spr, RE Signals attached 1st Div. AIF:[RR]

Verschoyle, Maj. T., MC, 5th Royal Inniskilling Fusiliers, 10th Div.:[D, RM, RR, O, and translation of 1915 Turkish letters]

Vetch, Cdr H.A., RNR, Midshipman, HMS *Prince of Wales*:[VP, P, RR]

Walker, N., Pte, Manchester Rgt:[B]

Ward, A.L., Pte, 2/10th Middlesex Rgt, 53rd Div.:[RM]

Ward, F., Spr, RE Signals, 29th Div.:[P]

Ward, M., Tpr, Dorset Yeomanry:[RT]

Watkins, C., 6th Lancs. Fusiliers, 42nd Div.:[RT, RR]

Watson, Lieut-Col. D.B., MC, 2nd Lieut, 2/10th Middlesex Rgt, 53rd Div.:[D, P, VP, RR]

Weakford, S.A., Spr, RE Signals, 29th Div.:[RM]

Weaver, E., HMS *Amethyst*:[RT]

Wettern, Capt. E., Spr, No. 2 Fld Coy RND Engineers:[VP, O, B,P, D, L, RT, RR, maps]

Whittall, Maj. H. M., DSO, Lieut. R.M., RND, attached 29th Div.:[RM, RT, RR]

Whyte, A. L. G., S/S, RAMC, 1/3rd E. Anglian Fld Amb., 54th Div.:[D, L, RT, B, RR]

Wicks, Maj., Sgt, 2nd Royal Fusiliers, 29th Div.:[RR]

William-Powlett, Vice-Admiral Sir Peveril., DSO, Midshipman, HMS *Vengeance* and HMS *Beagle*:[D, P, RR]

Williams, Cdr A.M., CBE, DSC, Midshipman, HMS *Euryalus*:[RT, RR, P]

Williamson, Capt. W. Corbett, Pte, R.M., RND Corps HQ:[VP, RT, RR]

Willis, E.F., Pte, RMLI (Chatham):[D, P, VP, RR]

Wilsdon, Mrs S.:[P]

Wilson, A.E., Able Seaman, Nelson Bn RND:[VP, D, RR]

Wilson, Cdr H., OBE, DSC, Midshipman, HMS *Euryalus*:[P, D, RR, L]

Winkcup, S., Pte, ASC:[RR]

Wolton, Capt. E.D., Lieut, 1/5th Suffolk Rgt TF, 43rd Bde:[L, RR, B, RT, RM]

Wood, H.C., Quartermaster Sergeant, RND Engineers:[D]

Wood, J., Able Seaman, Anson Bn RND:[RR]

Wood, W.G., Gnr, RFA:[RM]

Woodworth, F.T.K., Lieut, 7th Manchester Rgt, 42nd Div.:[O and papers of F. Bamber, 7th Manchester Rgt]

Australian

Alexander, Maj. A., Lieut, 10th Bn:[RR]

Allchin, Lieut-Col. E.F., Sig. Sgt, 10th Bn:[RR]

Alston, the Rev. E.C, Pte, 12th Bn:[VP, RM]

Andrews, Canon M., Pte, 1st Fld Amb.:[RR]

Arnold, C.J., Pte, 4th Bn:[RR]

Bachtold, Brig. H., Capt, 1st Fld Coy Engineers, 1st Div.:[RR, L, P]

Bailey, H.R., Pte, 19th Bn:[RR]

Bain, E., Sgt, 10th Light Horse:[RT, RR]

Barton, W., Bugler, 2nd Bn:[RM, RR]

Bell, Mrs J.R.:[letters, photos, equipment and various papers of her husband (Lieut, 12th Bn reinforcements in 1915)]

Berrisford, F., Pte, 8th Bn:[RR]

Bertwistle, W.H., Lieut, 27th Bn, Machine-Gun Section:[D, RR]

Bevan, T.G., Tpr, 3rd Light Horse:[RM]

Birtwistle, I.T., Lieut, 22nd Bn:[D, RR]

Bradford, J.C, Acting Sgt, 7th Light Horse:[RR]

Bradshaw, W.A., L/Cpl, 10th Bn:[RR]

Brearley, S., Sgt, 8th Bn, 1st Australian Div.:[RM]

Briggs, C.H., Gnr, 9th Btn, 1st Australian Div.:[RR]

Brown, A.E.: Tpr, 12th Light Horse:[RR]

Brown, J.A., Lieut, 10th Light Horse:[RM]

Brownell, Mrs P.J.:[diary of her husband, Gnr Brownell, AIF]

Burgess, Pte, 17th Bn:[RR, B]

Burrows, G., Spr, 1st Fld Coy Engineers, 1st Div.:[RR, P]

Butcher, Maj. M.G, Tpr, 3rd Light Horse:[RR, P, O]

Champion, Dr B., Pte, 1st Bn:[RR]

Clark, W.M., Pte, 10th Bn:[D, RT]

Mackenzie, W., Chaplain, 4th Bn:[L, O]

McKinlay, Col. J.L., MM, Spr, 1st Div. Sig. Coy:[P, RT, RR]

Mackintosh, S.J., Pte, 2nd Bn:[RR]

McLennan, W., Tpr, 2nd Light Horse:[P, RR, RM]

McNeill, Brig. J.G.D., Capt, 5th Light Horse:[RR, P]

Manuel, Mrs:[letters of father, Pte., 11th Bn]

Mayne, E.L., Gnr, 1st Brigade Ammunition Column, AFA:[RR]

Minogue, F., 10th Light Horse:[B]

Molloy, T.J., Pte, 1st Bn:[RR]

Moore, E., 1st A. A. M. C.:[P, VP, D]

Morris, A.P., 1st Light Horse Fld Amb.:[RM]

Nicholas, R.A., Pte, Hospital Transport Corps, AIF:[L, RR, VP]

Oakes, D.S.M., Spr, 1st Field Coy. Engineers, 1st Div.:[RR]

Oliver, A.J., Tpr, 3rd Light Horse:[P]

Orr, H., Sgt, 16th Bn:[RR]

Parkes, Cobden, 2nd Lieut, 1st Bn:[D, RM, RR]

Paterson, W.W., 3rd Infantry Bde:[L]

Pickford, Mrs:[letter to, and diary of, V. Frankcombe, 15th Bn]

Pinkerton, R., Gnr, 3rd Battery AFA, 1st Div.:[RR]

Rabbidge, A., Tpr, 2nd Light Horse:[P, RM]

Radnell, G.A., Pte, 8th Bn:[RM, RT, D, B, VP]

Ross, A.W., Staff Sgt., Australian Postal Corps:[P]

Rutter, A.L., Sgt, 26th Bn:[RR]

Scudds, H., Pte, 10th Bn:[RM]

Sharman, C.A., Pte, 26th Bn, Machine-Gun Section:[P, VP, RR]

Sharp, F.H., L/Cpl, Sig., 12th Bn:[B, RR, P, VP]

Shaw, Lieut-Col. G.D., MC, Lieut, 28th Bn:[RT, RR]

Sinclair, C.G., Pte, 24th Bn:[RT, L]

Skinner, E.C., Pte, 16th Bn:[L]

Smith, T.S., Pte, 2nd Bn:[RR, RT]

Smythe, H.A., Pte, 3rd Bn:[L]

Smythe, V., Lieut, 4th Bn:[RM]

Stagles, W., Pte, 11th Bn:[VP, P, O, RT, RR]

Sutton, S.:[P]

Sykes, P.W., Pte, 4th Australian Fld Amb.:[RT, RR]

Syme, J., Tpr, 10th Light Horse:[RR]

Thyer, Brig. W., officer, 2nd Div. Sig. Coy:[RT, L]

Turner, F.G., Pte, 3rd Infantry Bde:[RM]

Waite, A.F., Spr, 3rd Field Coy. Engineers:[P, VP]

Walker, J.A., Cpl, 19th Bn:[RR]

Watson, Lieut-Col. S.H., Capt., 2nd Div. Sig. Coy:[RR, RT, and diary extracts from Sgt Both]

Westbrook, F.E., Gnr, 2nd Battery AFA:[RR and 1915 poetry]

White, W.F., Tpr, 7th Light Horse:[RR, P]

Williams, C.H., Tpr, 10th Light Horse:[RR]

Williams, S.M., L/Cpl, 11th Bn:[VP, O, RR]

Wilson, W.J., Pte, 12th Bn:[VP, RR]

Wordsworth, Maj.-Gen. R.H., Lieut, 1st Light Horse:[RR, P]

Young, Mrs H.:[letters of her father, G.C. Killner, 1st Light Horse Fld Amb]

Young, O.C., Bugler, 16th Bn:[B, RR, P]

New Zealand

Aiken, F.W., Sgt, Div. Sig. Coy, NZ Engineers:[RT, RR]

Algie, C.S., Lieut., Auckland Bn:[D, VP]

Anderson, J.A., Pte, Canterbury Bn:[RR]

Angus, W.M., Pte, 2nd Div. Train (later attached to RNAS):[RR, P]

Armstrong, N.J., Tpr, Auckland Mtd Rifles:[RR, VP]

Baker, R.D., Canterbury Bn:[RM]

Barclay, W.P., Pte, Div. HQ:[RR]

Bassett, C.R.G., VC, Cpl, NZ Div. Sig. Coy:[RR, RT]

Batchelor, E.H.S., Lieut, Canterbury Bn:[RR]

Bayne, A., Bugler, Wellington Bn:[D]

Bell, W.A., Pte, 1st Wellington Bn:[RR]

Berry, H.N., Tpr, Auckland Mtd Rifles:[D, O]

Bishop, Lieut-Col. Gibson, MC, 1st Lieut, Otago Bn:[VP, RM, P, RR]

Blanks, A.D., Tpr, Auckland Mtd Rifles:[RR, P]

Blue, J., Pte, Canterbury Bn, Machine-Gun Section:[RR]

Brown, C.H.J.: Canterbury Bn:[L]

Brown, A.S., Pte, 1st Otago Bn:[RR]

Canton, C.H., Pte, Wellington Bn:[RR, map, B]

Cardno, G., Sgt. NZ Medical Corps:[D, donated by daughter, Mrs HK Claridge]

Cates, C., NZ Medical Corps:[D]

Chambers, S., Wellington Mtd Rifles:[L]

Claridge, C.J., Pte, 3rd Auckland Bn:[VP, D, RR, RM]

Clark, N, Driver, NZASC:[RT, RM]

Clunies Ross, S., Gnr, 1st Battery NZFA:[RR]

Comyns, C.L., L/Cpl., 1st Wellington Bn:[D, L]

Cooper, A.F., Pte, Wellington Bn:[D, L]

Currey, A.A., Bdr, 1st Battery NZFA:[L, RM, RR, map]

Davie, R., Pte, Wellington Bn:[RT]

Davies, Mrs:[typescript memoirs of her husband, a NZ infantryman taken P.O.W. on the Peninsula]

Dunner, N.C., NZFA:[RT, B]

Elsom, C., Spr, 1st Fld Coy, NZ Engineers:[RR]

Evans, Mrs C.A., Gallipoli veteran's widow:[P]

Fagan, J.A., Pte, Auckland Bn:[RR, D, VP and diary extracts from Pte H.B. Raudrop, Auckland Bn, and letter of F.W. Watson, Auckland Bn]

Fenwick, P.C., Lieut-Col.NZ Medical Corps, Deputy Assistant Director Medical Services:[D]

Fielden, H.R., Bdr. 3rd Battery NZFA:[D]

Fleming, N., Sgt, NZ Medical Corps, 1st Fld Amb.:[RR]

Foord, W.H., Cpl, 1st Field Coy, NZ Engineers:[RR]

Foote, F.J., Tpr, Auckland Mtd Rifles:[RT, RR, VP]

Furby, Maj. W.E.S., Capt., 1st Wellington Bn:[RR]

Galloway, Capt. M.S., MC, Sgt, 1st Wellington Bn:[RR]

Garrett, H.G., Pte, Auckland Mtd Rifles:[RR]

Gasparich, J.G., Sgt, Canterbury Bn:[RM]

Geary, Capt. S.J., Cpl, 1st Auckland Bn:[RR]

Gollop, C.T., NZFA:[D]

Gressen, Sir Kenneth, Major, 1st Canterbury Bn:[RR]

Griffin, Miss L.:[photograph of her brother on the Peninsula]

Harrigan, C.T., Pte, 1st Otago Bn:[RR, VP, B]

Harris, Capt. R.H., Sgt, 1st Auckland Bn:[RR, RM, RT, O]

Hatrick, H.K., Cpl, Auckland Mtd Rifles:[L, VP, map]

Hawke, E., Cpl, 1st Canterbury Bn:[D]

Hayden, C.R., Infantryman:[RM]

Hilston, Mrs A.:[VP]

Honnor, E.H.: Infantry officer:[L]

Hood, J., Pte, NZ Medical Corps:[RR]

Horneman, J., Infantryman:[RM]

Howard, H.:[P]
Howe, O.W., Pte, Auckland Bn:[RR]
Hughes, F.W., L/Cpl, NZFA:[RR]
Hunter, H.G., Pte, 1st Canterbury Bn:[D, P, RR]
Jenkin, H.C, Sgt, NZFA:[RR]
Jenkins, M.E., Sgt, Canterbury Mtd Rifles:[RR]
Jennings, A.G., MC, Sgt, 1st Wellington Bn:[D, VP, P, RR]
Jennings, Col. W. I. K., DSO, Capt., Otago Bn:[RR]
Keesing, H.W., Pte, NZ Medical Corps:[D]
Latimer, L.H., Pte, 1st Otago Bn:[RR]
Leaman, A.W.H., Tpr, Canterbury Mtd Rifles:[RR, map, P]
Leary, L., Pte, 1st Wellington Bn:[RT]
Little, D.A., 1st Canterbury Bn:[D, P]
Littlejohn, G.E., Wellington Bn:[D]
Lush, A., Spr, NZ Engineers:[RT]
Lyddiard, A.W., Pte, NZFA:[RR]
McBeath, G., Sgt, Auckland Bn:[RR, O]
McBride, J., Auckland Bn:[P]
McCarthy, D.G., Pte, Otago Bn:[RR]
McKeith, E.G., Pte, 1st Canterbury Bn:[RM]
McMillan, J., Cpl, Canterbury Mtd Rifles:[RT, P]
McPherson, R., Gnr, NZFA:[RR]
McRobie, J.D., Cpl, NZ Engineers:[D, VP, RR]
Mansfield, D.R., Sgt, 1st Fld Coy, NZ Engineers:[RM, RR, D]
Marris, Capt. A., Pte, Canterbury Bn, Machine-Gun Section:[RR, P, B, VP, D, O]
Maxwell, N.R., Pte, 1st Auckland Bn:[RR, VP, L]
May, G., Auckland Bn:[P]
Morgan, G.M., L/Cpl, Canterbury Mtd Rifles:[RR]
Morton, Captain A.B., Staff Captain NZ Corps:[D, VP re his death]
Muir, Mrs A., widow of a Gallipoli veteran:[B]
Murphy, Col. W., MC, Pte, 1st Otago Bn:[RT]
Murray, A., Infantryman:[RT]
Murton, W., Pte, 1st Fld Amb., NZ Medical Corps:[RM]
Oakey, Lieut-Col. A. N., M.C., Lieut, NZ Engineers:[RR]
Palmer, H.V., Pte, Canterbury Bn:[B, D, RT, RR]
Palmer, J., Tpr, Auckland Mtd Rifles:[RR, VP, B]
Park, Air Marshal Sir Keith, MC, DFC, 2nd Lieut, NZFA and attached RFA:[RR]
Parker, Lieut-Col. F.W., Capt., RNZASC:[RM, RR, P]
Parsons, M., Tpr, Canterbury Mtd Rifles:[RR]
Pennefather, Capt. S S., DCM, Pte Wellington Bn:[RR]
Price, T.H., Spr, 3rd Fld Coy, NZ Engineers:[RM]
Potts, H.W., Pte, 1st Otago Bn:[RR]
Priestley, H.G.M., Cpl, NZ Medical Corps Fld Amb.:[D]
Rasmussen, H.P., Tpr, Canterbury Mtd Rifles:[RR]
Rawlings, Capt. C.H., MC:[D, O, RR]
Reece, J.C, Pte, 3rd Auckland Bn:[RM]
Richards, M.A., Tpr Otago Mtd. Rifles:[D, VP, O]
Roberts, J.J., Pte, 1st Wellington Bn:[RR, VP]
Robinson, A.E., Pte, Auckland Bn:[B, L, RR]
Rogers, F., Sgt, 1st Otago Bn:[RM, P]
Rogers, P., 1st Otago Bn:[RR, RM]
Rudd, J.F., L/Cpl, Canterbury Mtd Rifles, Machine-Gun Section:[RM, D, P, RR]

Ryan, W.C., Sgt Clerk, NZ Pay Corps:[P, B]
Seddon, G.H., Pte, 1st Otago Bn:[RR]
Skinner, J. S., Sgt, Otago Bn:[RR]
Smith, A., Pte, Wellington Bn:[RT]
Smith, A.E.W., Pte, Canterbury Bn:[RR]
Smith, F.G.:[Sapper Moore-Jones prints]
Spence, F.G., 2nd Lieut, 5th Battery NZFA:[RM]
Stacey, D. E., Pte, 1st Auckland Bn:[RR]
Stevens, K. M., Tpr, Auckland Mtd Rifles:[VP, D, RR and published memoirs]
Sutherland, T.H., Gunner, NZFA:[P]
Taverndale, F.W., Sgt, Wellington Bn:[RR]
Taylor, L.G., Pte, Canterbury Bn:[D, RR]
Thomas, C.W., Tpr, Auckland Mtd Rifles:[RT, RM]
Thompson, A.C., Pte, Canterbury Bn:[VP, P]
Twisleton, Miss N.G.:[letters of her father, an officer in the Otago Mtd Rifles, and diary of NZ Nursing Sister Speedy]
Walsh, C.J., Pte, 1st Auckland Bn:[D, RR]
Watson, O.L., Pte, Canterbury Bn:[P, RR]
Weir, R. J., Pte, Wellington Bn:[RR]
Westenra, J.:[RR]
Whitcombe, A.:[RR]
Whiting, E.H., Pte, Canterbury Bn:[RR]
Williams, Mrs:[B]
Wilson, A.M., Pte, 1st Wellington Bn:[RR]
Winter, J.H., Tpr, Wellington Mtd Rifles:[RR]
Wyatt, A., Pte, Auckland Bn:[P, RM]
Wyatt, W.C.:[P]
Young, Mrs A.:[widow of a Gallipoli veteran: 1915 gas mask]

French
Albert, Augustin, Machine-Gun Coy, 312 Brigade:[L, RT, RR]
Bareille, J., Sgt, 4ième Rég. Mixte Colonial:[VP, P, B]
Baroli, Simple Soldat, 4ième Rég. de Zouaves:[RR]
Beurier, Dr F.:[photographs of his father, a French army doctor, on the Peninsula, P, B]
Bollon, François, Simple Soldat, 6ième Rég. Colonial:[VP, RM, RR]
Bory, Jean Pierre, 105ième d'Artillerie Lourde:[RM, RR]
Deffez, Jean, Cannonier, battleship *Gaulois*:[VP, D]
Delaye, Contre Amiral, Enseigne de Vaisseau de Première Classe, French Air Squadron at Tenedos:[RT, P, D, RR]
Doin, Louis, Mountain Artillery:[VP, RT, RR]
Élie, Armand, Simple Soldat, 4ième Rég. Mixte Colonial:[RM, RR]
Evans, Maillard, battleship *Gaulois*:[RM]
Eymard, Jules, Radio Telegraphist at Kum Kale landing and on the Peninsula:[P, RM, RR]
Favot, L., Caporal, 175ième Rég. d'lnfanterie:[RR]
Fournel, Adrien, Simple Soldat, 175ième Rég:[RR, VP, RM]
Galline, F., Pharmacien at Seddel Bahr field hospital:[RM, RR, L]
Galoche, E.M., Caporal, 6ième Reg. d'lnfanterie Colonial:[RR]
Gamier, Maitre, 181ième Rég. d'Artillerie:[RR]
Giauffret, Simple Soldat, 4ième Rég. de Zouaves:[RR]
Gilormini, Jean, Sgt, 175ième Rég. de Marche:[RR, B]
Gondard, Maitre, 6ième Reg. d'lnfanterie Colonial:[VP, RT, RR]
Grammond, MmeViricel de:[diary of a member of the family who served on the Peninsula in the 2ième Zouaves]
Gras, Henri, 3ième Bn, 1er Rég. de Marche d'Afrique:[RT, RR]

Guédet-Guépratte, Mme:[complete private and official papers of Admiral Guépratte]

Herkenne, Mme:[documents and notes on service of her father in 3ième Zouaves]

Hoaire, P. de la, Marine on *Argenfels*:[RR]

Jauras, Frederic, Matelot, battleship *Gaulois*:[RM]

Jomain, Simple Soldat, 6ième Rég. Colonial:[RM, RR]

Lucas, Contre Amiral, Enseigne de Vaisseau Première Classe, battleship *Gaulois*:[P, RT, RR]

Malcailloz, Émile, Caporal, 8ième Rég. du Genie (Télégraphistes):[B, P, RT, RR]

Massia, Simple Soldat, 4ième Rég. de Zouaves:[RR]

Medard, L., Simple Soldat, 30ième d'Artillerie Lourde:[RR]

Motreff, Ernest, minesweeper *Charrue*:[P, B]

Pastinelli, Matelot, battleship *St Louis*:[RR]

Payro, Sauveur, Matelot, battleship *Bouvet*:[RR]

Pegard, Marcel, Chef de Pièce, 45ième Batterie (75mm.), 17ième Rég:[D, P, L, VP, RM, RR]

Pellet, Simple Soldat, 58ième Reg. d'Infanterie Mixte Colonial:[RR]

Petit, Marcel, battleship *Jaureguiberry*:[VP, RT, RR]

Pion, Fernand, minesweeper *Pioche*:[L, RT]

Roger, L., 176ième Rég. d'lnfanterie:[RM]

Roux, Ernest, Caporal, 1er Reg. d'Artillerie, 33ième Batterie:[RR, P]

Roux, M.:[RR]

Sagnier, René, Enseigne de Vaisseau de Première Classe, battleship *Suffren*:[RT, RR]

Seyeux, M., Midshipman, battleship *Gaulois*:[D, RR]

Sylvestre, A., Maréchal des Logis, 56ième Batterie d'Artillerie Lourde:[VP, RT, RR, P, B]

Thierry, Charles, Caporal, 176ième Rég. d'Infanterie:[p, l, d. b. RR, O]

Tournebise, Henri, Radio Télégraphiste:[VP, p, RT, RR]

Vallet, Pierre, Enseigne de Vaisseau Premiére Classe, battleship *Gaulois*:[RT, RR]

Vallières, S., Officier, 5ième Rég. Chasseurs d'Afrique:[RR]

Varcollier, H., Enseigne de Vaisseau in command of a supply vessel:[RT, RR]

Vincenti, M., Simple Soldat, Service de Sante:[original water colours done while serving in French infantry on Peninsula]

Weil, Commandant R., S. Lieut, 32ième Batterie, 8ième Rég. d'Artillerie:[D, P, VP, RT, RR]

Turkish

Abdurrahman, Mr:[RR]

Altay, General Fahrettin:[L, RR]

Arkayan, General Askir:[RT, RR]

Artun, Colonel S.:[RR]

Belen, General F.:[RR]

Ben, General O.:[RR]

Demirsu, Colonel:[RR]

Dilmen, Mr S.:[RM, RR]

Ozgen, Captain:[RR]

Savasman, Lieut-Col. A.:[RR]

German

Organisational/Institutional Sources of Information

Bundesministerium der Verteidigung (Bonn)

Militärgeschichtliches Forschungsamt (Freiburg im Briesgau)

Bundesarchiv Militärarchiv (Bonn)

Deutsches Rotes Kreuz

Stadt Kiel: Der Magistrat Hauptamt

Verband Deutscher Soldaten (Bonn)

Marine Offizier Vereinigung (Bonn – Bad Godesberg)

Alte Adler Gemeinschaft (Bad Kissingen)

Alte Kameraden

Deutscher Soldatenbund Kyffhauser e.v. (Wiesbaden)
Deutscher Marinebund e.v. (Wilhelmshaven)
Kameradschaftliche Vereinigung der Marineflieger
Dr Ervin Liptai, Col. Cdr, War Museum and Institute, Budapest

Personal Contact
Hoffman, Jakob, SMS *Goeben*:[RT]
Mertz, Heinz, SMS *Goeben*:[RT]
Mohl, Hans von, SMS *Breslau*, later on Admiral Souchon's staff:[RT, RR]
Pieper, Kontreadmiral Waldemar, Chief of Ordnance Inspection:[Ordnance Report]
Thomsen-Oldenswort, Dr Waldemar, Hamidieh Battery and later A.D.C. to Admiral Pieper:[RT]

2. Other Archives
(Precise references are given in the footnotes for all documents quoted in the text and not from the Liddle Collection)

British
National Archives, London
Notes on meetings of the War Council, the Dardanelles Committee and the War Committee, with Cabinet memoranda.
War Office and Admiralty papers: appreciations, Kitchener-Hamilton correspondence, reports etc.
Mediterranean Expeditionary Force: orders, various papers and war diaries.
Allied Squadron in Eastern Mediterranean: orders, various papers and ships' logs.

Imperial War Museum, London
Mediterranean Expeditionary Force: orders and various papers.
Allied Squadron in Eastern Mediterranean: orders and various papers.
Dardanelles Commission Report, 1917.
Acheson, Lieut, 2 letters (naval action in Dardanelles, 1915).
Berridge, Midshipman W.L., notes and letters.
Birdwood, General, letters from Anzac to Col. Rintoul, Rtd.
Bremner, F.D.H., No. 3 Squadron, RNAS, log book.
Burge, Lieut-Col. N.O., RMLI, letters.
Clough, H., ship's surgeon, letters.
Dawnay, Major G.P., MEF HQ Staff officer, letters.
Douglas-Jones, Capt. E.D., memoir of Suvla.
Drewry, Midshipman, VC, letters (V Beach, Helles and Suvla landings).
Ford, J.E., RMLI, diary.
Jones, Rev. D., privately published diary (Suvla).
King-Wilson, Lieut, 'A Medical Officer's Memoirs'.
Lisle, Gen. B. de, letter.
Moreton, H.W., diary.
Nightingale, Captain G. Warneford, 1st Royal Munster Fusiliers, letters.
Samson, Air Commodore C.R., DSO, AFC, notes and various papers.
Thompson, J., 42nd East Lancs. Div., memoirs.

Centre for Military Archives, King's College, London
Letters and papers of General Sir Ian Hamilton.

National Maritime Museum, Greenwich
Vice-Admiral Sir Arthur Limpus, correspondence with de Robeck, Wemyss, Lord Methuen etc.
Captain Kelly of HMS *Dublin*, proceedings and correspondence.
Sir James Porter, Principal Hospital Transport Officer, various papers.

Gloucestershire County Record Office
Letters of George Moss to the Rector of Dyrham (Blathwayte Papers).

Roxburgh Museum
Papers relating to the KOSB Regiment.

Museum of the Kings Own Scottish Borderers, Berwick
Letters of Pte John Lavelle.
Diary of Captain A.M. Shaw.
Letter of Pte David Harper.
Photographs of Capt R.R. Lumgair.

The Gurkha Museum, Winchester
Diary of Colonel A.B. Tillard.
Photograph Collection.

The Museum of the Manchester Regiment, Ashton under Lyne
Photographic Collection.

The Museum of the Lancashire Fusiliers, Bury
Photographic Collection.

The Museum of the Green Howards, Richmond, North Yorkshire
Photographic Collection.

The Museum of the Royal Welsh Regiment, Brecon
Photographic Collection – South Wales Borderers.

The Museum of the Dorset Regiment, Dorchester
Photographic Collection, Dorset Yeomanry (Wingfield Digby Estate).

J.M. Bruce, J.S. Leslie Aeroplane Photographic Collection, Scarborough

French
French Military Archives, Chateau de Vincennes, Paris
Documentation on every aspect of the leadership and administration of the Corps Expéditionnaire d'Orient, its relations with the French Ministry of Defence and with the overall command of the MEF HQ, including plans of the Kum Kale landing of 25 April, reports on the Helles landing and fighting, reports on the French aerodrome at Tenedos, discipline, etc.

French Naval Archives, Paris
Official documentation on the Allied naval attack of 18 March, especially the loss of the *Bouvet*. (The Musée de la Marine also has material on the *Bouvet*.)

Australian
The State Library, Adelaide, South Australia
Carew Reynell Papers: letters of 7 September 1915 from Birdwood to D.J. Byard on death of Reynell (PRG 29/22); letter written as a diary by Reynell, May 1915 (PRG 29/22).
A. S. Hutton diary for 1915 (D 4975).
Red Cross Repatriation Papers (227 SRG 76).
10th Battalion AIF War Diary (PRG 272/8/1).
10th Battalion AIF File of unofficial letters 1914–15 (PRG 272/9).
Gallipoli photographs.

La Trobe Library, Victoria State Library, Melbourne
Letter of Sgt R.M. Collins, 23rd Bn, to Minister of Defence, Senator Pearce, a friend of the
Collins family, 8 November 1915 (Box 940/1 MS 8 133).
Special Instructions for action during suspension of arms, 24 May 1915 (Box 225/4 A). Presented
by Sergeant A. Nicholas, 1st AIF.
John Monash, letters to wife and daughter, December 1915 (MS 9456).
Letters from Robert M. Calder describing May attack at Cape Helles and August offensive at
Anzac (MS 9003).

National Archives, National Library, Canberra
Vasey Papers.
Fisher Papers, Dardanelles Commission Evidence (MS 2919 Series 7).
Murdoch Papers, correspondence with George Pearce, Minister of Defence, September 1915, and
with Lloyd George, October 1915 (MS 2823).
Lord Novar Papers. (Lord Novar, as Sir Ronald Ferguson, was the Australian Governor-General
in 1914–15. He corresponded with both General Birdwood and General Bridges.)
General Bridges' letter of 5 May 1915 to Lady Bridges.

Royal Military College, Duntroon, Canberra
Letters of Capt. Christopher Carrington, RNZFA, 1914–15 (Carrington Papers, 7-11).

Australian War Memorial, Canberra
John Simpson Kirkpatrick, letters (AWM 749/80/7).
Diary of General Bridges (AWM 749/12/4).
Lieut-Col. Watson Papers (AWM 419/111/2).
Lord Birdwood Collection, diary for 1915, letters to Bridges, letter from Hamilton.
Sgt R.H. Adams, M.M., 8th Bn, letters (AWM 181.11).
Lieut W.E. Addison, 18th Bn, letter written as a diary (AWM 181.11).
CQMS A.L. Guppy, 14th Bn, typed extracts from diary (AWM 12.1.16).
Photographic archives.

Mitchell Library, Sydney, NSW
Cook, Thomas Murphy, Sgt, 1st Bn, diary.
Evans, N.C, 1st Light Horse Fld Amb., letter.
Gordon, A.D., 1st Fld Amb., diary account.
Hall, Peter, 2nd Stationary Hospital, letter of 2 May 1915 describing voyage of *Seang Choon* to
Alexandria.
Hellman, A.L., 1st Div. Sig. Coy, diary.
Keary, J., 18th Bn, diary.
McKinlay, T.J., 8th Bn, letter describing August attack at Lone Pine.
Marks, Col. D., 13th Bn, diary.
Morris, Sgt. A.P.K., 1st Light Horse, stretcher-bearer, diary.
Nixon, Robert Rex, 4th Bn, letters.
Nixon, Rupert, 13th Bn, letters.
O'Hare, A., 19th Bn, diary.
Pearce, M.E., 1st Light Horse, diary.
Ruskin, Alfred, of HMAS *Sydney*, log for 1914 re SMS *Emden*.
Wagstaff, Brig.-Gen. C.M., report of attack of 18/19 May to 6 a.m., 20 May.

New Zealand
The Alexander Turnbull Library, Wellington
Browne, H.E., Wellington Mtd Rifles, diary (Misc. M.S. 1196).

Clifton, Spr E.C., 1st Fld Coy, NZEF, diary.

Gascoigne, J.W., letters, diary, pay book (Misc. Papers 1007, File 5).

Jones, A. T., diary, January 1915.

Marshall, J.W. (M.S. Papers 137, folder 12 B).

Melvill, William, papers (M.S. Papers 244, File 10) (NZ and Aust. Div. Evacuation Orders).

Paul, J., letter to E.C. Walmsley, 1 June 1915 (Misc. Man. ALS161).

Ritchie, T.R., diary and evidence to the Dardanelles Commission (Misc. M.S. 1428).

Tuck, G.A., diary for 1914–15 (M.S. 1914–18).

Wilson, Sir James A., papers, letters from Gen. Godley, in command NZ and Aust. Div., and letter from

New Zealand National Archives, Wellington

War Diary, General Staff, NZ and Aust. Div.: Nibrunesi Point Raid report, Birdwood/Godley correspondence, Godley/Sir James Allan (Min. of Defence) correspondence.

RND GSO2 War Diary (Lieut-Cdr B. Freyberg, o/c/ Hood Bn, report 26 April 1915).

NZ and Aust. Div., General Routine Orders, daily reports, General Staff messages.

Private diary of General Braithwaite.

The Auckland Bn War Diary.

Christchurch Public Library, The New Zealand Room, Christchurch, South Island

The Canterbury Infantry Bn War Diary.

J. L. Anderson, 1915 diary.

Editions of *The Press*, Christchurch daily newspaper.

Index

In the main, ranks and honours are not shown but where it is considered helpful to list a rank or post it is for the year 1915.